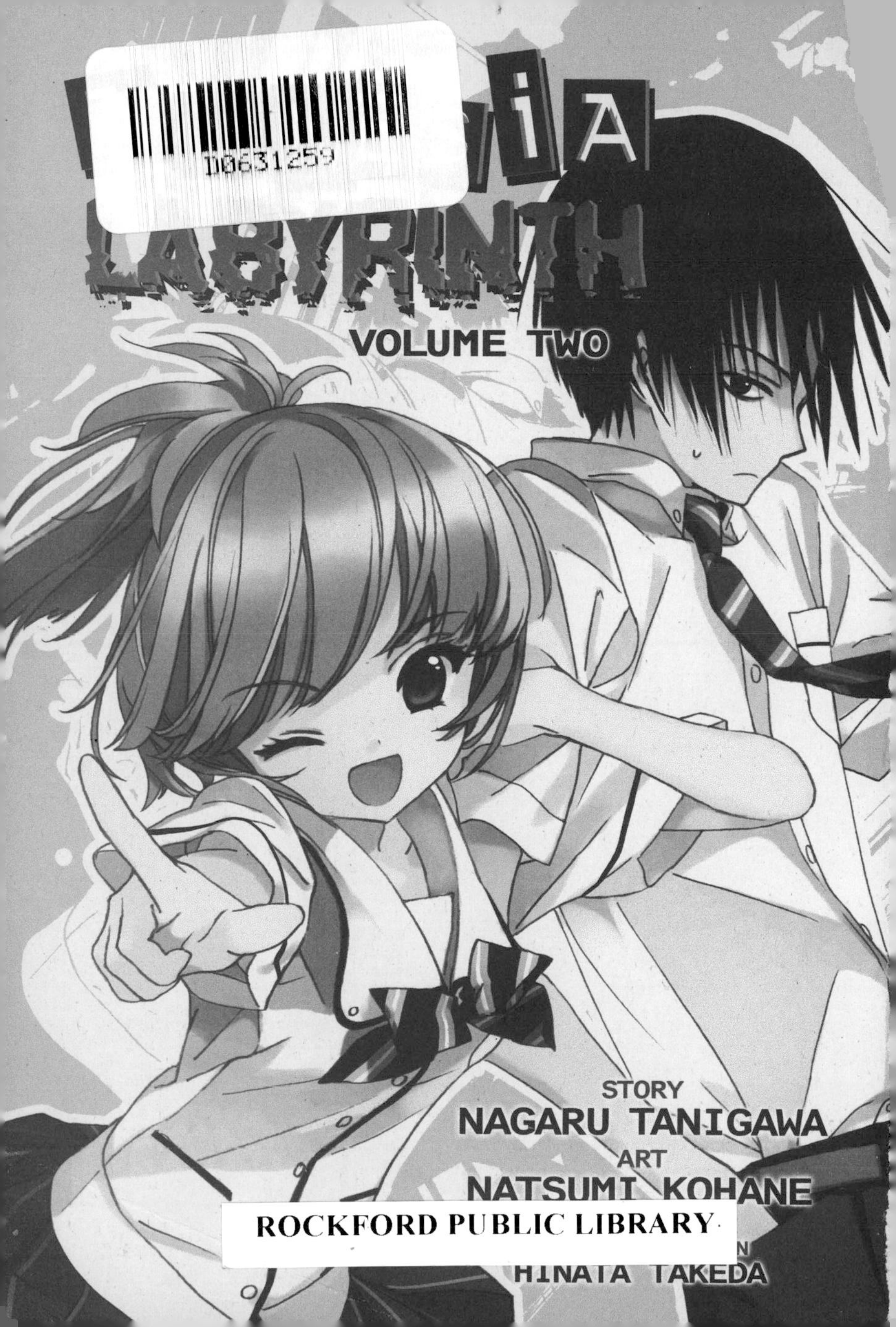
iA
LABYRINTH
VOLUME TWO
STORY
NAGARU TANIGAWA
ART
NATSUMI KOHANE
HINATA TAKEDA

AMNESIA LABYRINTH VOL. 2

story by Nagaru Tanigawa   art by Natsumi Kohane

STAFF CREDITS

translation	**Nan Rymer**
adaptation	**Shannon Fay**
lettering & layout	**Nicky Lim**
cover design	**Nicky Lim**
copy editor	**Shanti Whitesides**
editor	**Adam Arnold**
publisher	**Jason DeAngelis**
	Seven Seas Entertainment

AMNESIA LABYRINTH VOL. 2
© 2009 Nagaru Tanigawa
© 2009 Kohane Nasumi
First published in 2009 by Media Works Inc., Tokyo, Japan.
English translation rights arranged with ASCII MEDIA WORKS.

Visit us online at www.gomanga.com.

ISBN: 978-1-934876-37-4

Printed in Canada

First Printing: June 2011

10 9 8 7 6 5 4 3 2 1

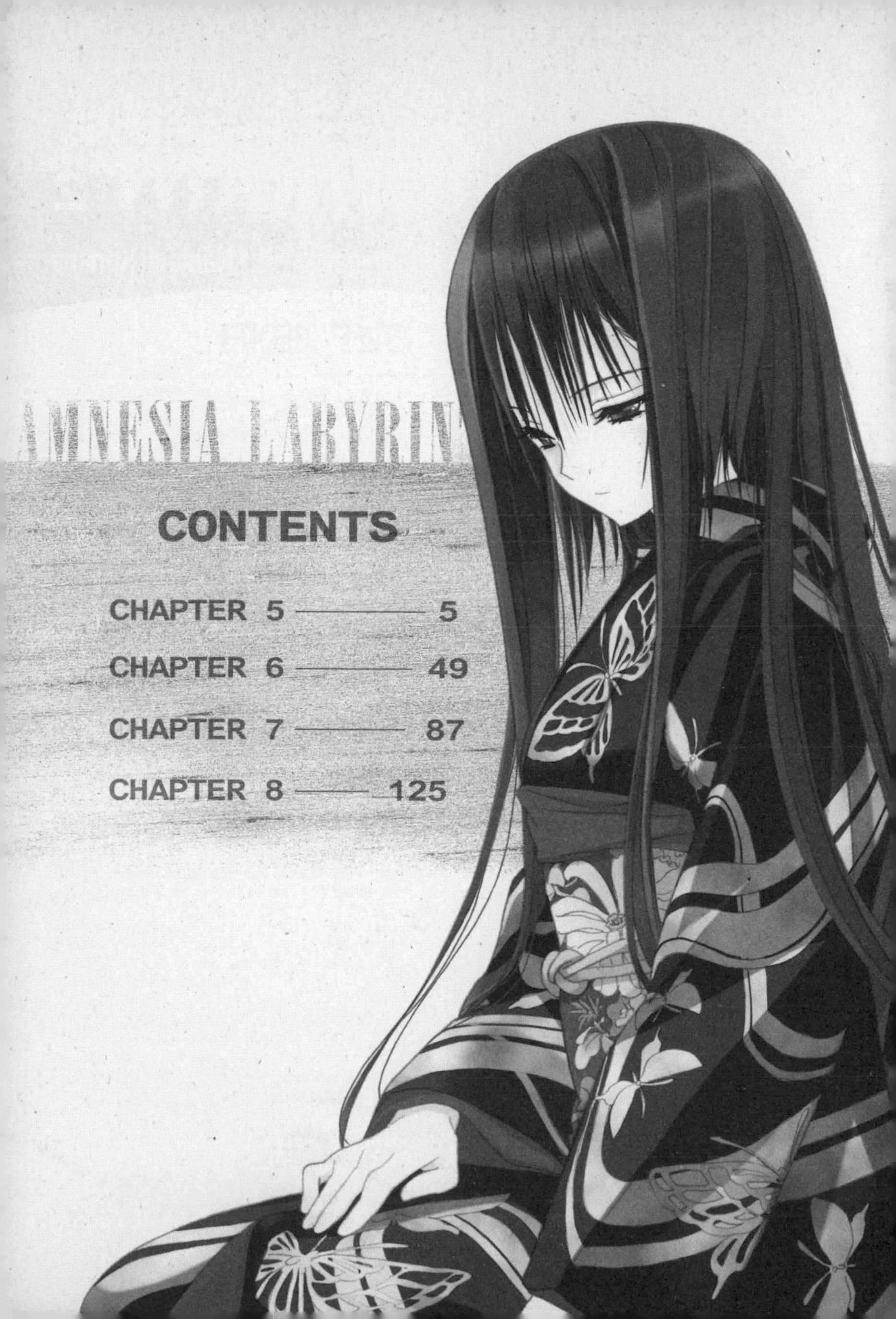
AMNESIA LABYRIN

CONTENTS

AMNESIA
LABYRINTH

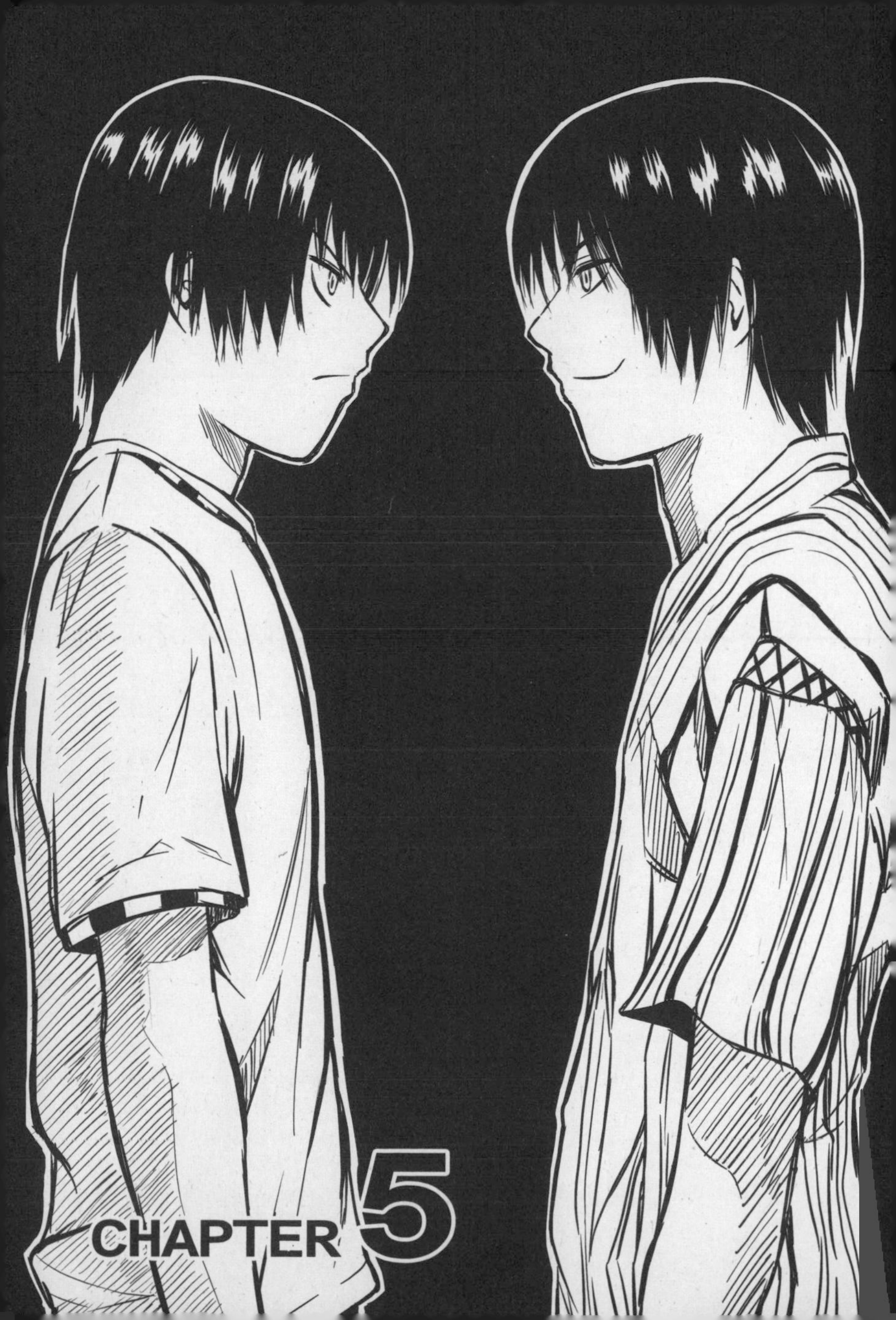
CHAPTER 5

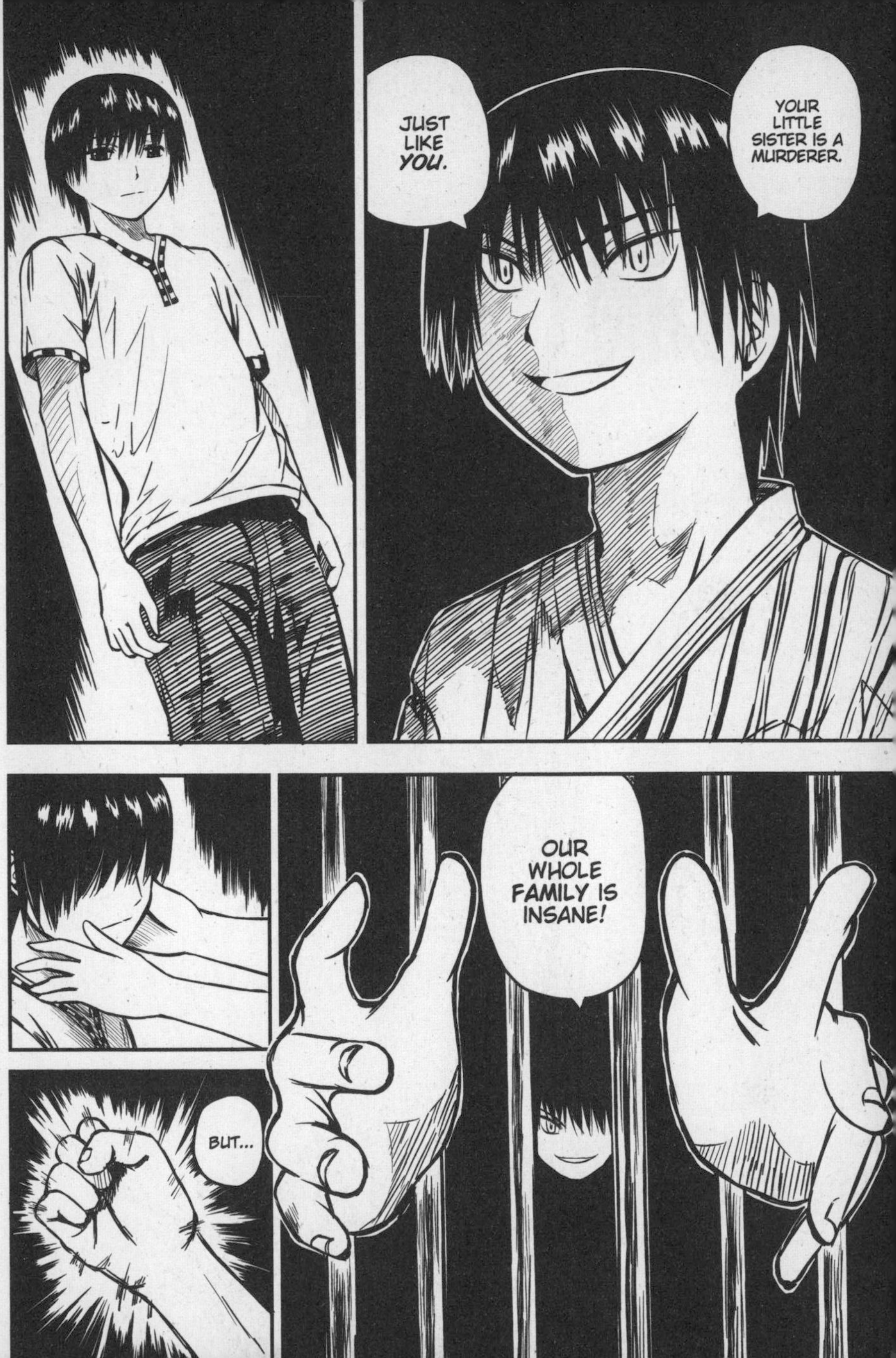
YOUR LITTLE SISTER IS A MURDERER.
JUST LIKE YOU.
OUR WHOLE FAMILY IS INSANE!
BUT...

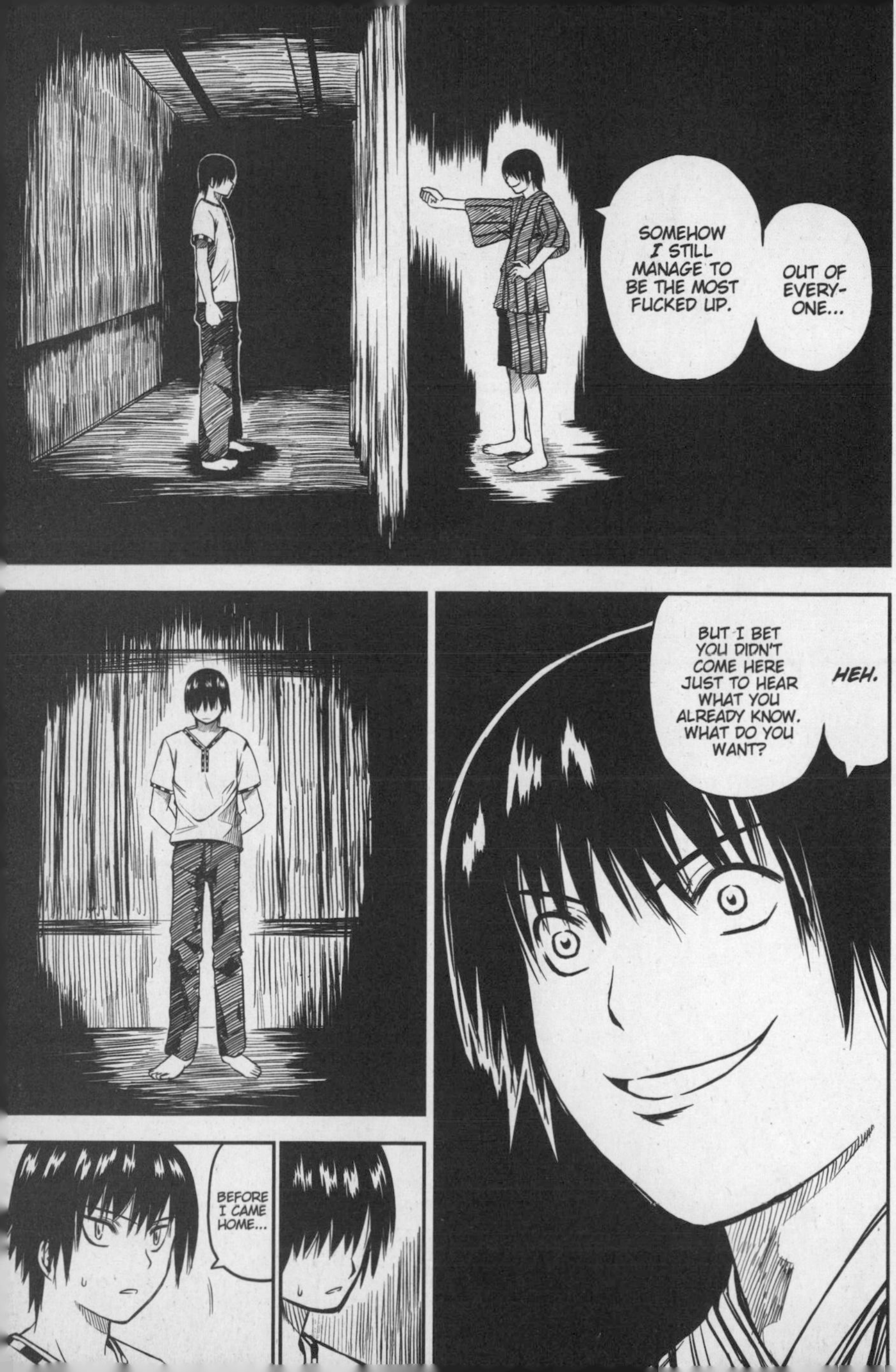
OUT OF EVERY-ONE...
SOMEHOW I STILL MANAGE TO BE THE MOST FUCKED UP.
HEH.
BUT I BET YOU DIDN'T COME HERE JUST TO HEAR WHAT YOU ALREADY KNOW. WHAT DO YOU WANT?
BEFORE I CAME HOME...

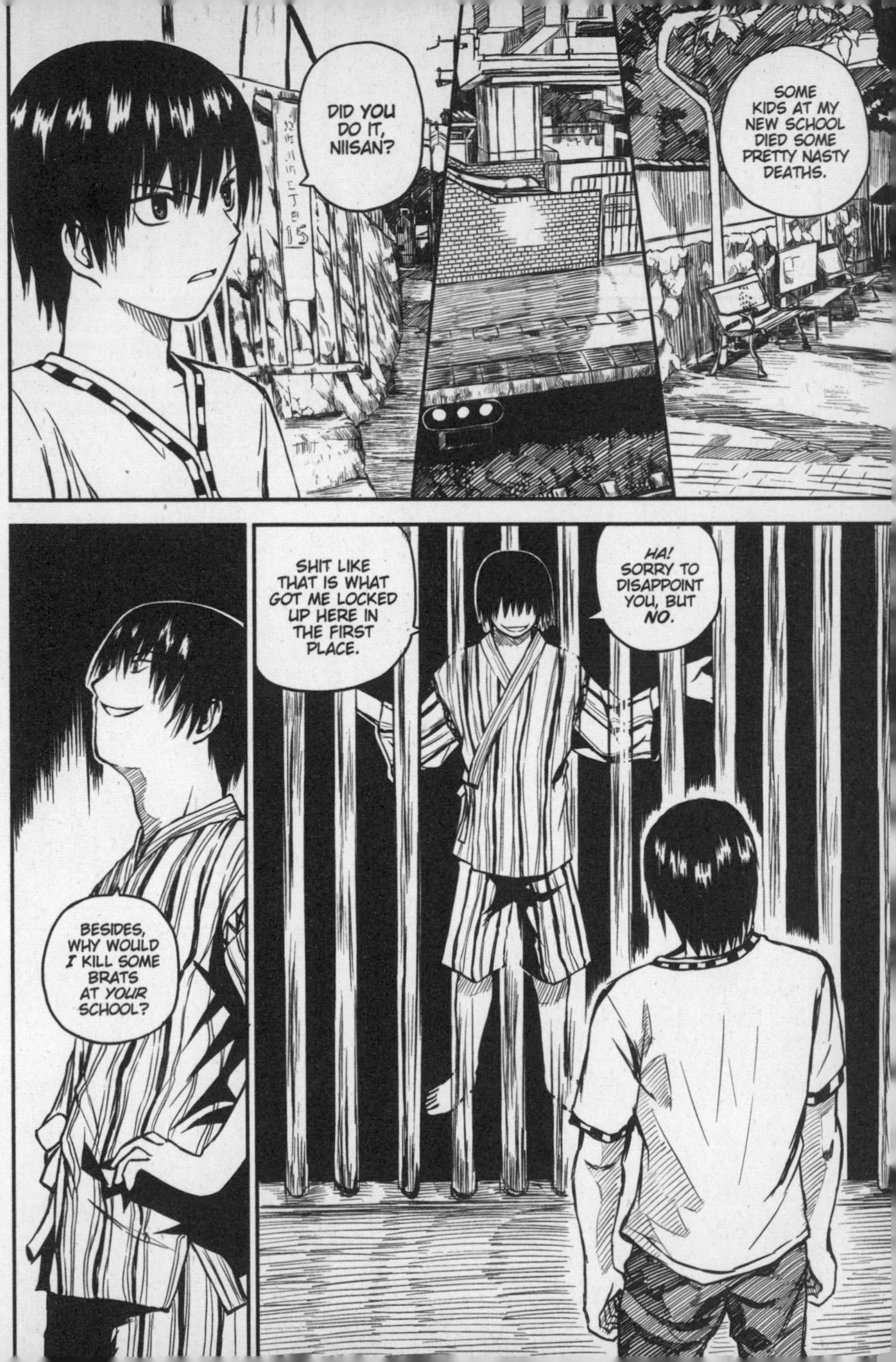
SOME KIDS AT MY NEW SCHOOL DIED SOME PRETTY NASTY DEATHS.
DID YOU DO IT, NIISAN?
HA! SORRY TO DISAPPOINT YOU, BUT NO.
SHIT LIKE THAT IS WHAT GOT ME LOCKED UP HERE IN THE FIRST PLACE.
BESIDES, WHY WOULD I KILL SOME BRATS AT YOUR SCHOOL?

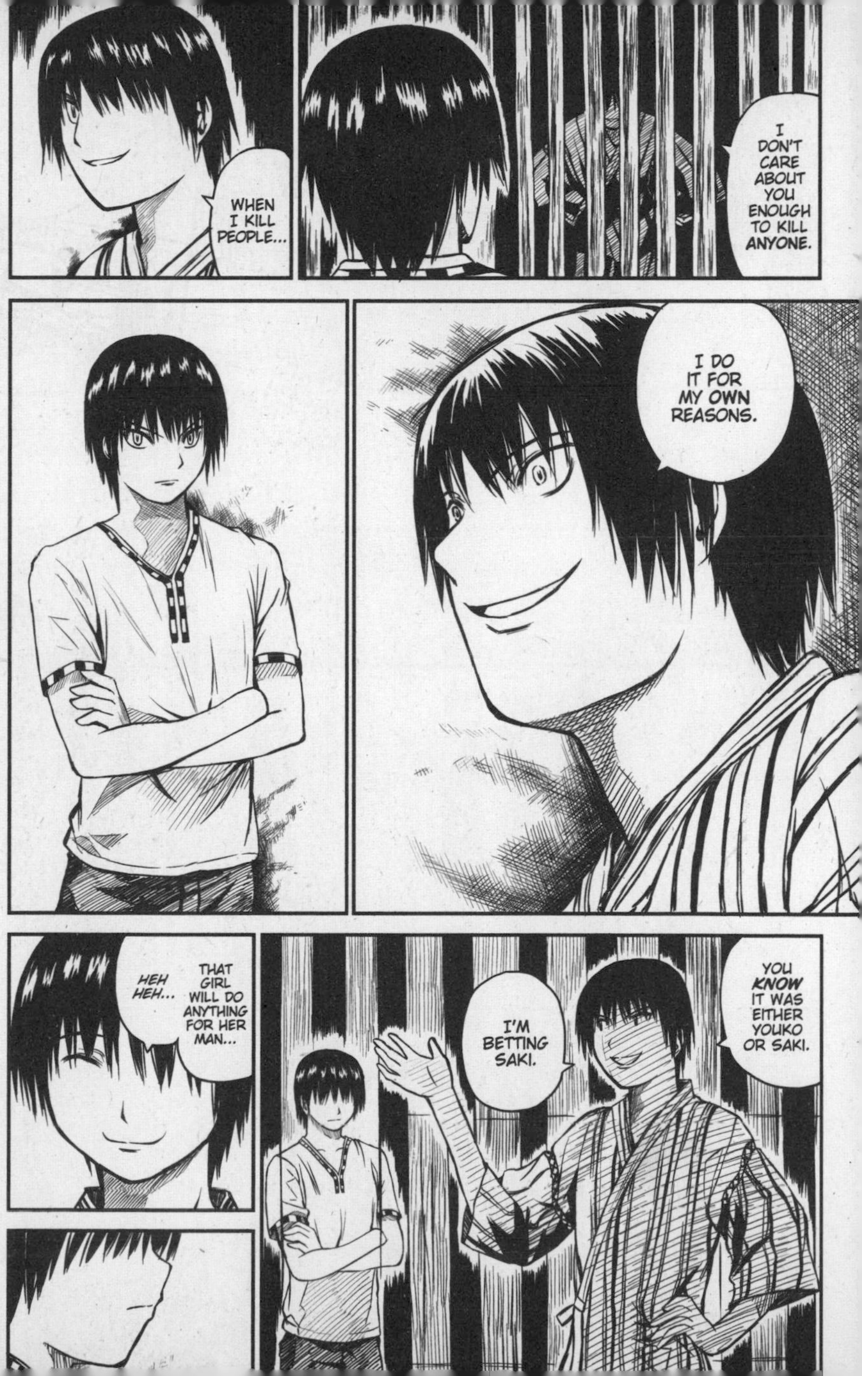
I DON'T CARE ABOUT YOU ENOUGH TO KILL ANYONE.
WHEN I KILL PEOPLE...
I DO IT FOR MY OWN REASONS.
YOU *KNOW* IT WAS EITHER YOUKO OR SAKI.
I'M BETTING SAKI.
THAT GIRL WILL DO ANYTHING FOR HER MAN...
HEH HEH...

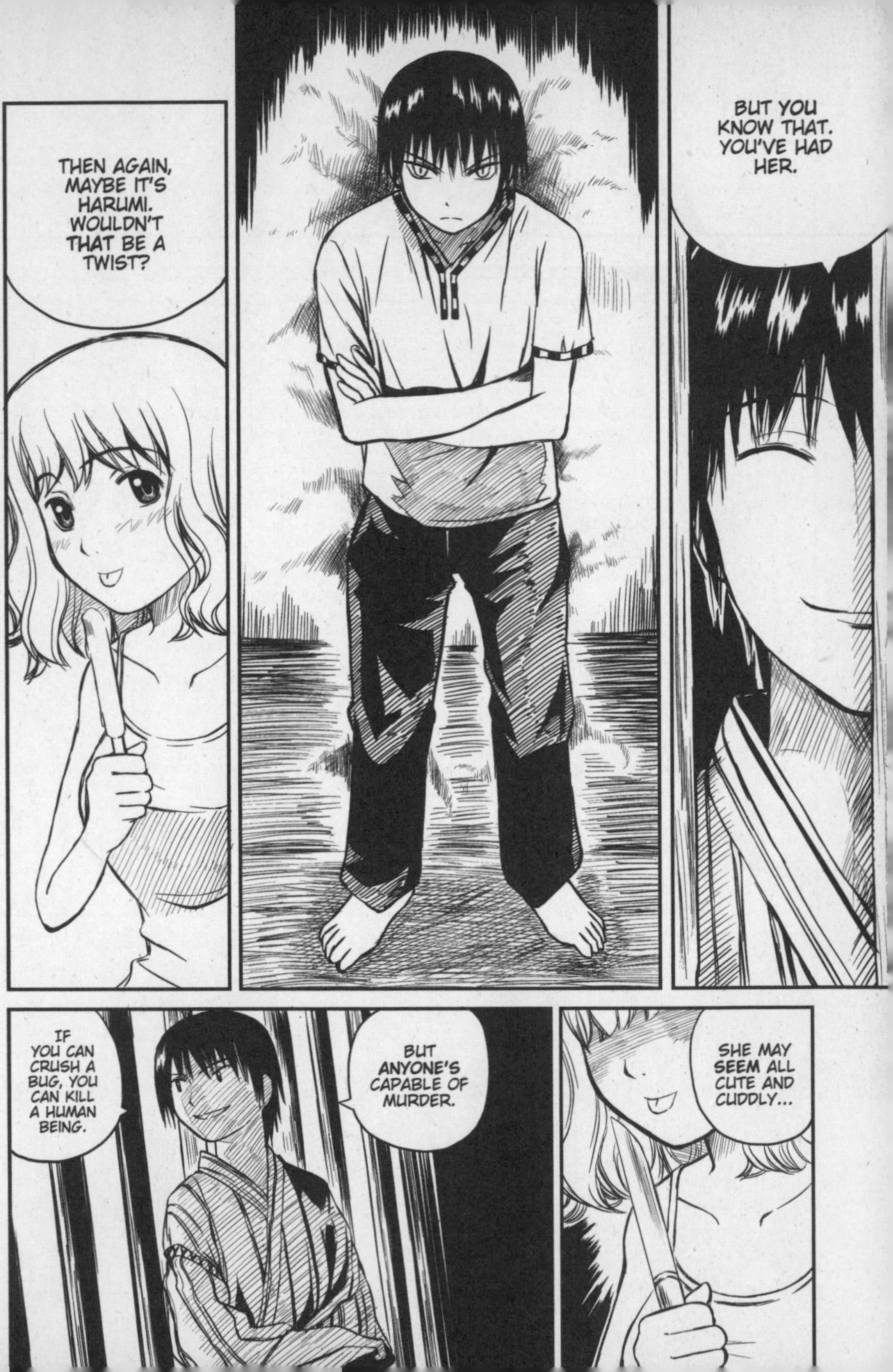
BUT YOU KNOW THAT. YOU'VE HAD HER.
THEN AGAIN, MAYBE IT'S HARUMI. WOULDN'T THAT BE A TWIST?
SHE MAY SEEM ALL CUTE AND CUDDLY...
BUT ANYONE'S CAPABLE OF MURDER.
IF YOU CAN CRUSH A BUG, YOU CAN KILL A HUMAN BEING.

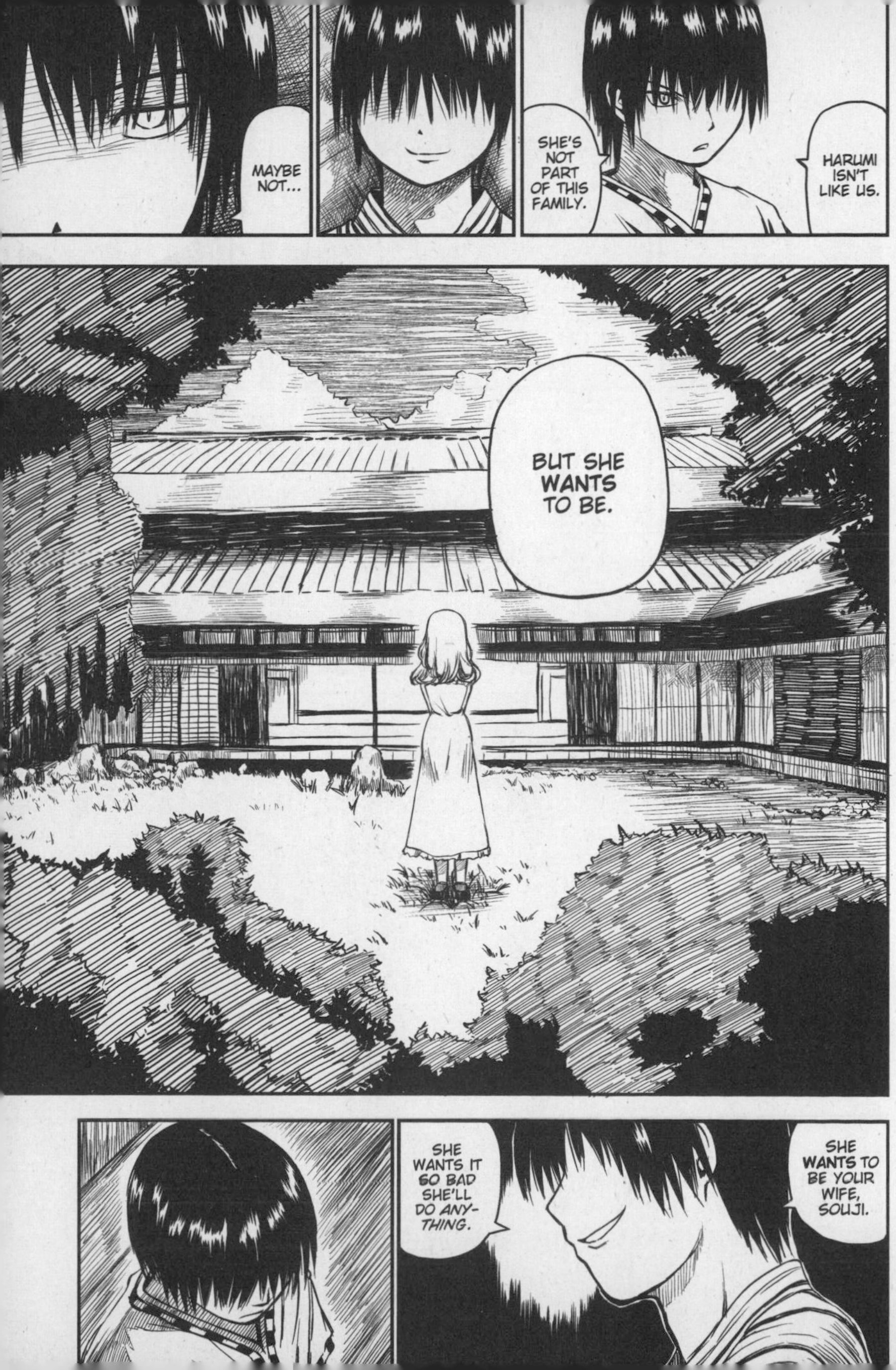
HARUMI ISN'T LIKE US.
SHE'S NOT PART OF THIS FAMILY.
MAYBE NOT...
BUT SHE WANTS TO BE.
SHE WANTS TO BE YOUR WIFE, SOUJI.
SHE WANTS IT SO BAD SHE'LL DO *ANY-THING*.

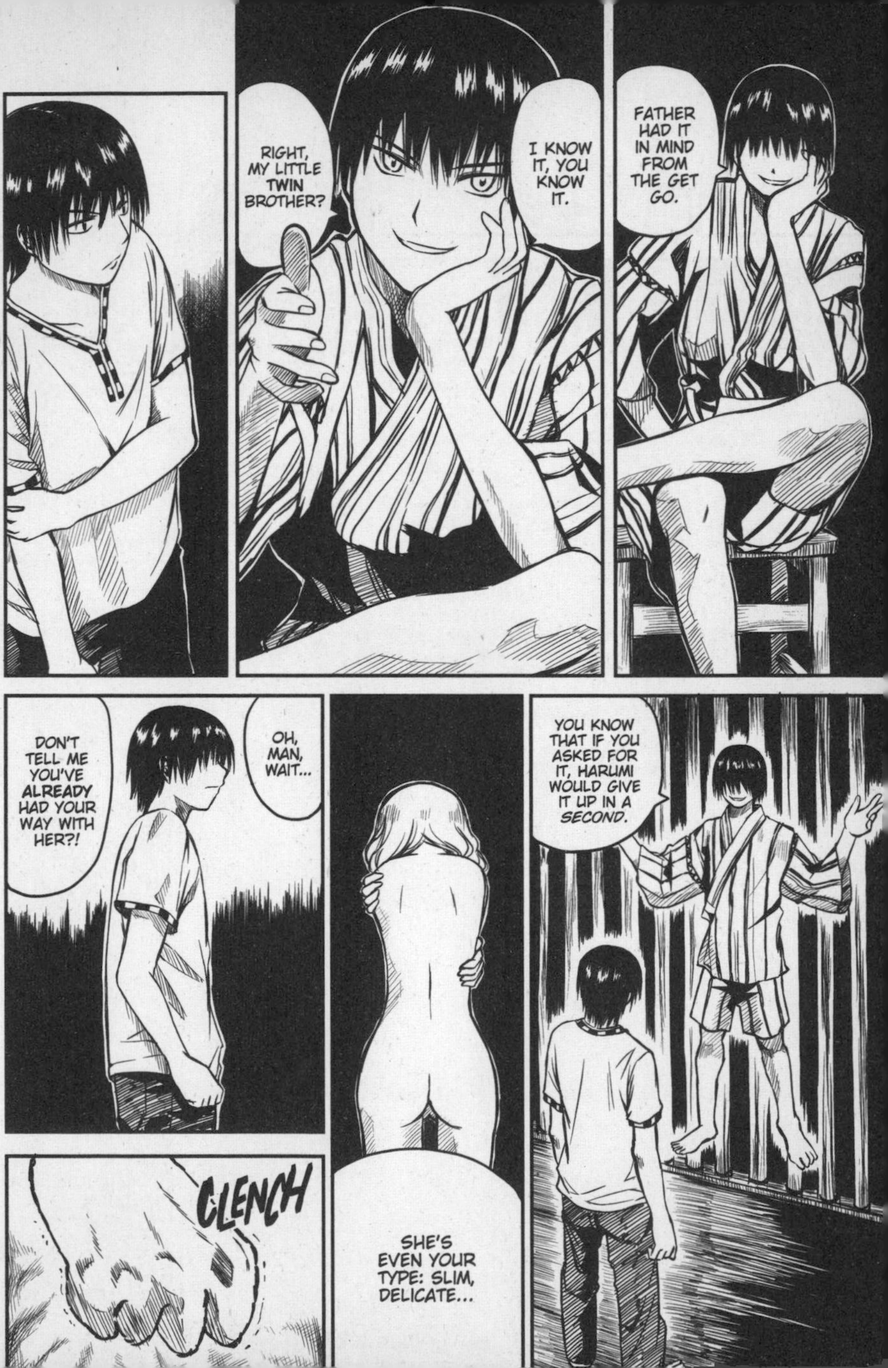
FATHER HAD IT IN MIND FROM THE GET GO.
I KNOW IT, YOU KNOW IT.
RIGHT, MY LITTLE TWIN BROTHER?
YOU KNOW THAT IF YOU ASKED FOR IT, HARUMI WOULD GIVE IT UP IN A SECOND.
OH, MAN, WAIT...
DON'T TELL ME YOU'VE ALREADY HAD YOUR WAY WITH HER?!
SHE'S EVEN YOUR TYPE: SLIM, DELICATE...
CLENCH

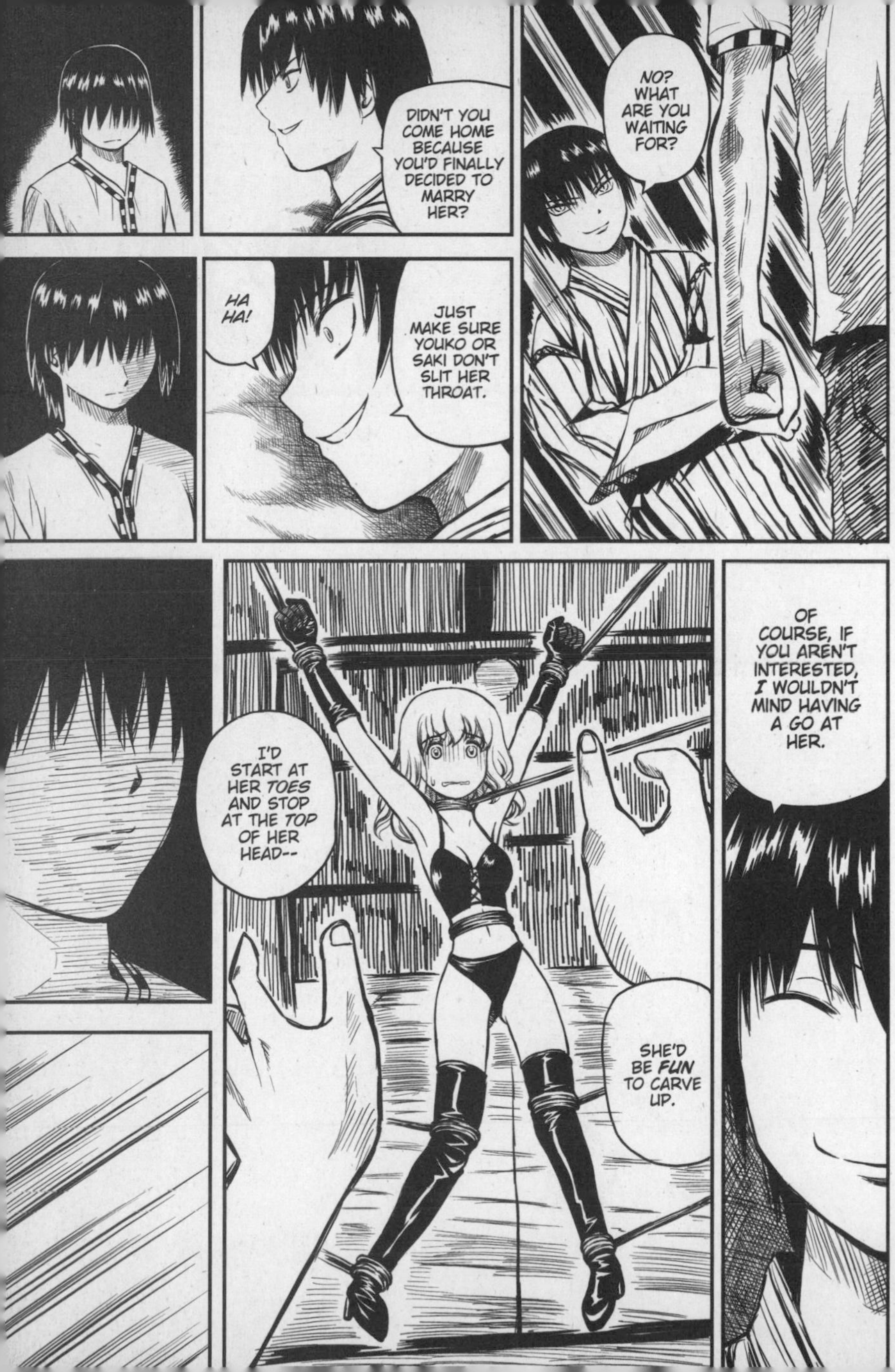
NO? WHAT ARE YOU WAITING FOR?
DIDN'T YOU COME HOME BECAUSE YOU'D FINALLY DECIDED TO MARRY HER?
JUST MAKE SURE YOUKO OR SAKI DON'T SLIT HER THROAT.
HA HA!
OF COURSE, IF YOU AREN'T INTERESTED, I WOULDN'T MIND HAVING A GO AT HER.
I'D START AT HER TOES AND STOP AT THE TOP OF HER HEAD--
SHE'D BE FUN TO CARVE UP.

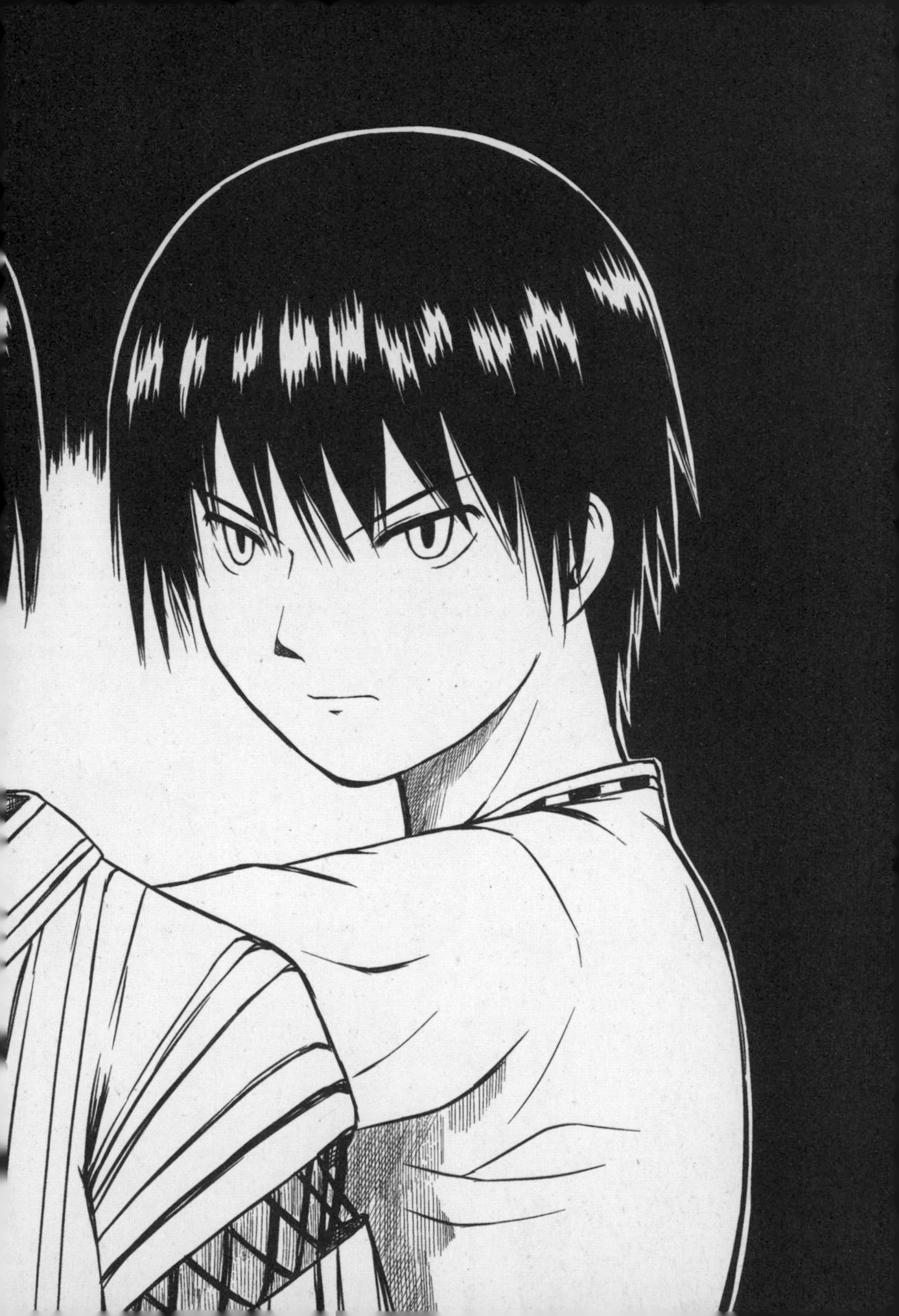

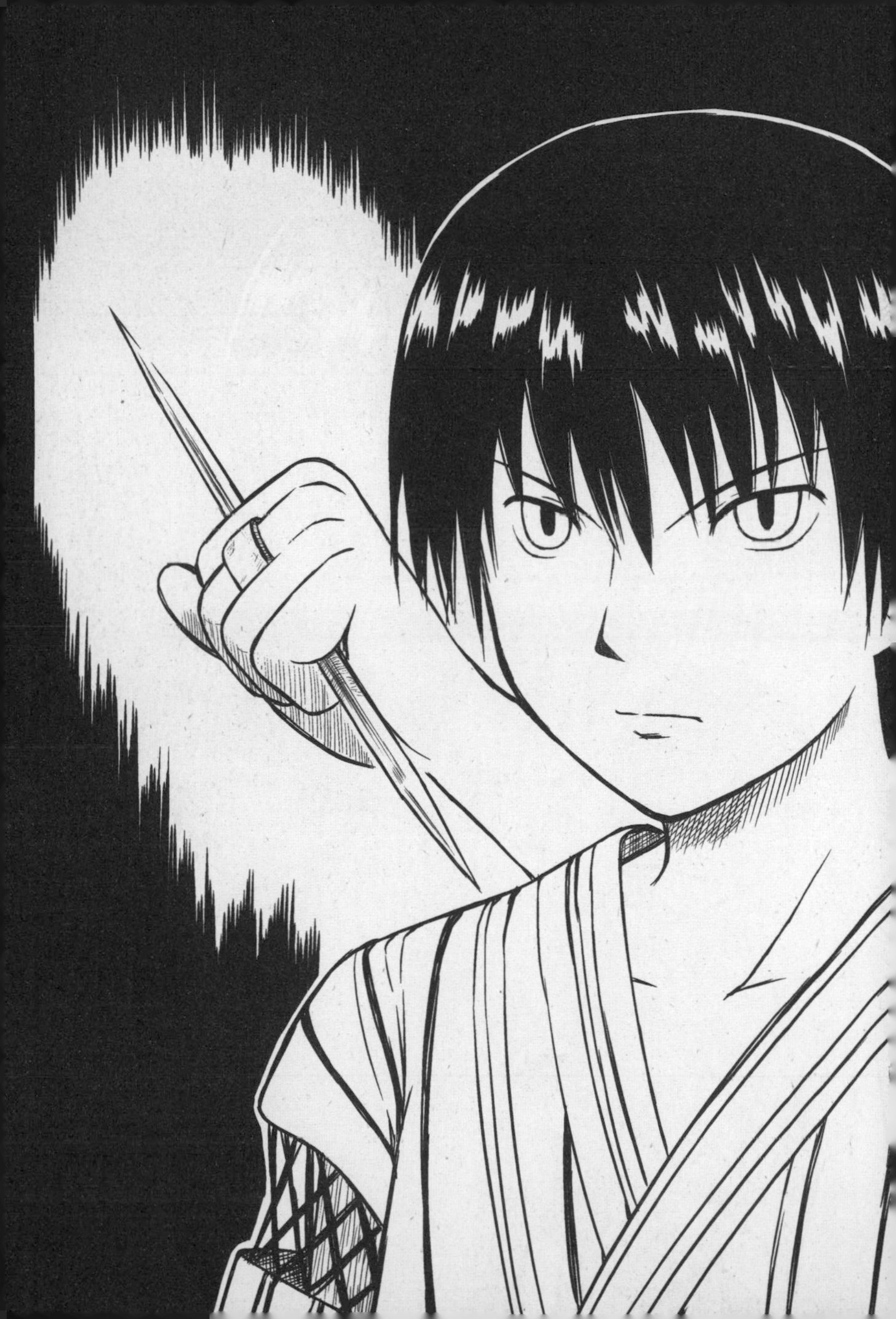

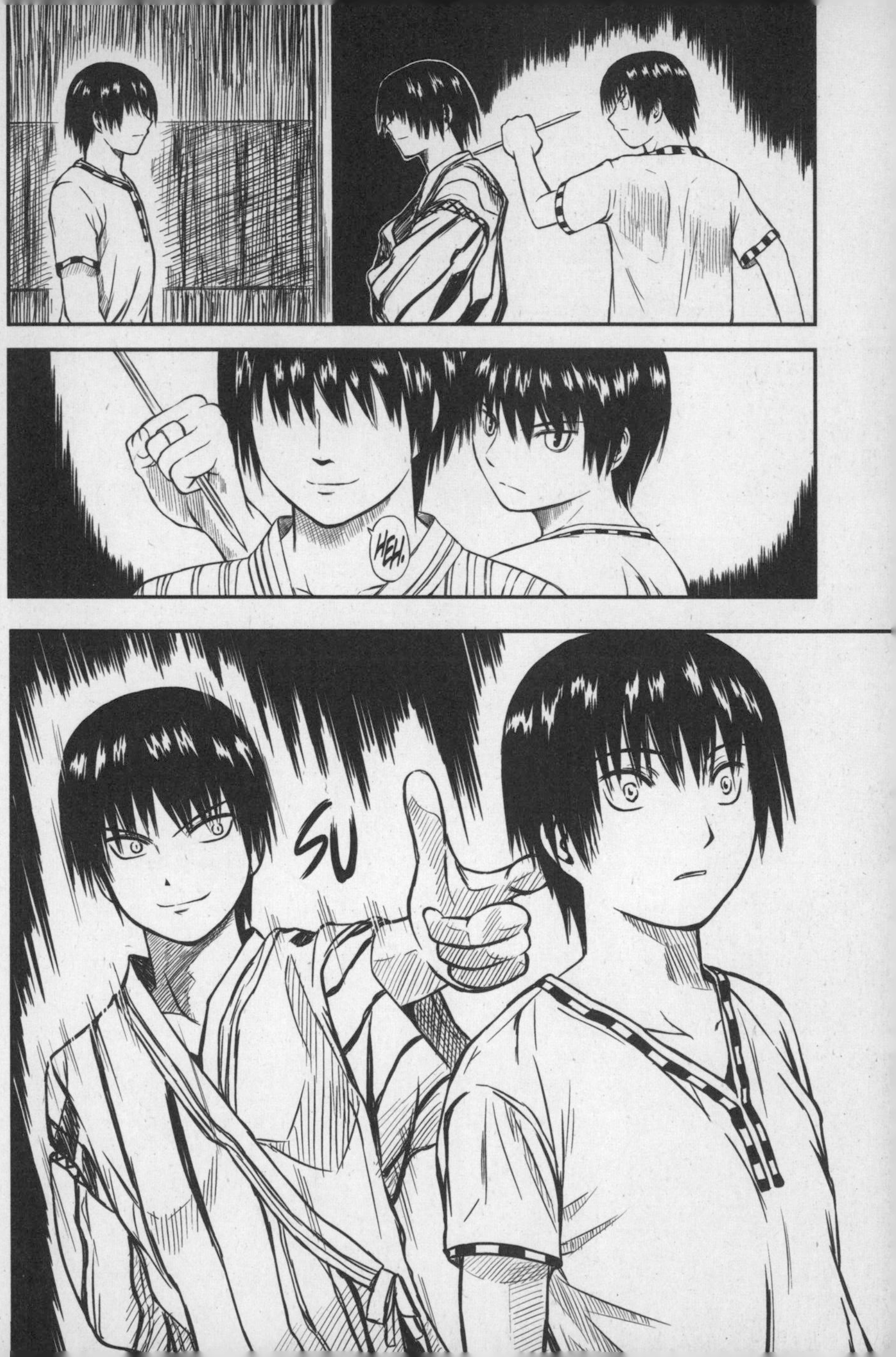
HEH.
SU

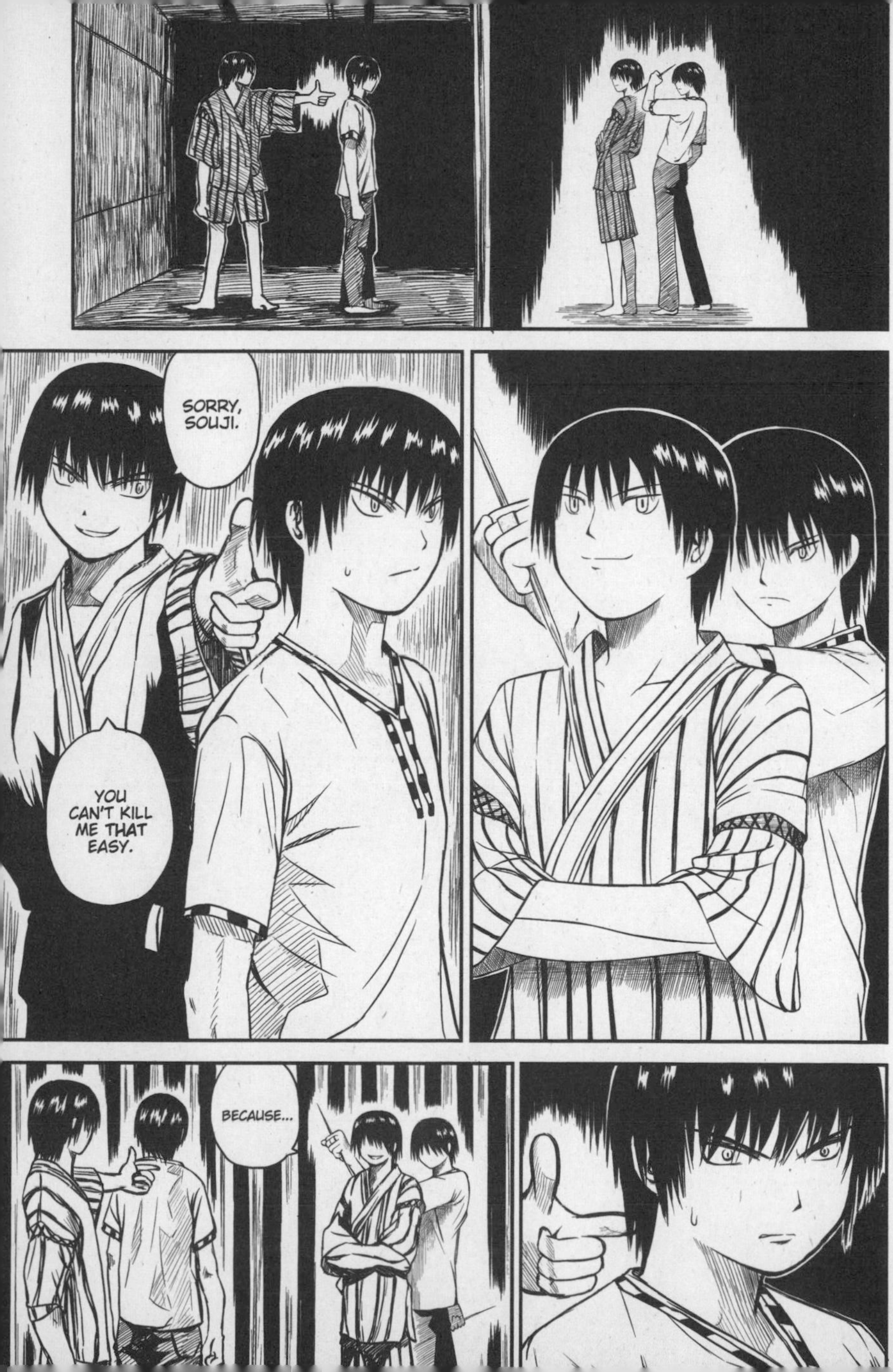
SORRY, SOUJI.
YOU CAN'T KILL ME THAT EASY.
BECAUSE...

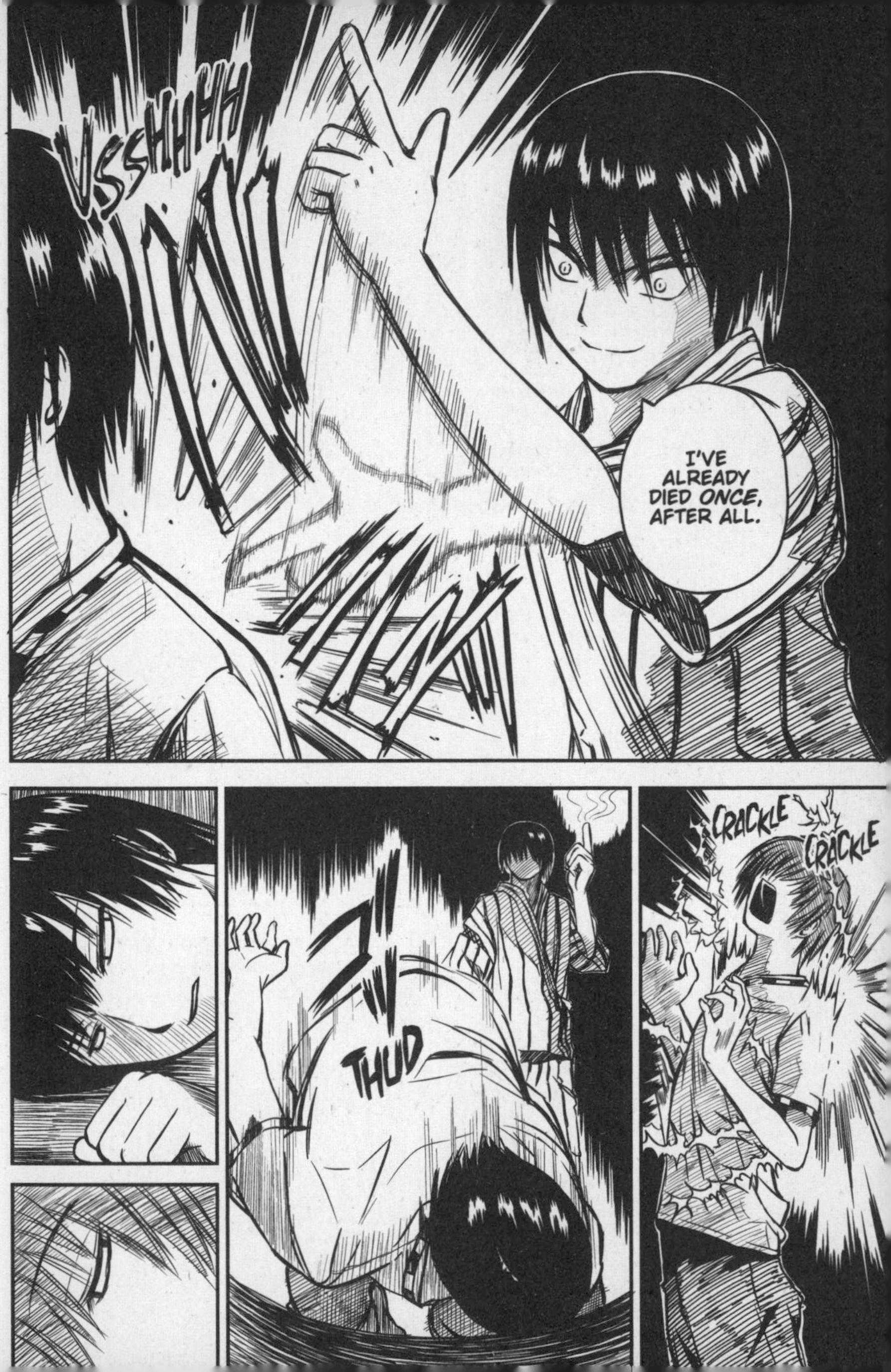
VSSHHHH
I'VE ALREADY DIED ONCE, AFTER ALL.
CRACKLE
CRACKLE
THUD

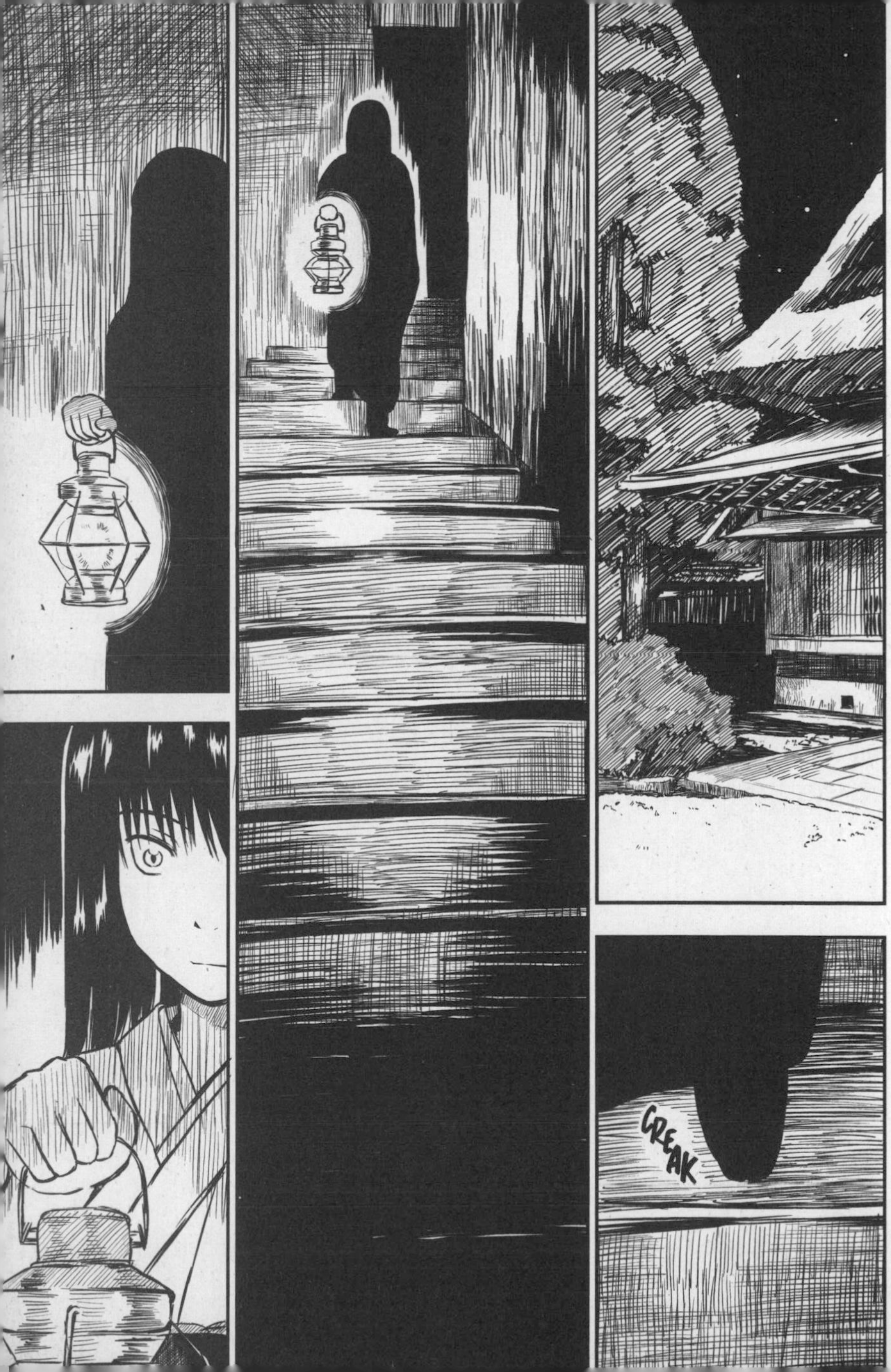
CREAK

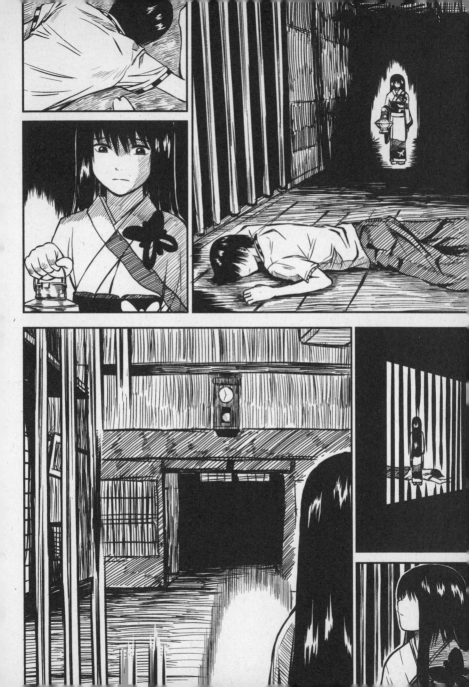

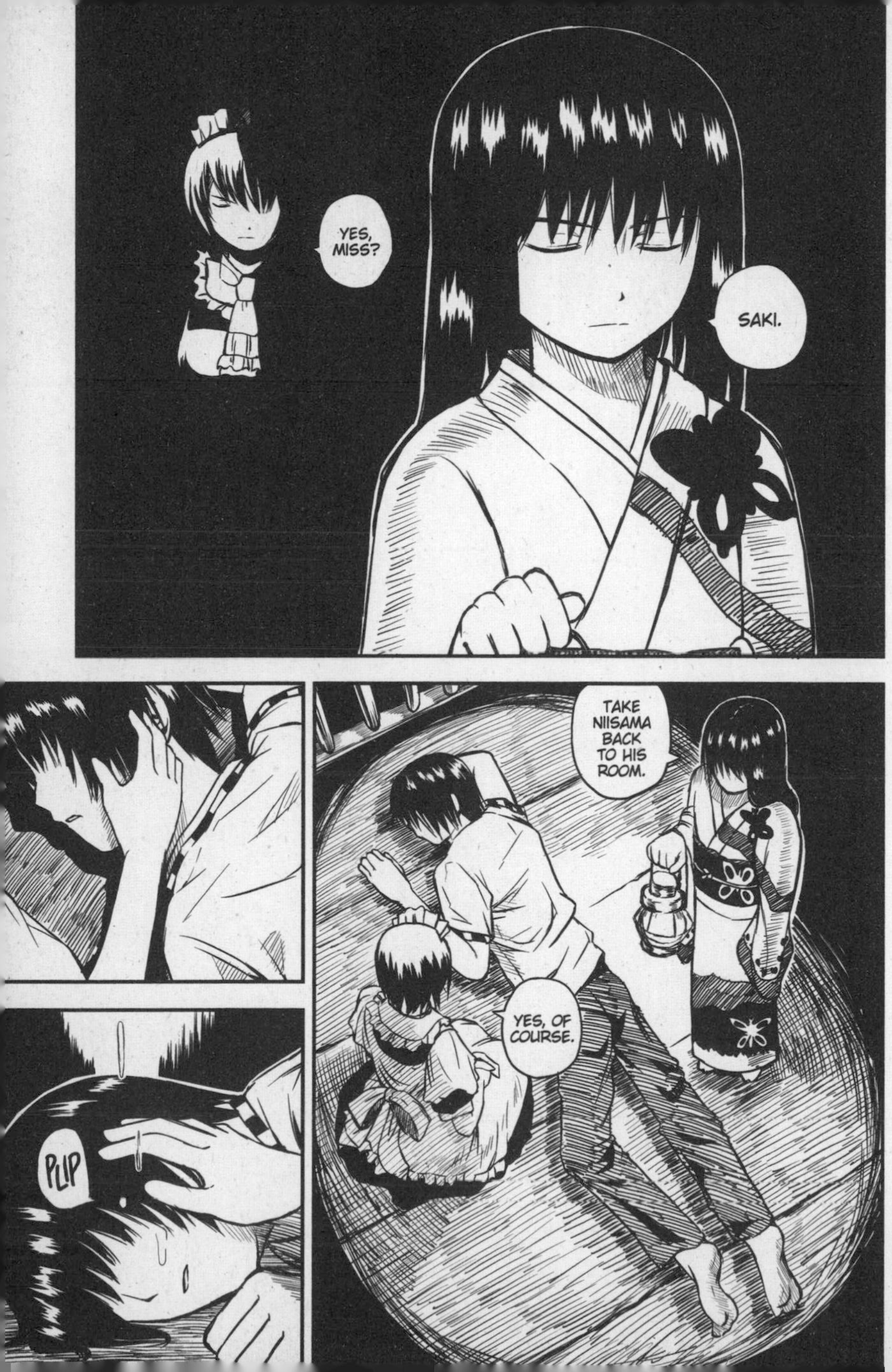
SAKI.
YES, MISS?
TAKE NIISAMA BACK TO HIS ROOM.
YES, OF COURSE.
PLIP

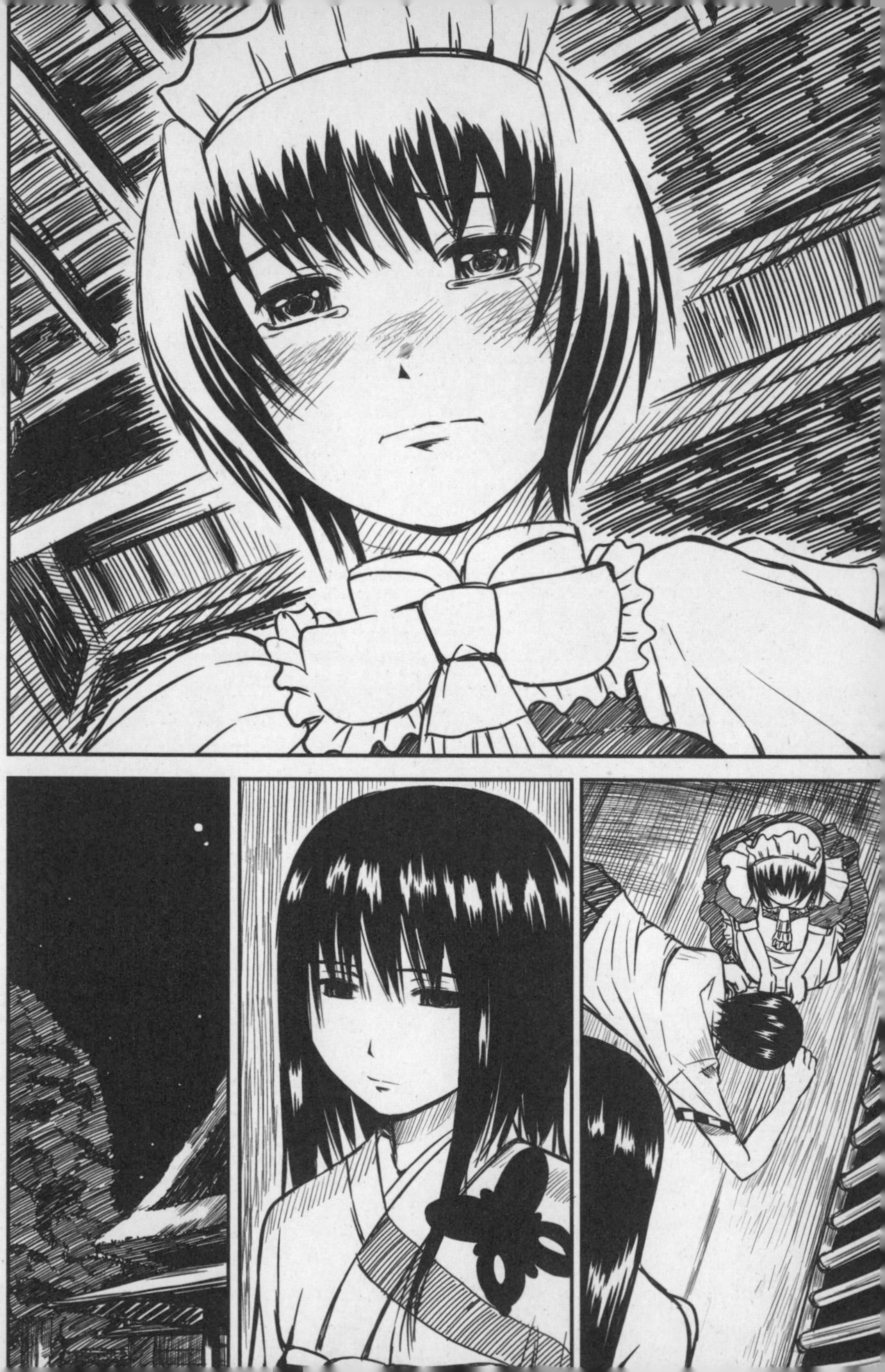

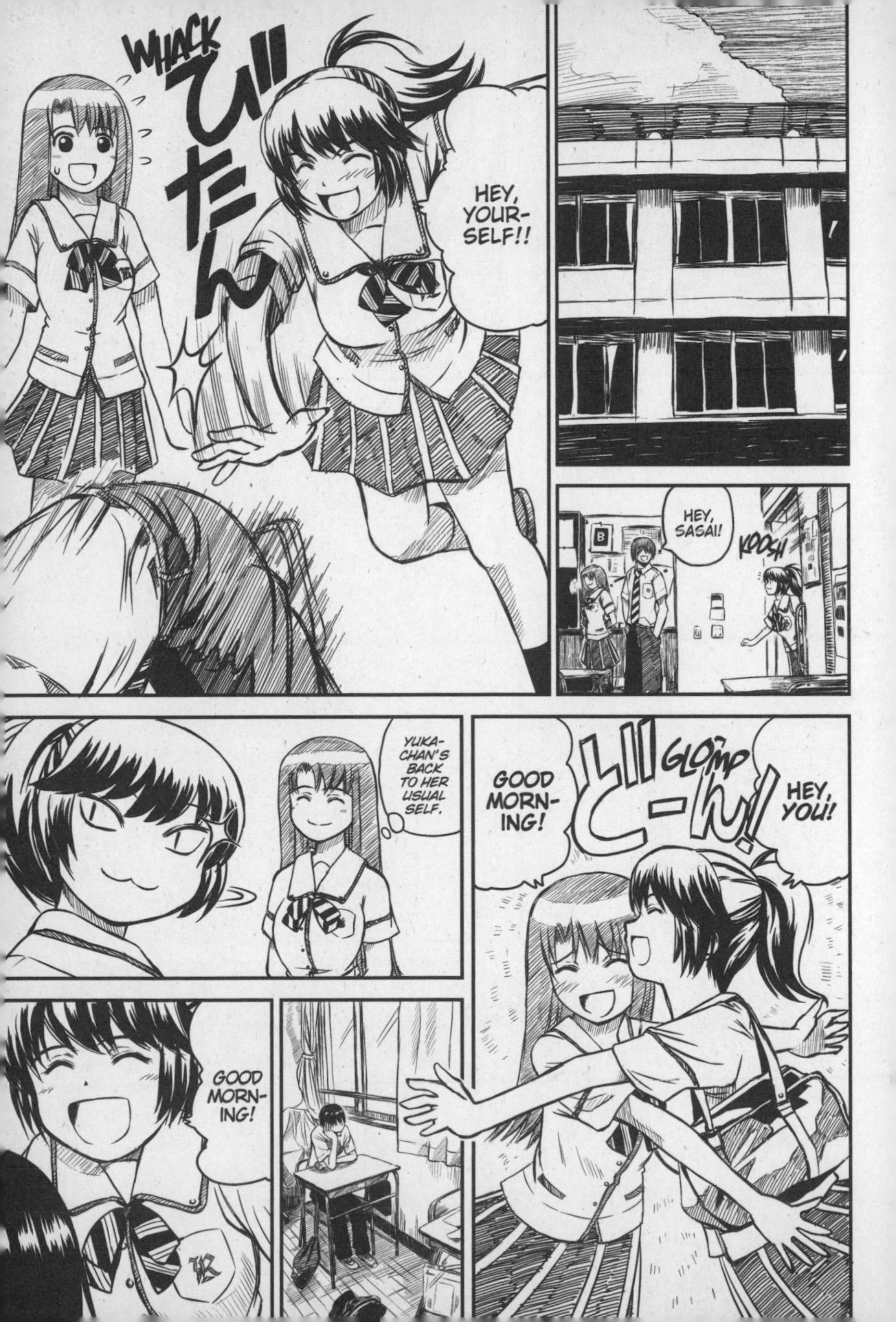
KOOSH
HEY, SASAI!
HEY, YOURSELF!!
WHACK
びたん
HEY, YOU!
GLOMP
どーん!
GOOD MORNING!
YUKA-CHAN'S BACK TO HER USUAL SELF.
GOOD MORNING!

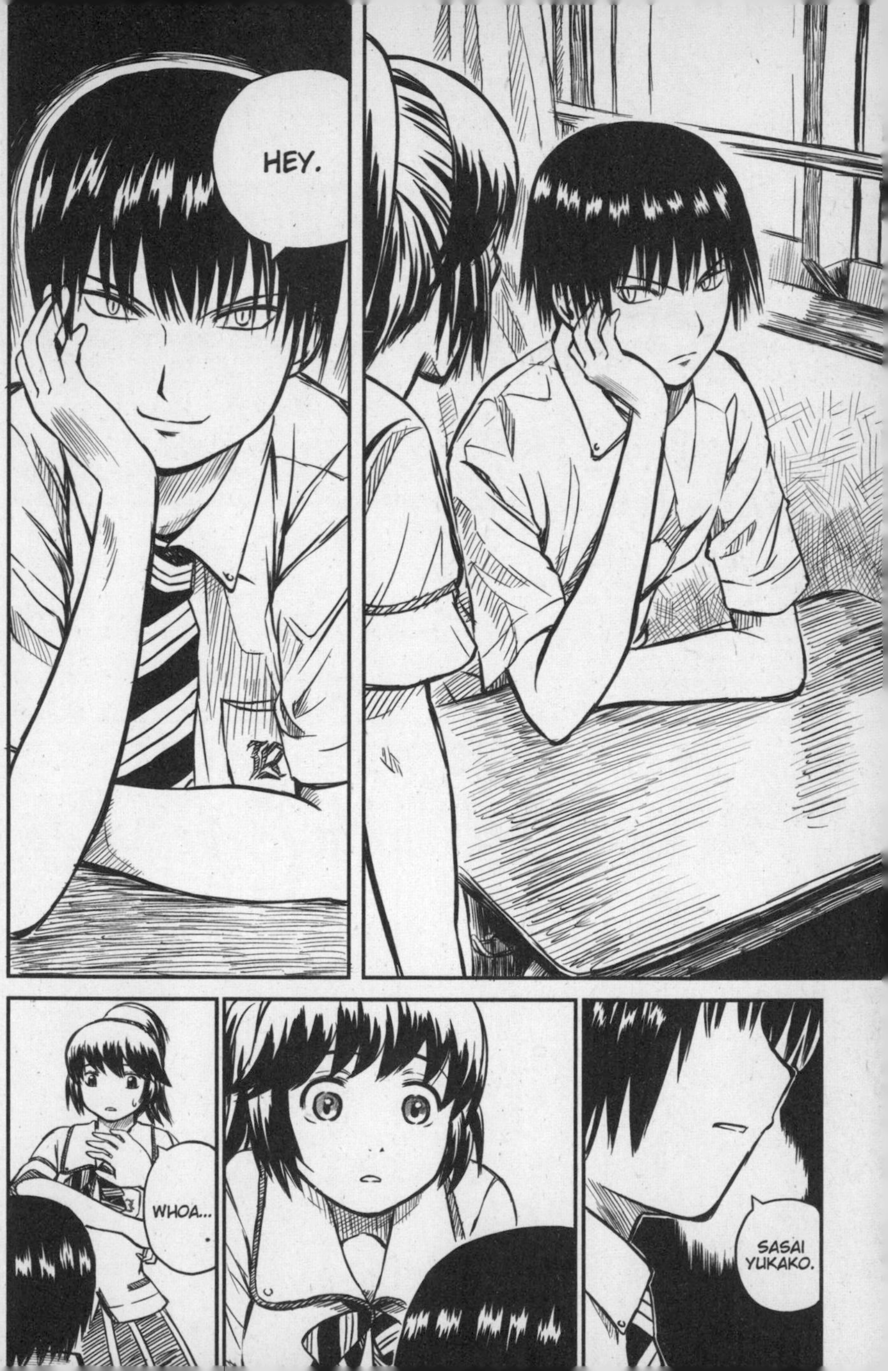
HEY.
SASAI YUKAKO.
WHOA...

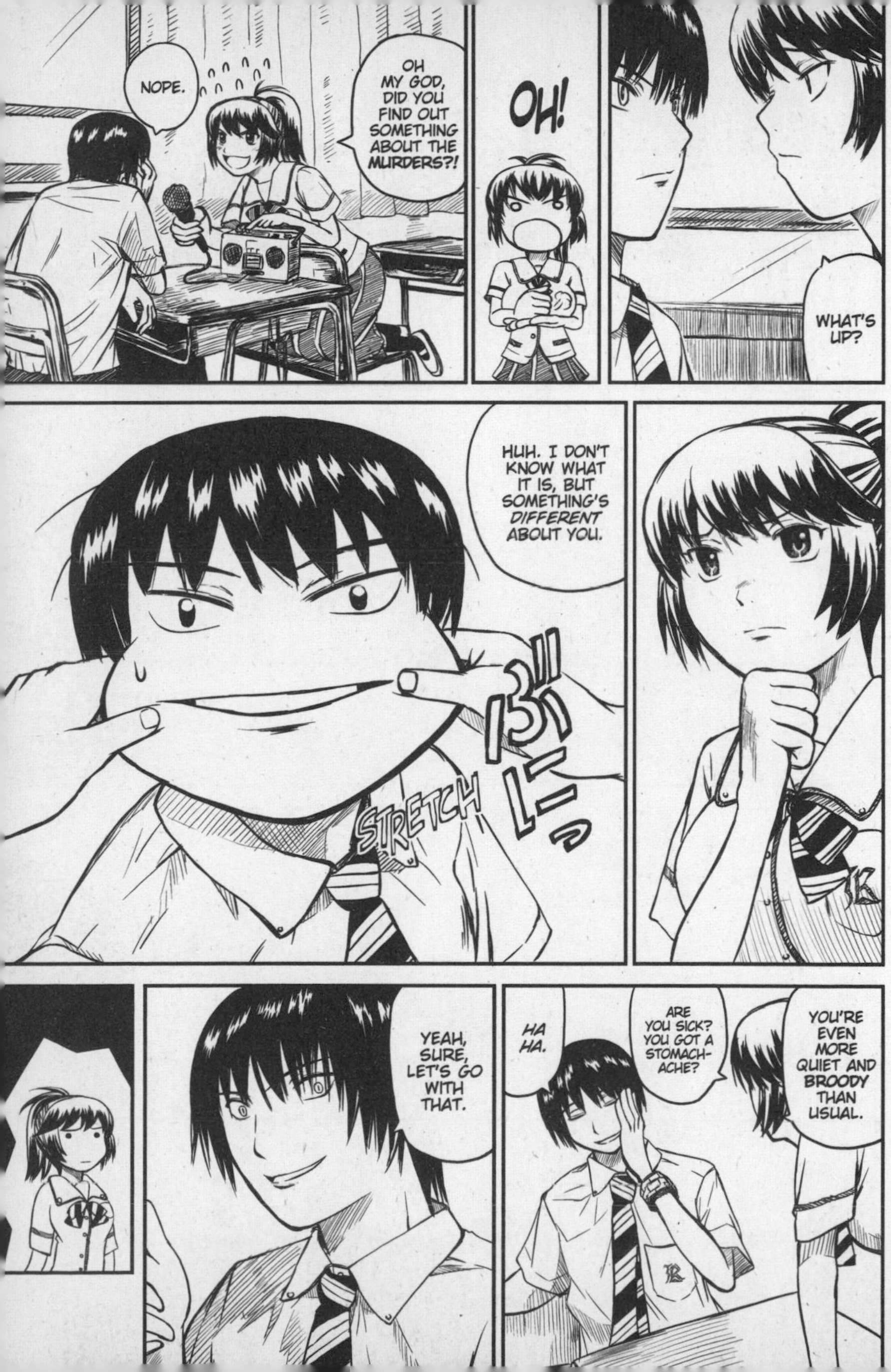
WHAT'S UP?
OH!
OH MY GOD, DID YOU FIND OUT SOMETHING ABOUT THE MURDERS?!
NOPE.
HUH. I DON'T KNOW WHAT IT IS, BUT SOMETHING'S *DIFFERENT* ABOUT YOU.
ぶにーっ
STRETCH
YOU'RE EVEN MORE QUIET AND BROODY THAN USUAL.
ARE YOU SICK? YOU GOT A STOMACH-ACHE?
HA HA.
YEAH, SURE, LET'S GO WITH THAT.

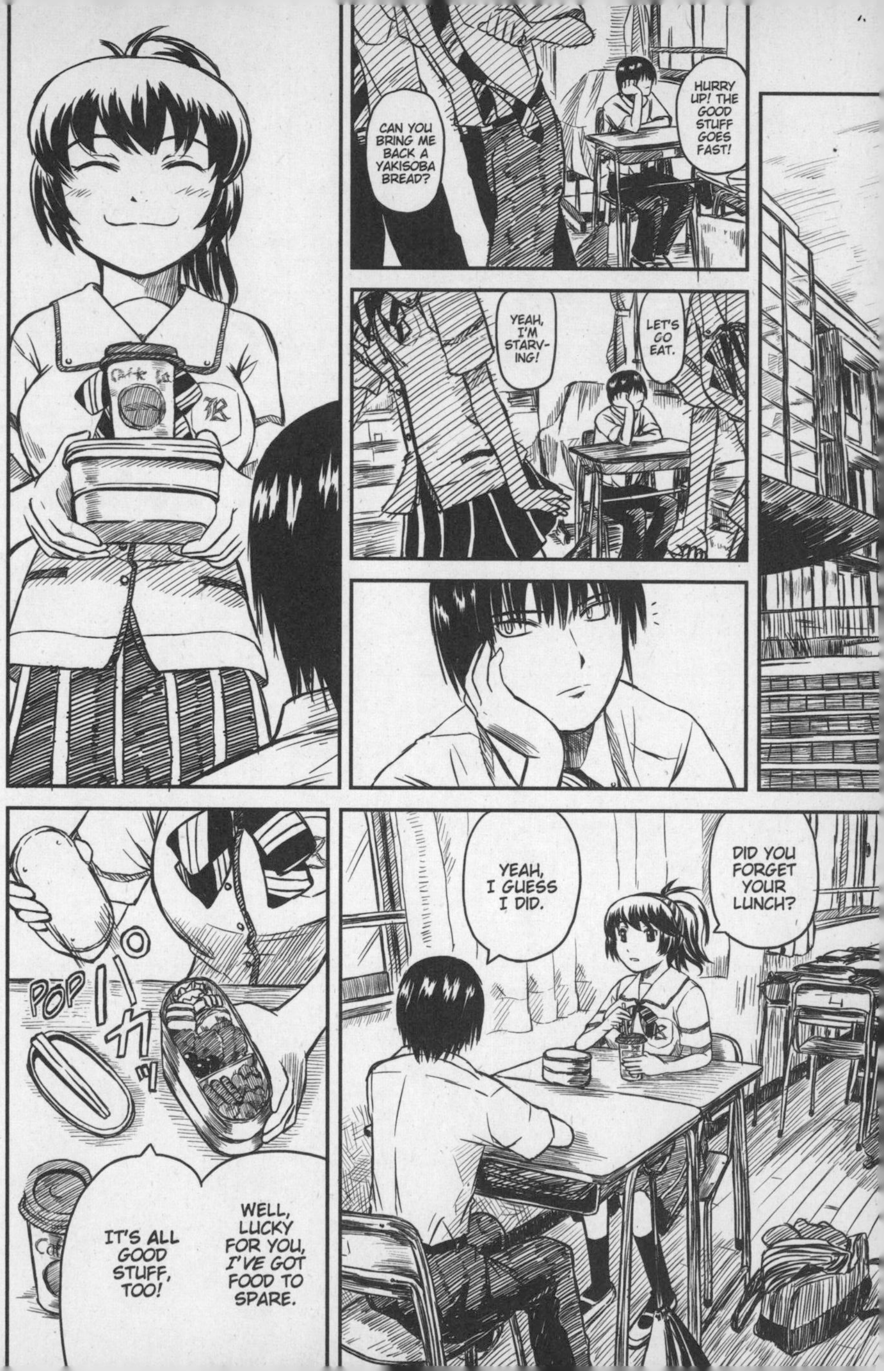
HURRY UP! THE GOOD STUFF GOES FAST!
CAN YOU BRING ME BACK A YAKISOBA BREAD?
LET'S GO EAT.
YEAH, I'M STARVING!
DID YOU FORGET YOUR LUNCH?
YEAH, I GUESS I DID.
POP
WELL, LUCKY FOR YOU, I'VE GOT FOOD TO SPARE.
IT'S ALL GOOD STUFF, TOO!

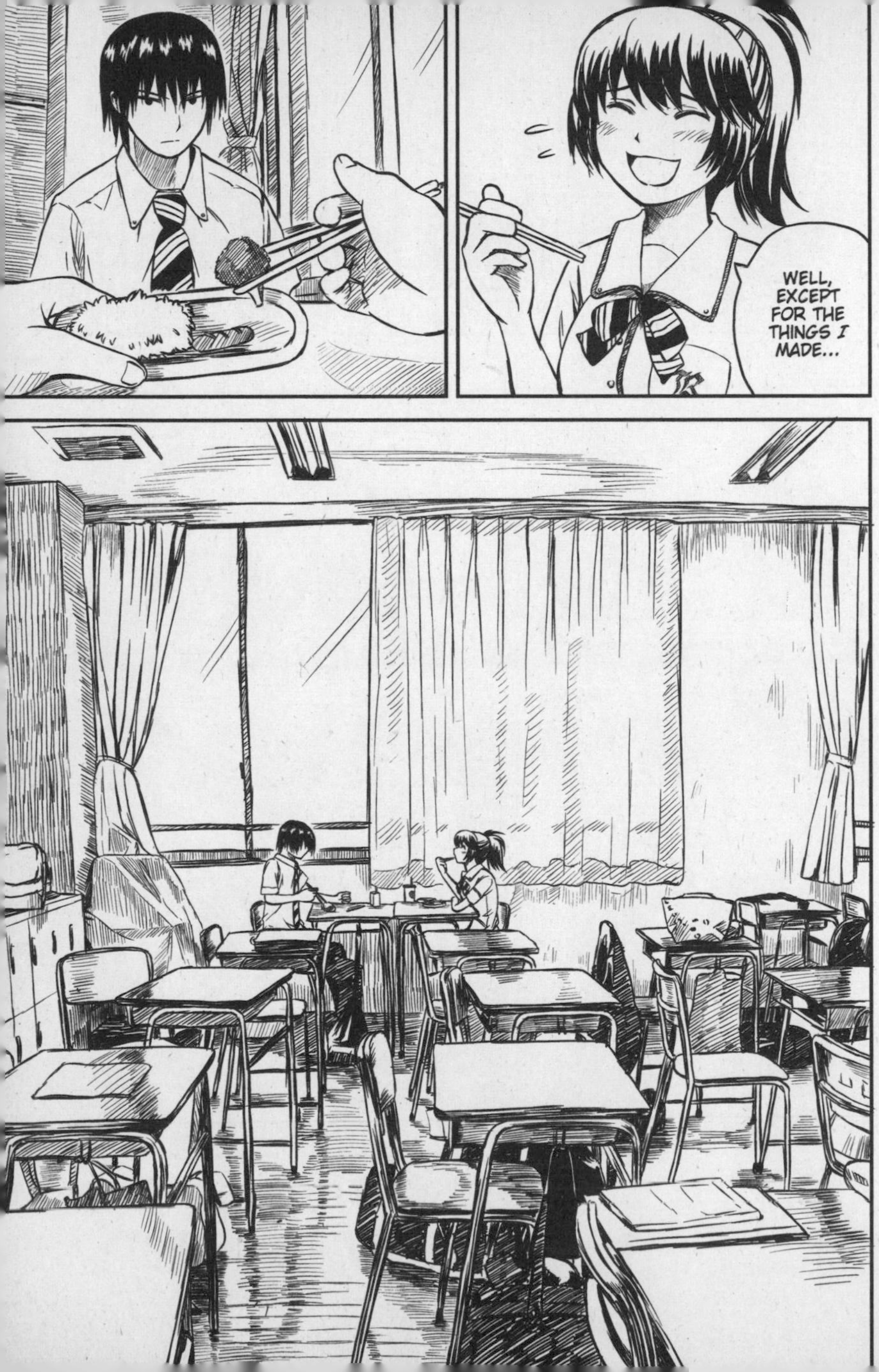
WELL, EXCEPT FOR THE THINGS I MADE...

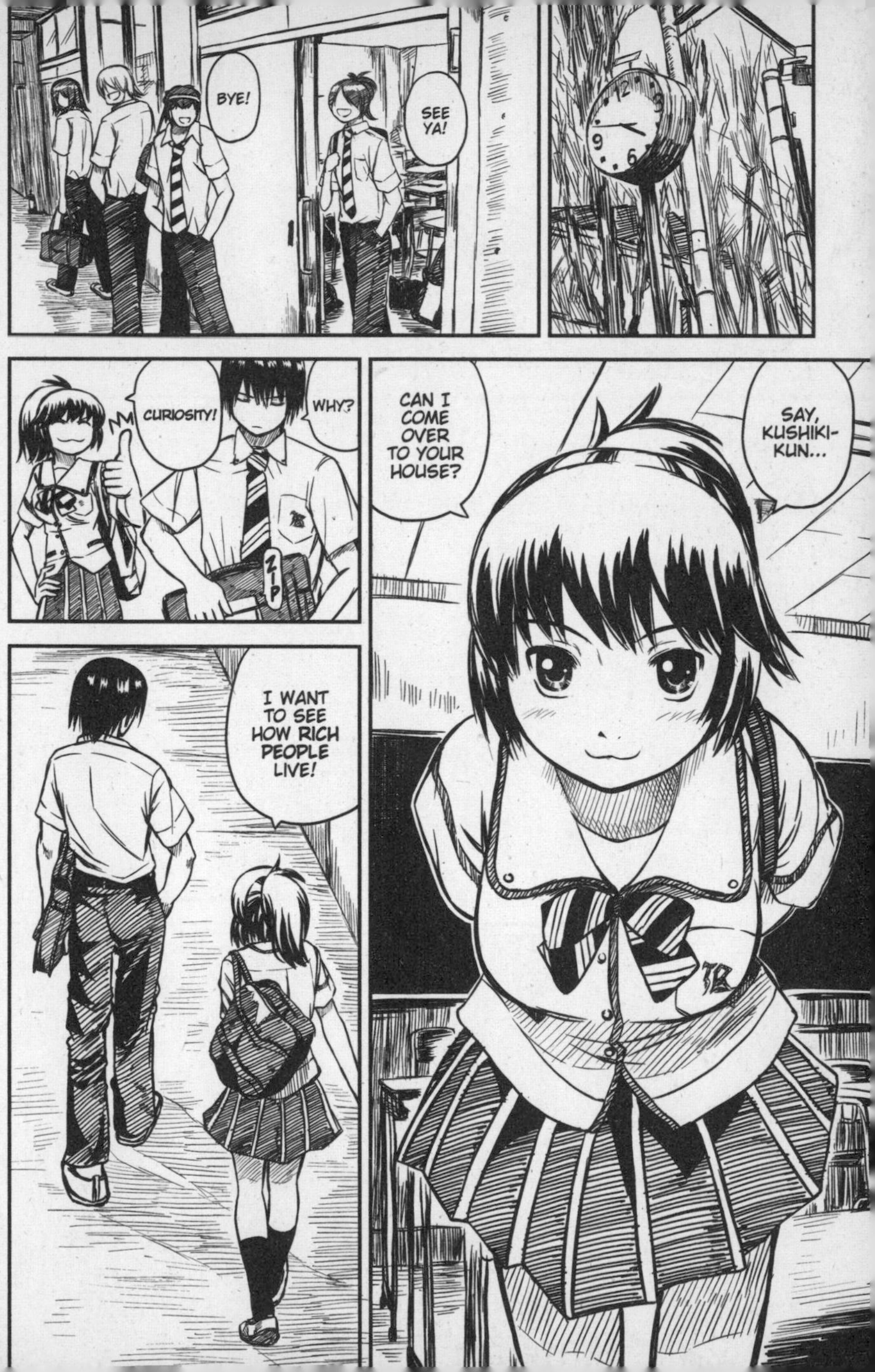
SEE YA!
BYE!
SAY, KUSHIKI-KUN...
CAN I COME OVER TO YOUR HOUSE?
WHY?
CURIOSITY!
ZIP
I WANT TO SEE HOW RICH PEOPLE LIVE!

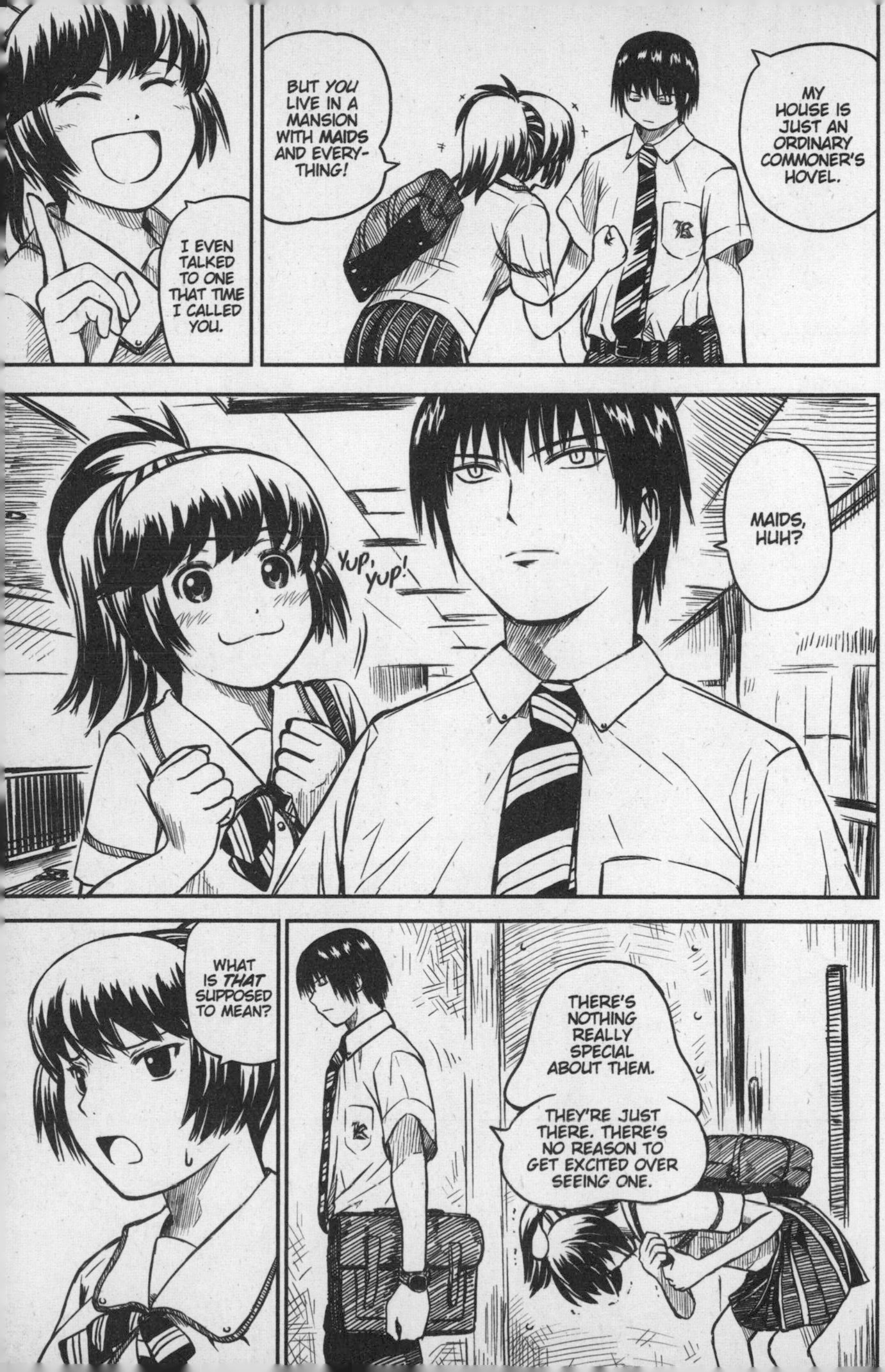
MY HOUSE IS JUST AN ORDINARY COMMONER'S HOVEL.
BUT YOU LIVE IN A MANSION WITH MAIDS AND EVERYTHING!
I EVEN TALKED TO ONE THAT TIME I CALLED YOU.
MAIDS, HUH?
YUP, YUP!
THERE'S NOTHING REALLY SPECIAL ABOUT THEM.
THEY'RE JUST THERE. THERE'S NO REASON TO GET EXCITED OVER SEEING ONE.
WHAT IS THAT SUPPOSED TO MEAN?

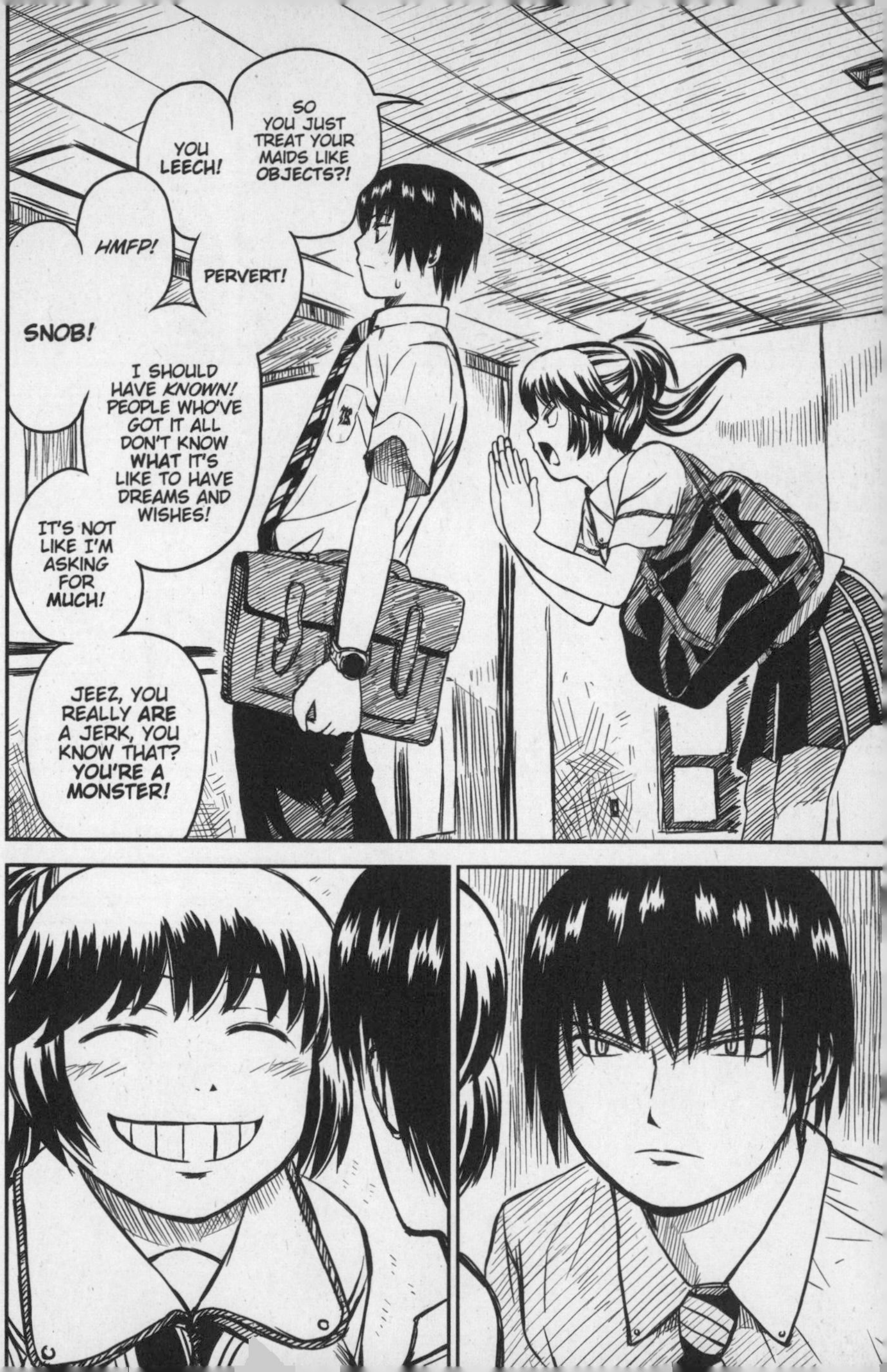
SO YOU JUST TREAT YOUR MAIDS LIKE OBJECTS?!
YOU LEECH!
PERVERT!
HMFP!
SNOB!
I SHOULD HAVE *KNOWN!* PEOPLE WHO'VE GOT IT ALL DON'T KNOW WHAT IT'S LIKE TO HAVE DREAMS AND WISHES!
IT'S NOT LIKE I'M ASKING FOR MUCH!
JEEZ, YOU REALLY ARE A JERK, YOU KNOW THAT? YOU'RE A MONSTER!

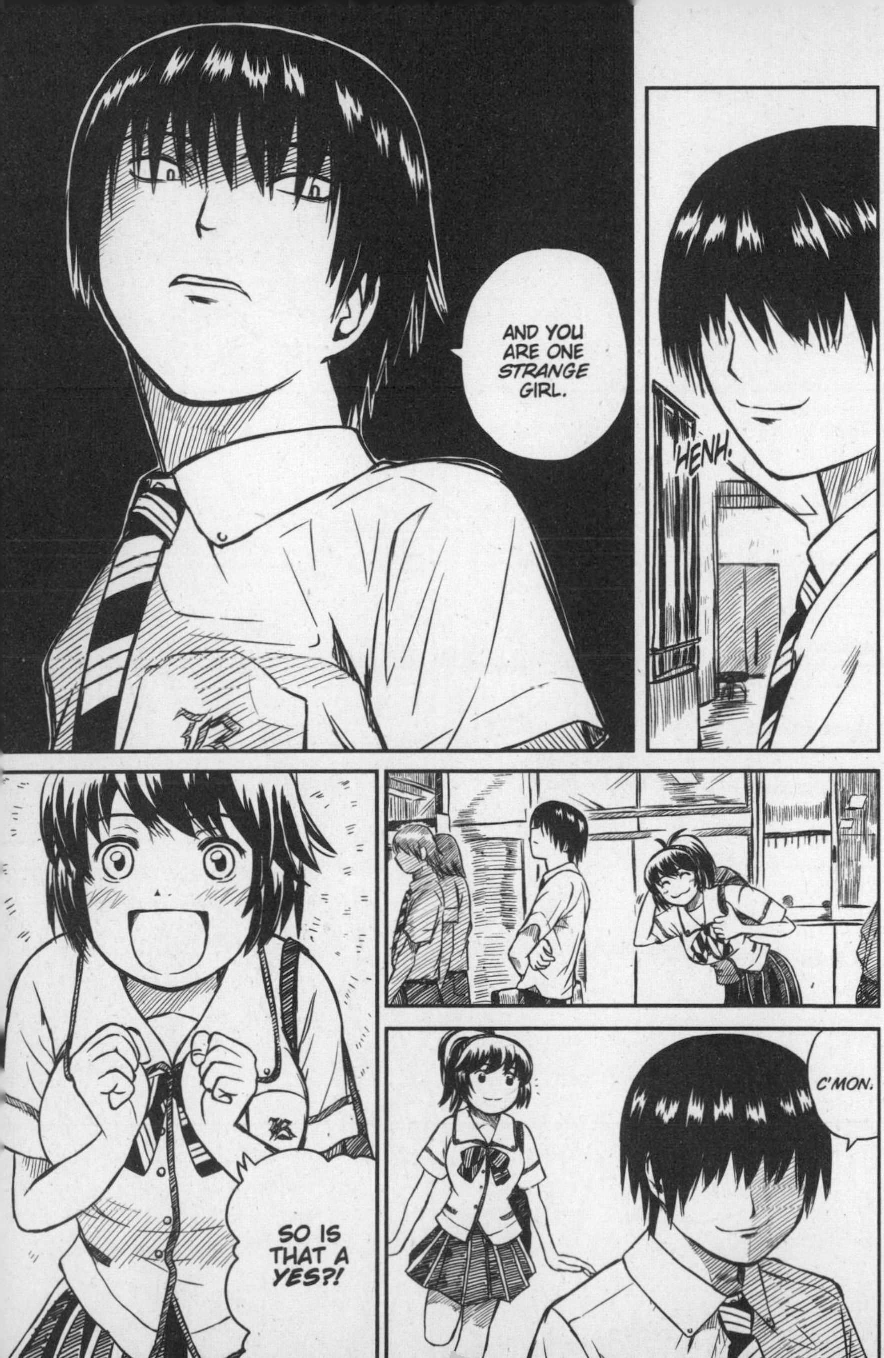
HENH.
AND YOU ARE ONE STRANGE GIRL.
C'MON.
SO IS THAT A YES?!

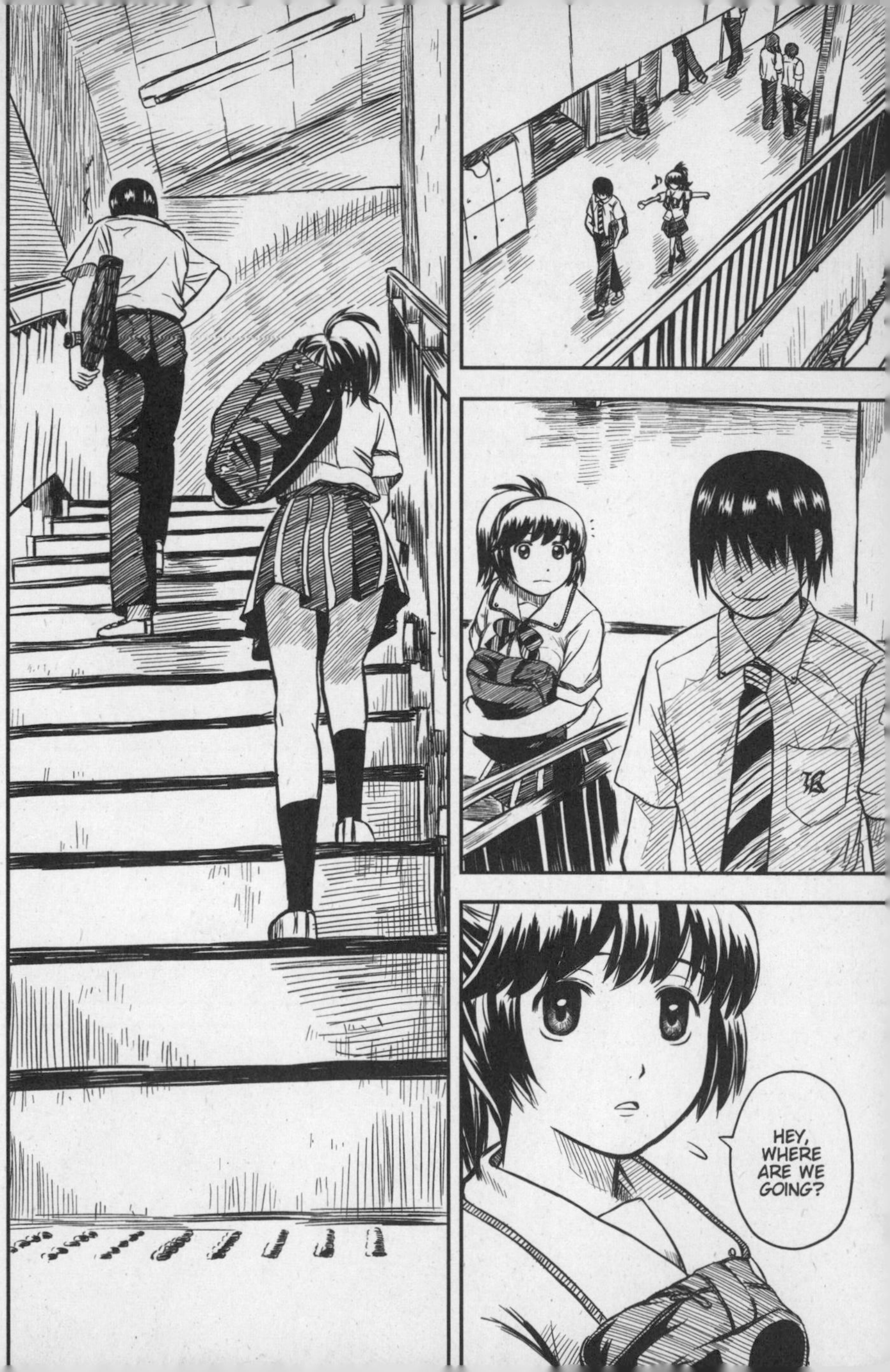
HEY, WHERE ARE WE GOING?

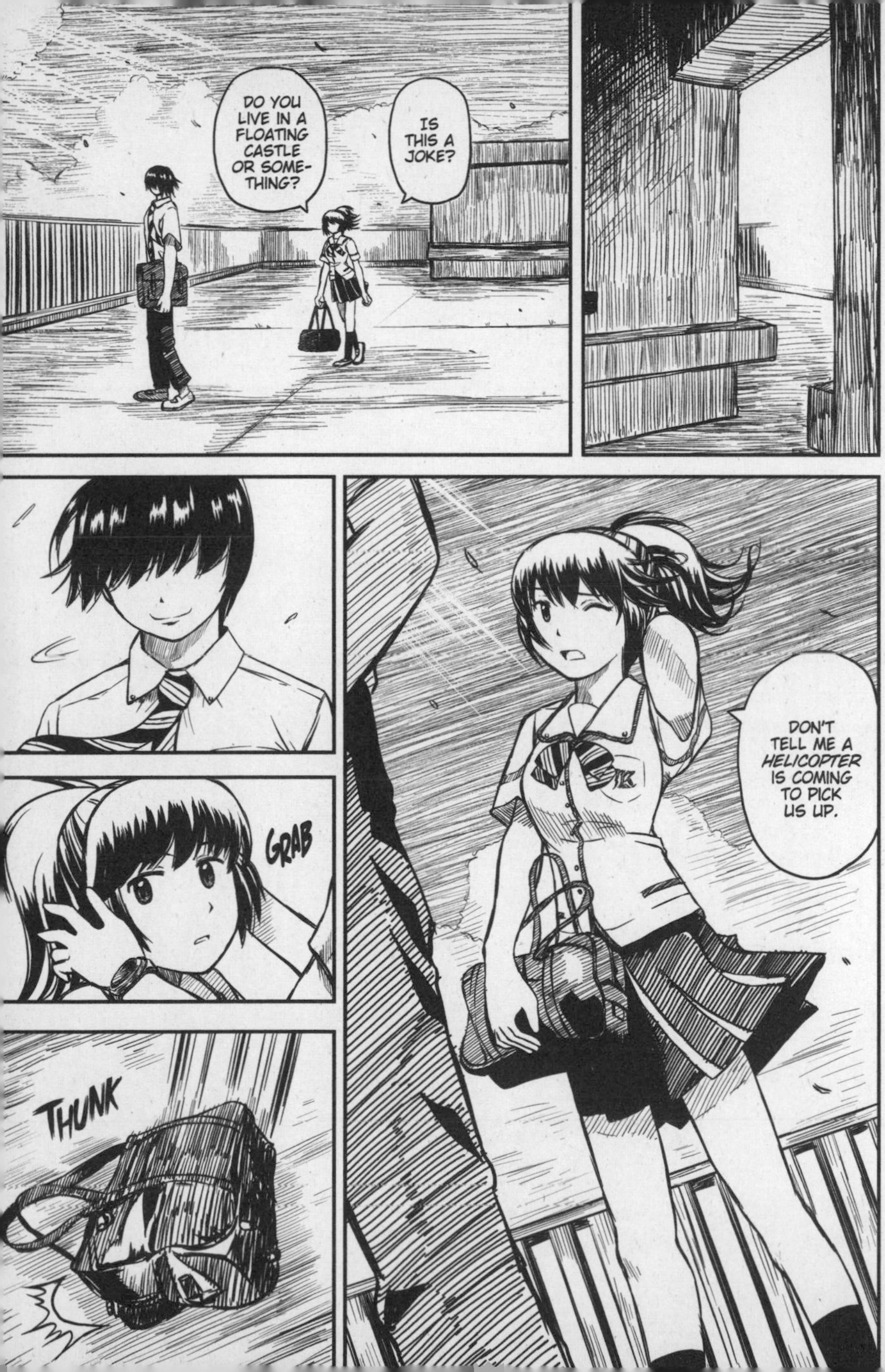
IS THIS A JOKE?
DO YOU LIVE IN A FLOATING CASTLE OR SOME-THING?
DON'T TELL ME A *HELICOPTER* IS COMING TO PICK US UP.
GRAB
THUNK

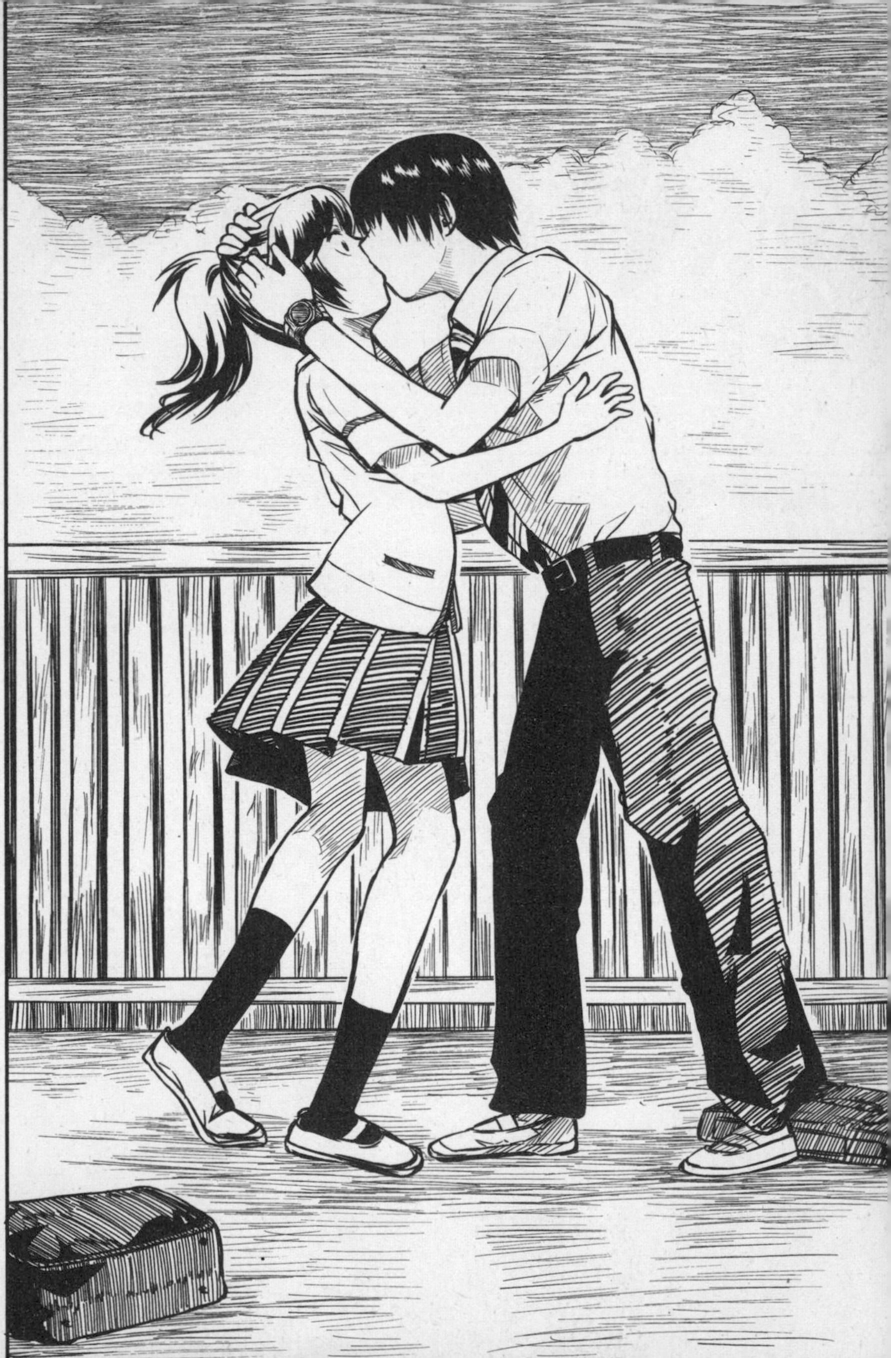

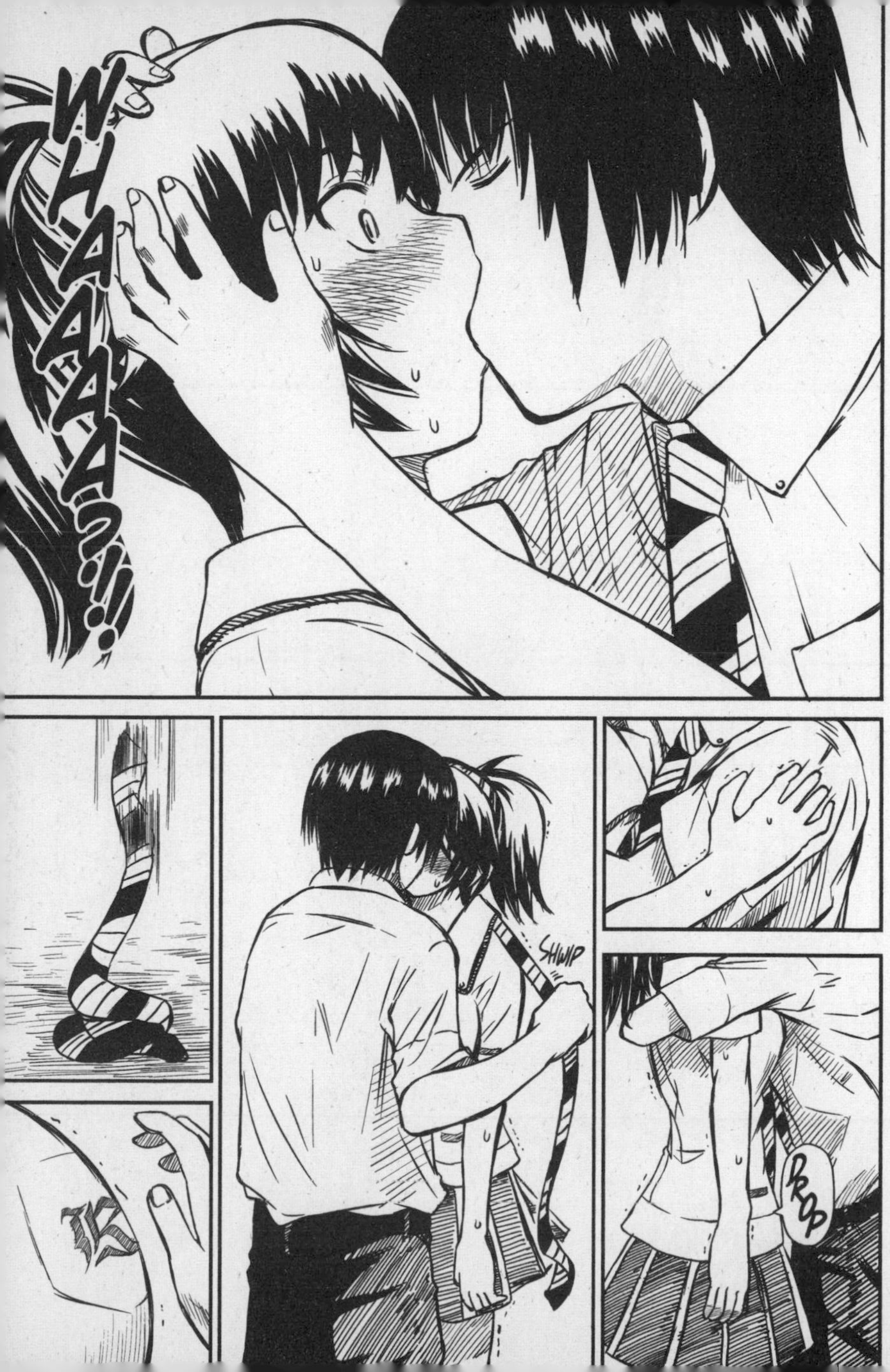
WHAAAAA?!!
DROP
SHWIP

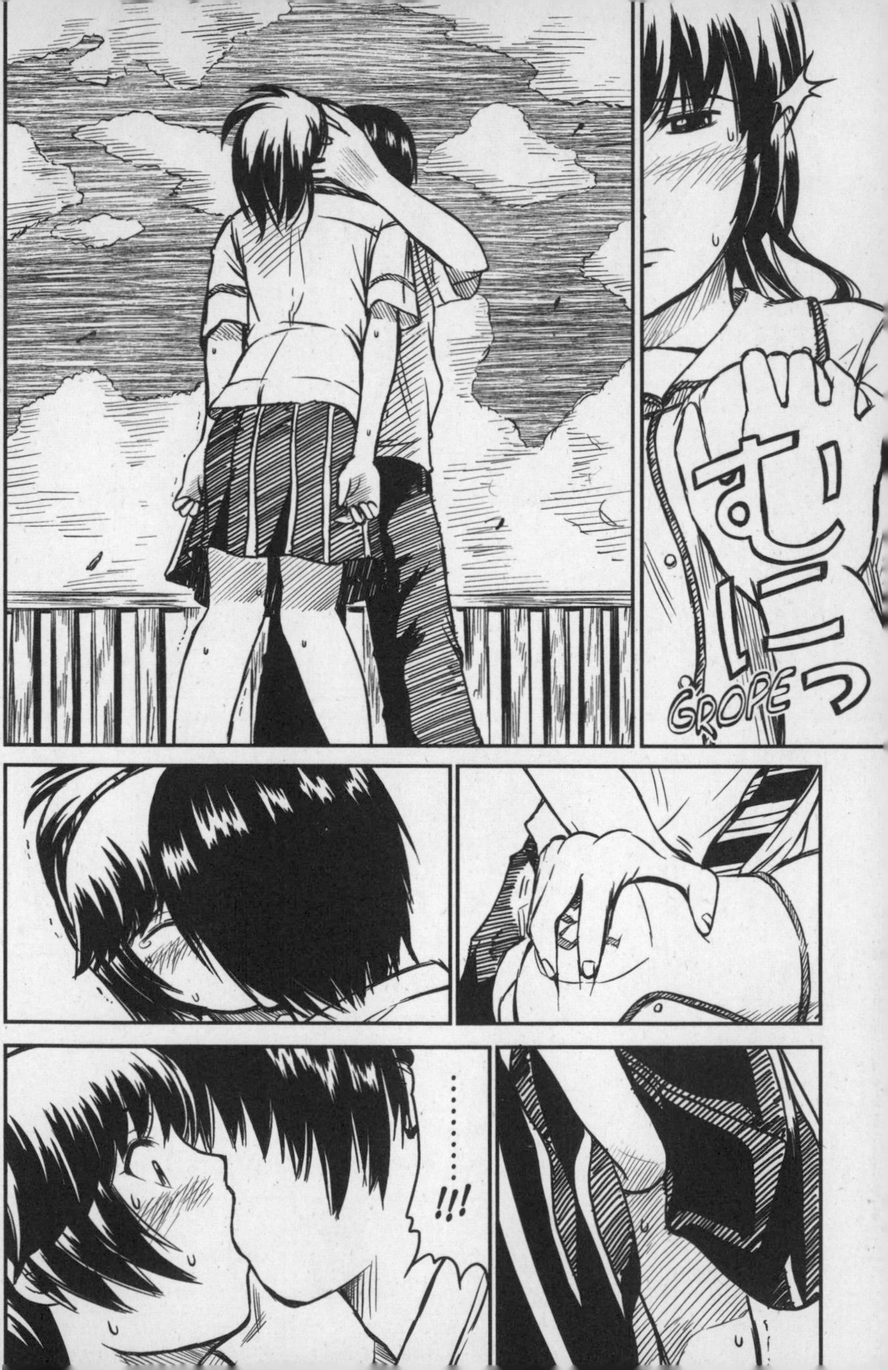
むにっ
GROPE
......
!!!

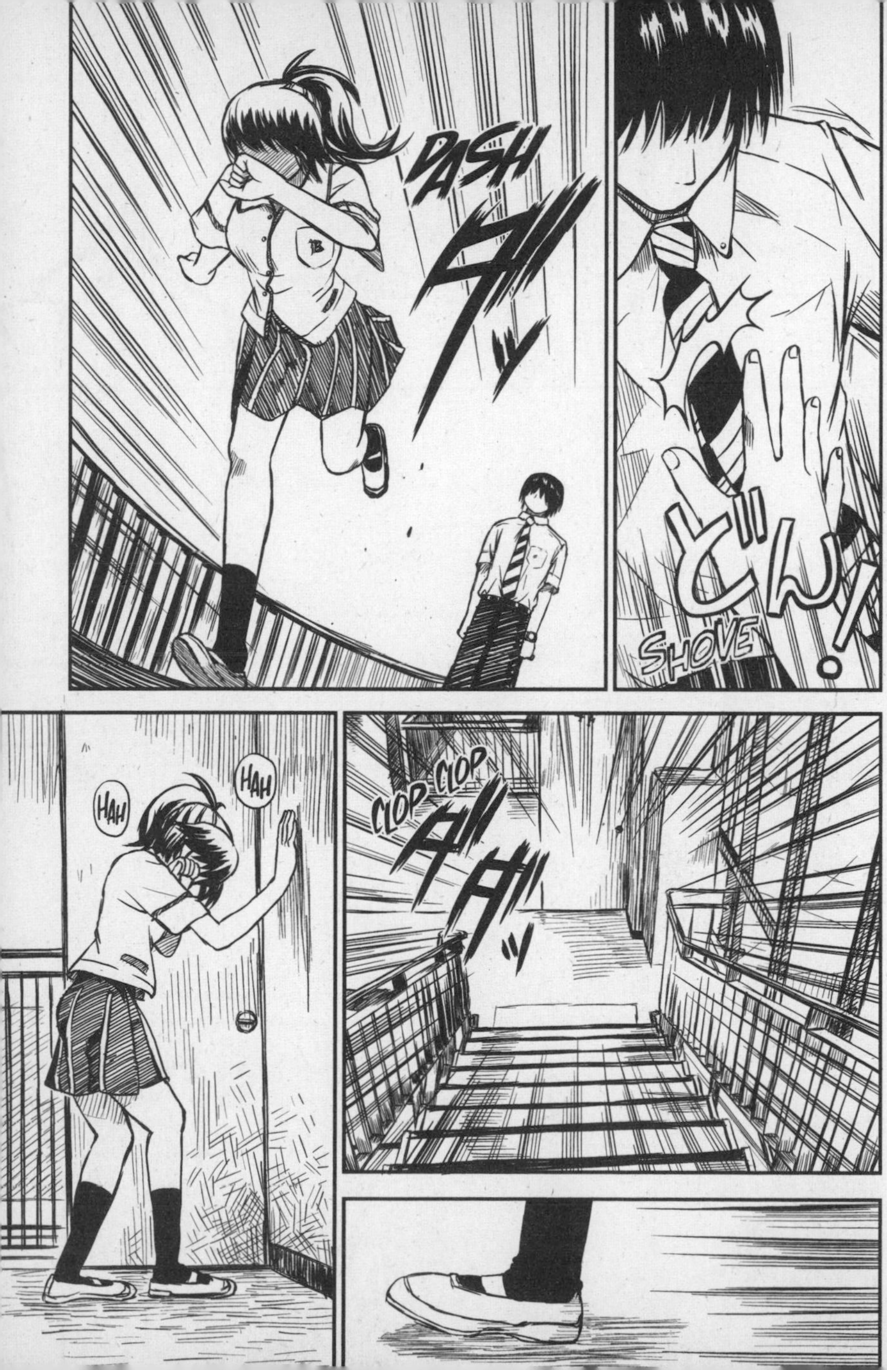
どん!
SHOVE
DASH
ダッ
CLOP CLOP
ダッ ダッ
HAH
HAH

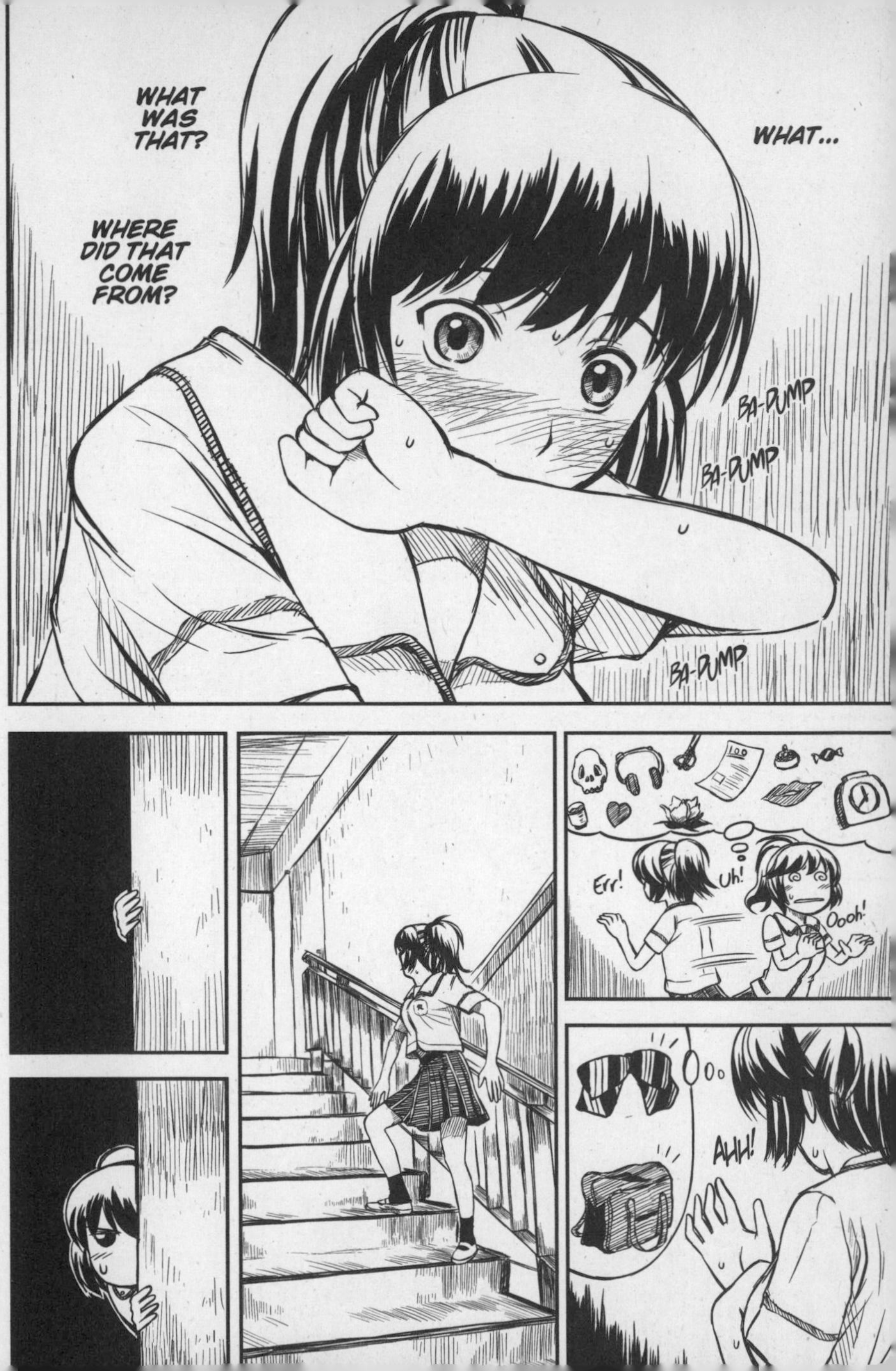
WHAT...
WHAT WAS THAT?
WHERE DID THAT COME FROM?
BA-DUMP
BA-DUMP
BA-DUMP
Oooh!
Uh!
Err!
AHH!
Ooo

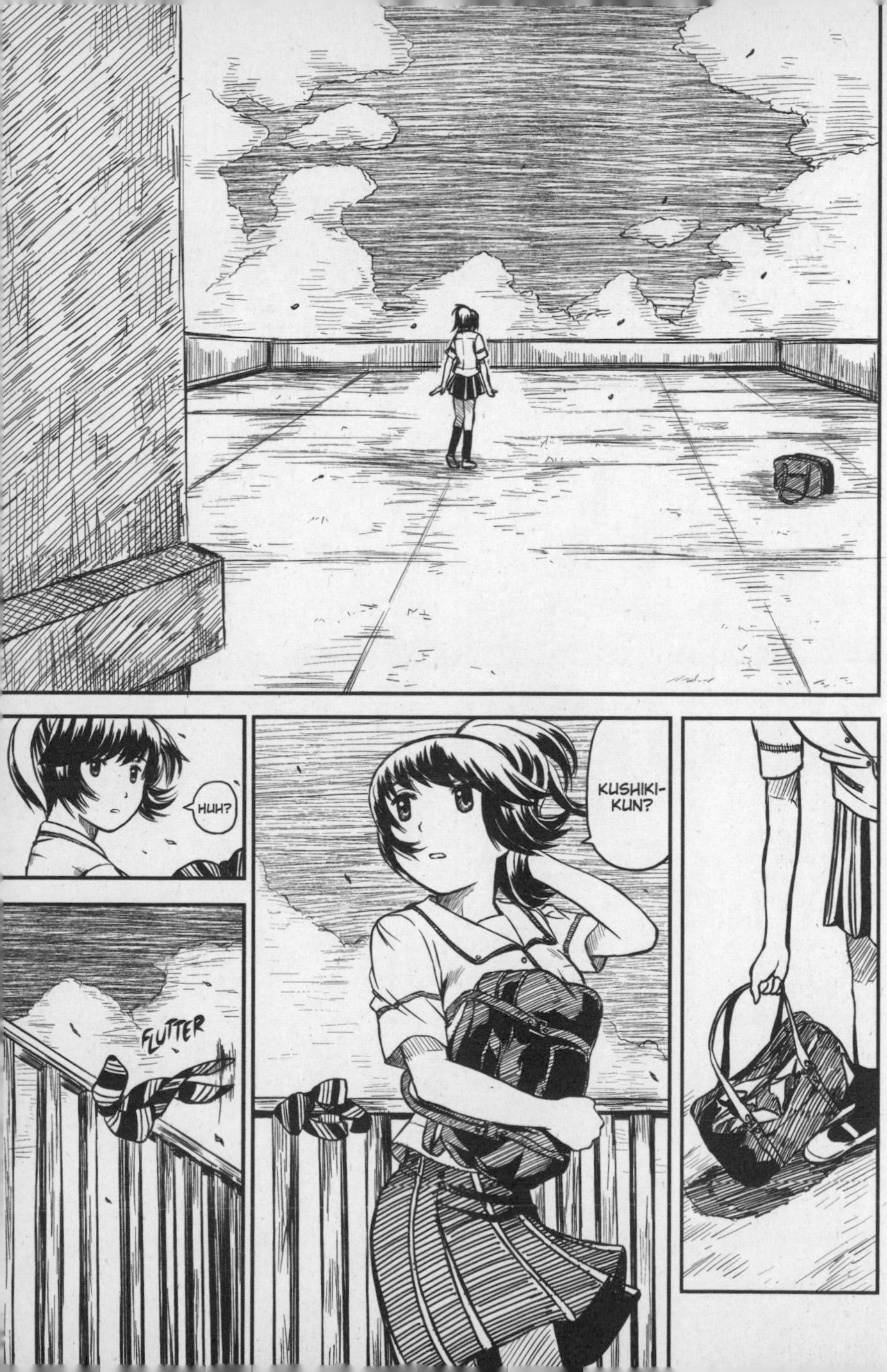
KUSHIKI-KUN?
HUH?
FLUTTER

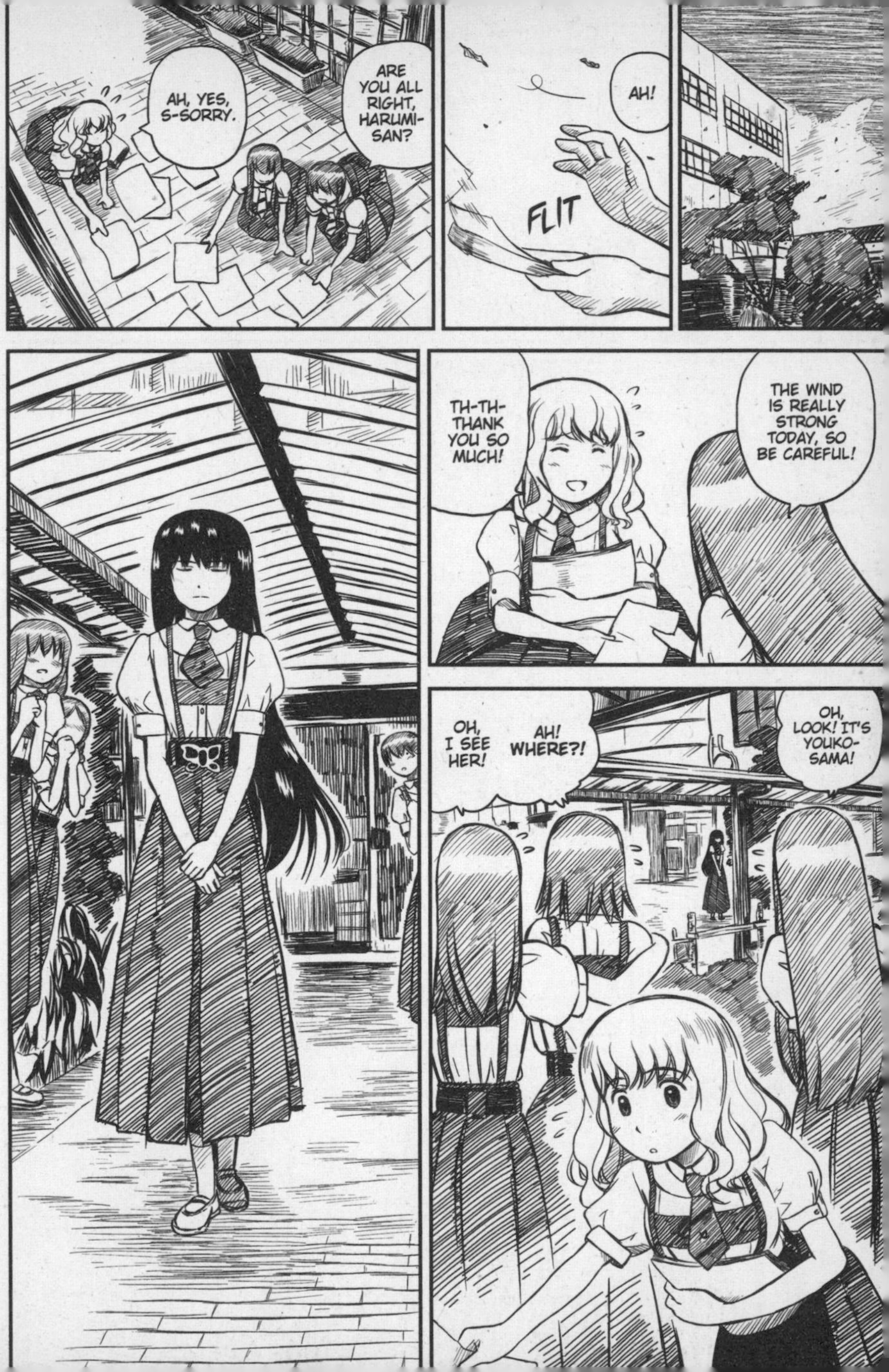
AH!
FLIT
ARE YOU ALL RIGHT, HARUMI-SAN?
AH, YES, S-SORRY.
THE WIND IS REALLY STRONG TODAY, SO BE CAREFUL!
TH-TH-THANK YOU SO MUCH!
OH, LOOK! IT'S YOUKO-SAMA!
AH! WHERE?!
OH, I SEE HER!

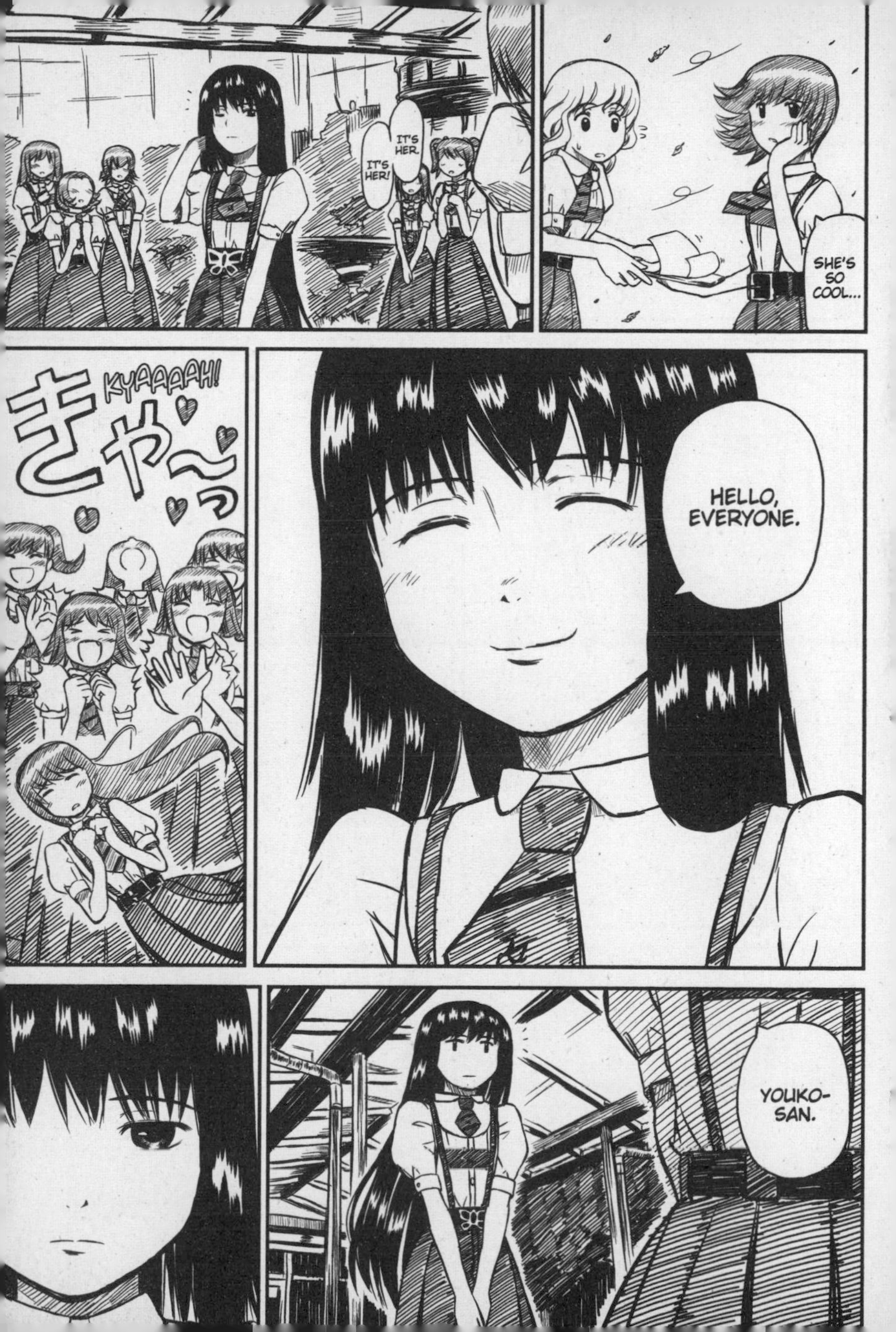
SHE'S SO COOL...
IT'S HER.
IT'S HER!
HELLO, EVERYONE.
KYAAAAH!
きゃ～っ
YOUKO-SAN.

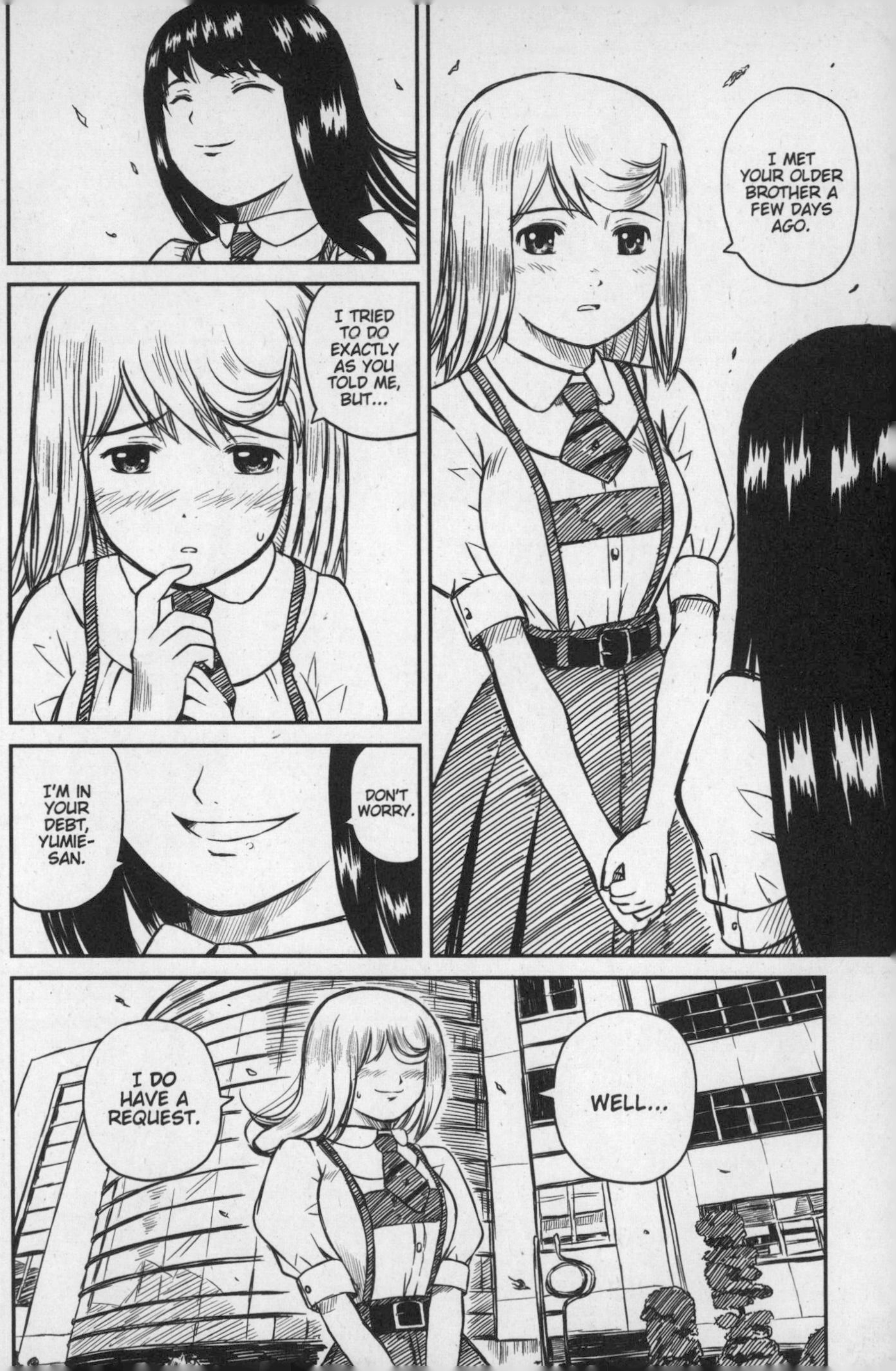
I MET YOUR OLDER BROTHER A FEW DAYS AGO.
I TRIED TO DO EXACTLY AS YOU TOLD ME, BUT...
DON'T WORRY.
I'M IN YOUR DEBT, YUMIE-SAN.
WELL...
I DO HAVE A REQUEST.

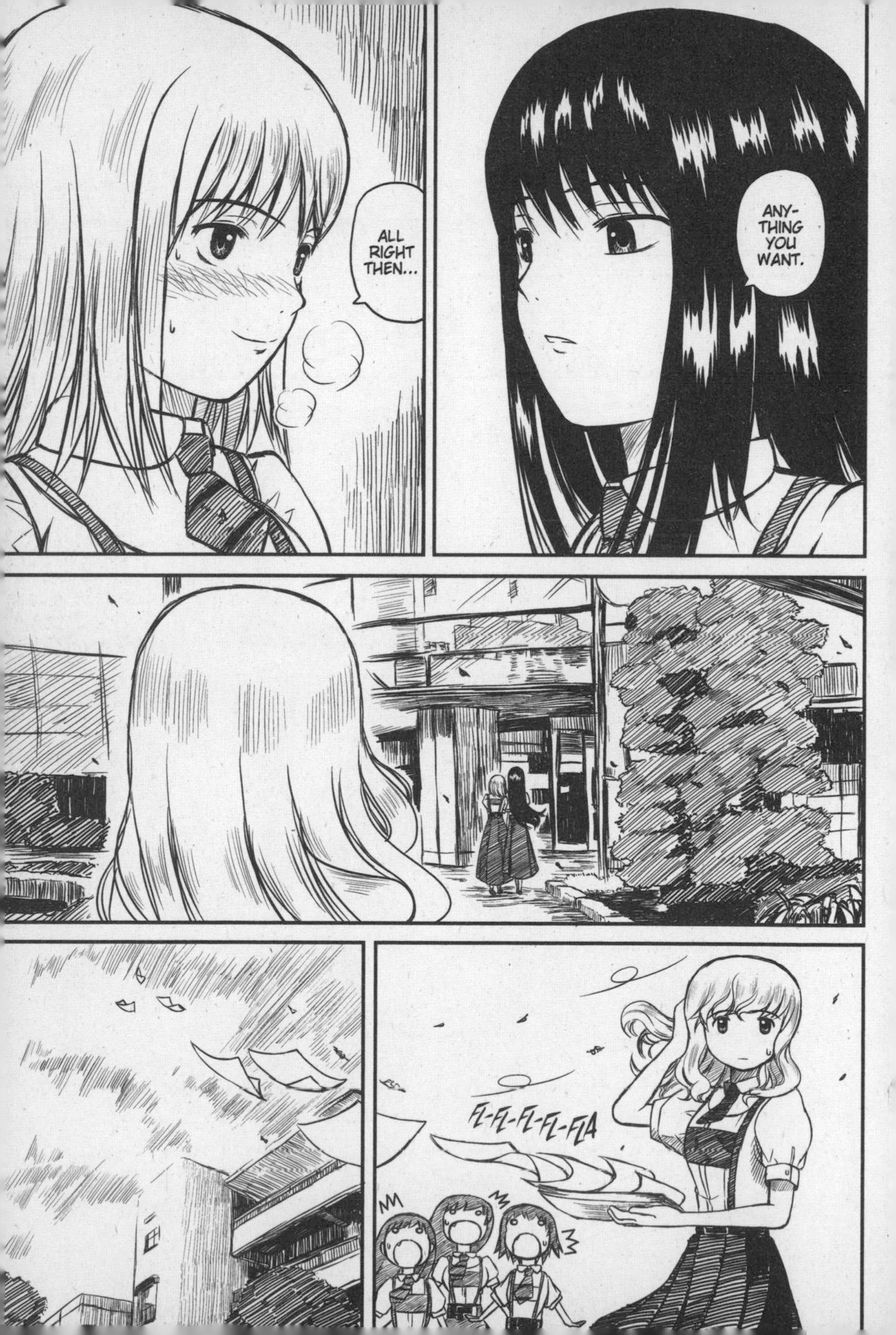
ANY-THING YOU WANT.
ALL RIGHT THEN...
FL-FL-FL-FL-FLA

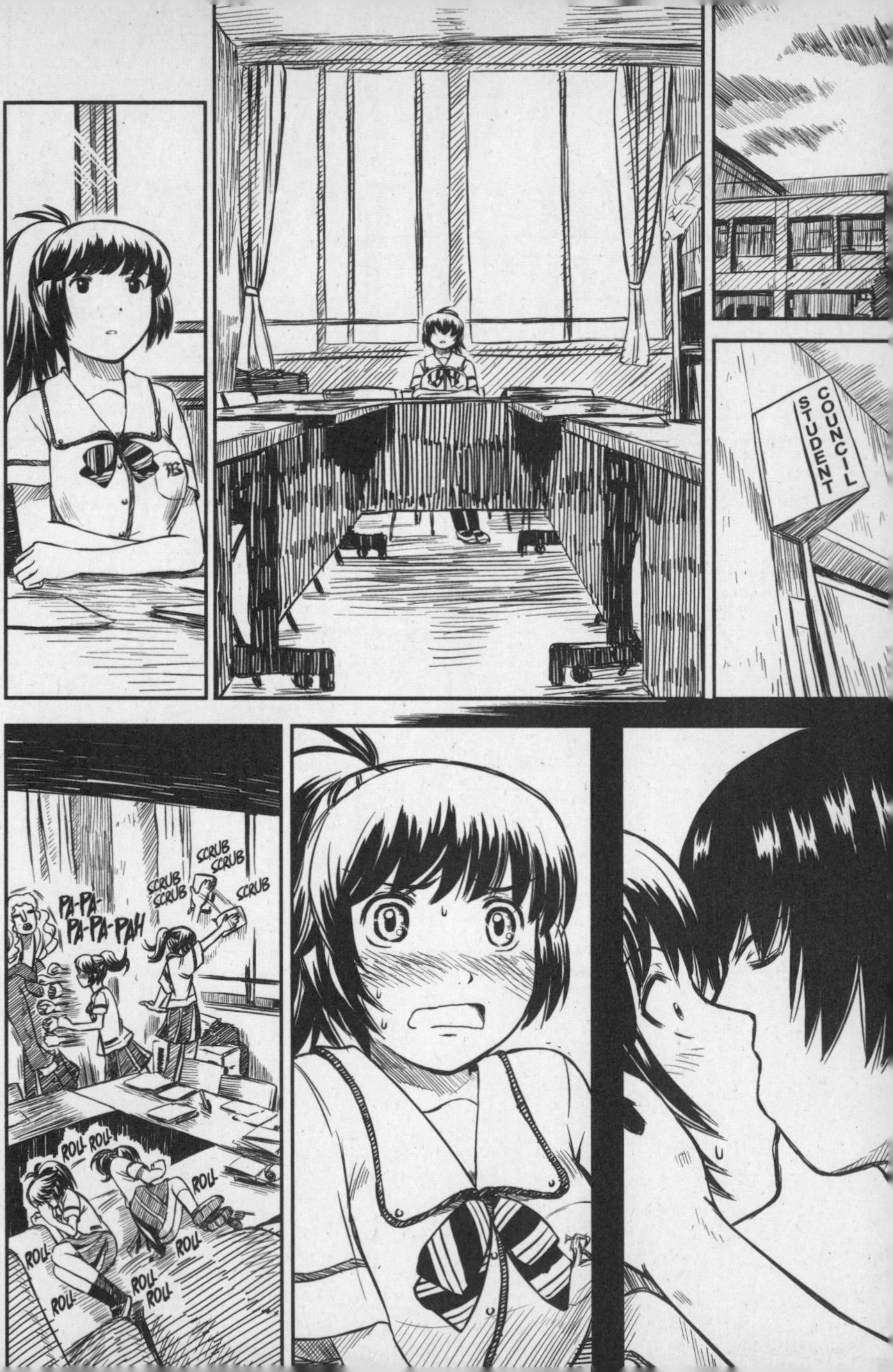
STUDENT COUNCIL
SCRUB SCRUB
SCRUB SCRUB
SCRUB
PA-PA-PA-PA-PAH
ROLL- ROLL-
ROLL-
ROLL-
ROLL-ROLL
ROLL-
ROLL

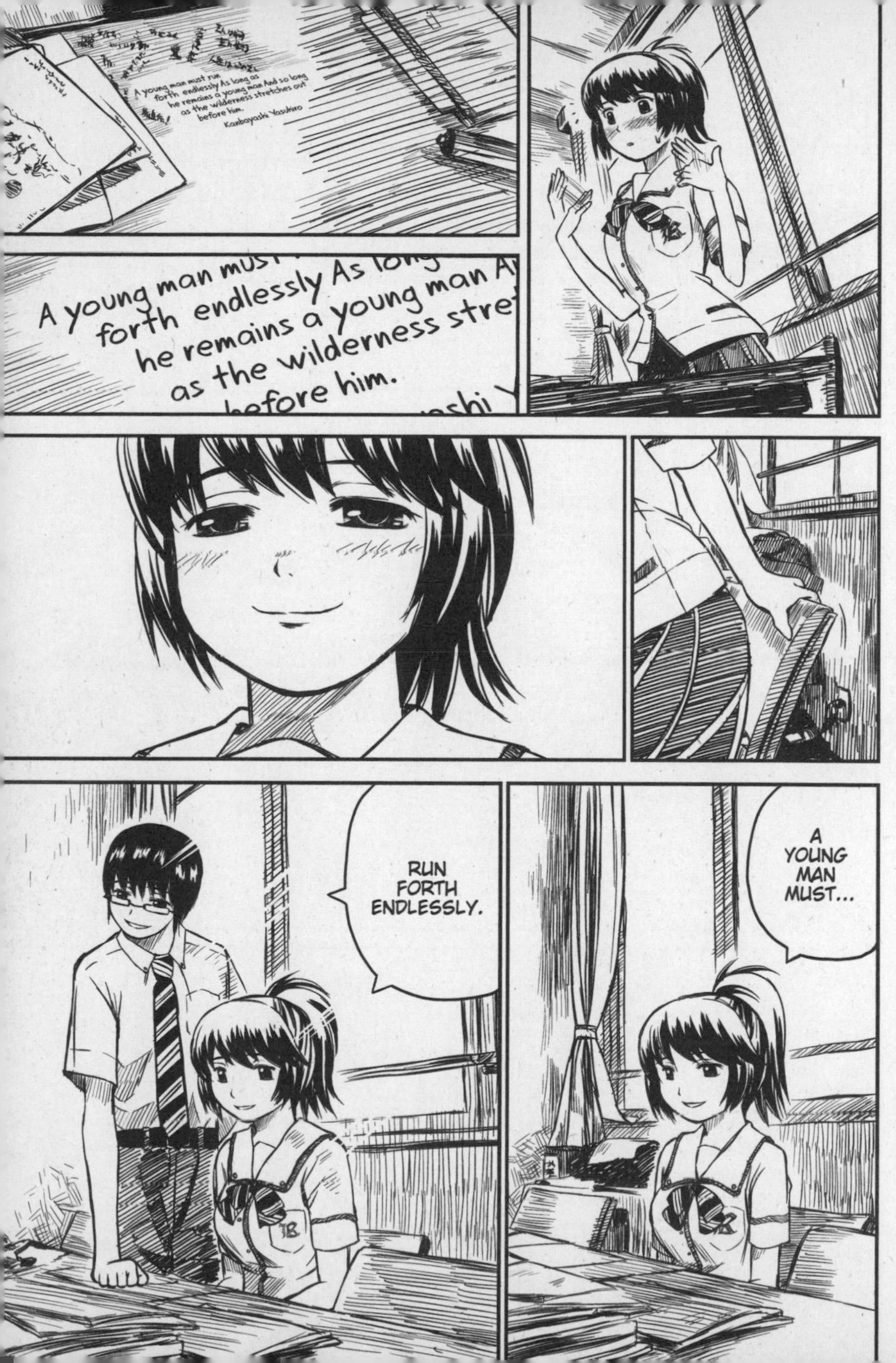
A young man must run forth endlessly As long as he remains a young man And so long as the wilderness stretches out before him.
Kanbayashi Yasuhiro
A young man must
forth endlessly As long
he remains a young man A
as the wilderness stret
before him.
A YOUNG MAN MUST...
RUN FORTH ENDLESSLY.

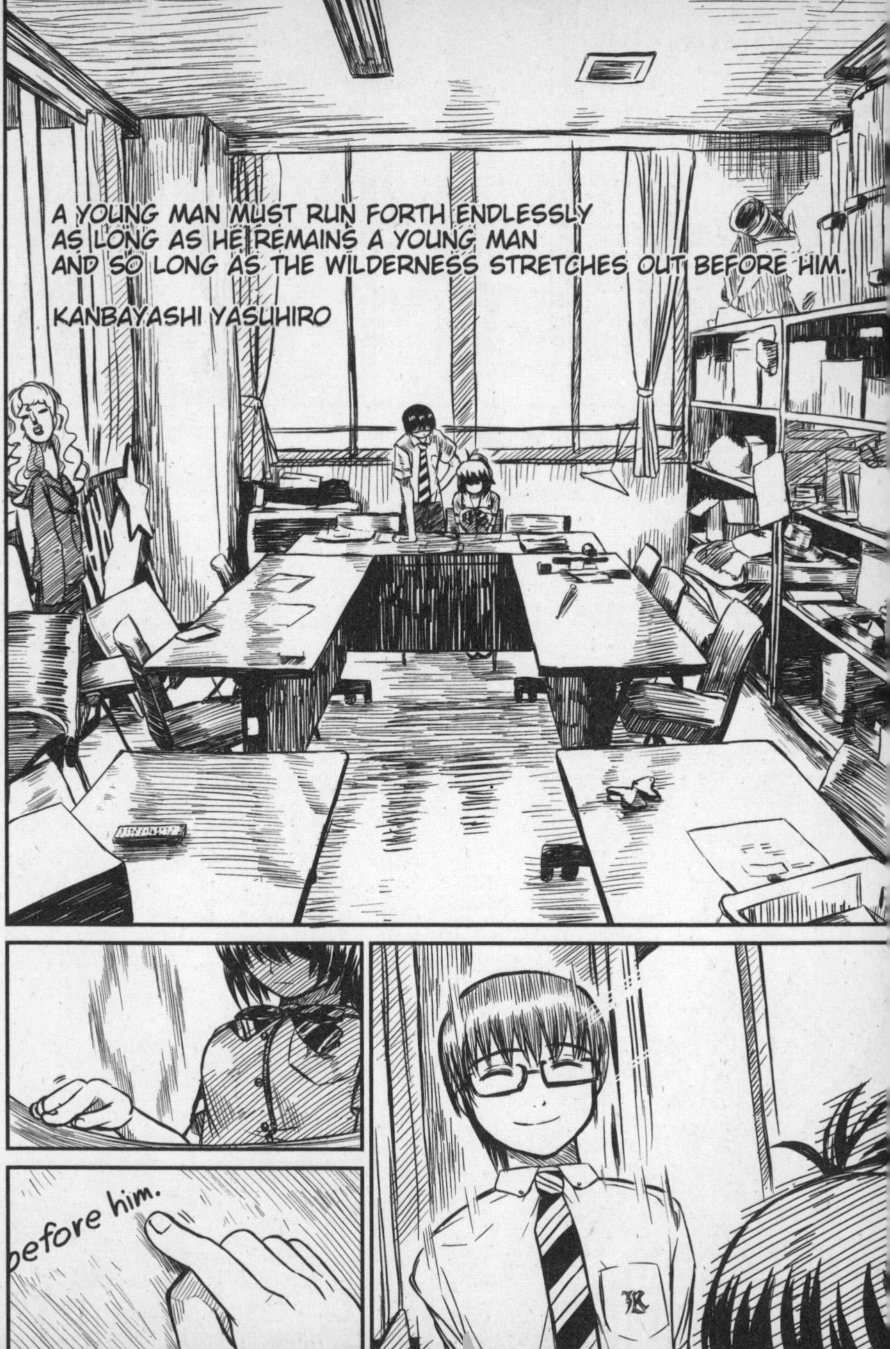
A YOUNG MAN MUST RUN FORTH ENDLESSLY
AS LONG AS HE REMAINS A YOUNG MAN
AND SO LONG AS THE WILDERNESS STRETCHES OUT BEFORE HIM.
KANBAYASHI YASUHIRO
before him.

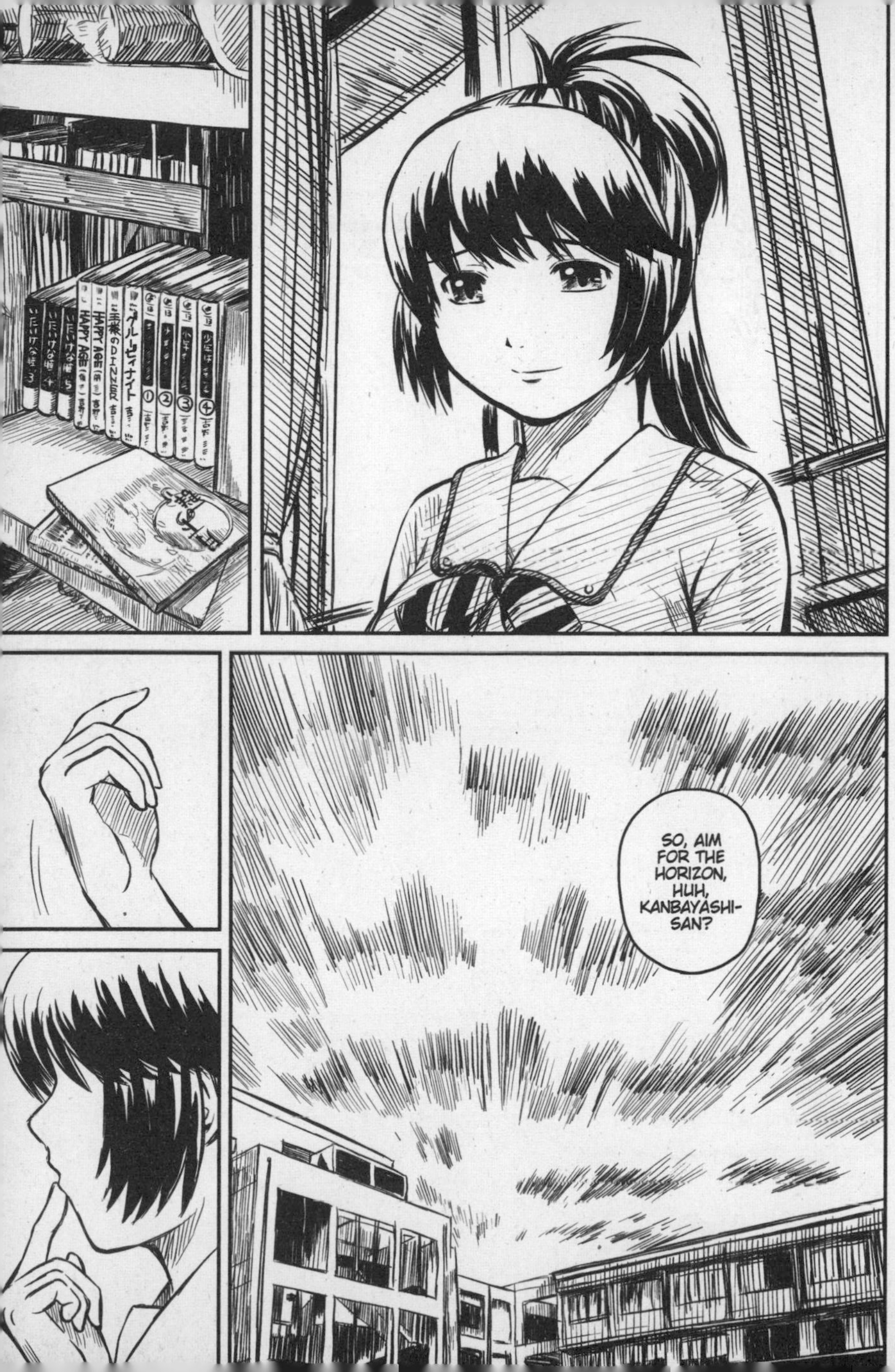
SO, AIM FOR THE HORIZON, HUH, KANBAYASHI-SAN?

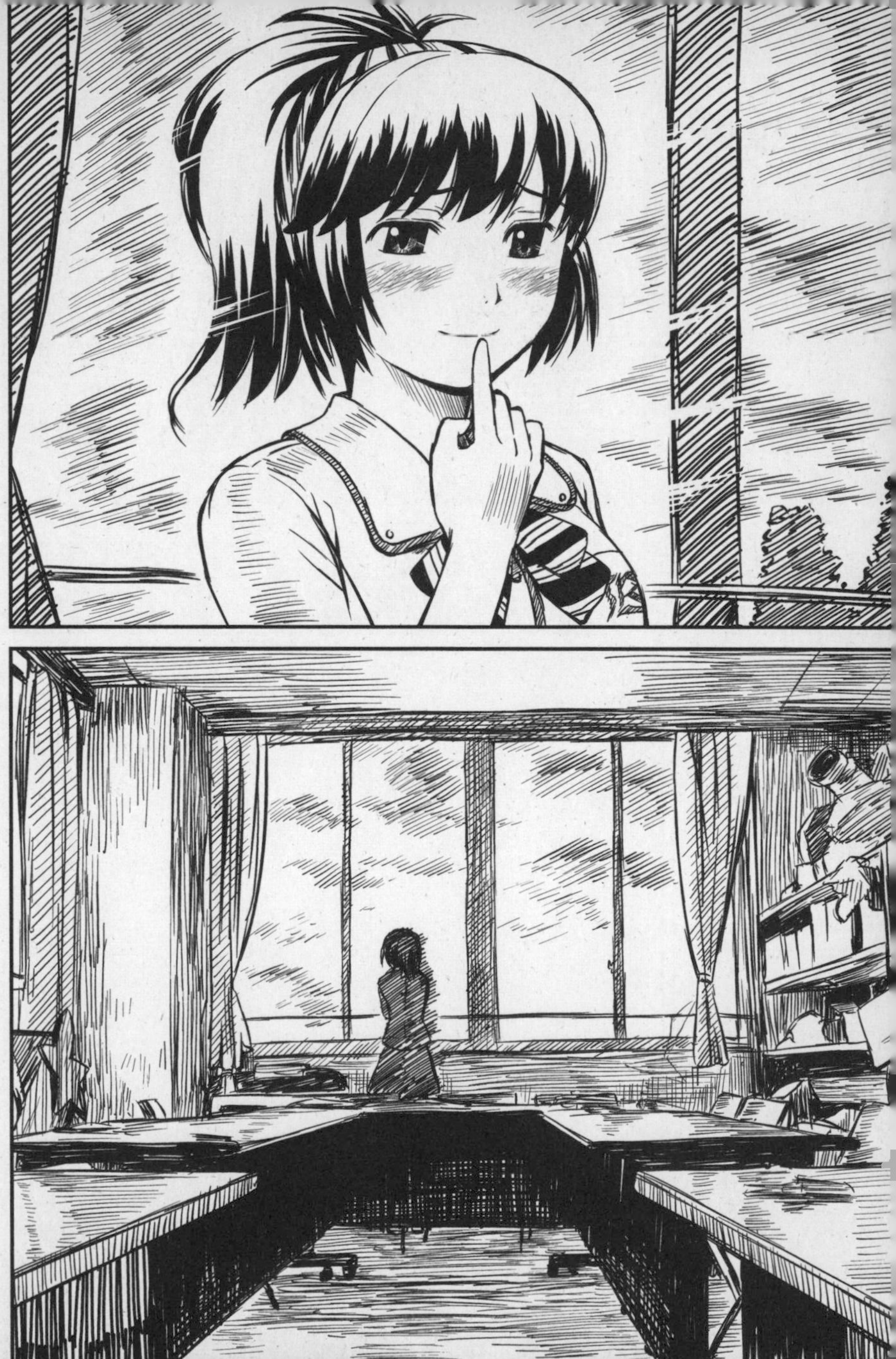

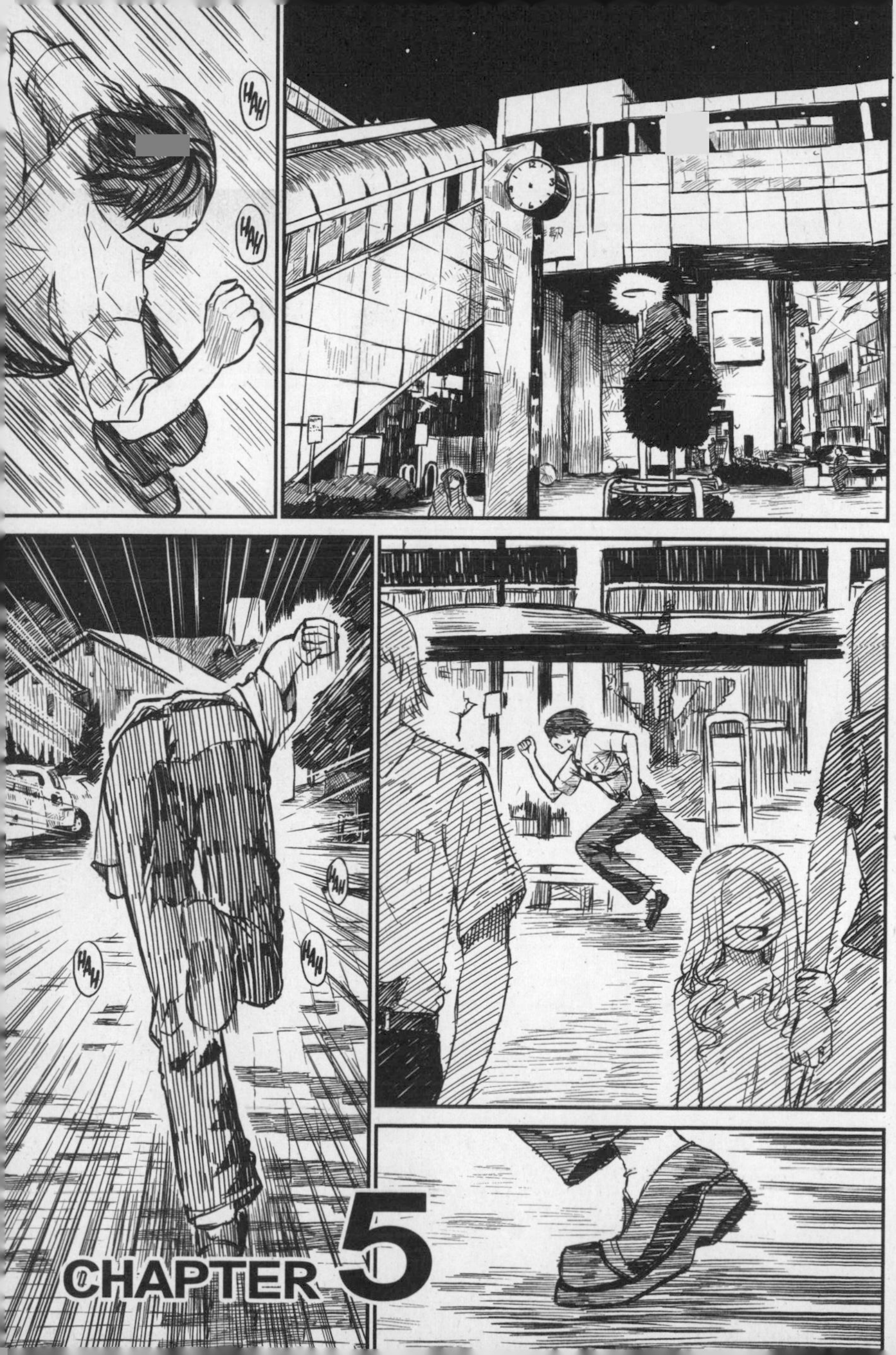
HAH
HAH
HAH
HAH
HAH
CHAPTER 5

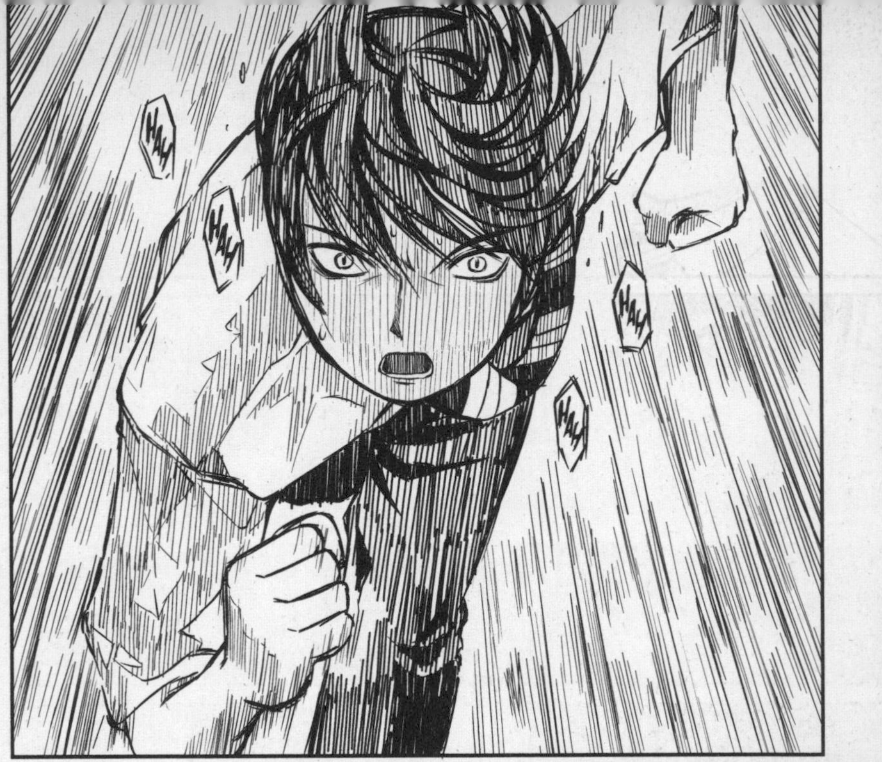
HAH
HAH
HAH
HAH
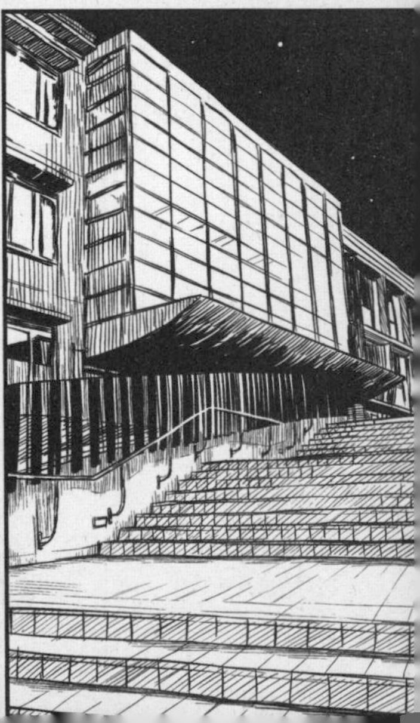
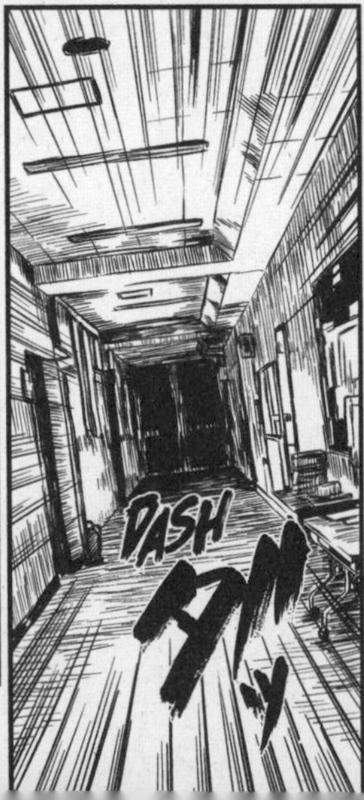
DASH
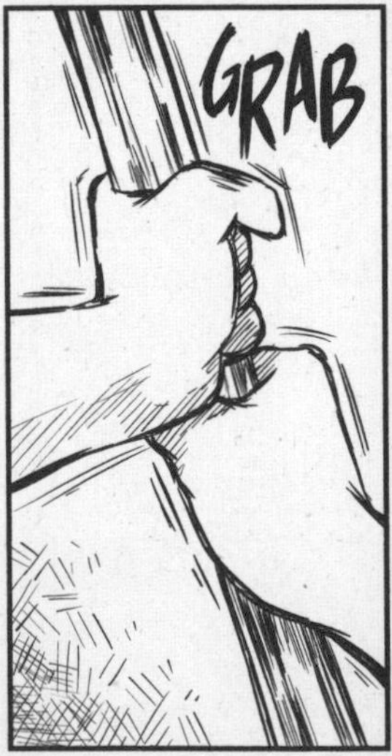
GRAB

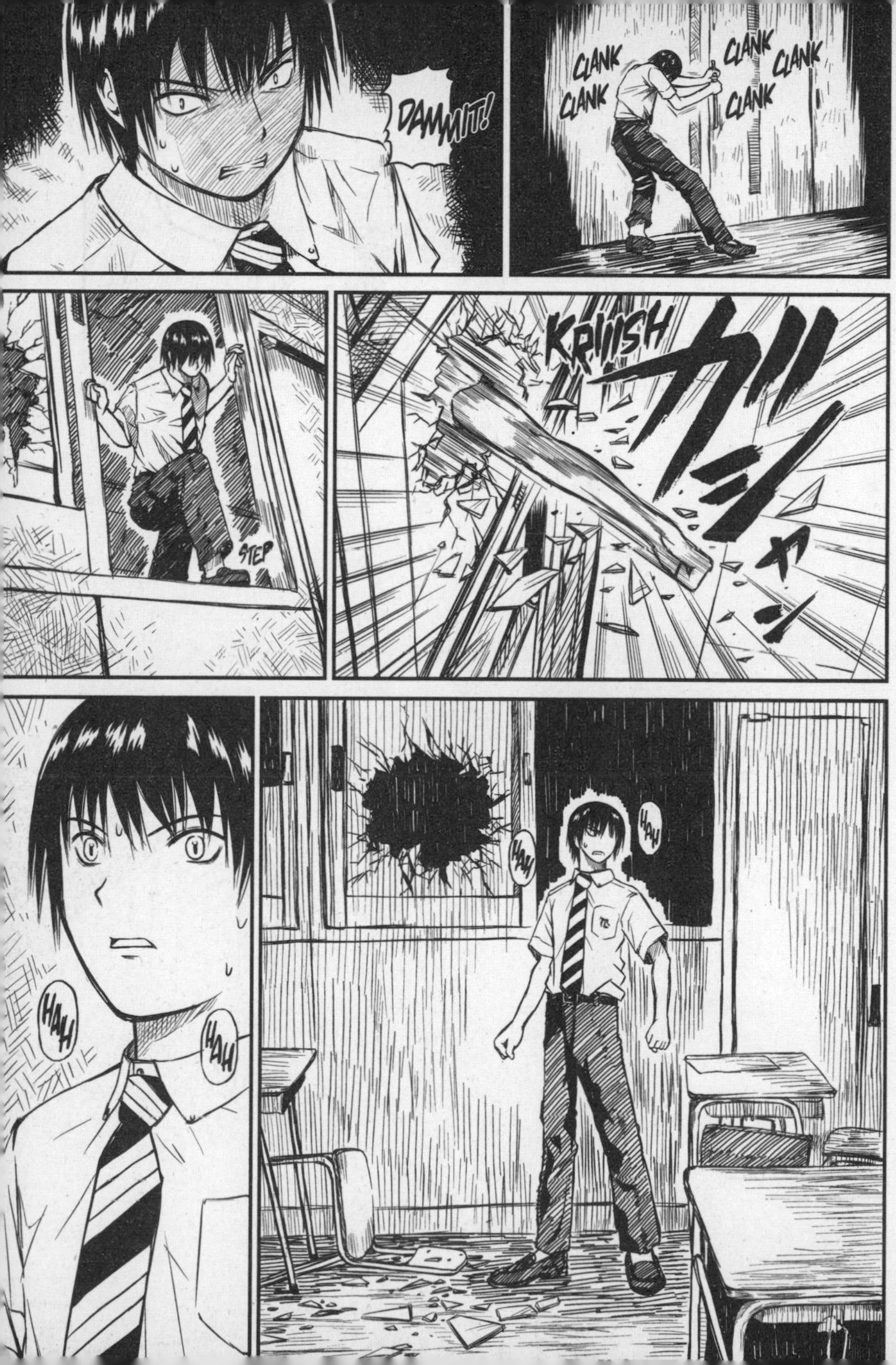
CLANK
CLANK
CLANK
CLANK
CLANK
CLANK
DAMMIT!
KRIIISH
ガシャーン
STEP
HAH
HAH
HAH
HAH

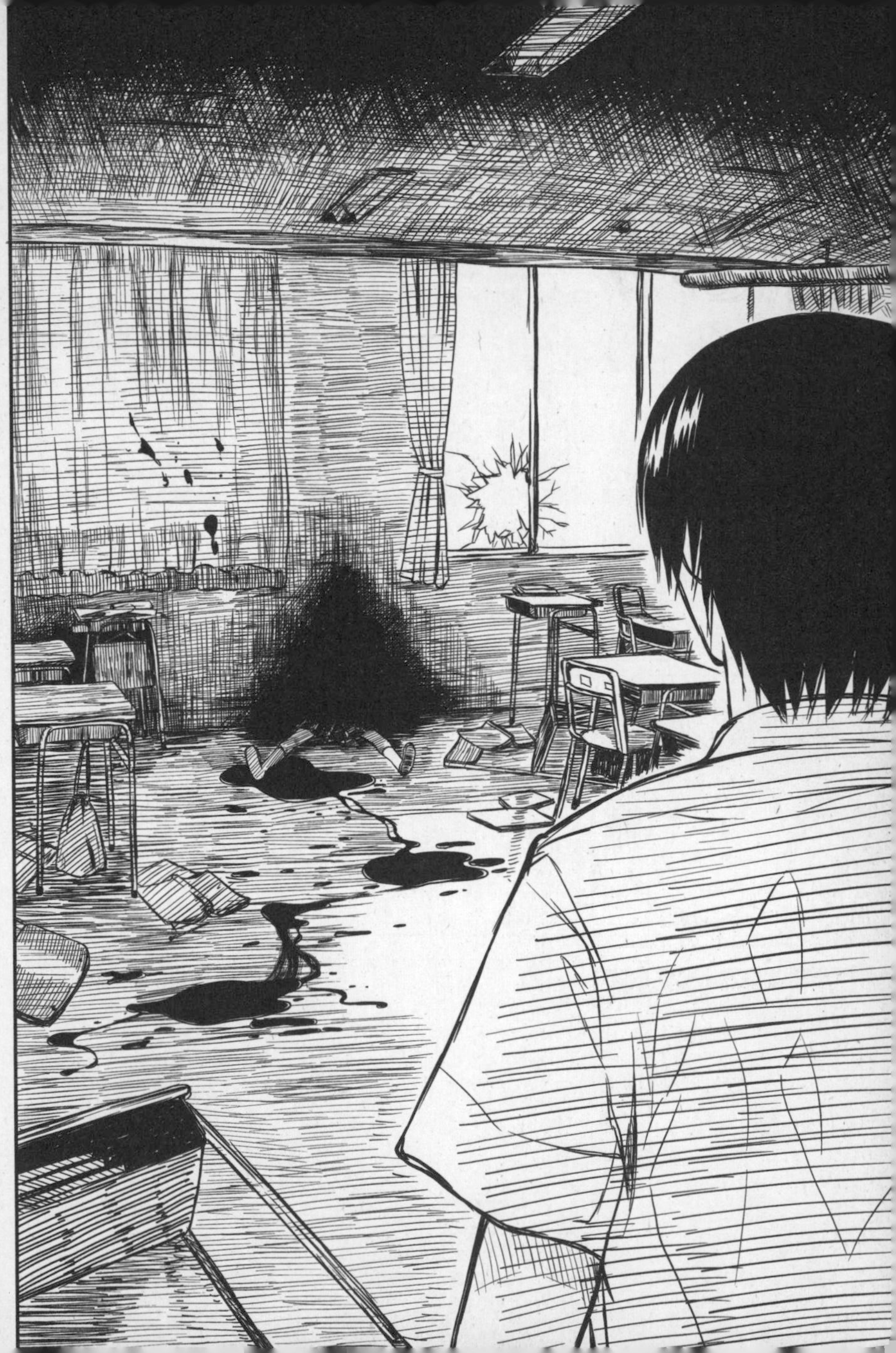

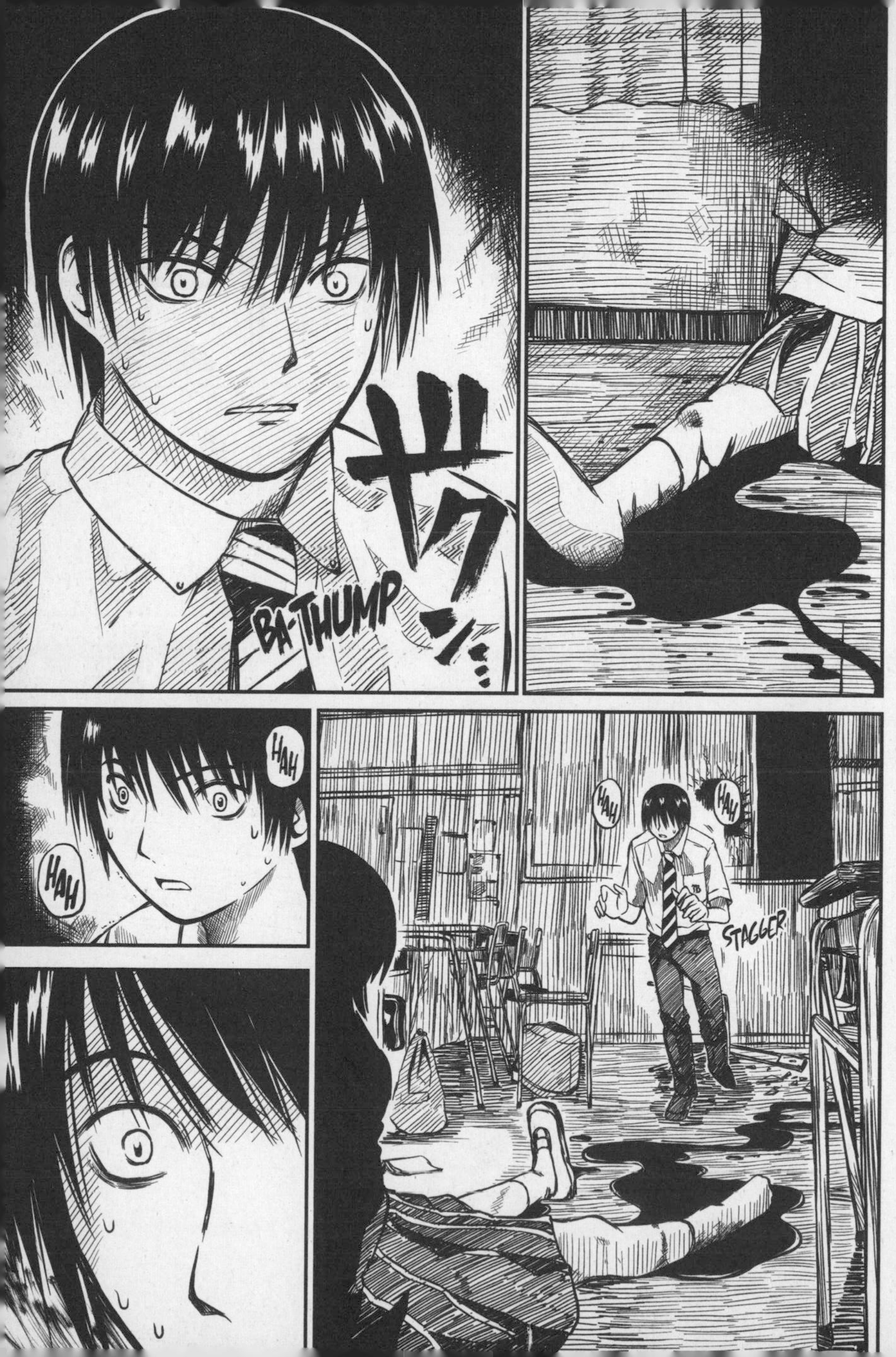
ザク
BA-THUMP
HAH
HAH
STAGGER
HAH
HAH

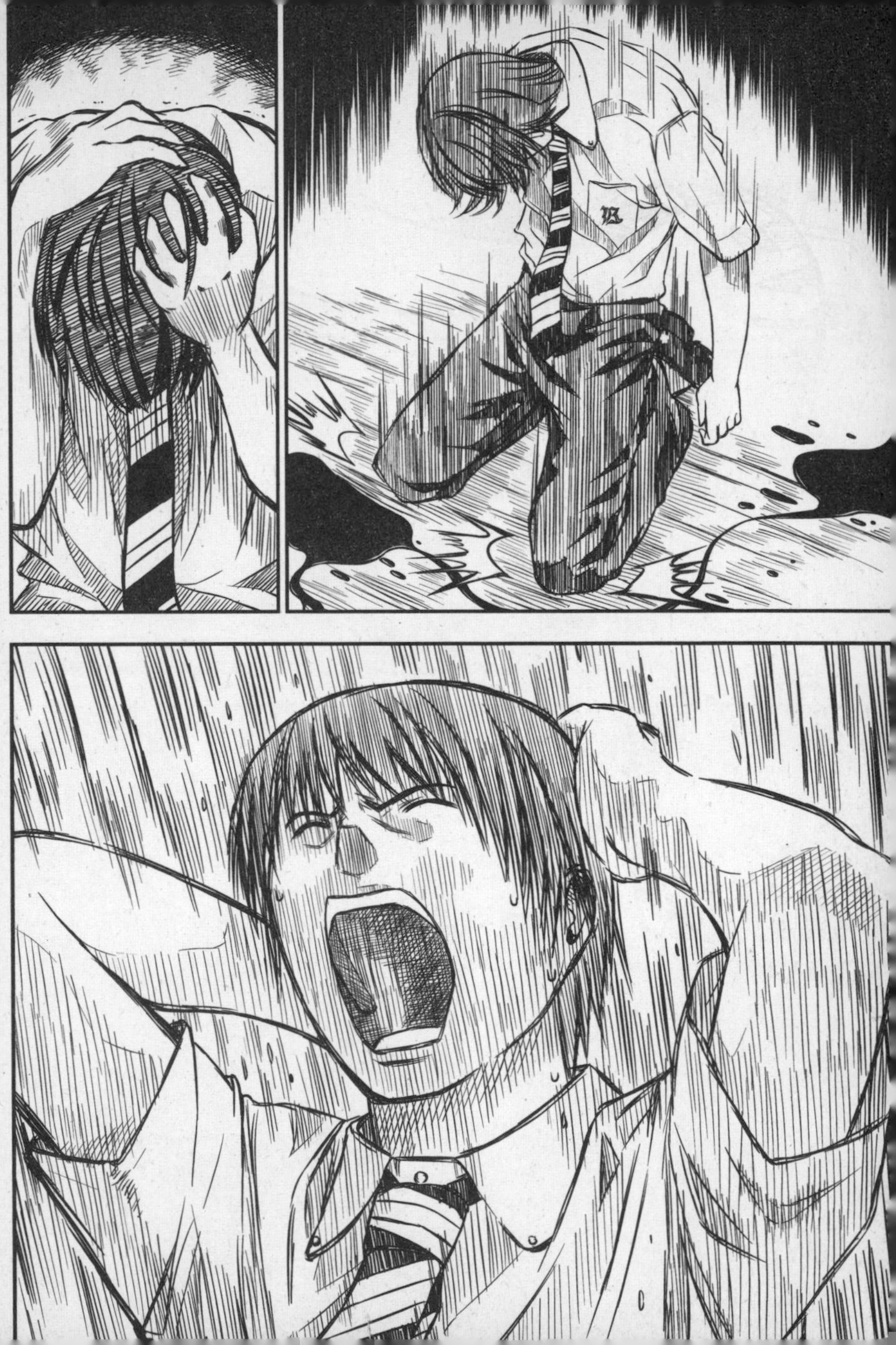

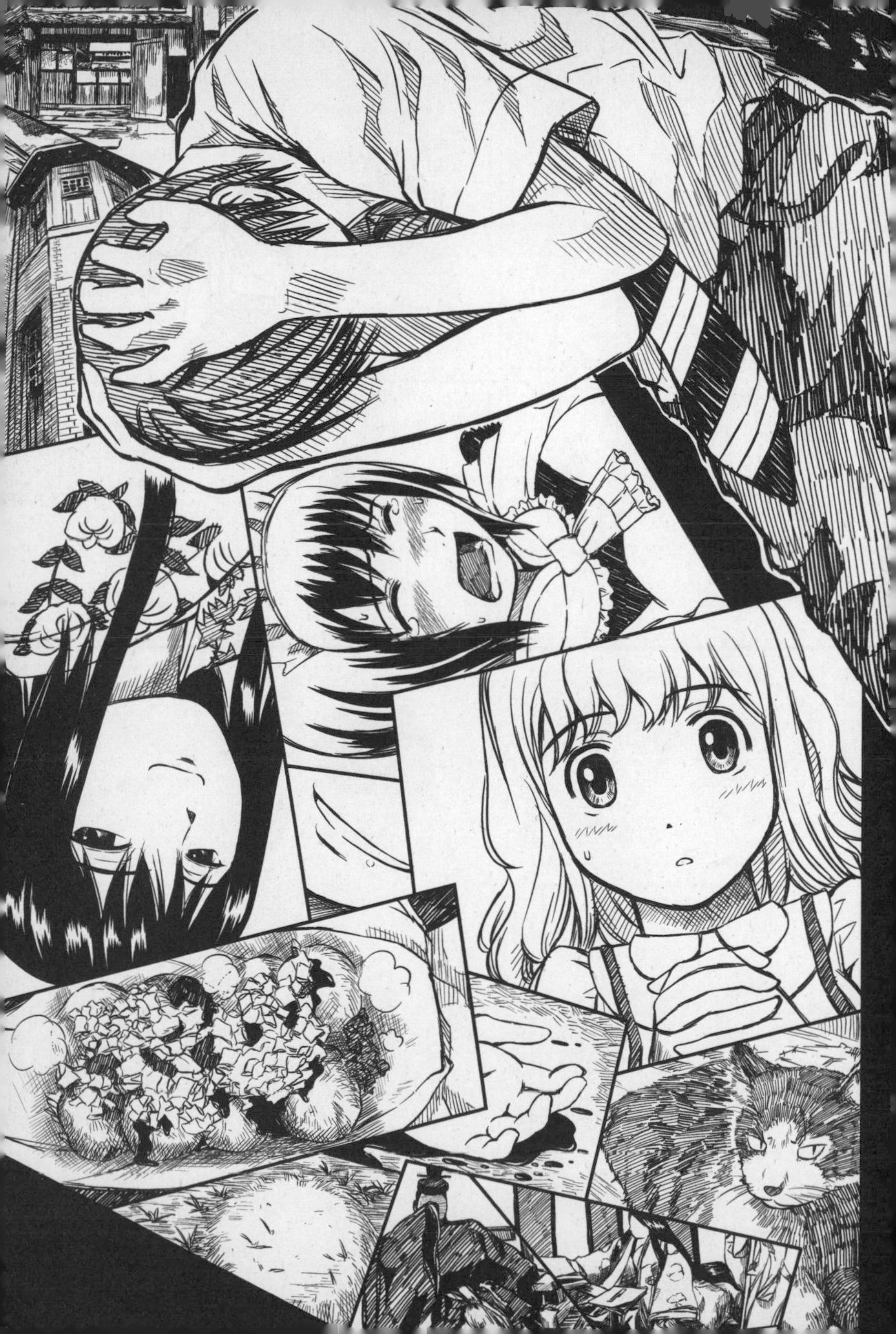

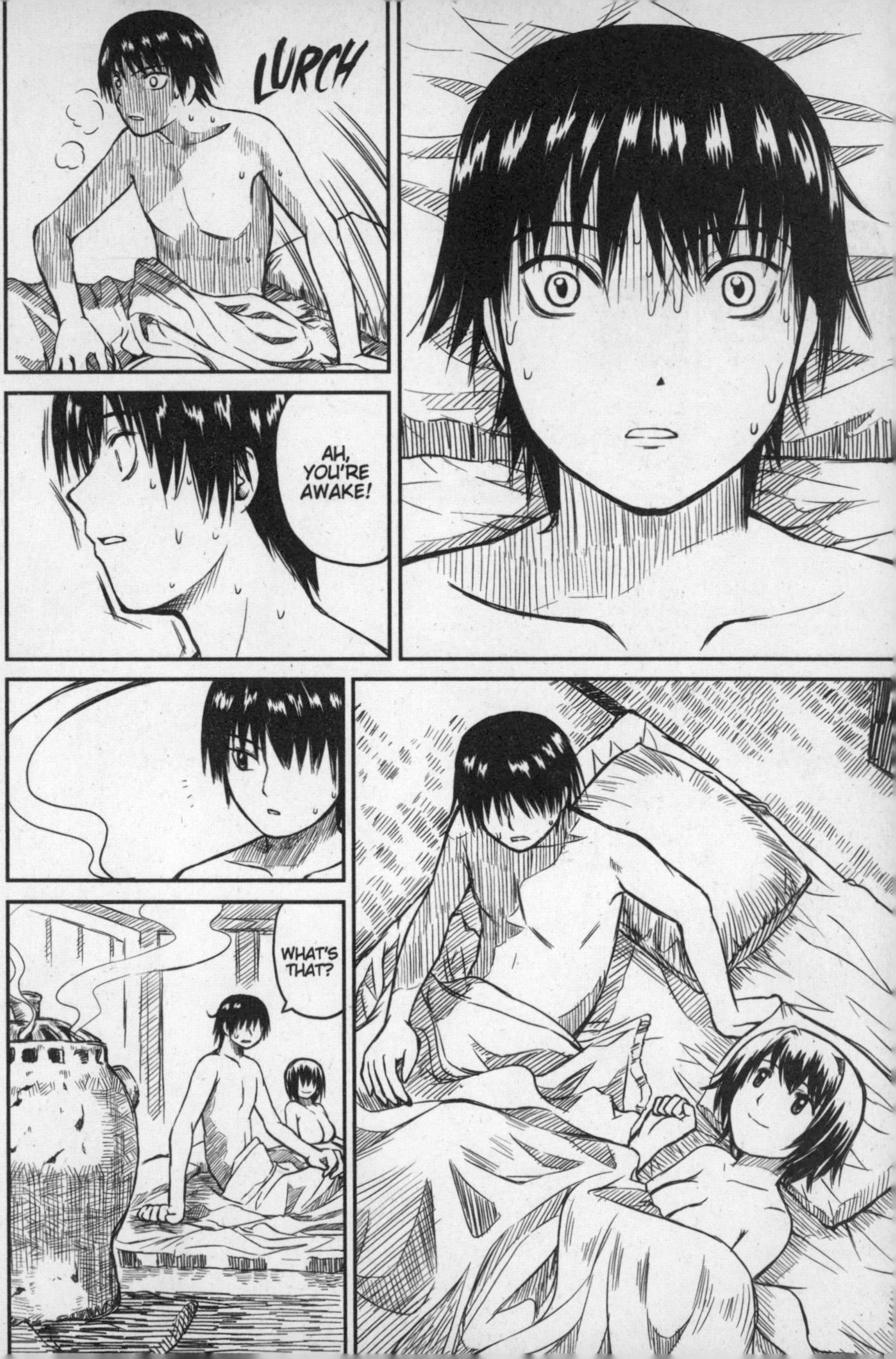
LURCH
AH, YOU'RE AWAKE!
WHAT'S THAT?

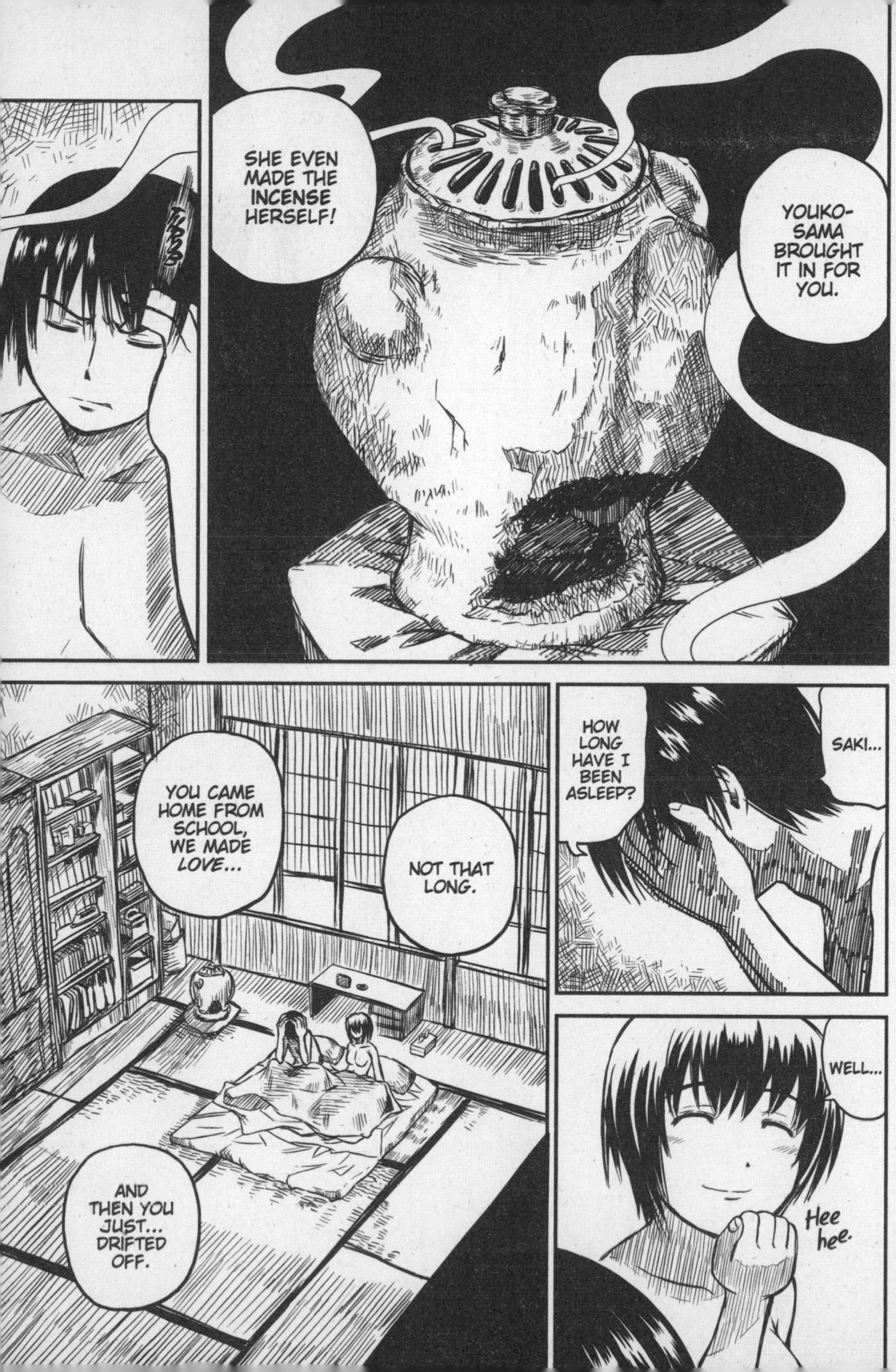
YOUKO-SAMA BROUGHT IT IN FOR YOU.
SHE EVEN MADE THE INCENSE HERSELF!
SAKI...
HOW LONG HAVE I BEEN ASLEEP?
WELL...
Hee hee.
NOT THAT LONG.
YOU CAME HOME FROM SCHOOL, WE MADE LOVE...
AND THEN YOU JUST... DRIFTED OFF.

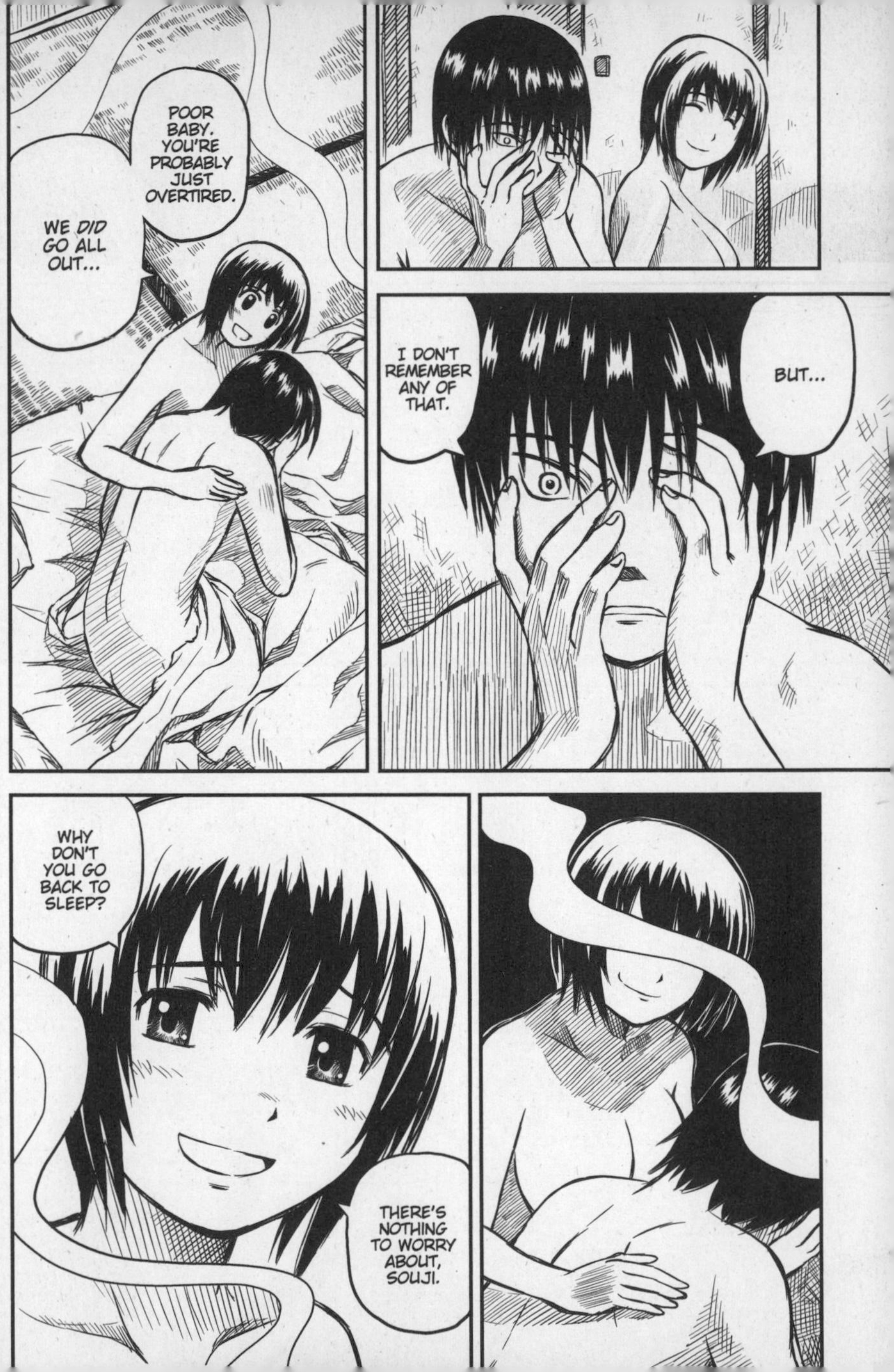
BUT...
I DON'T REMEMBER ANY OF THAT.
POOR BABY. YOU'RE PROBABLY JUST OVERTIRED.
WE *DID* GO ALL OUT...
WHY DON'T YOU GO BACK TO SLEEP?
THERE'S NOTHING TO WORRY ABOUT, SOUJI.

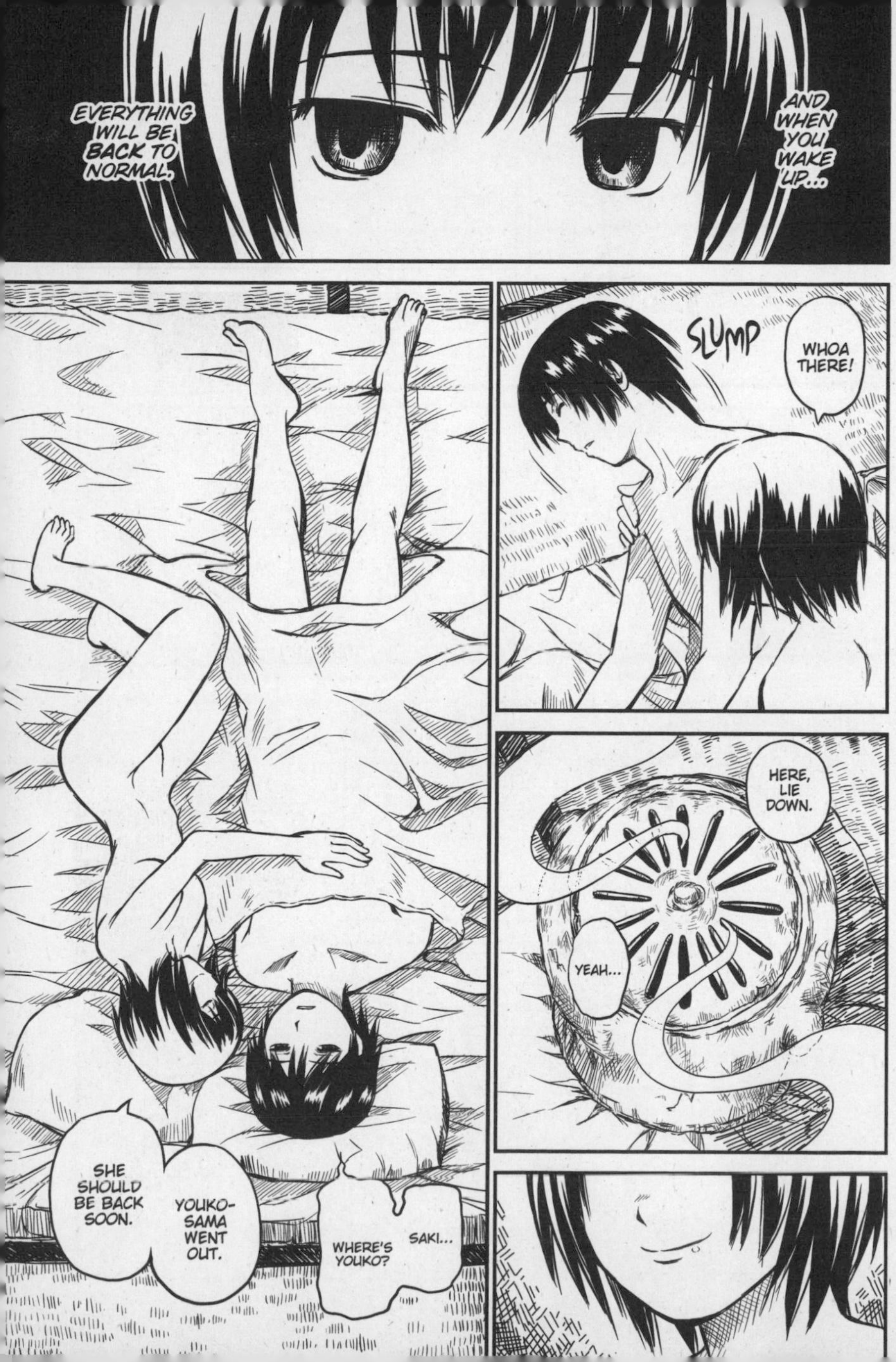
AND WHEN YOU WAKE UP...
EVERYTHING WILL BE BACK TO NORMAL.
WHOA THERE!
SLUMP
HERE, LIE DOWN.
YEAH...
SAKI...
WHERE'S YOUKO?
YOUKO-SAMA WENT OUT.
SHE SHOULD BE BACK SOON.

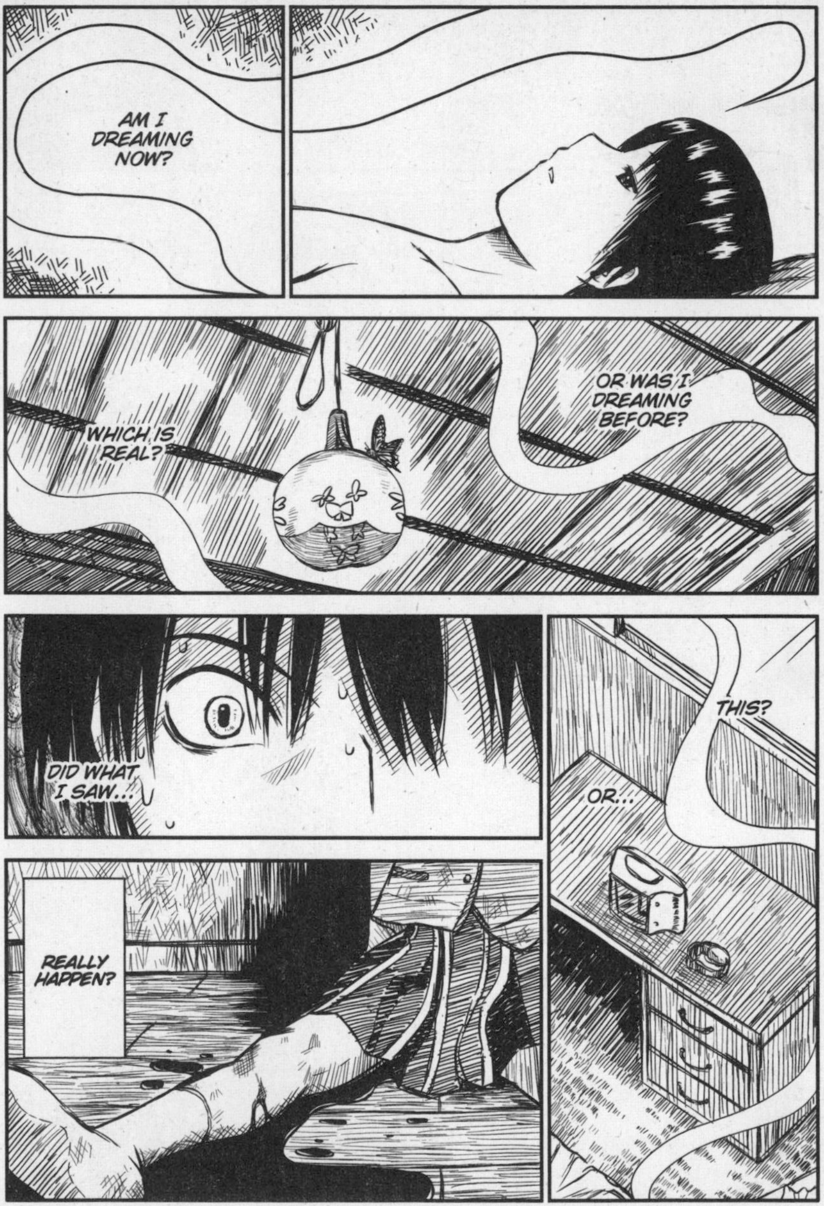
AM I DREAMING NOW?
OR WAS I DREAMING BEFORE?
WHICH IS REAL?
THIS?
OR...
DID WHAT I SAW...
REALLY HAPPEN?

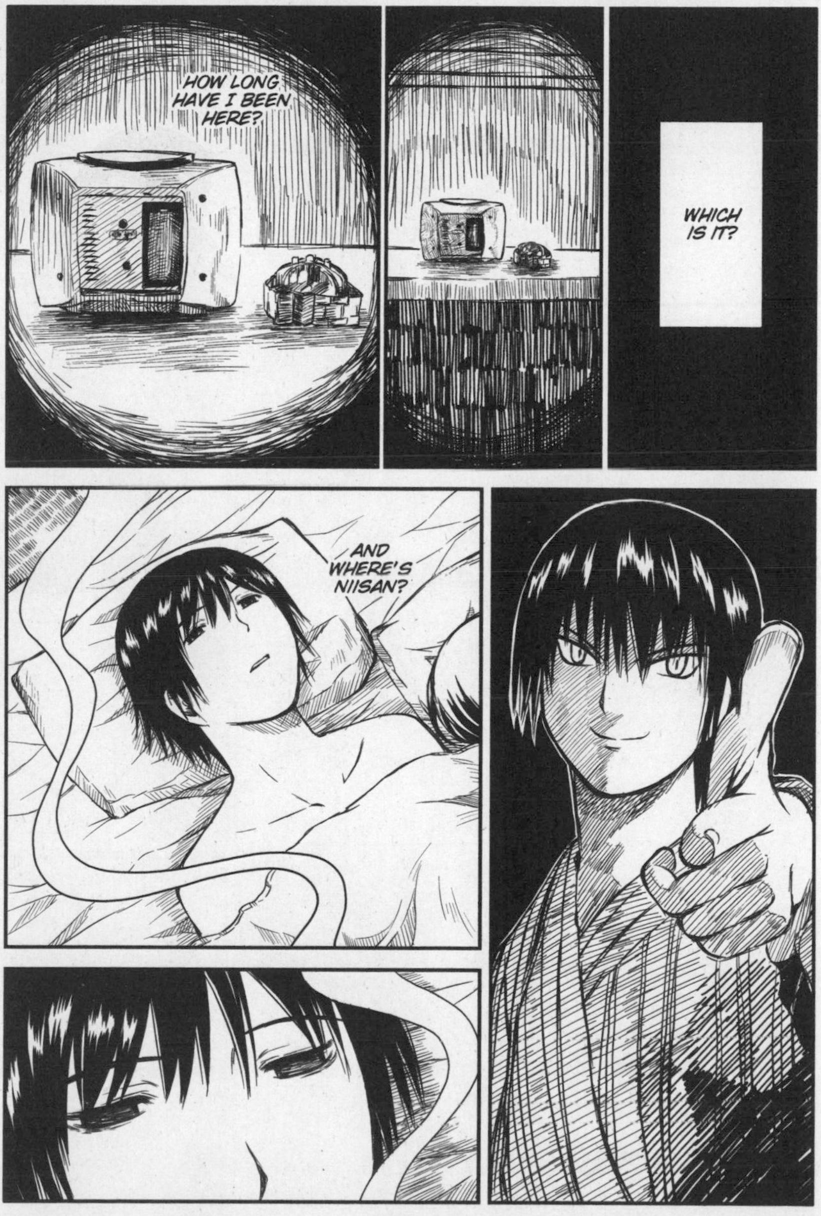
WHICH IS IT?
HOW LONG HAVE I BEEN HERE?
AND WHERE'S NIISAN?

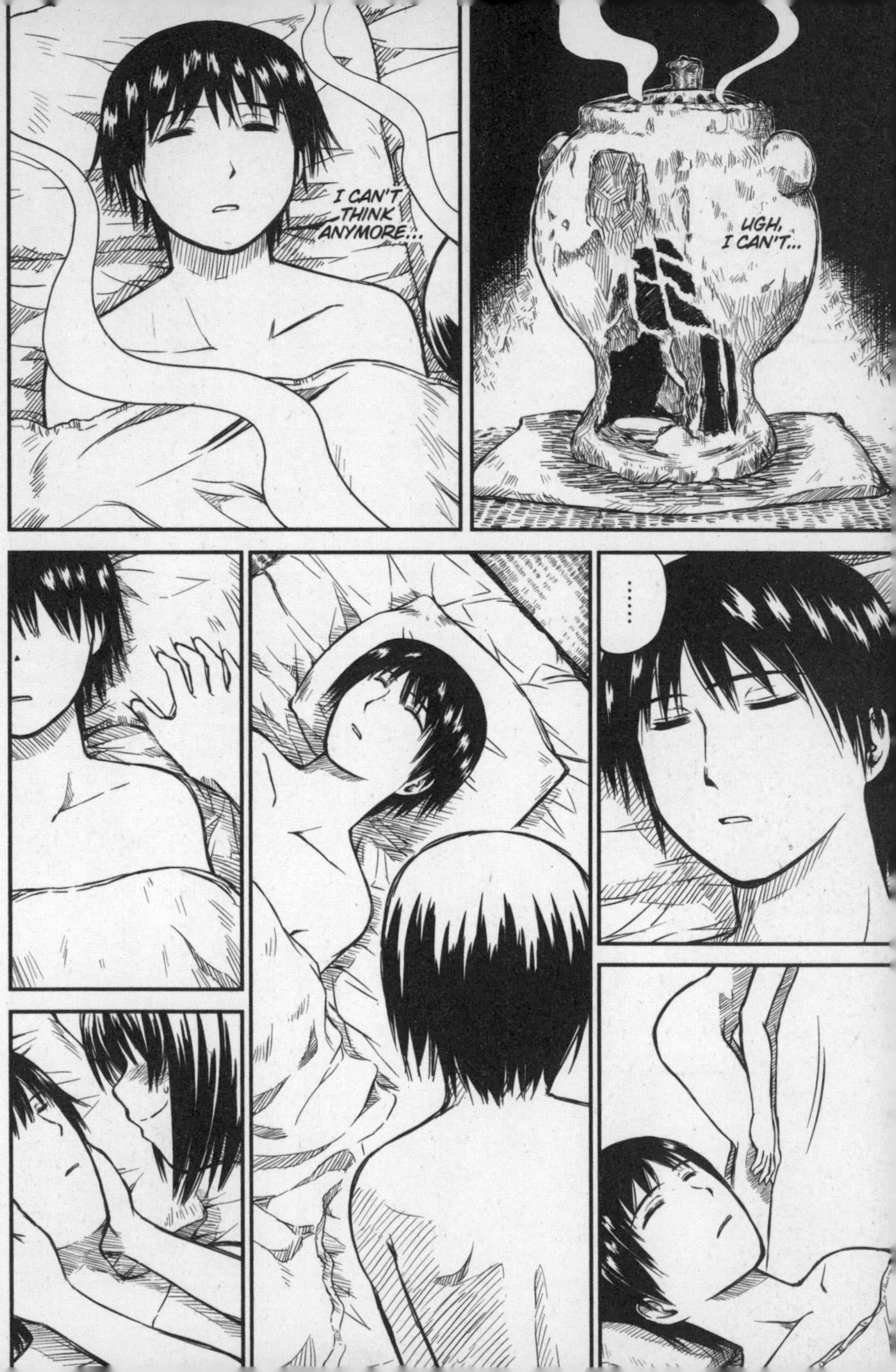
UGH, I CAN'T...
I CAN'T THINK ANYMORE...
......

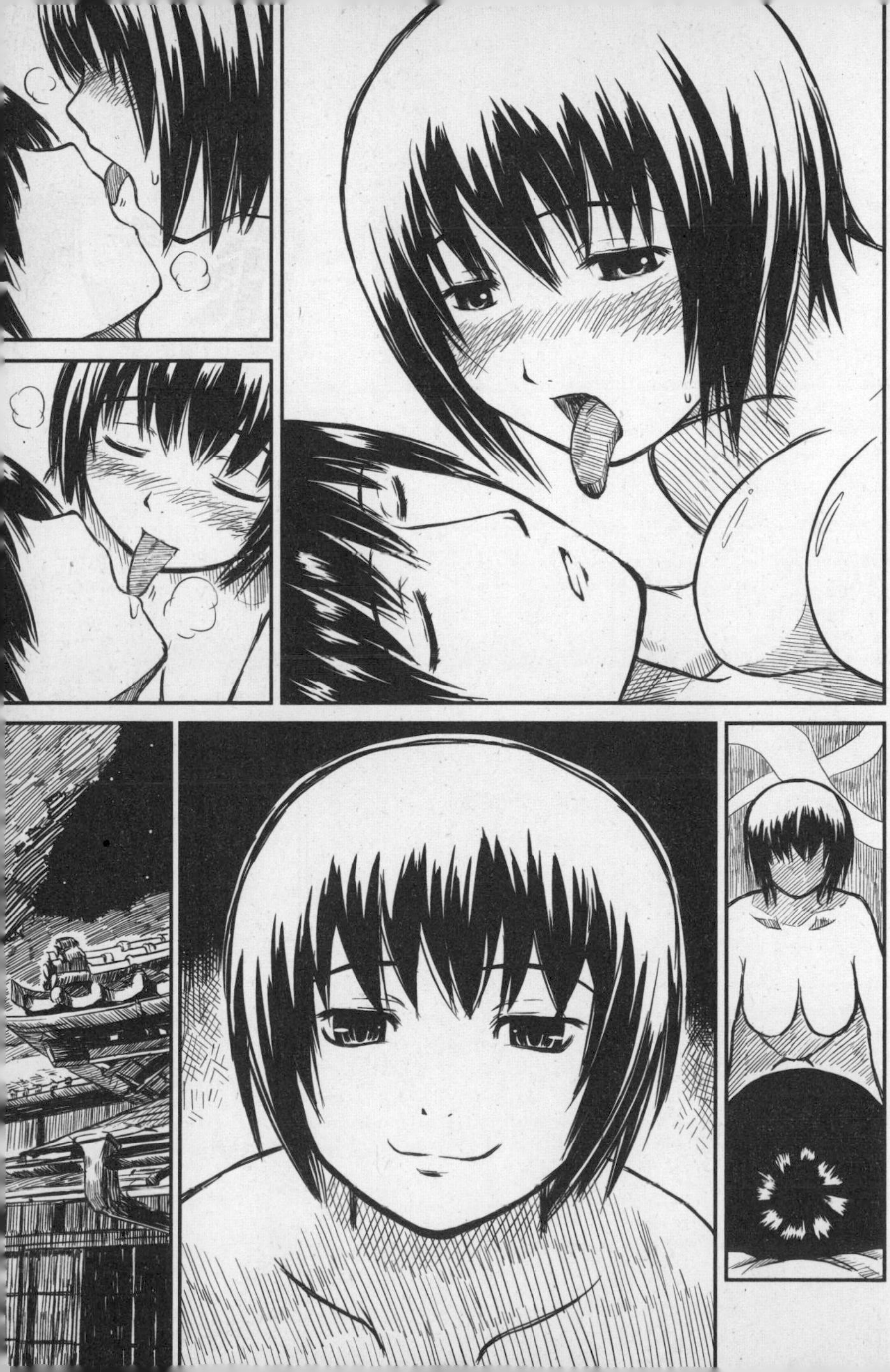

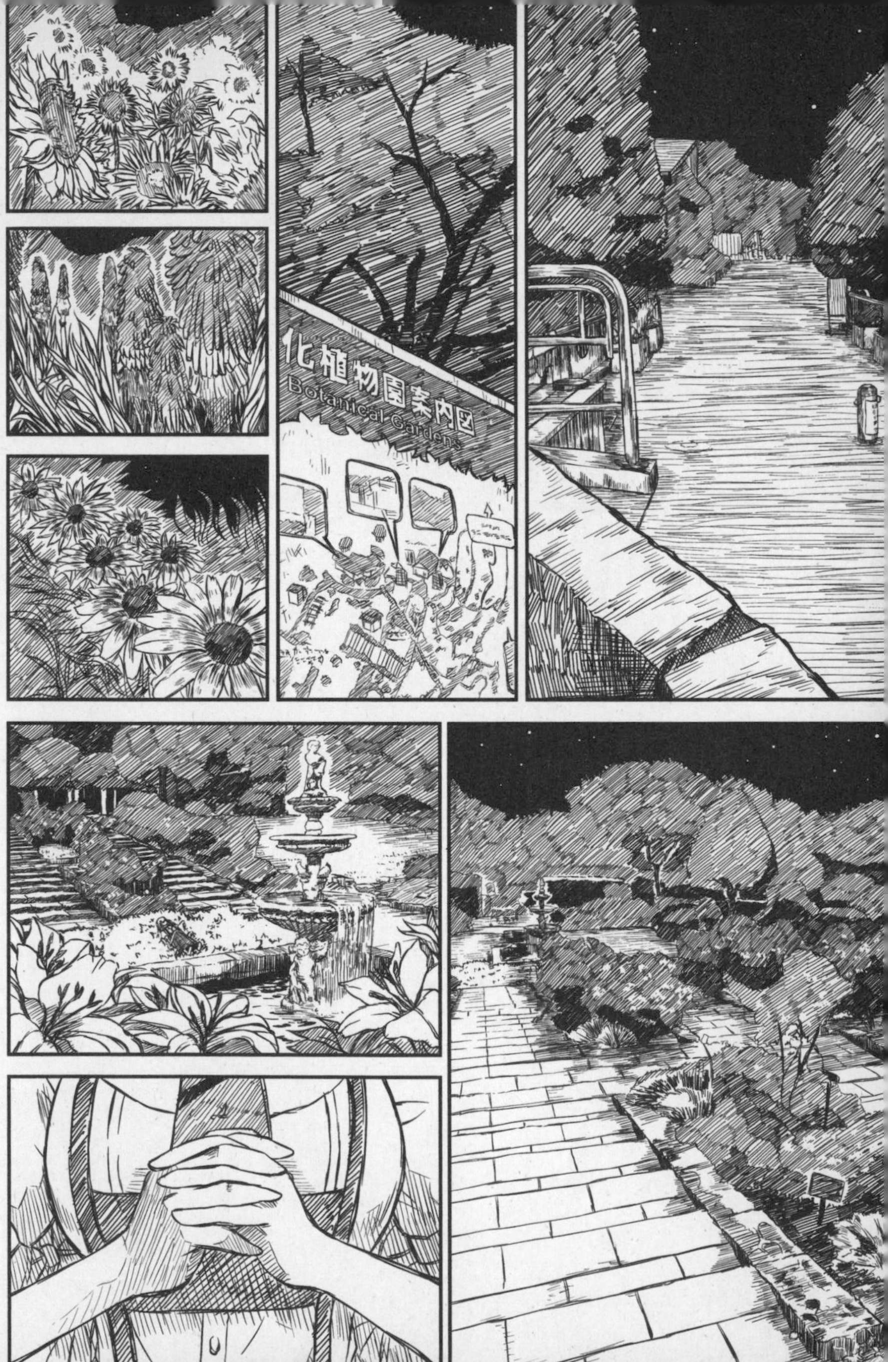
化植物園案内図
Botanical Gardens

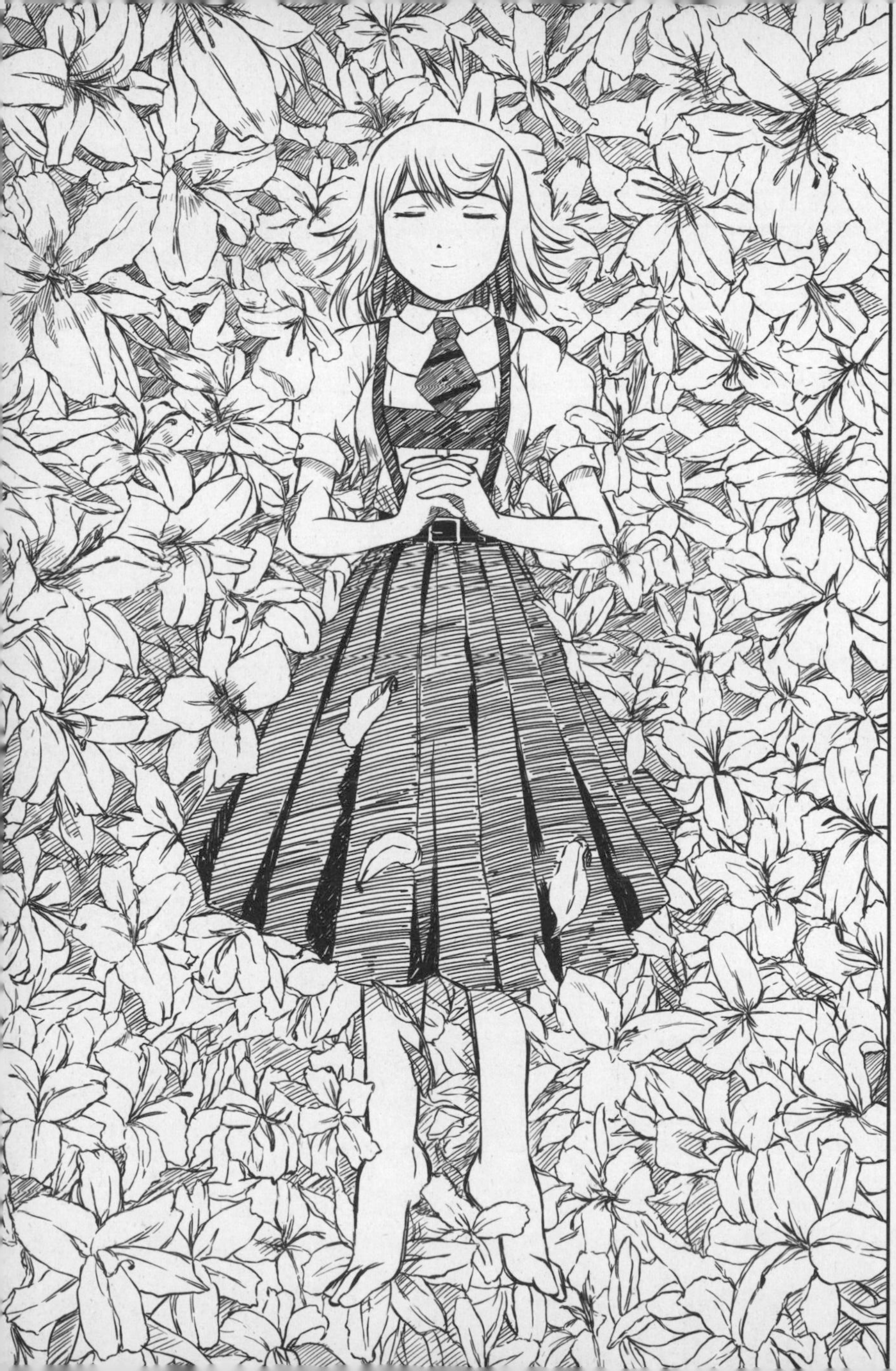

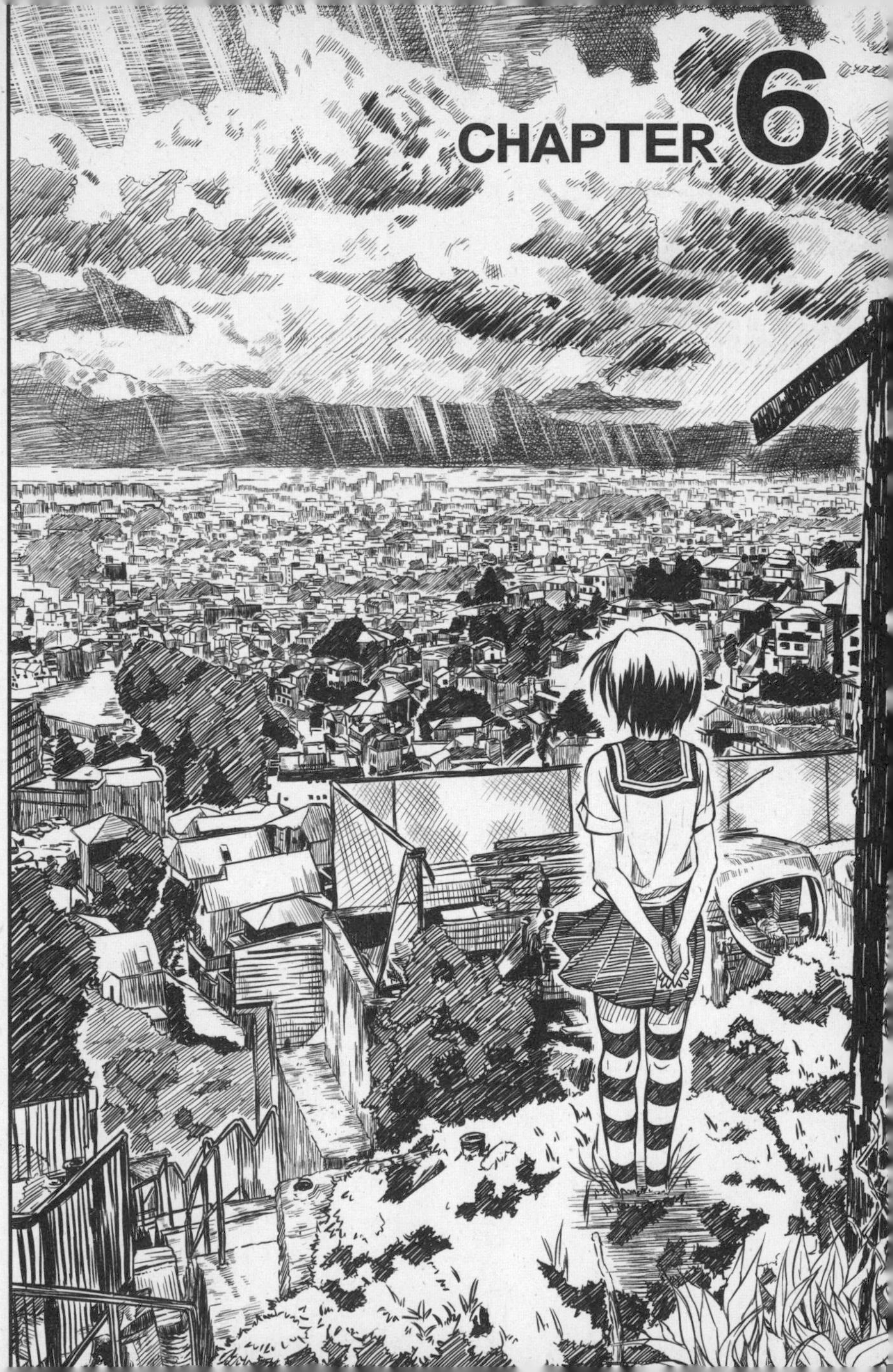
CHAPTER 6

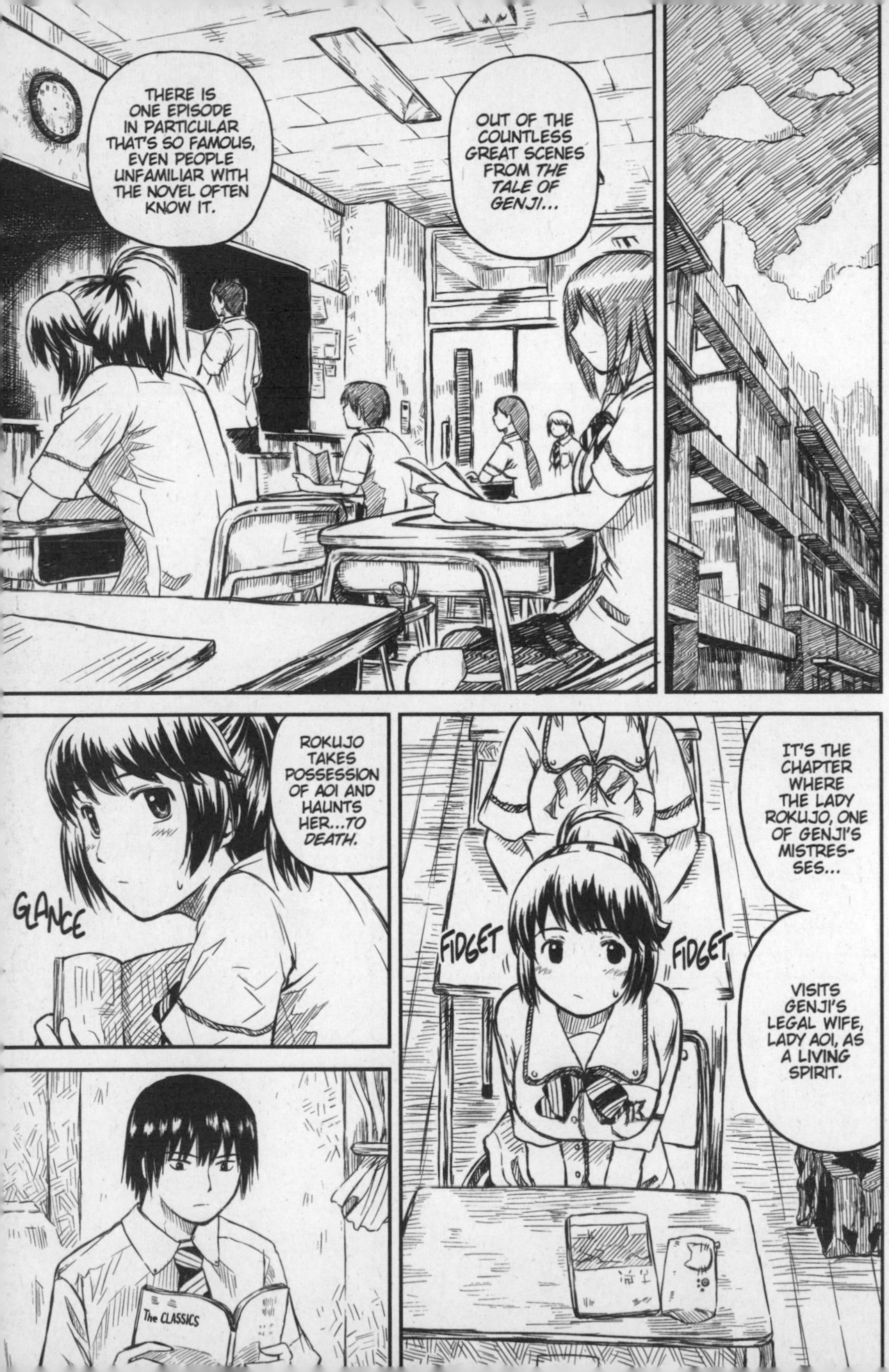
OUT OF THE COUNTLESS GREAT SCENES FROM *THE TALE OF GENJI*...
THERE IS ONE EPISODE IN PARTICULAR THAT'S SO FAMOUS, EVEN PEOPLE UNFAMILIAR WITH THE NOVEL OFTEN KNOW IT.
IT'S THE CHAPTER WHERE THE LADY ROKUJO, ONE OF GENJI'S MISTRES-SES...
VISITS GENJI'S LEGAL WIFE, LADY AOI, AS A LIVING SPIRIT.
FIDGET
FIDGET
ROKUJO TAKES POSSESSION OF AOI AND HAUNTS HER...*TO DEATH.*
GLANCE
The CLASSICS

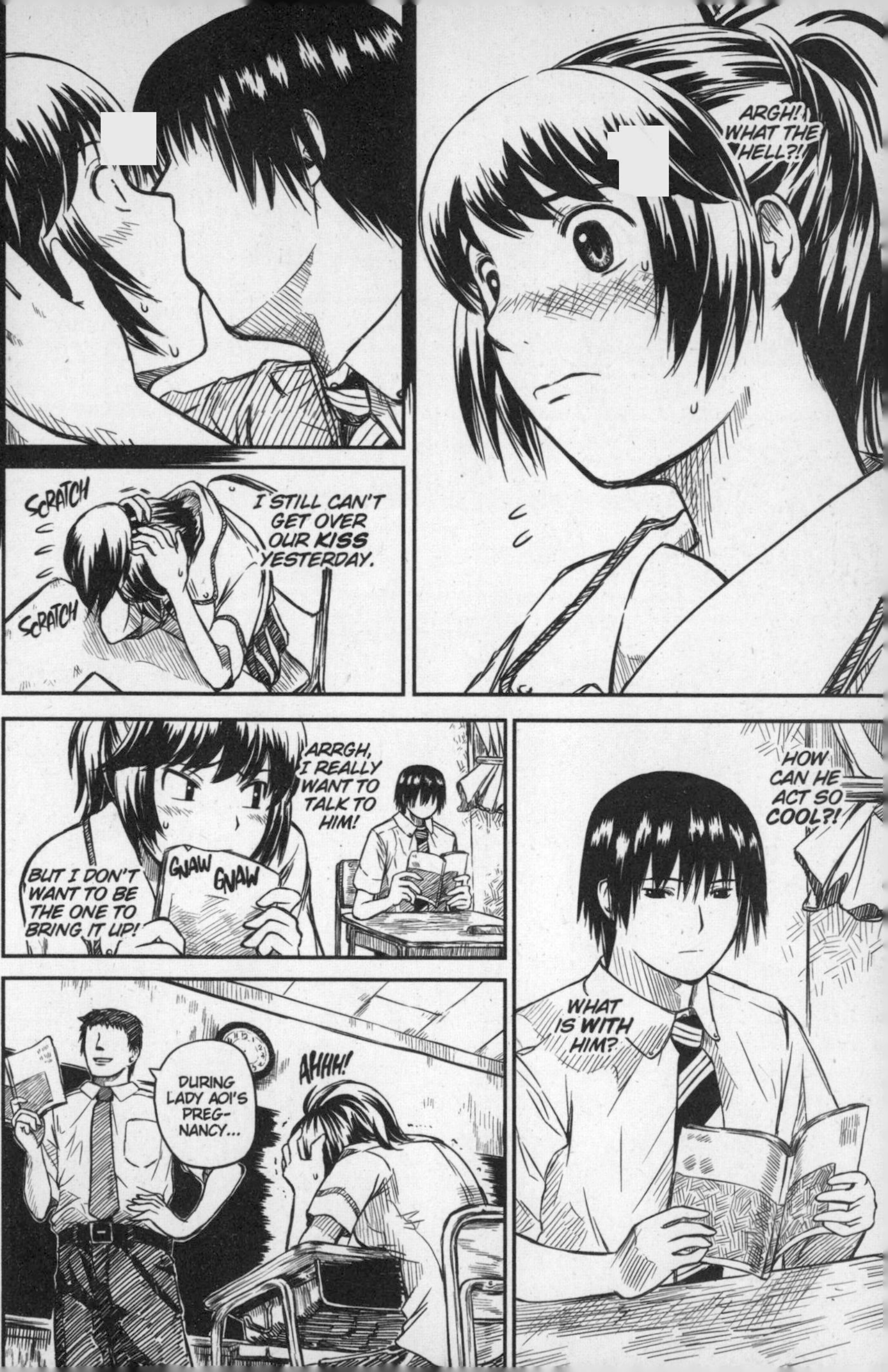
ARGH! WHAT THE HELL?!
SCRATCH
I STILL CAN'T GET OVER OUR KISS YESTERDAY.
SCRATCH
HOW CAN HE ACT SO COOL?!
WHAT IS WITH HIM?
ARRGH, I REALLY WANT TO TALK TO HIM!
BUT I DON'T WANT TO BE THE ONE TO BRING IT UP!
GNAW
GNAW
AHHH!
DURING LADY AOI'S PREG-NANCY...

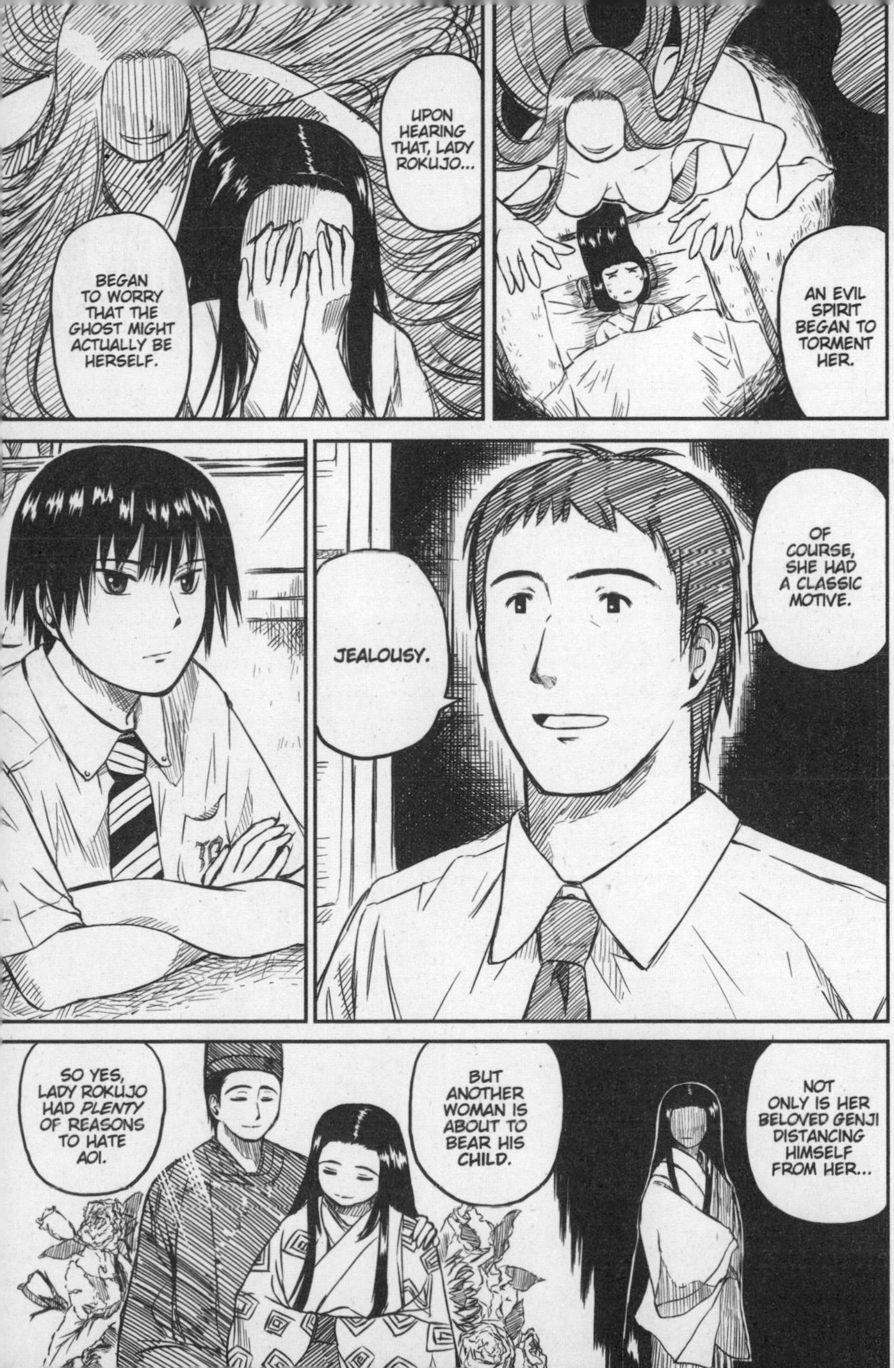
AN EVIL SPIRIT BEGAN TO TORMENT HER.
UPON HEARING THAT, LADY ROKUJO...
BEGAN TO WORRY THAT THE GHOST MIGHT ACTUALLY BE HERSELF.
OF COURSE, SHE HAD A CLASSIC MOTIVE.
JEALOUSY.
NOT ONLY IS HER BELOVED GENJI DISTANCING HIMSELF FROM HER...
BUT ANOTHER WOMAN IS ABOUT TO BEAR HIS CHILD.
SO YES, LADY ROKUJO HAD *PLENTY* OF REASONS TO HATE AOI.

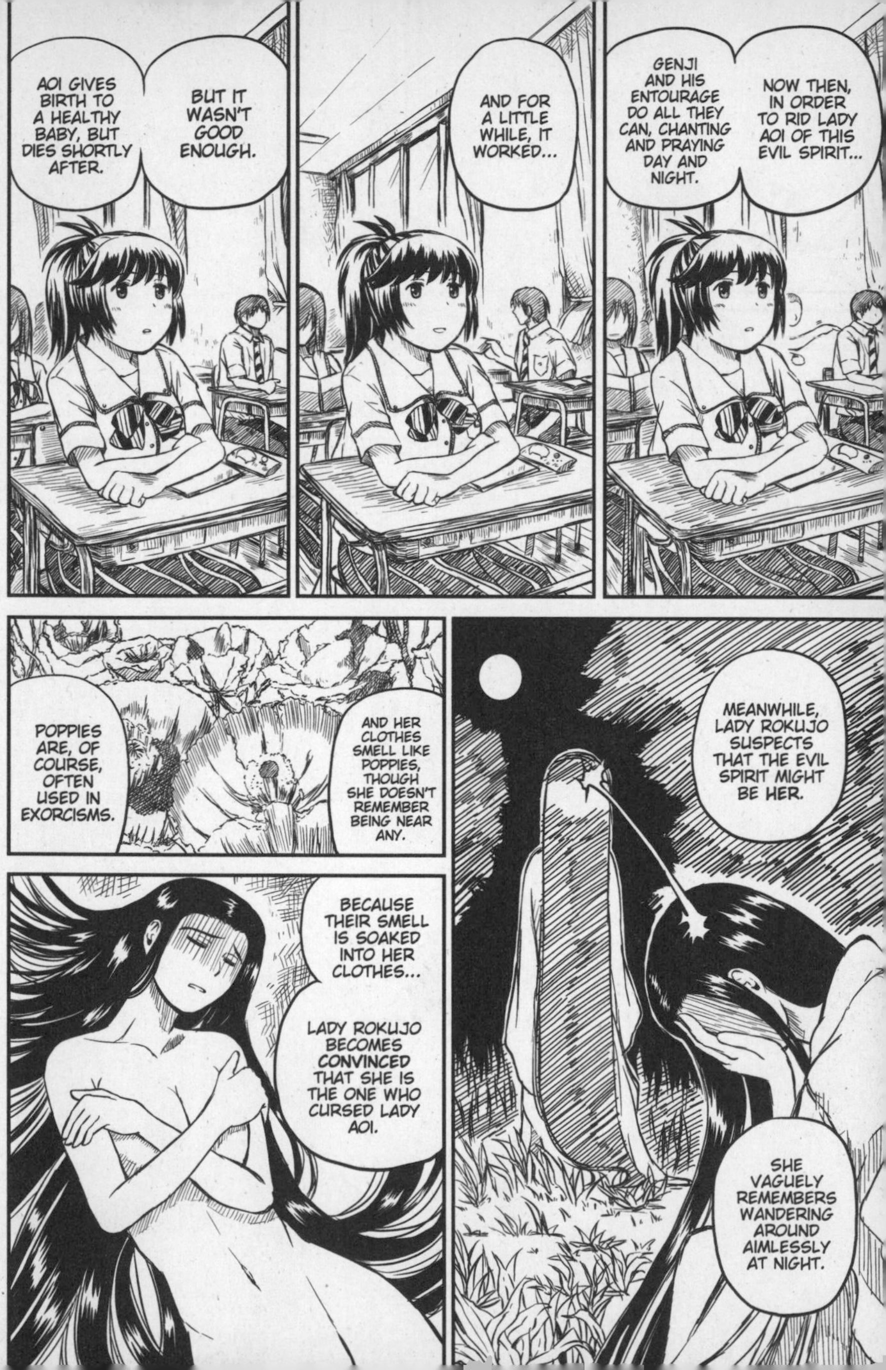
NOW THEN, IN ORDER TO RID LADY AOI OF THIS EVIL SPIRIT...
GENJI AND HIS ENTOURAGE DO ALL THEY CAN, CHANTING AND PRAYING DAY AND NIGHT.
AND FOR A LITTLE WHILE, IT WORKED...
BUT IT WASN'T GOOD ENOUGH.
AOI GIVES BIRTH TO A HEALTHY BABY, BUT DIES SHORTLY AFTER.
MEANWHILE, LADY ROKUJO SUSPECTS THAT THE EVIL SPIRIT MIGHT BE HER.
SHE VAGUELY REMEMBERS WANDERING AROUND AIMLESSLY AT NIGHT.
AND HER CLOTHES SMELL LIKE POPPIES, THOUGH SHE DOESN'T REMEMBER BEING NEAR ANY.
POPPIES ARE, OF COURSE, OFTEN USED IN EXORCISMS.
BECAUSE THEIR SMELL IS SOAKED INTO HER CLOTHES...
LADY ROKUJO BECOMES CONVINCED THAT SHE IS THE ONE WHO CURSED LADY AOI.

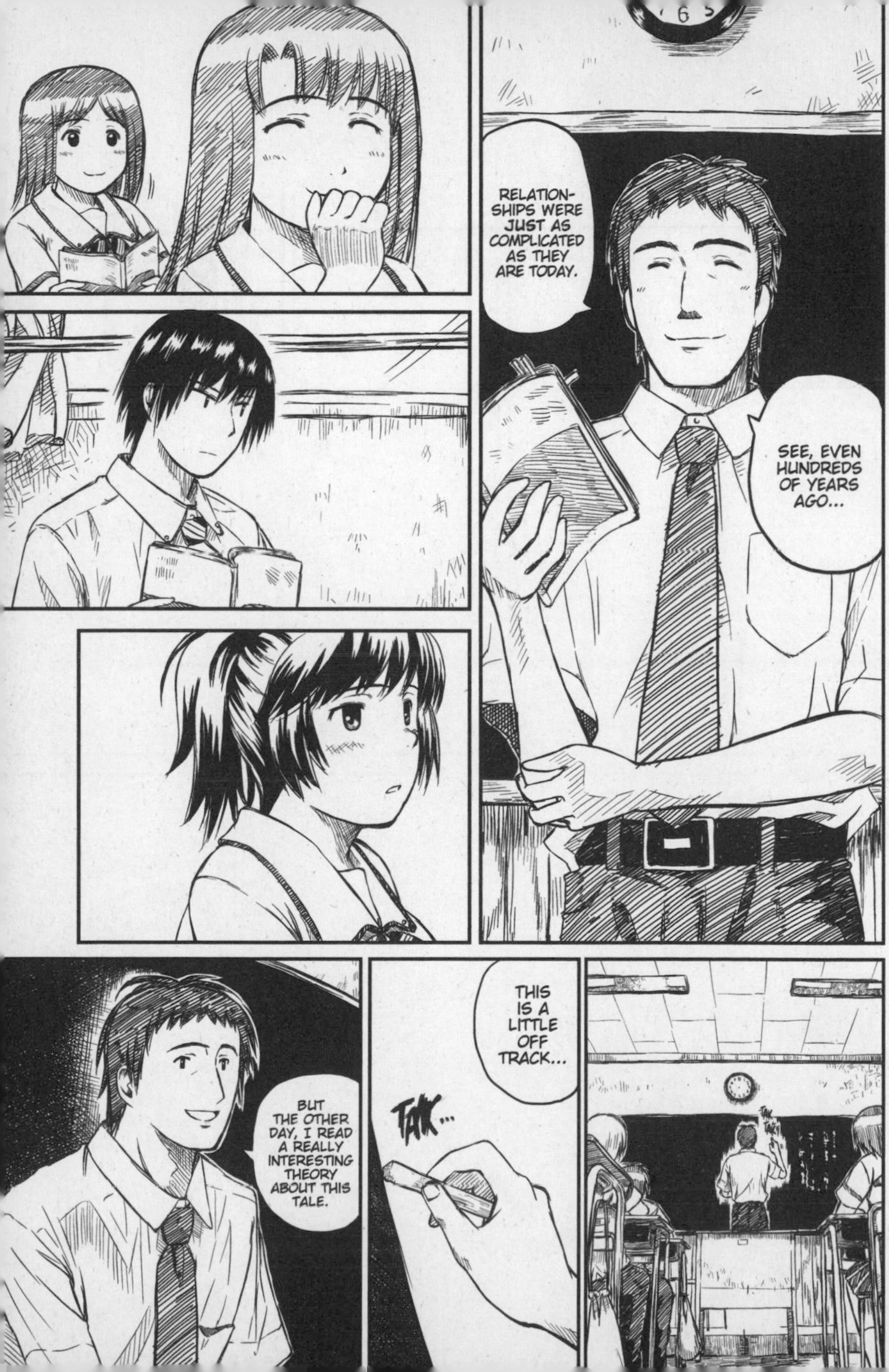
SEE, EVEN HUNDREDS OF YEARS AGO...
RELATION-SHIPS WERE JUST AS COMPLICATED AS THEY ARE TODAY.
THIS IS A LITTLE OFF TRACK...
TAK...
BUT THE OTHER DAY, I READ A REALLY INTERESTING THEORY ABOUT THIS TALE.

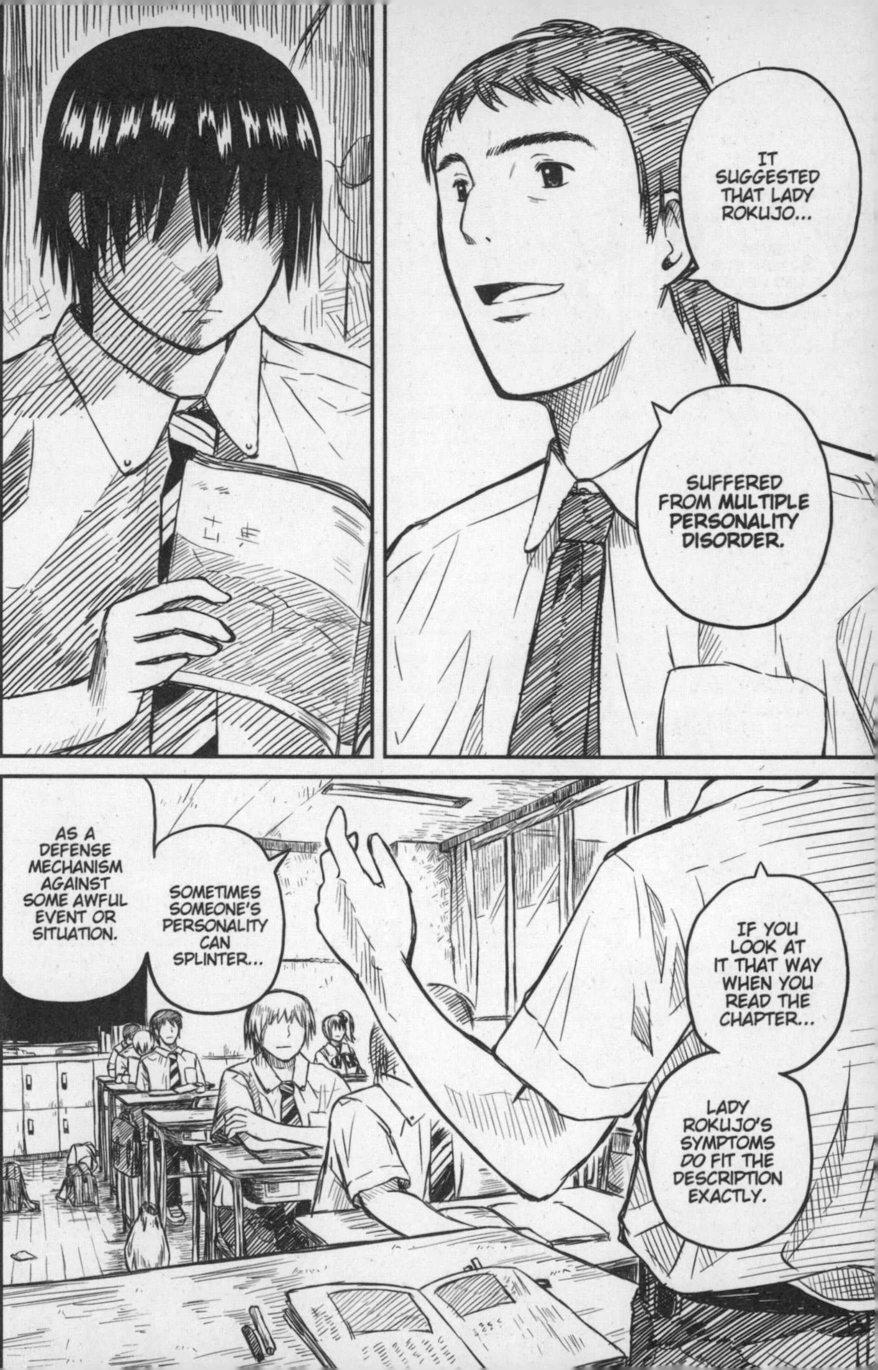
IT SUGGESTED THAT LADY ROKUJO...
SUFFERED FROM MULTIPLE PERSONALITY DISORDER.
IF YOU LOOK AT IT THAT WAY WHEN YOU READ THE CHAPTER...
LADY ROKUJO'S SYMPTOMS *DO* FIT THE DESCRIPTION EXACTLY.
SOMETIMES SOMEONE'S PERSONALITY CAN SPLINTER...
AS A DEFENSE MECHANISM AGAINST SOME AWFUL EVENT OR SITUATION.

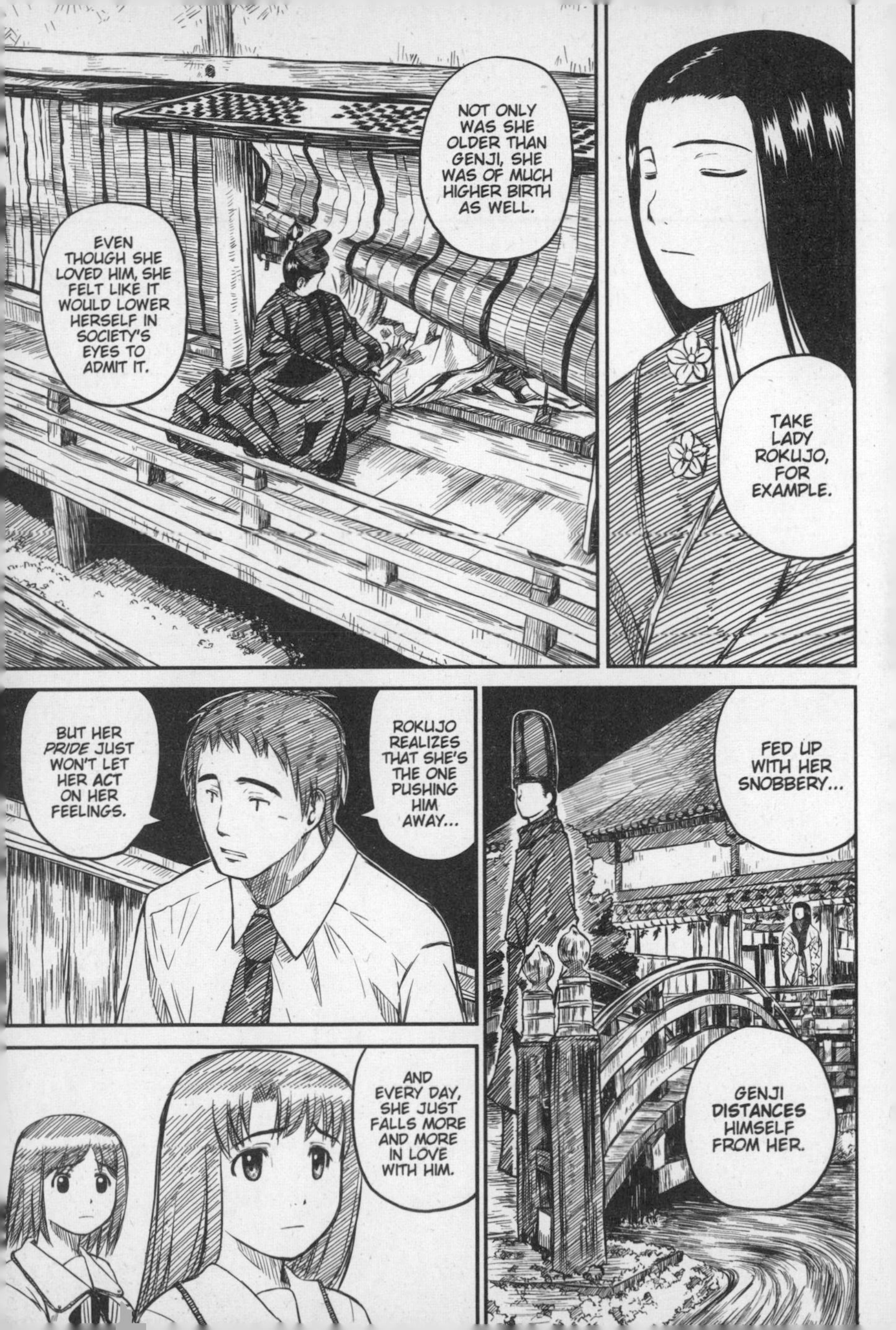
TAKE LADY ROKUJO, FOR EXAMPLE.
NOT ONLY WAS SHE OLDER THAN GENJI, SHE WAS OF MUCH HIGHER BIRTH AS WELL.
EVEN THOUGH SHE LOVED HIM, SHE FELT LIKE IT WOULD LOWER HERSELF IN SOCIETY'S EYES TO ADMIT IT.
FED UP WITH HER SNOBBERY...
GENJI DISTANCES HIMSELF FROM HER.
ROKUJO REALIZES THAT SHE'S THE ONE PUSHING HIM AWAY...
BUT HER *PRIDE* JUST WON'T LET HER ACT ON HER FEELINGS.
AND EVERY DAY, SHE JUST FALLS MORE AND MORE IN LOVE WITH HIM.

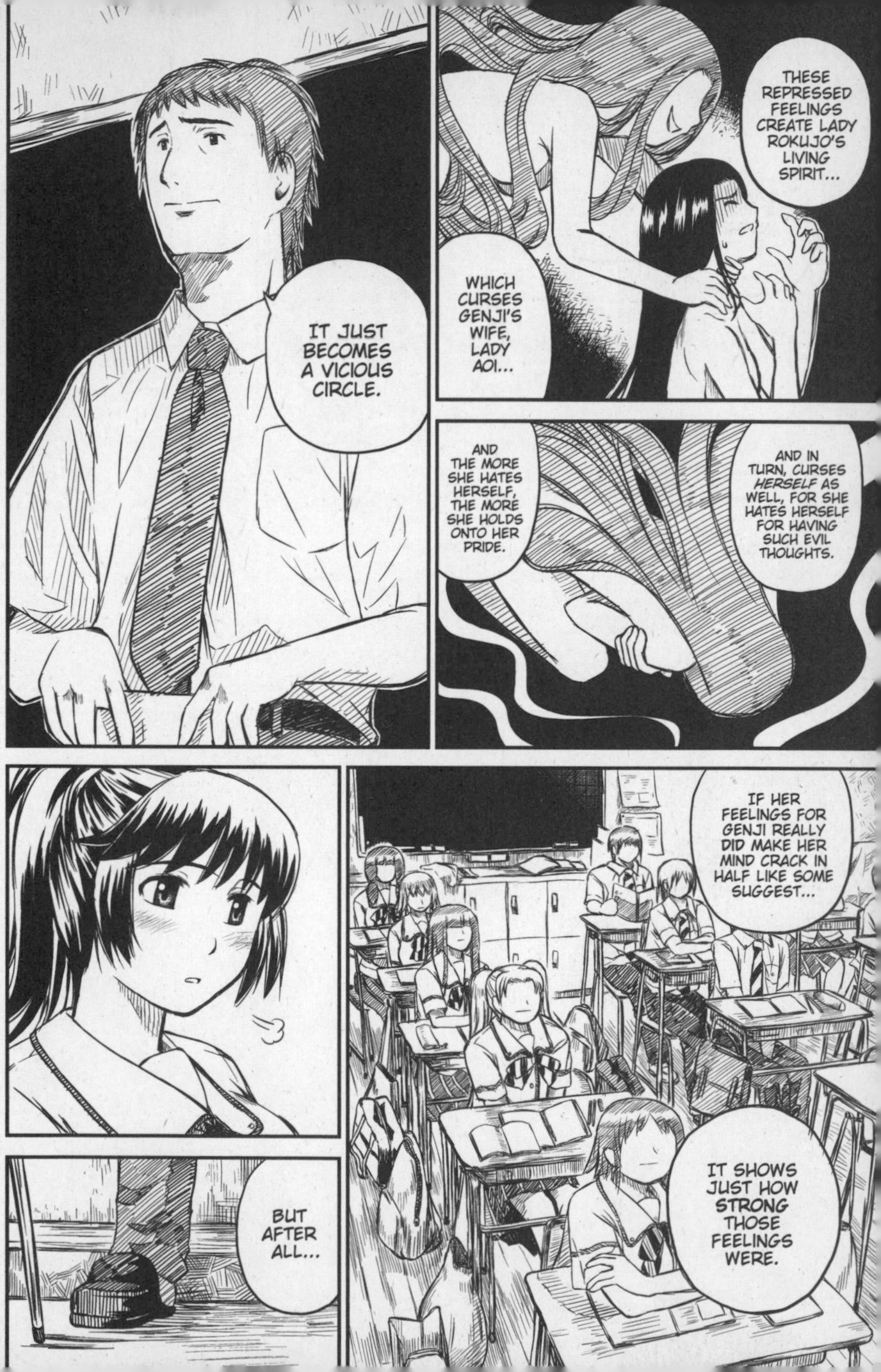
THESE REPRESSED FEELINGS CREATE LADY ROKUJO'S LIVING SPIRIT...
WHICH CURSES GENJI'S WIFE, LADY AOI...
AND IN TURN, CURSES *HERSELF* AS WELL, FOR SHE HATES HERSELF FOR HAVING SUCH EVIL THOUGHTS.
AND THE MORE SHE HATES HERSELF, THE MORE SHE HOLDS ONTO HER PRIDE.
IT JUST BECOMES A VICIOUS CIRCLE.
IF HER FEELINGS FOR GENJI REALLY DID MAKE HER MIND CRACK IN HALF LIKE SOME SUGGEST...
IT SHOWS JUST HOW STRONG THOSE FEELINGS WERE.
BUT AFTER ALL...

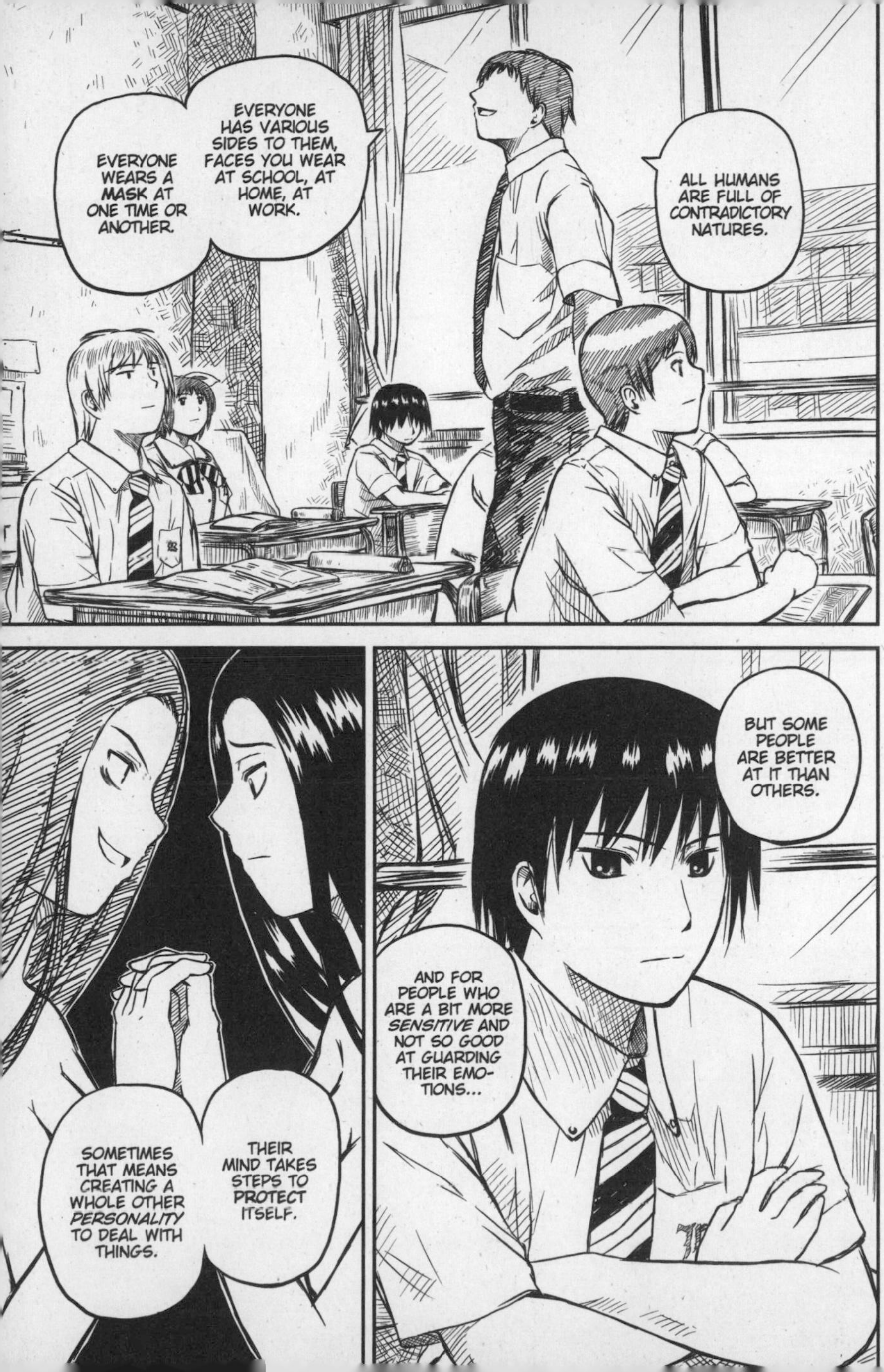
ALL HUMANS ARE FULL OF CONTRADICTORY NATURES.
EVERYONE HAS VARIOUS SIDES TO THEM, FACES YOU WEAR AT SCHOOL, AT HOME, AT WORK.
EVERYONE WEARS A MASK AT ONE TIME OR ANOTHER.
BUT SOME PEOPLE ARE BETTER AT IT THAN OTHERS.
AND FOR PEOPLE WHO ARE A BIT MORE *SENSITIVE* AND NOT SO GOOD AT GUARDING THEIR EMO-TIONS...
THEIR MIND TAKES STEPS TO PROTECT ITSELF.
SOMETIMES THAT MEANS CREATING A WHOLE OTHER *PERSONALITY* TO DEAL WITH THINGS.

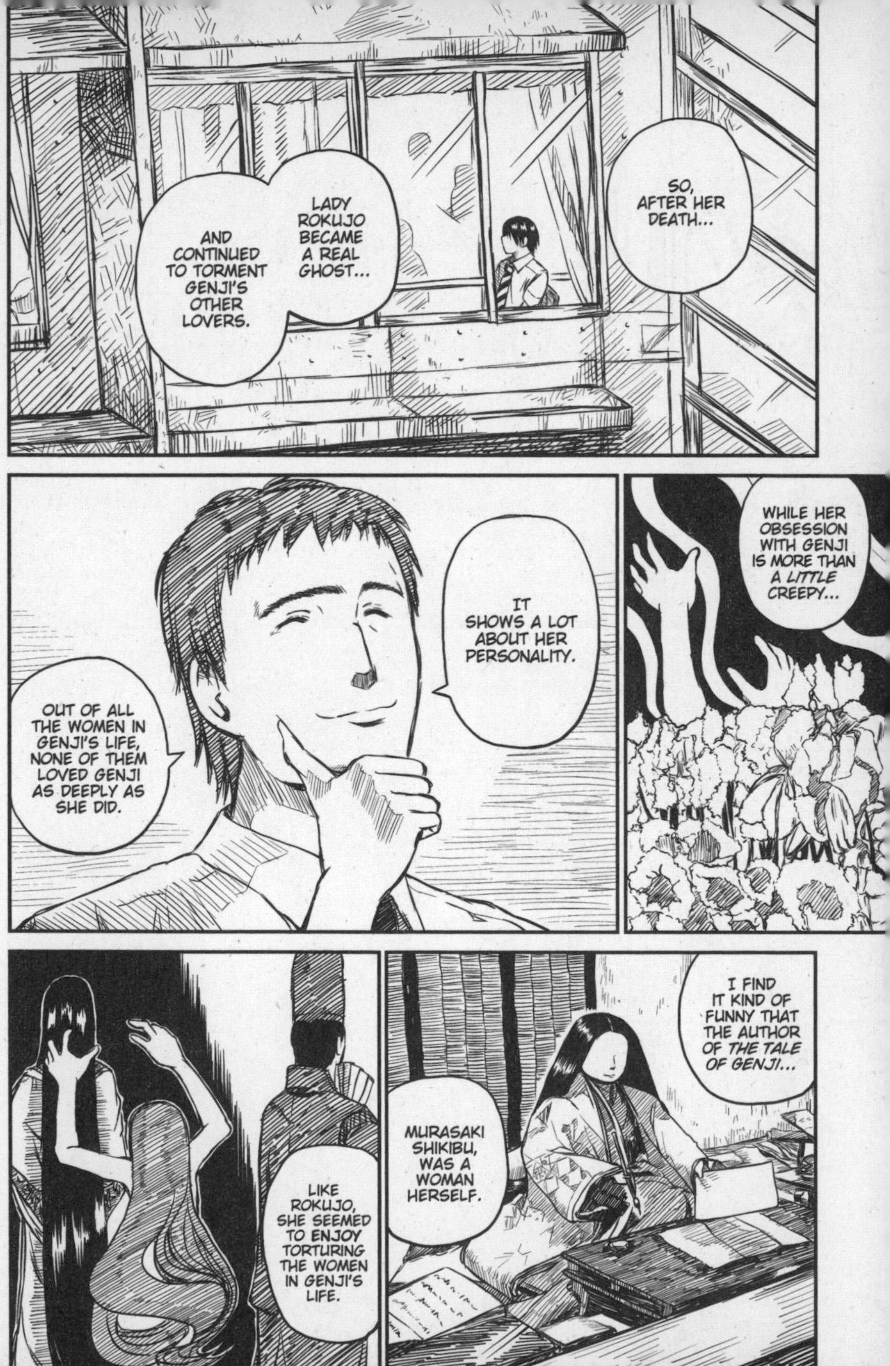
SO, AFTER HER DEATH...
LADY ROKUJO BECAME A REAL GHOST...
AND CONTINUED TO TORMENT GENJI'S OTHER LOVERS.
WHILE HER OBSESSION WITH GENJI IS MORE THAN A *LITTLE* CREEPY...
IT SHOWS A LOT ABOUT HER PERSONALITY.
OUT OF ALL THE WOMEN IN GENJI'S LIFE, NONE OF THEM LOVED GENJI AS DEEPLY AS SHE DID.
I FIND IT KIND OF FUNNY THAT THE AUTHOR OF *THE TALE OF GENJI*...
MURASAKI SHIKIBU, WAS A WOMAN HERSELF.
LIKE ROKUJO, SHE SEEMED TO ENJOY TORTURING THE WOMEN IN GENJI'S LIFE.

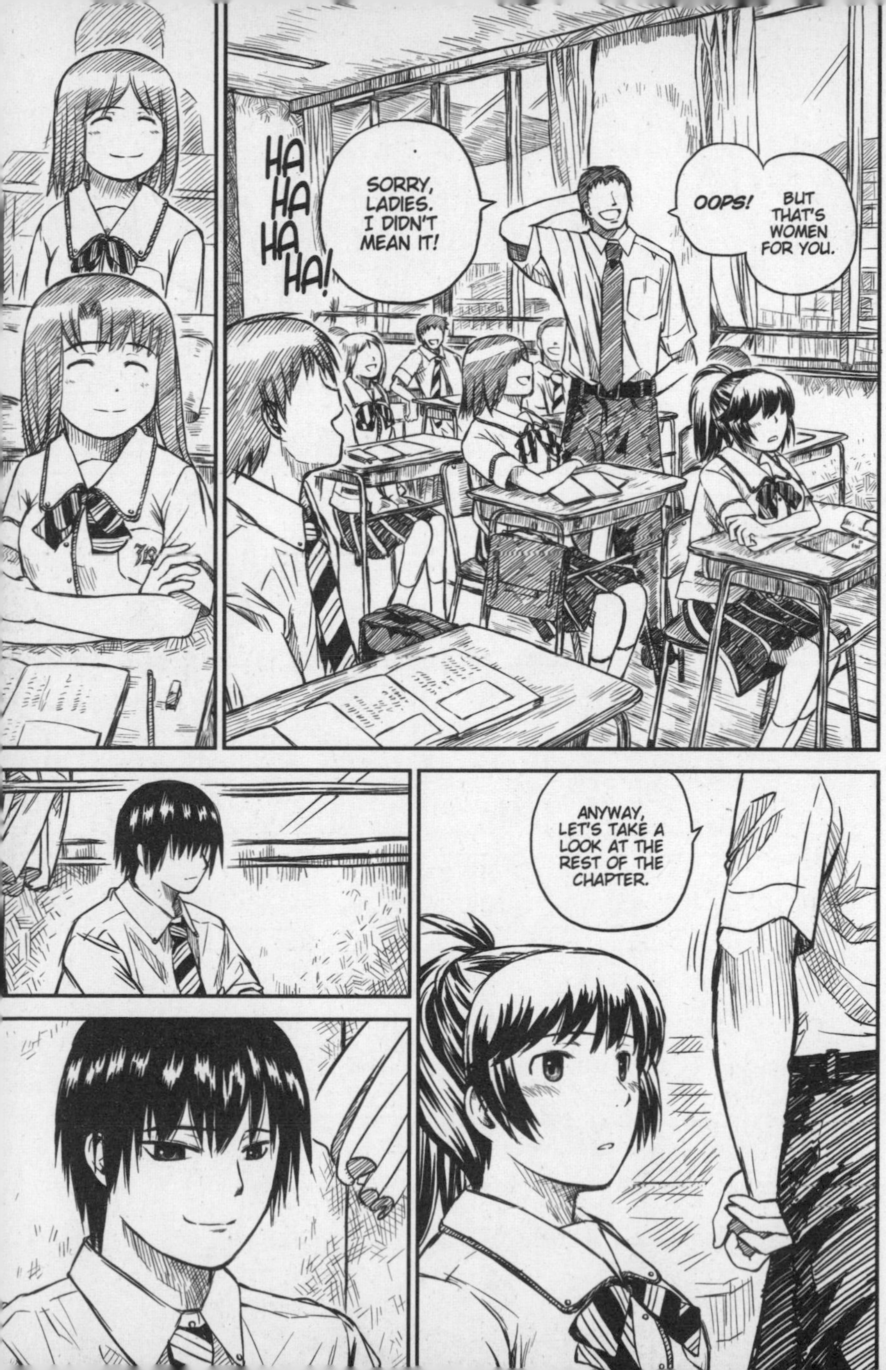
OOPS!
BUT THAT'S WOMEN FOR YOU.
SORRY, LADIES. I DIDN'T MEAN IT!
HA HA HA HA!
ANYWAY, LET'S TAKE A LOOK AT THE REST OF THE CHAPTER.

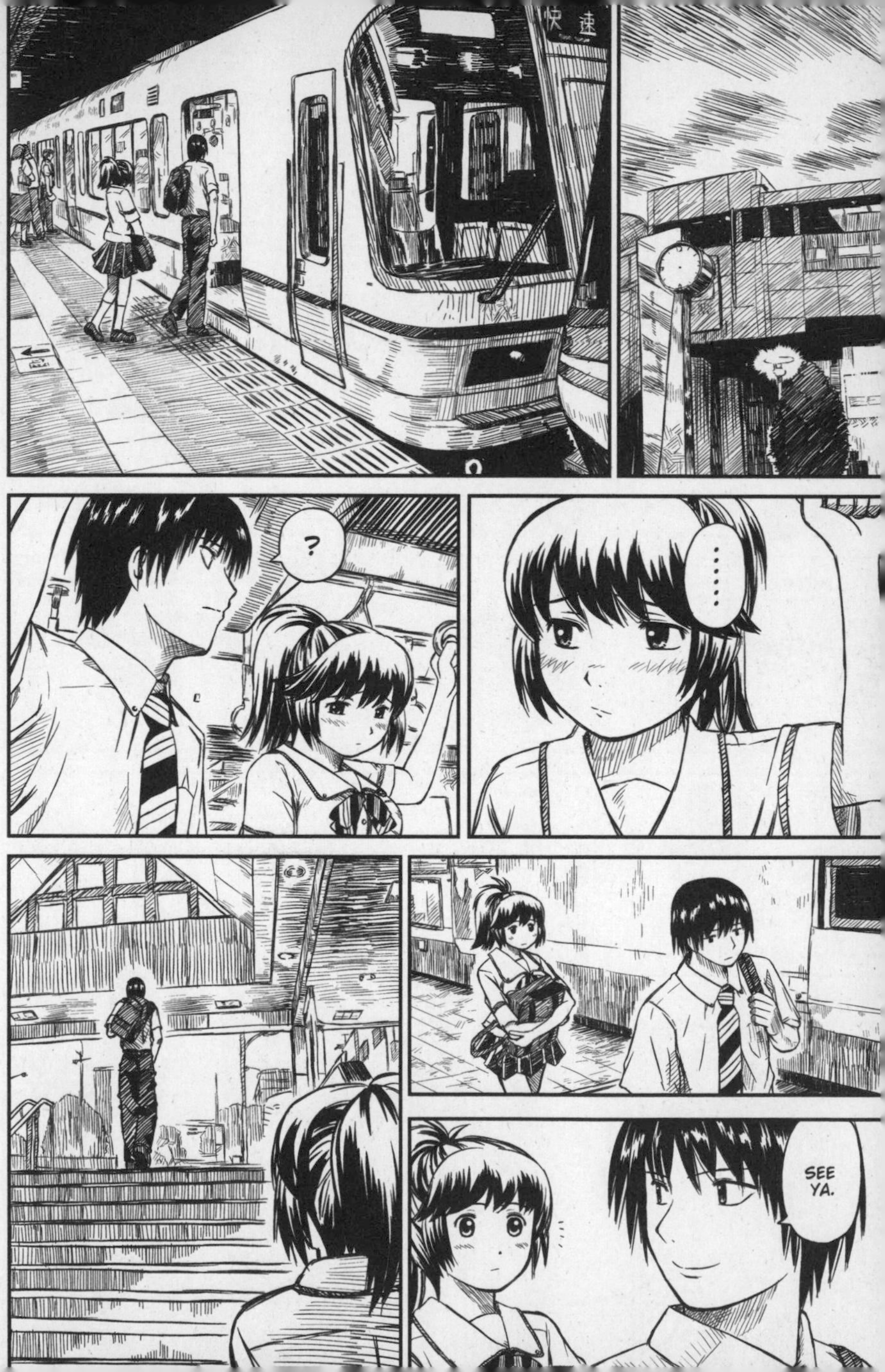
快速
......
?
SEE YA.

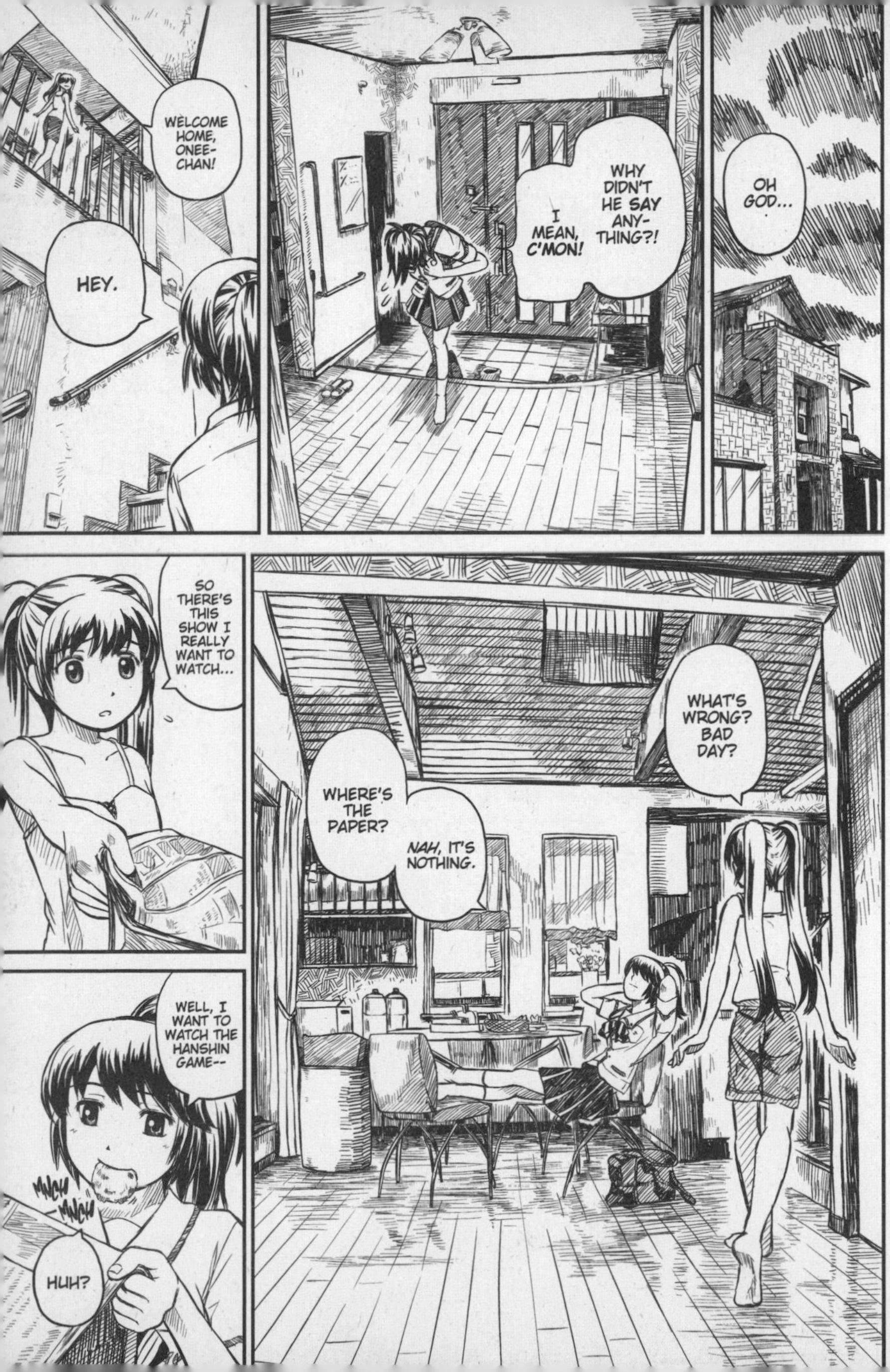
OH GOD...
WHY DIDN'T HE SAY ANY-THING?!
I MEAN, C'MON!
WELCOME HOME, ONEE-CHAN!
HEY.
WHAT'S WRONG? BAD DAY?
NAH, IT'S NOTHING.
WHERE'S THE PAPER?
SO THERE'S THIS SHOW I REALLY WANT TO WATCH...
WELL, I WANT TO WATCH THE HANSHIN GAME--
MNCH MNCH
HUH?

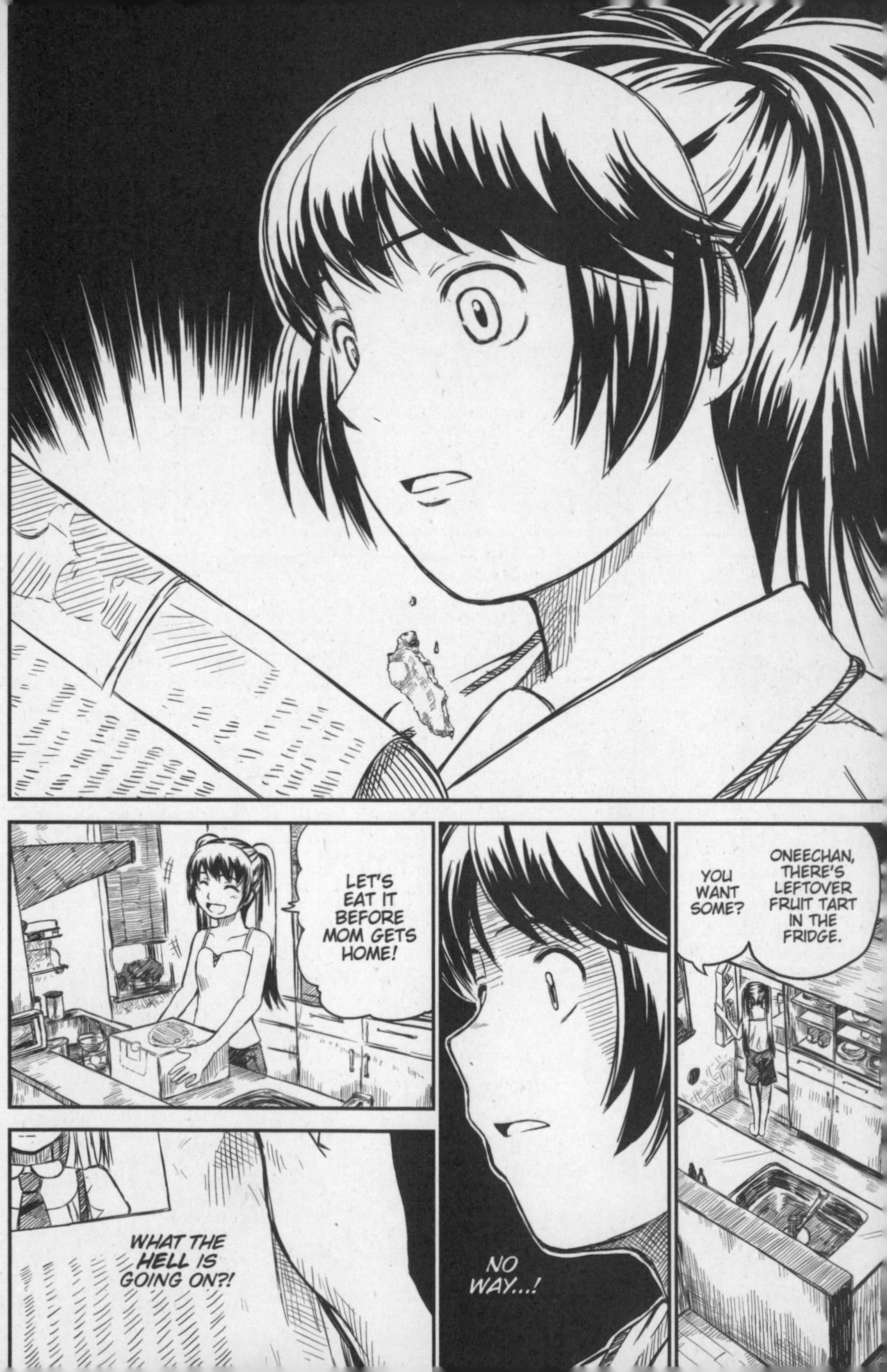
ONEECHAN, THERE'S LEFTOVER FRUIT TART IN THE FRIDGE.
YOU WANT SOME?
NO WAY...!
LET'S EAT IT BEFORE MOM GETS HOME!
WHAT THE HELL IS GOING ON?!

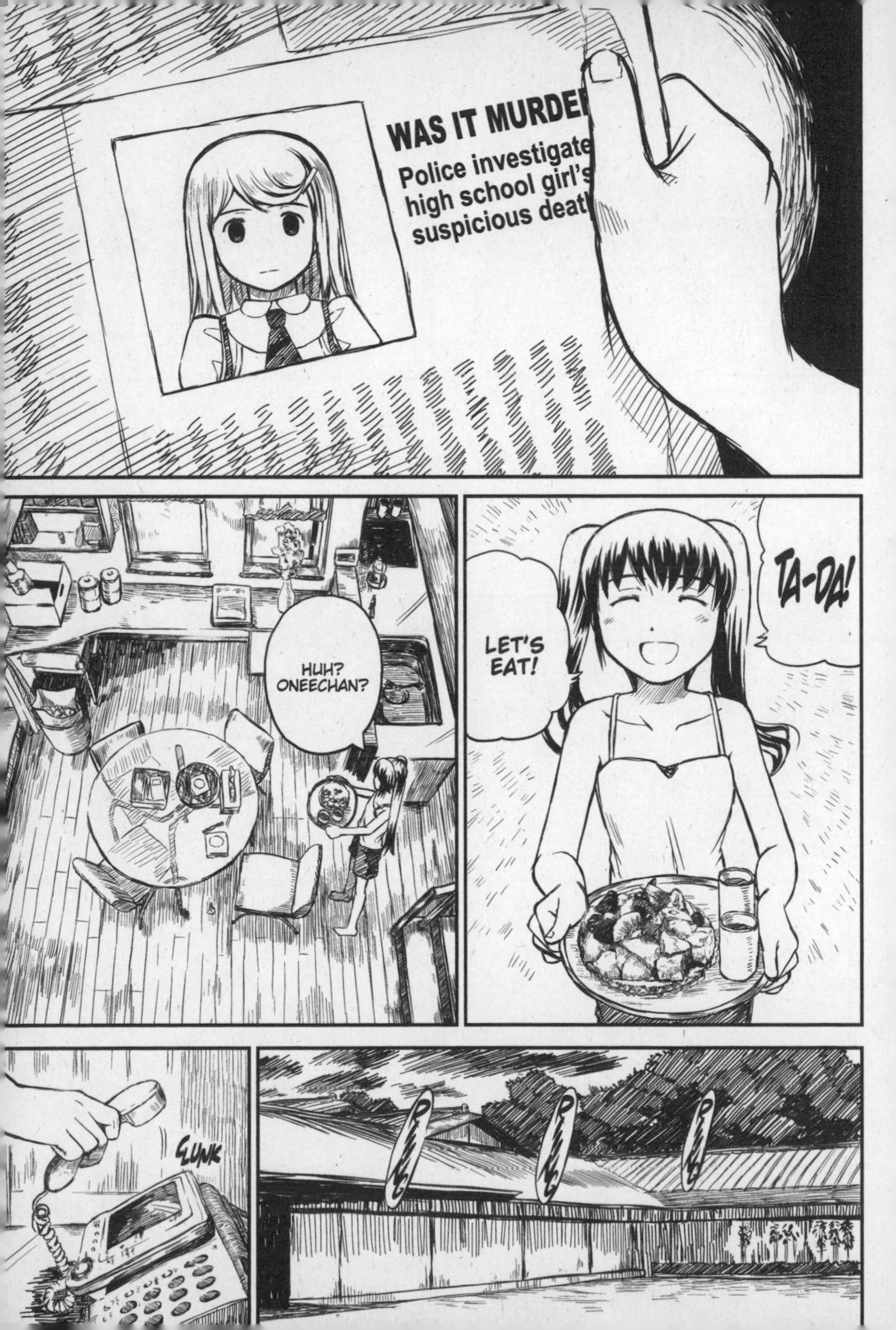
WAS IT MURDE
Police investigate
high school girl's
suspicious deat
TA-DA!
LET'S EAT!
HUH? ONEECHAN?
CLUNK

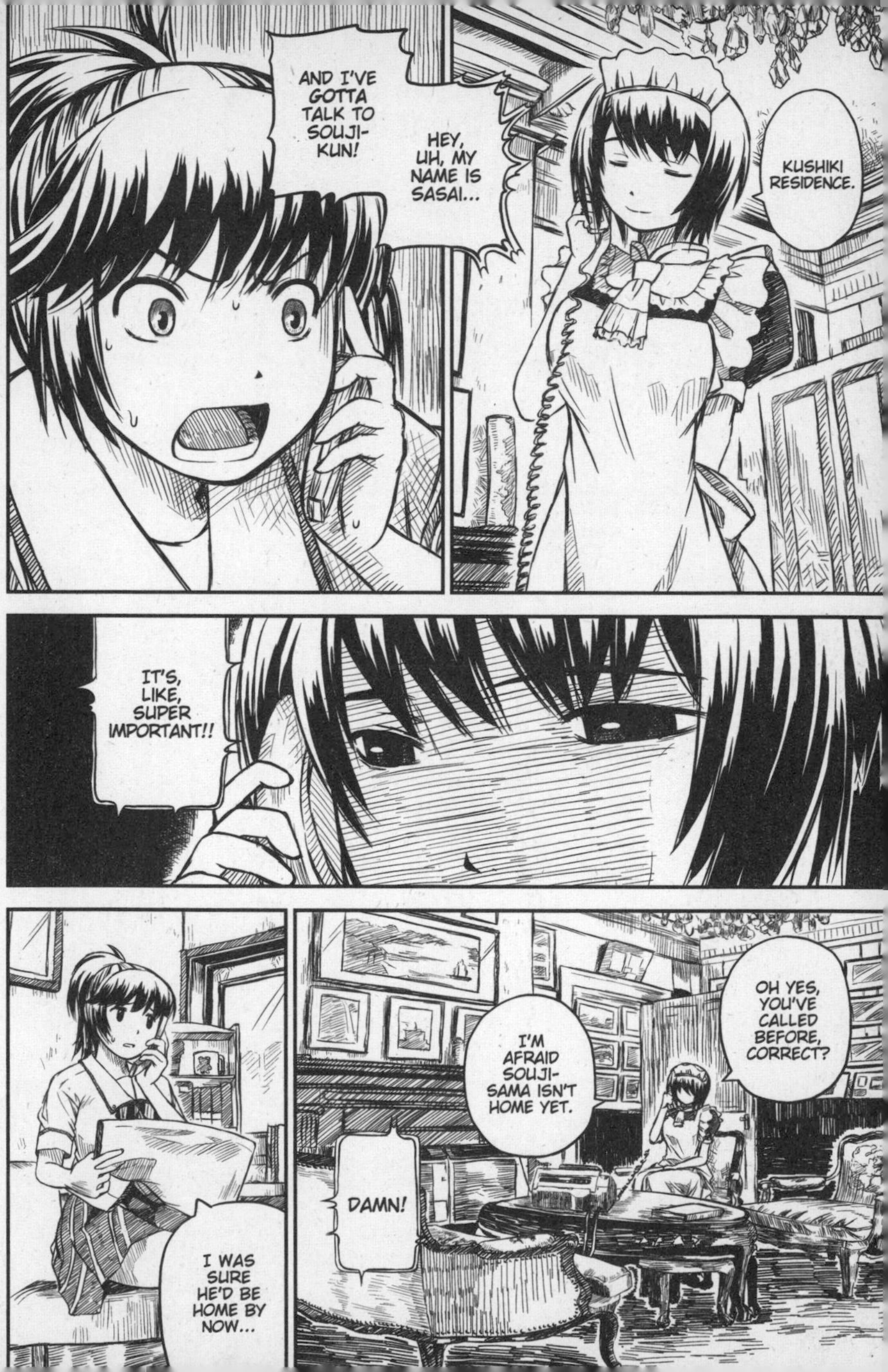
KUSHIKI RESIDENCE.
HEY, UH, MY NAME IS SASAI...
AND I'VE GOTTA TALK TO SOUJI-KUN!
IT'S, LIKE, SUPER IMPORTANT!!
OH YES, YOU'VE CALLED BEFORE, CORRECT?
I'M AFRAID SOUJI-SAMA ISN'T HOME YET.
DAMN!
I WAS SURE HE'D BE HOME BY NOW...

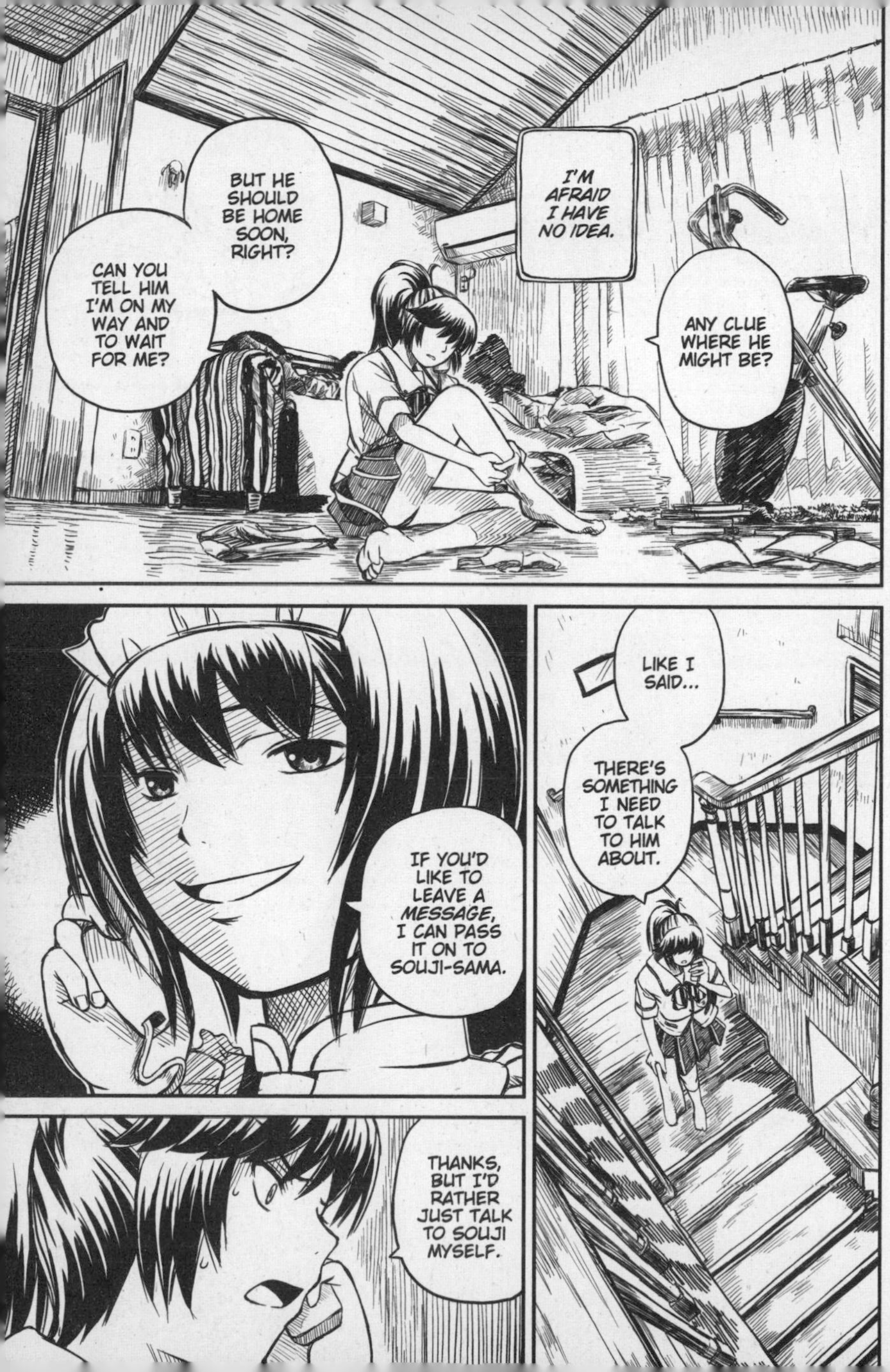
ANY CLUE WHERE HE MIGHT BE?
I'M AFRAID I HAVE NO IDEA.
BUT HE SHOULD BE HOME SOON, RIGHT?
CAN YOU TELL HIM I'M ON MY WAY AND TO WAIT FOR ME?
LIKE I SAID...
THERE'S SOMETHING I NEED TO TALK TO HIM ABOUT.
IF YOU'D LIKE TO LEAVE A *MESSAGE*, I CAN PASS IT ON TO SOUJI-SAMA.
THANKS, BUT I'D RATHER JUST TALK TO SOUJI MYSELF.

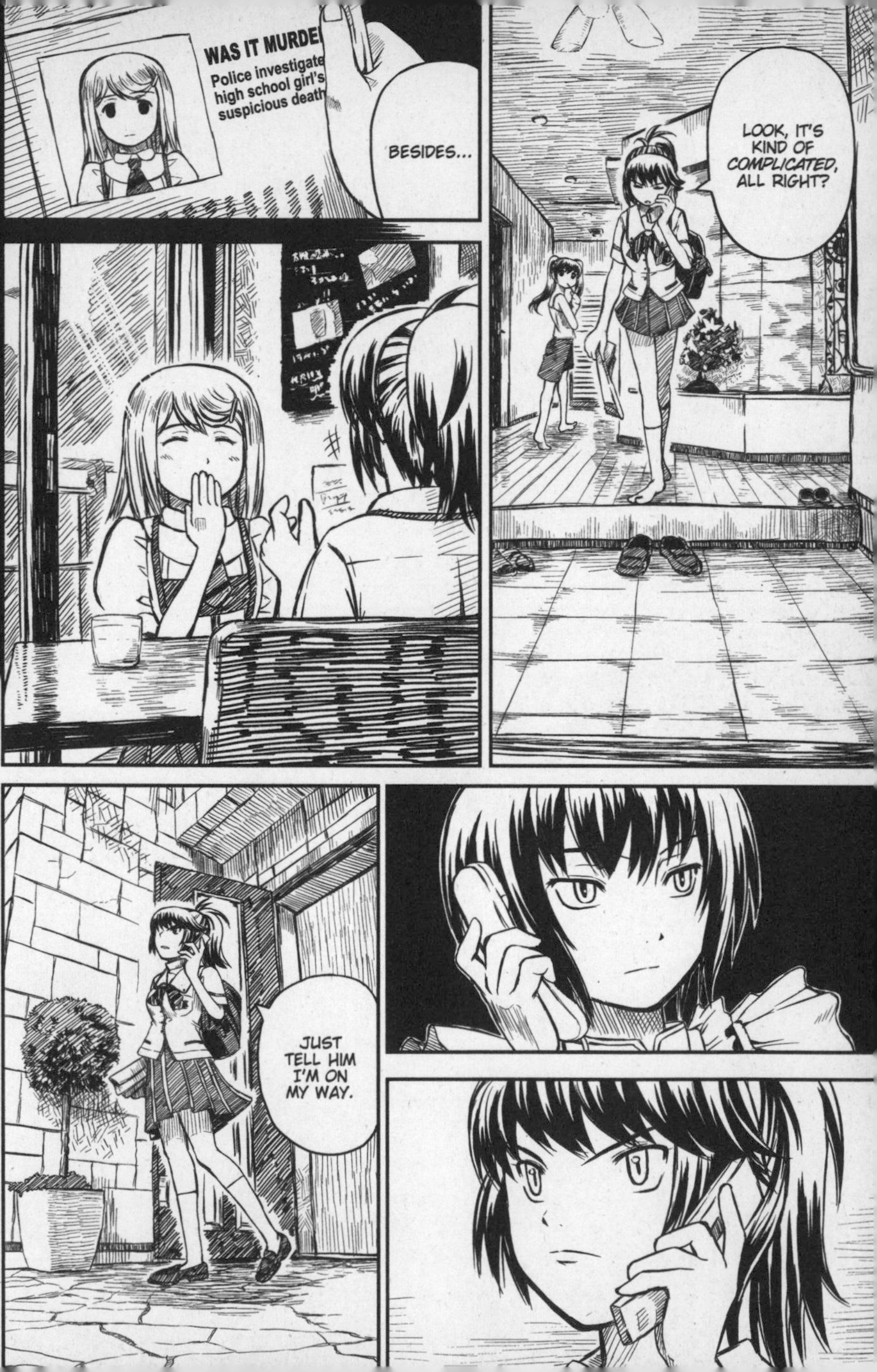
LOOK, IT'S KIND OF COMPLICATED, ALL RIGHT?
WAS IT MURDE
Police investigate
high school girl's
suspicious death
BESIDES...
JUST TELL HIM I'M ON MY WAY.

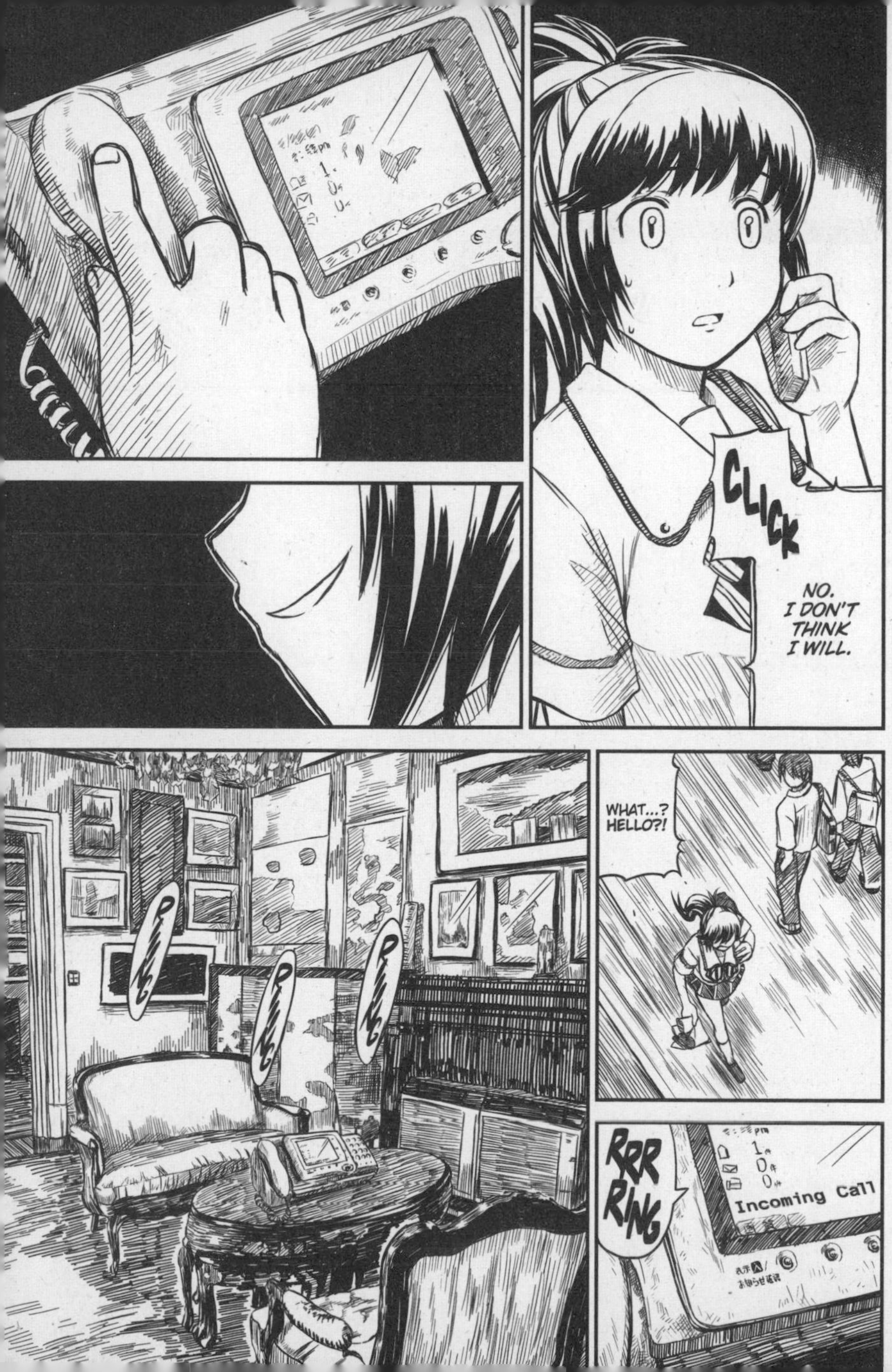
CLICK
NO. I DON'T THINK I WILL.
WHAT...? HELLO?!
RRR RING
Incoming Call
RING
RING
RING

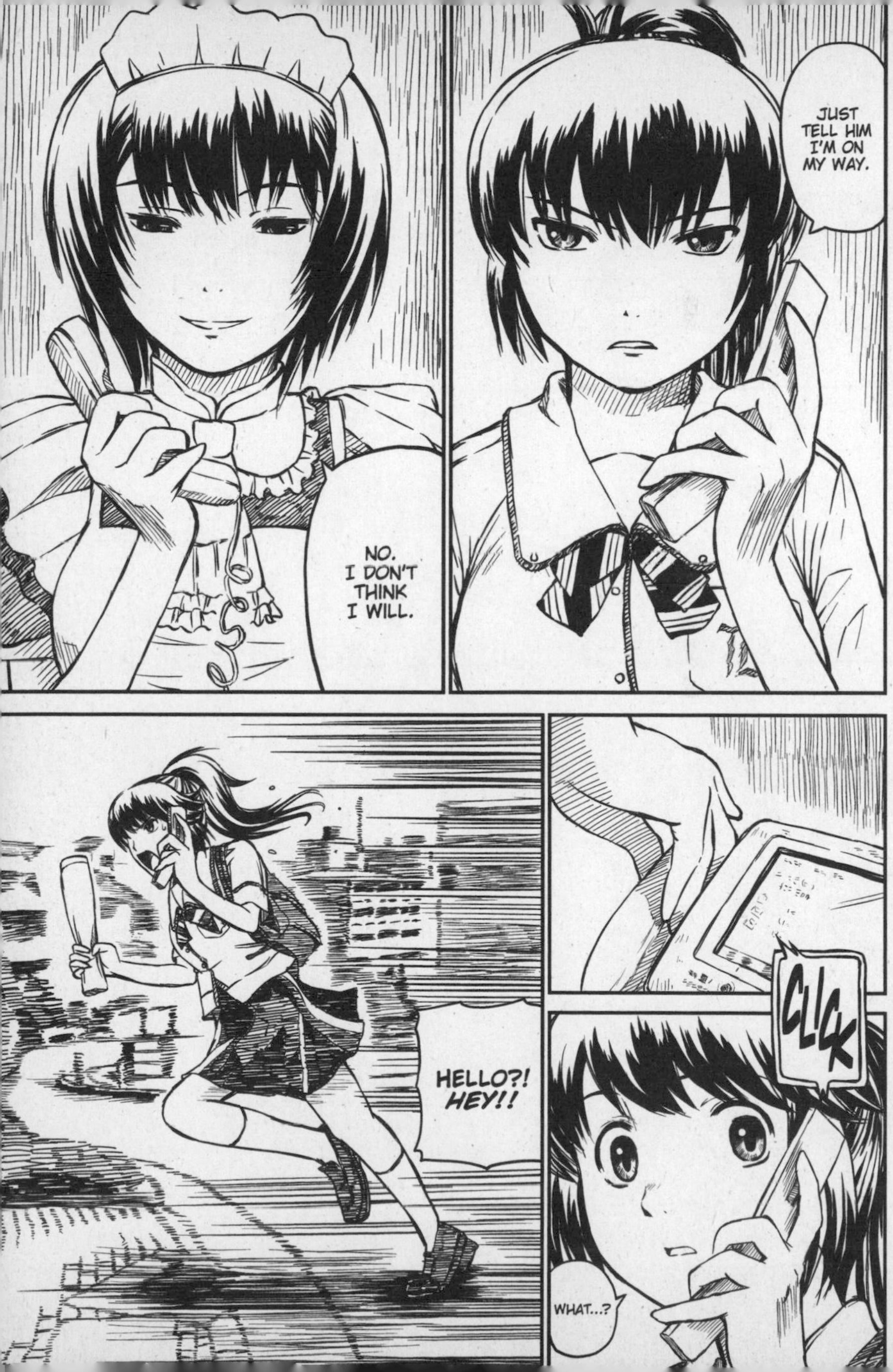
JUST TELL HIM I'M ON MY WAY.
NO. I DON'T THINK I WILL.
CLICK
WHAT...?
HELLO?! HEY!!

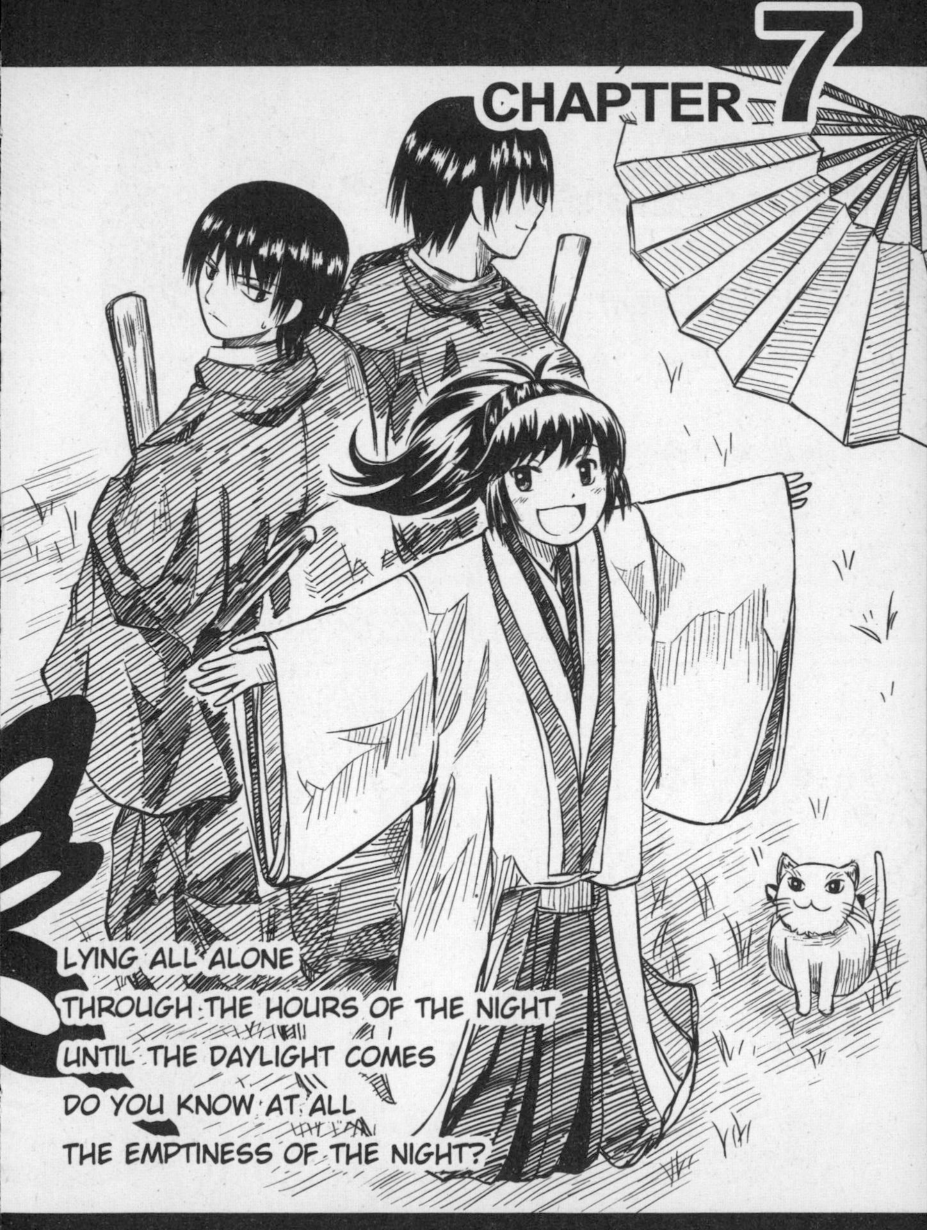
CHAPTER 7
LYING ALL ALONE
THROUGH THE HOURS OF THE NIGHT
UNTIL THE DAYLIGHT COMES
DO YOU KNOW AT ALL
THE EMPTINESS OF THE NIGHT?

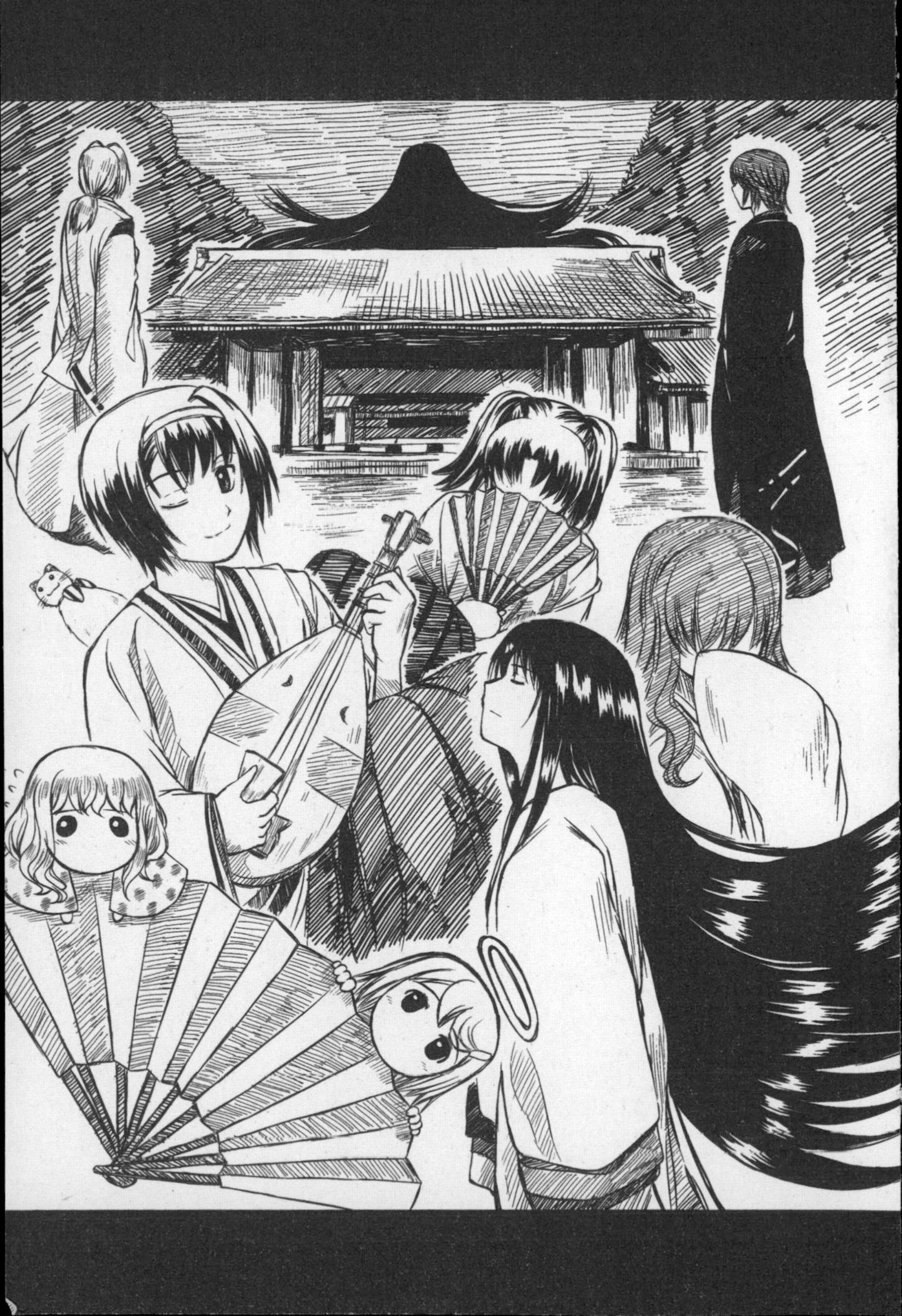

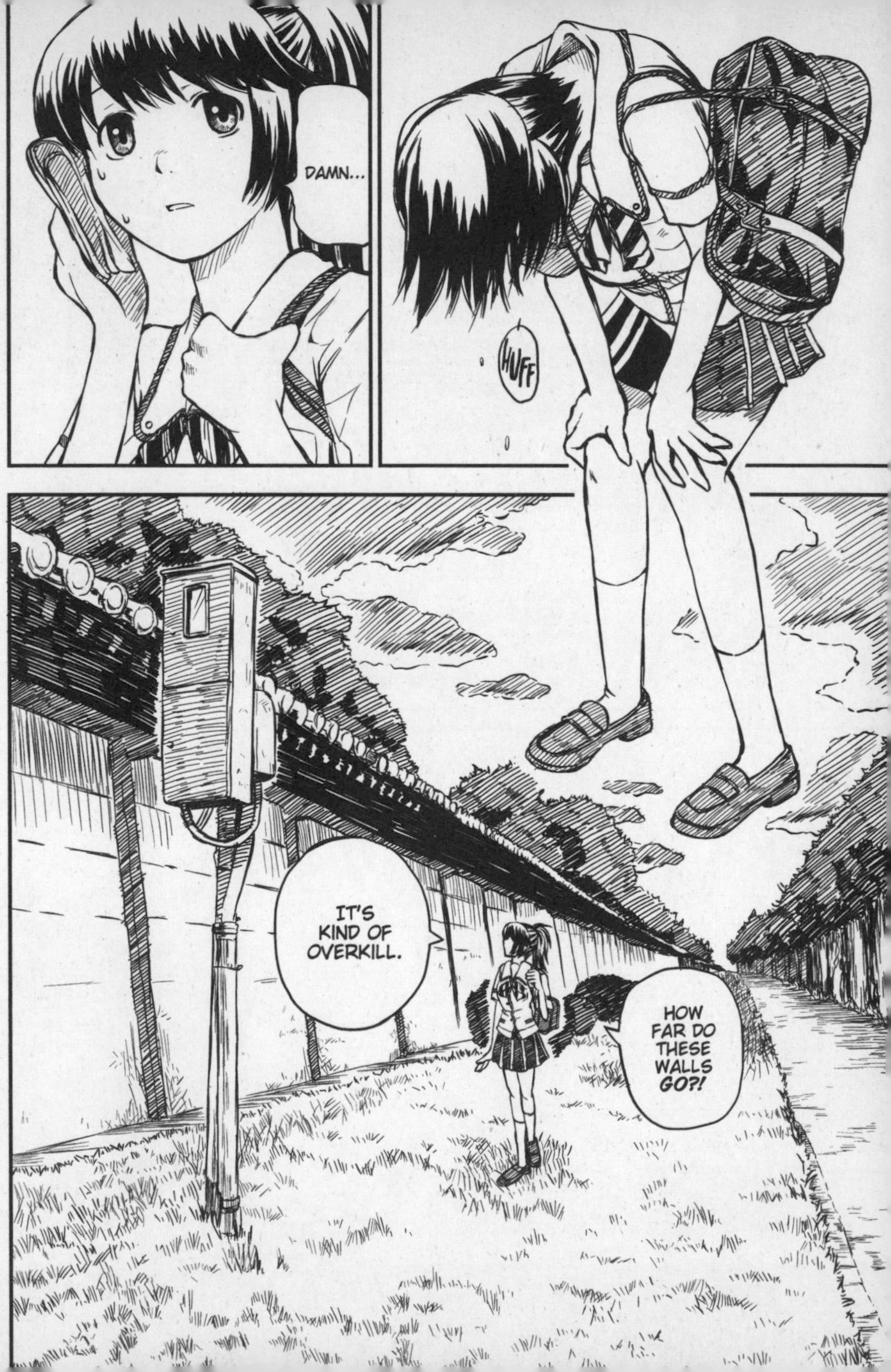
HUFF
DAMN...
HOW FAR DO THESE WALLS GO?!
IT'S KIND OF OVERKILL.

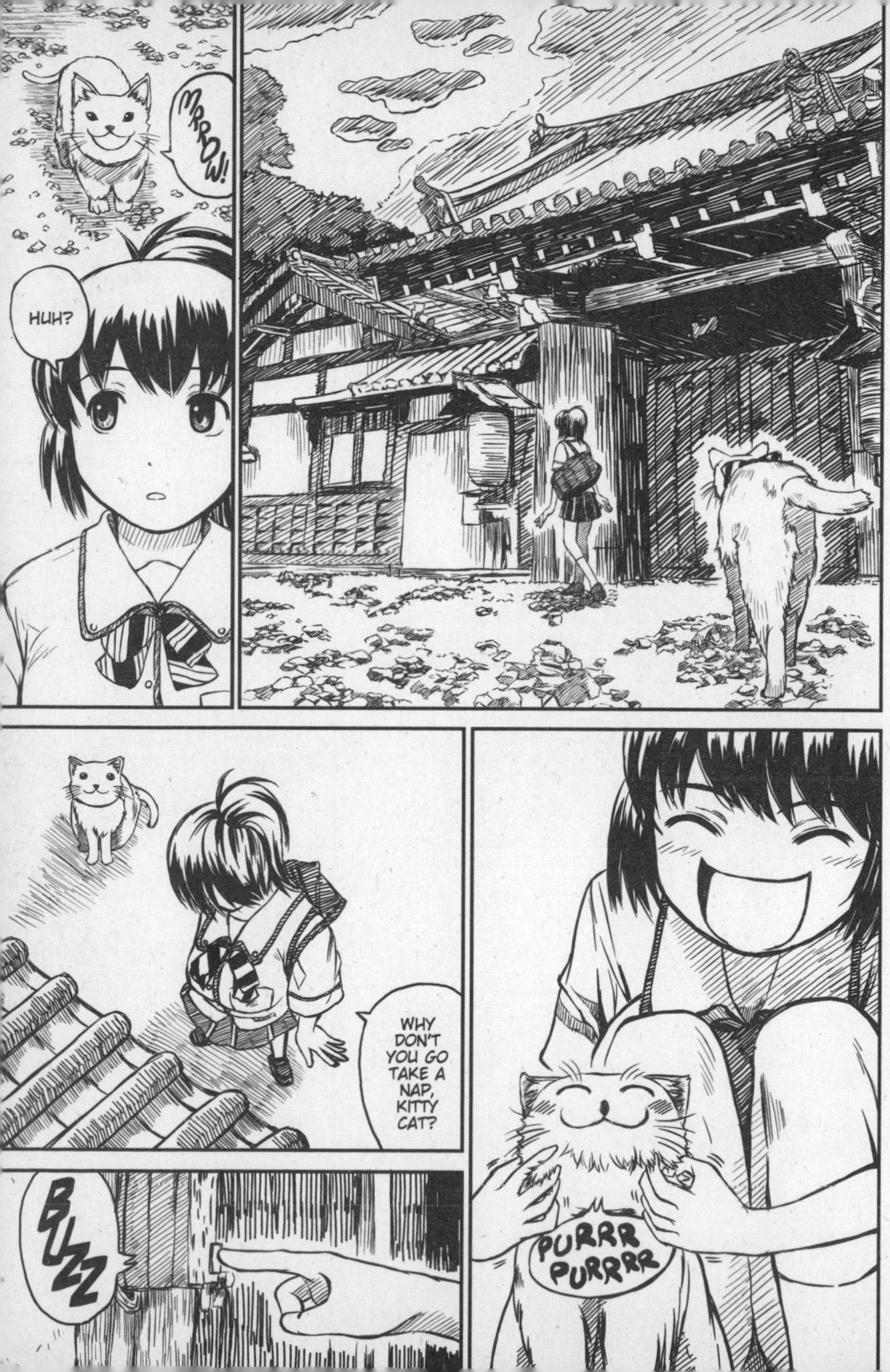
MRROW!
HUH?
PURRR PURRRR
WHY DON'T YOU GO TAKE A NAP, KITTY CAT?
BUZZ

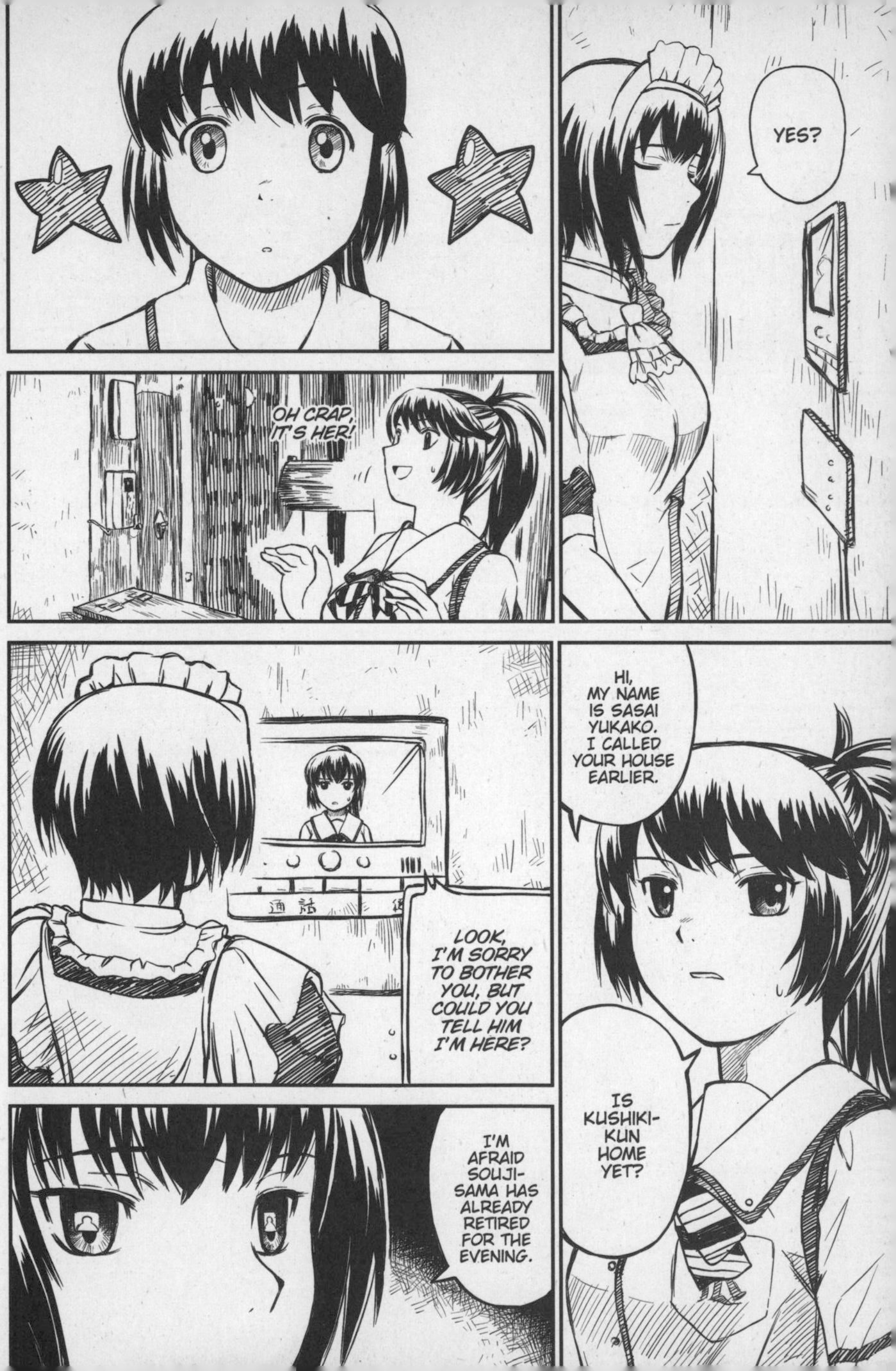
YES?
OH CRAP, IT'S HER!
HI, MY NAME IS SASAI YUKAKO. I CALLED YOUR HOUSE EARLIER.
IS KUSHIKI-KUN HOME YET?
通話
LOOK, I'M SORRY TO BOTHER YOU, BUT COULD YOU TELL HIM I'M HERE?
I'M AFRAID SOUJI-SAMA HAS ALREADY RETIRED FOR THE EVENING.

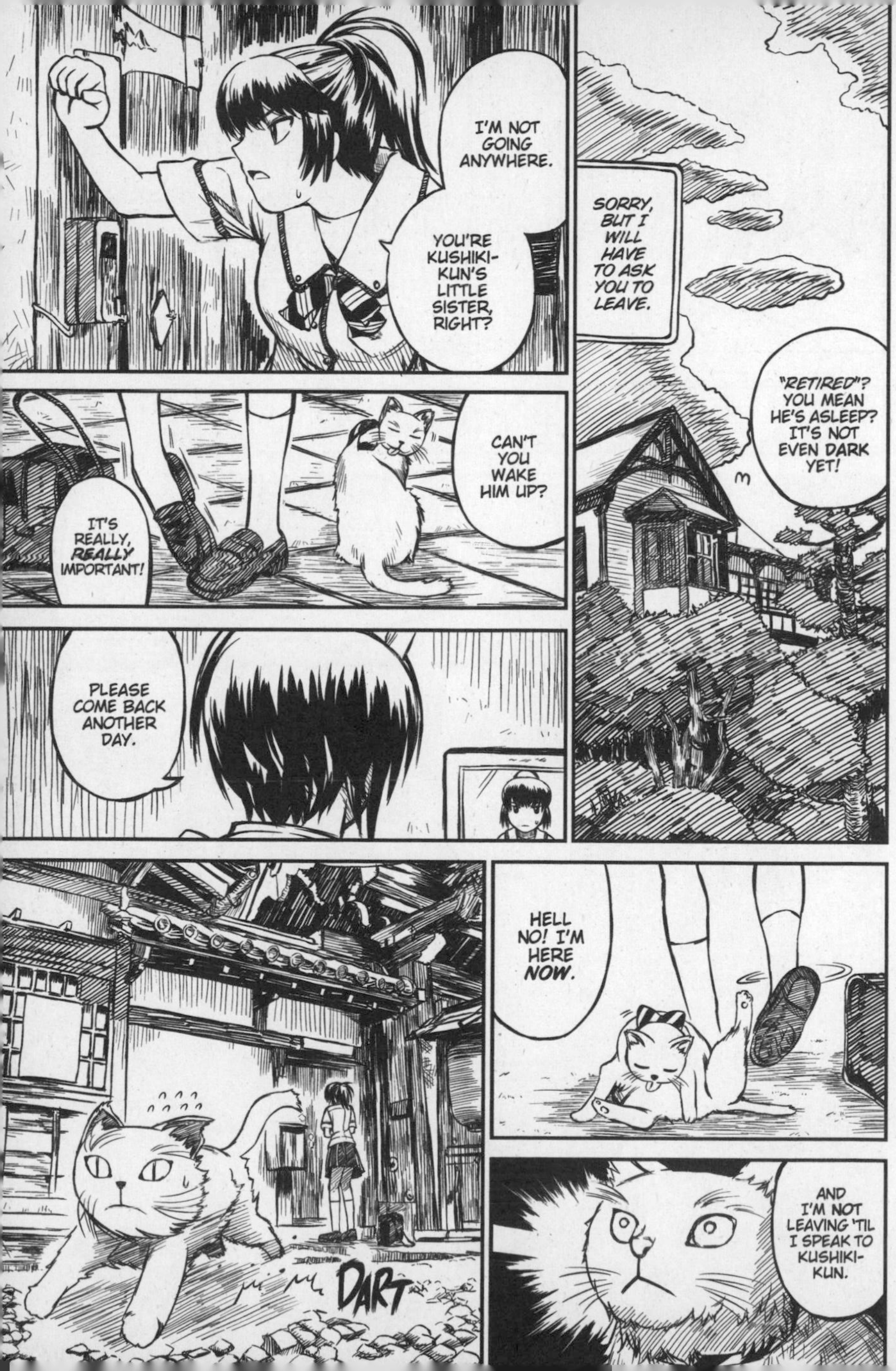
SORRY, BUT I WILL HAVE TO ASK YOU TO LEAVE.
"RETIRED"? YOU MEAN HE'S ASLEEP? IT'S NOT EVEN DARK YET!
I'M NOT GOING ANYWHERE.
YOU'RE KUSHIKI-KUN'S LITTLE SISTER, RIGHT?
CAN'T YOU WAKE HIM UP?
IT'S REALLY, *REALLY* IMPORTANT!
PLEASE COME BACK ANOTHER DAY.
HELL NO! I'M HERE *NOW*.
AND I'M NOT LEAVING 'TIL I SPEAK TO KUSHIKI-KUN.
DART

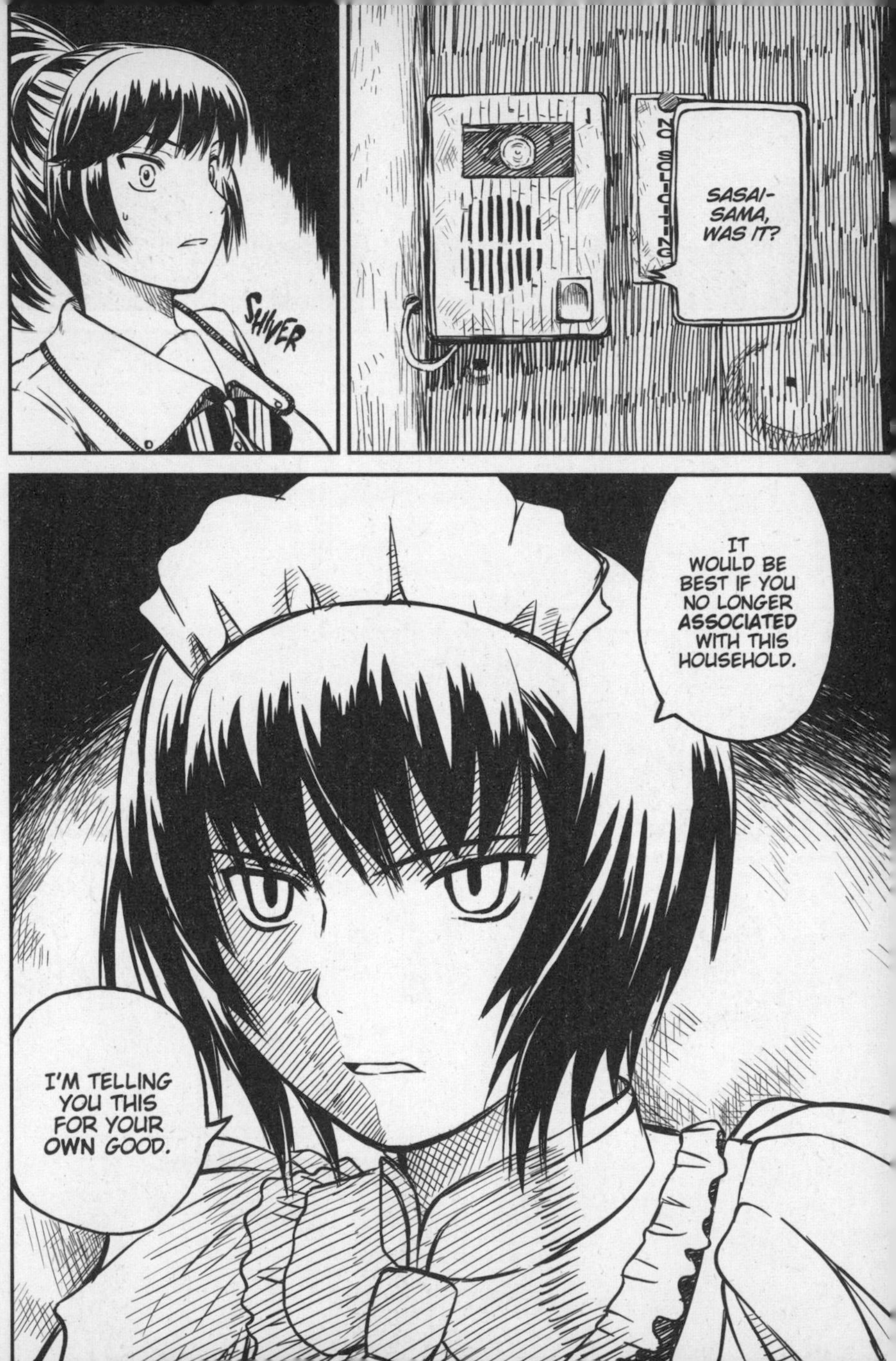
NO SOLICITING
SASAI-SAMA, WAS IT?
SHIVER
IT WOULD BE BEST IF YOU NO LONGER ASSOCIATED WITH THIS HOUSEHOLD.
I'M TELLING YOU THIS FOR YOUR OWN GOOD.

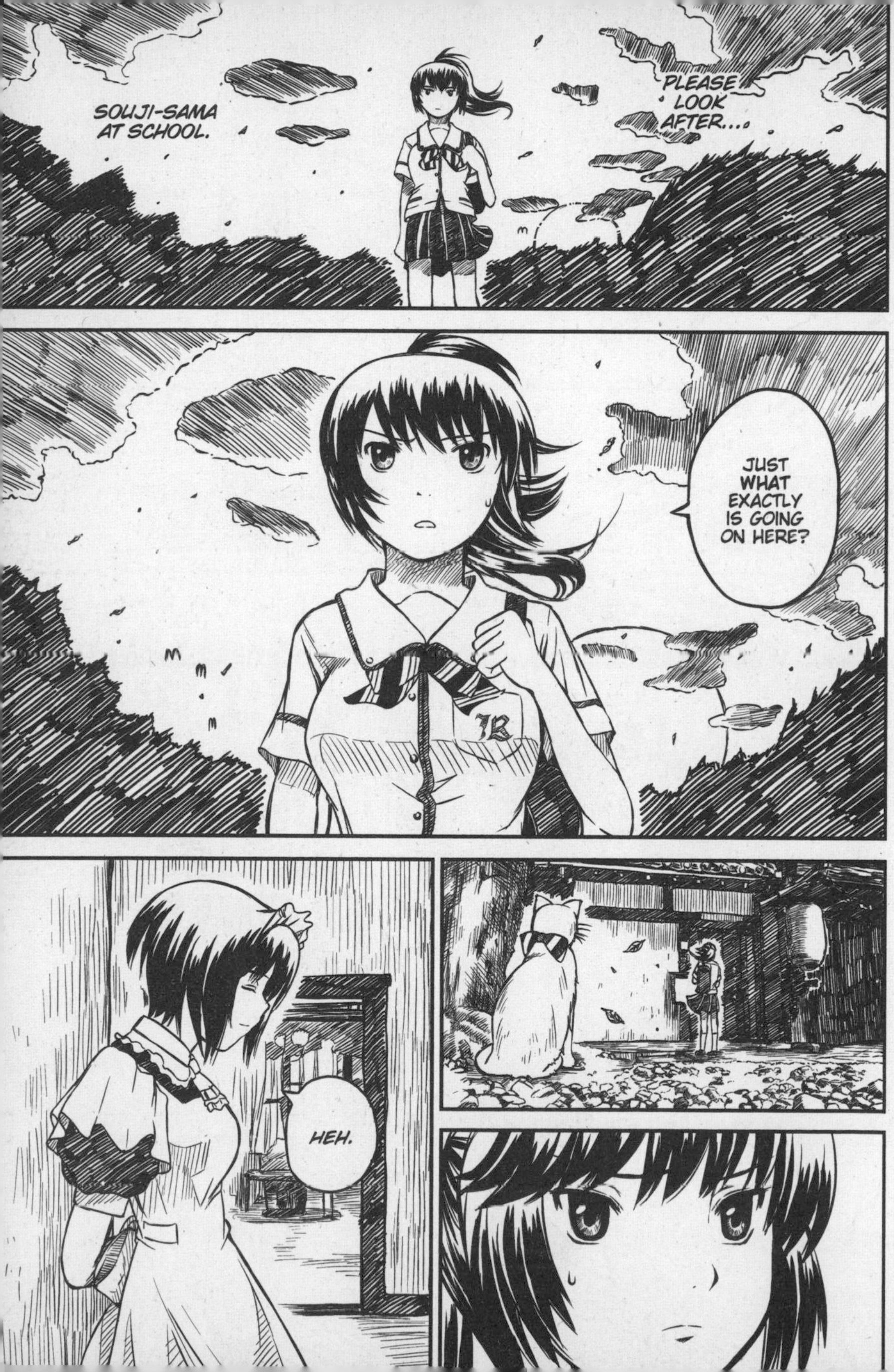
PLEASE LOOK AFTER...
SOUJI-SAMA AT SCHOOL.
JUST WHAT EXACTLY IS GOING ON HERE?
HEH.

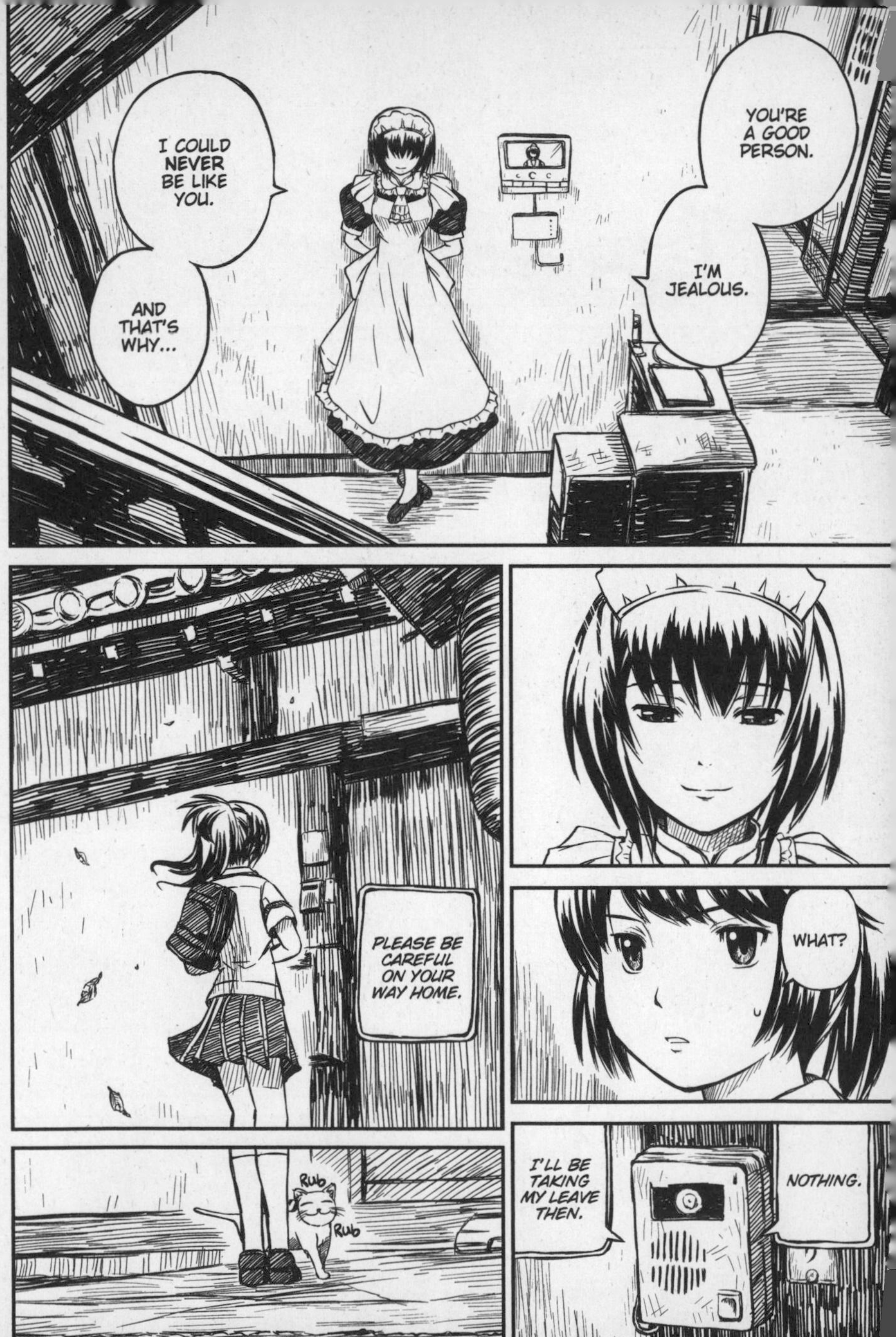
YOU'RE A GOOD PERSON.
I'M JEALOUS.
I COULD NEVER BE LIKE YOU.
AND THAT'S WHY...
WHAT?
PLEASE BE CAREFUL ON YOUR WAY HOME.
NOTHING.
I'LL BE TAKING MY LEAVE THEN.
Rub
Rub

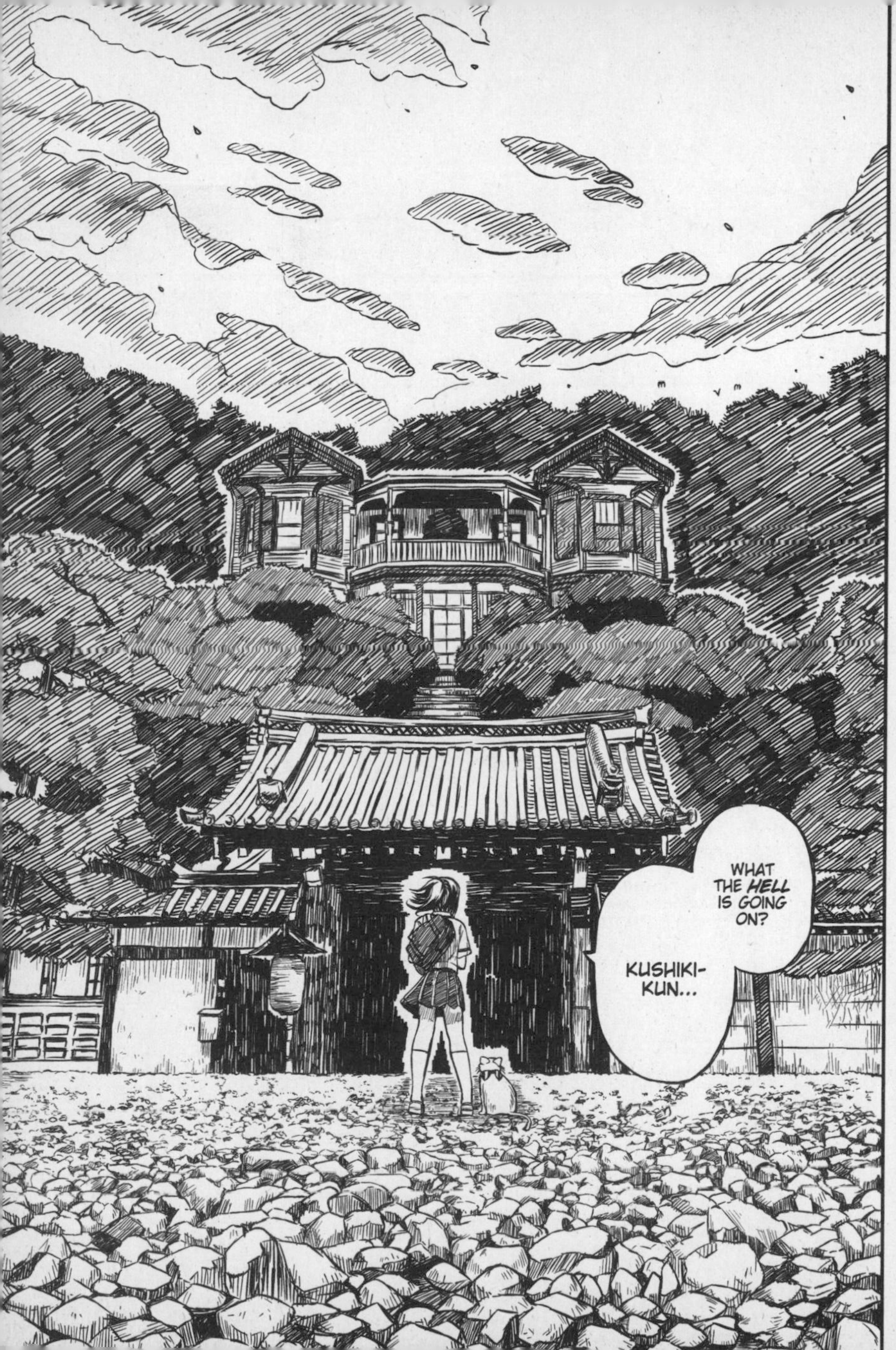
KUSHIKI-KUN...
WHAT THE HELL IS GOING ON?

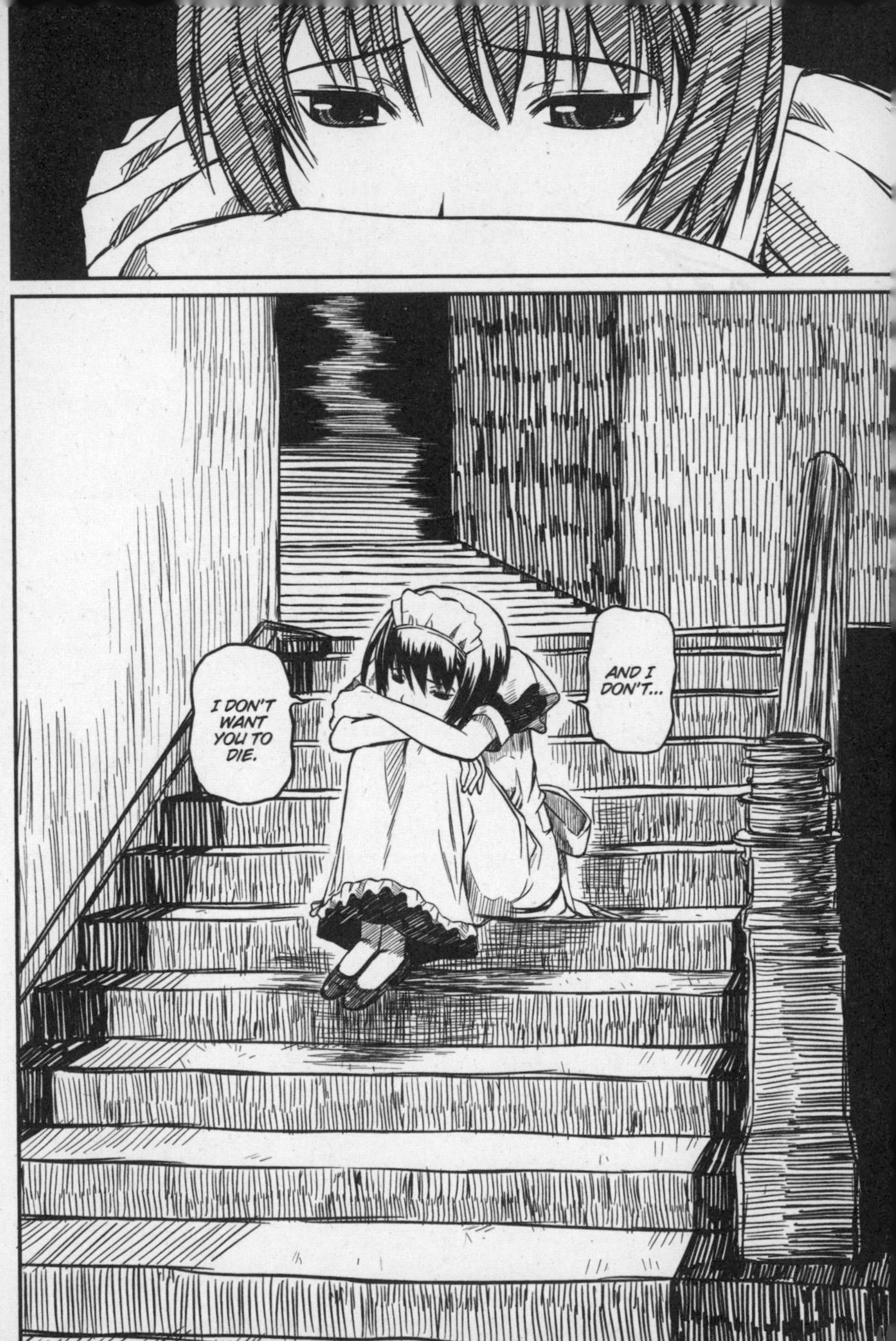
AND I DON'T...
I DON'T WANT YOU TO DIE.

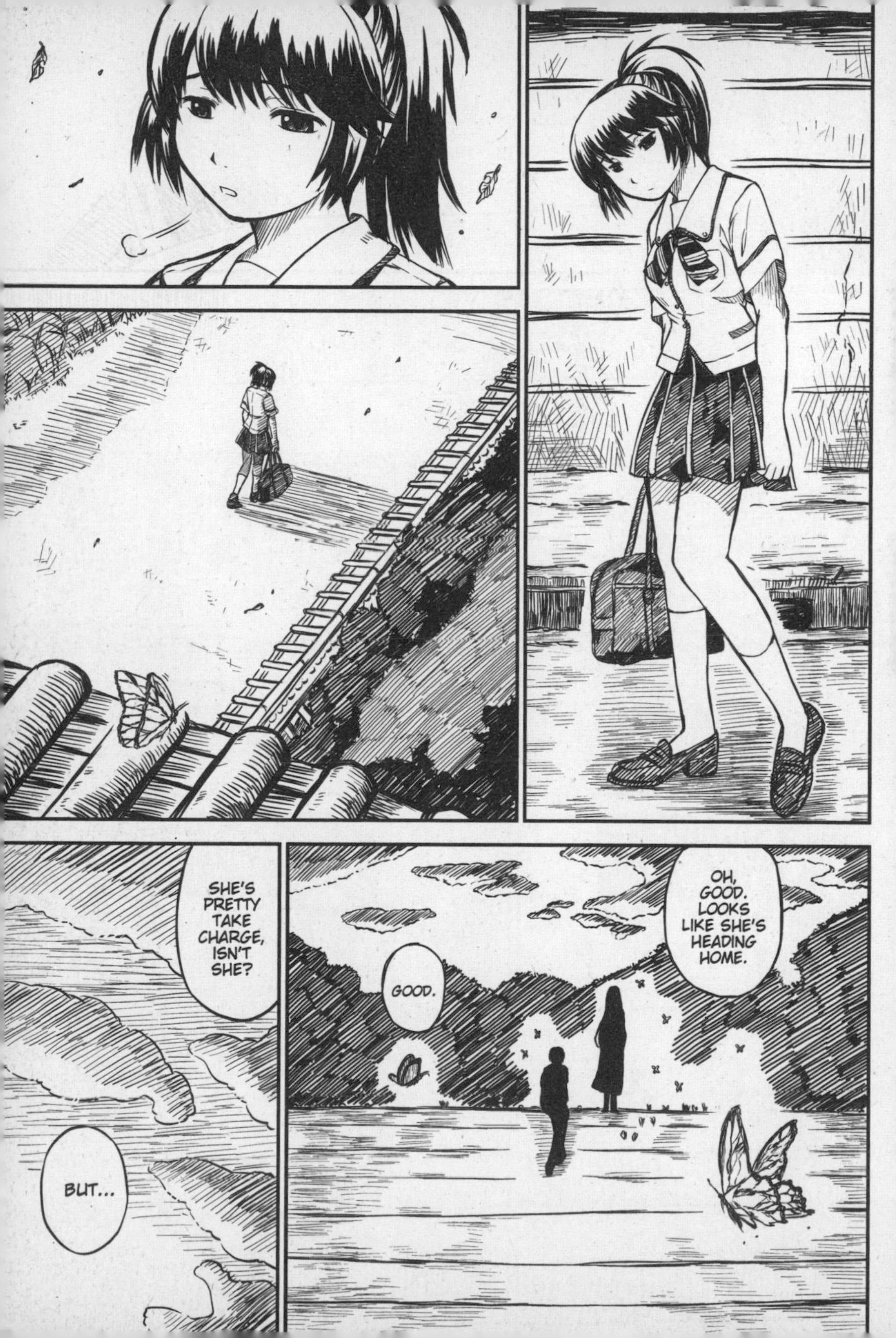
OH, GOOD. LOOKS LIKE SHE'S HEADING HOME.
GOOD.
SHE'S PRETTY TAKE CHARGE, ISN'T SHE?
BUT...

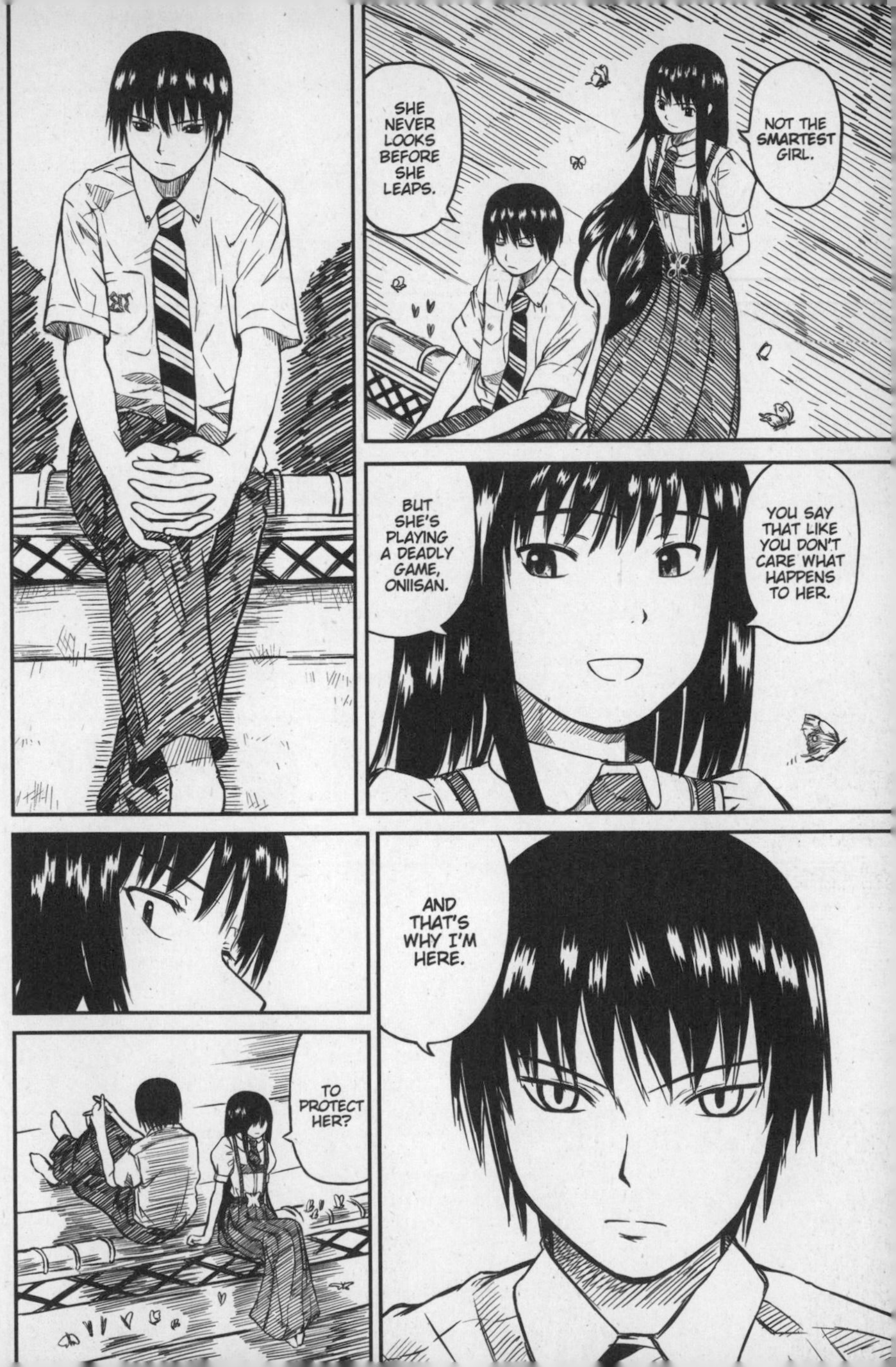
NOT THE SMARTEST GIRL.
SHE NEVER LOOKS BEFORE SHE LEAPS.
YOU SAY THAT LIKE YOU DON'T CARE WHAT HAPPENS TO HER.
BUT SHE'S PLAYING A DEADLY GAME, ONIISAN.
AND THAT'S WHY I'M HERE.
TO PROTECT HER?

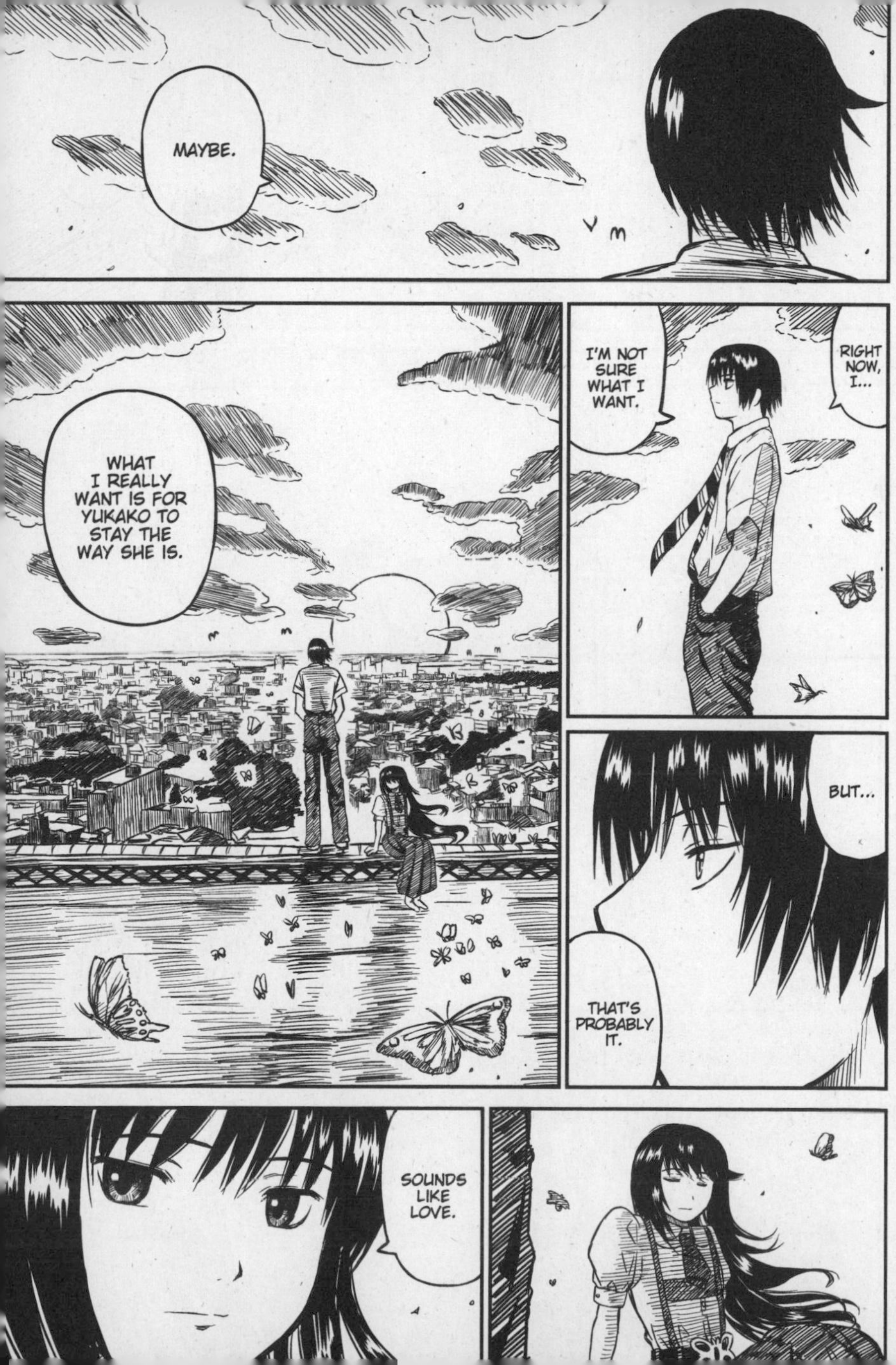
MAYBE.
RIGHT NOW, I...
I'M NOT SURE WHAT I WANT.
BUT...
THAT'S PROBABLY IT.
WHAT I REALLY WANT IS FOR YUKAKO TO STAY THE WAY SHE IS.
SOUNDS LIKE LOVE.

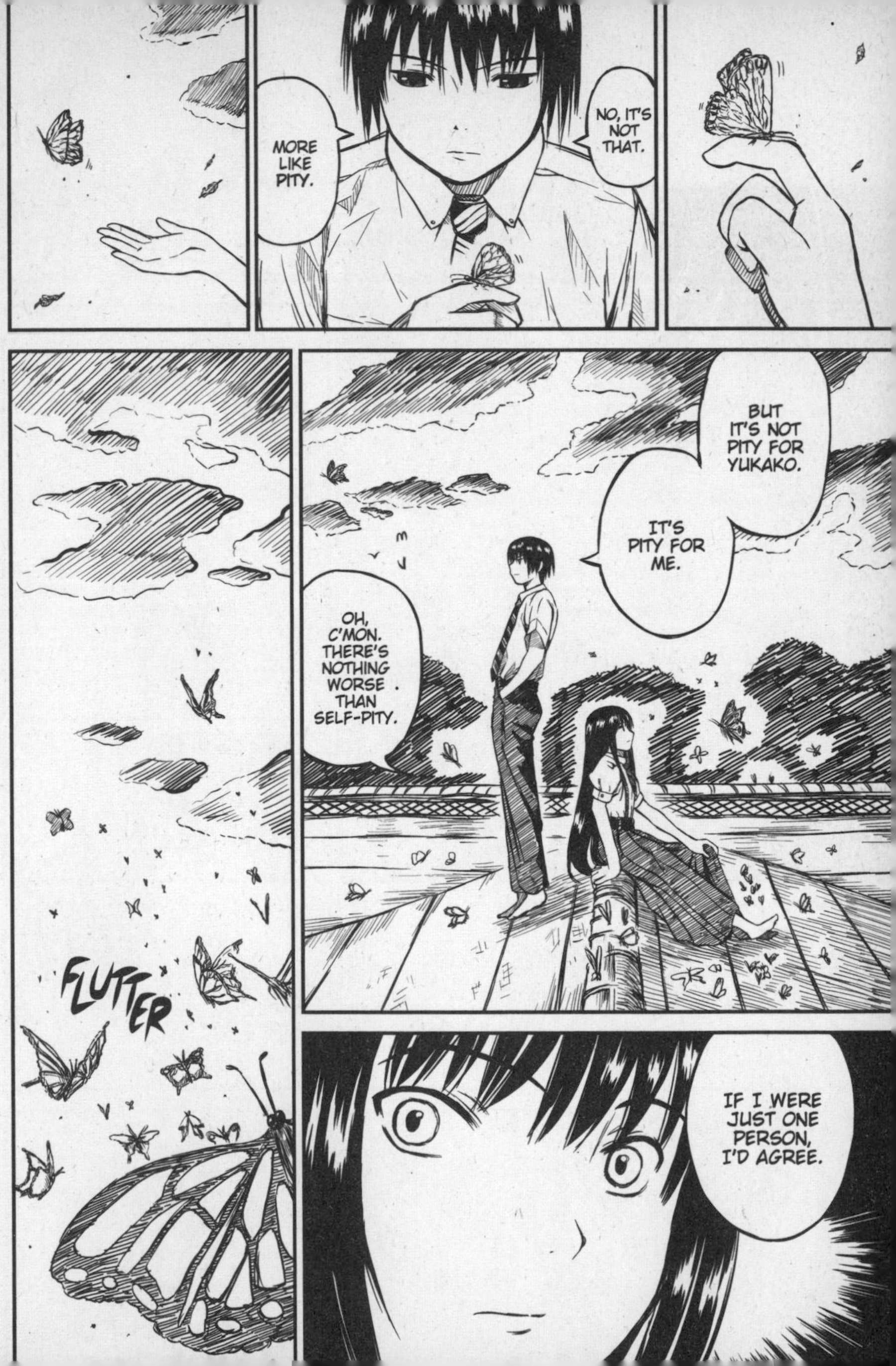
NO, IT'S NOT THAT.
MORE LIKE PITY.
BUT IT'S NOT PITY FOR YUKAKO.
IT'S PITY FOR ME.
OH, C'MON. THERE'S NOTHING WORSE THAN SELF-PITY.
IF I WERE JUST ONE PERSON, I'D AGREE.
FLUTTER

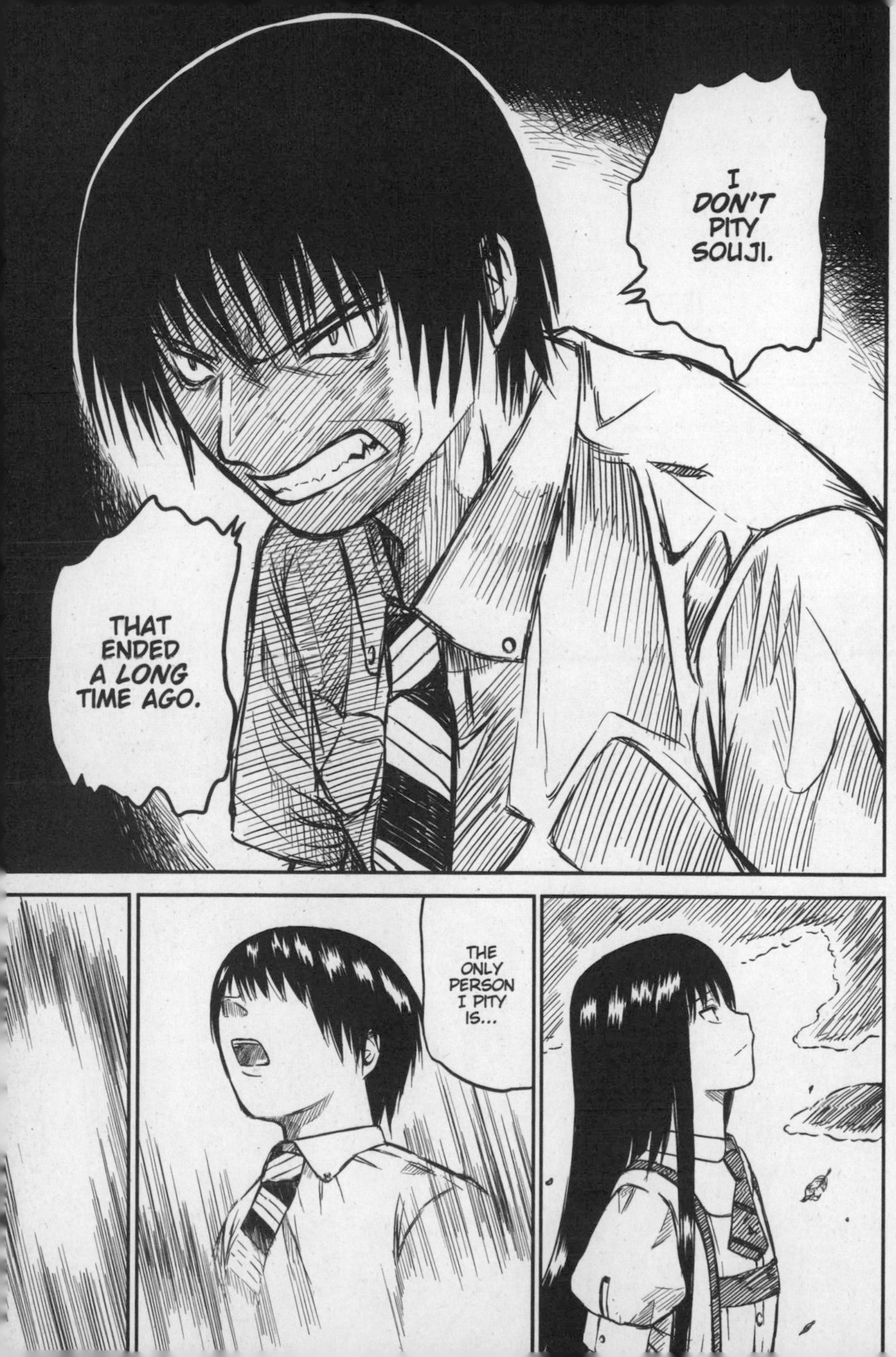
I *DON'T* PITY SOUJI.
THAT ENDED A *LONG* TIME AGO.
THE ONLY PERSON I PITY IS...

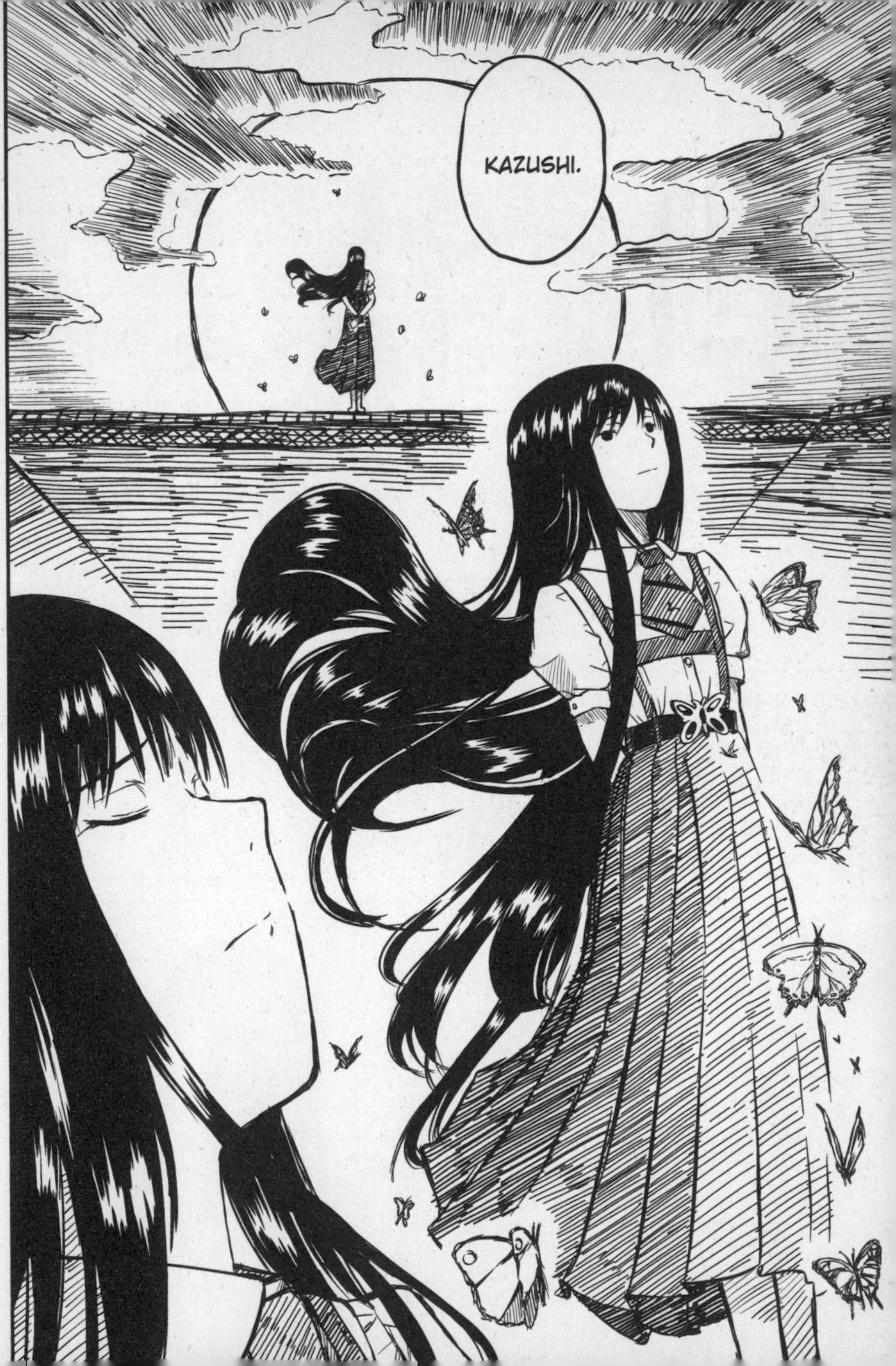
KAZUSHI.

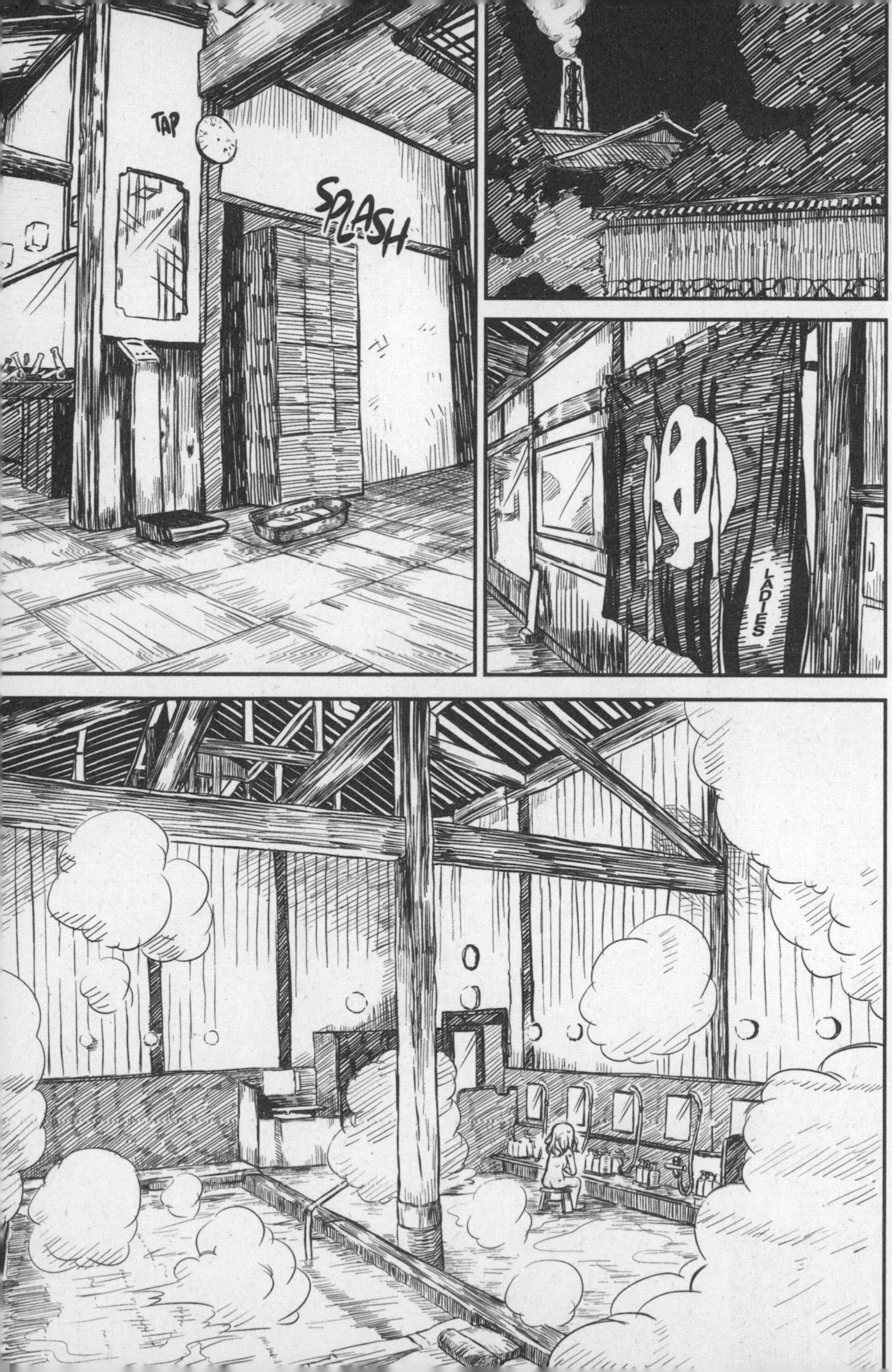
LADIES
TAP
SPLASH

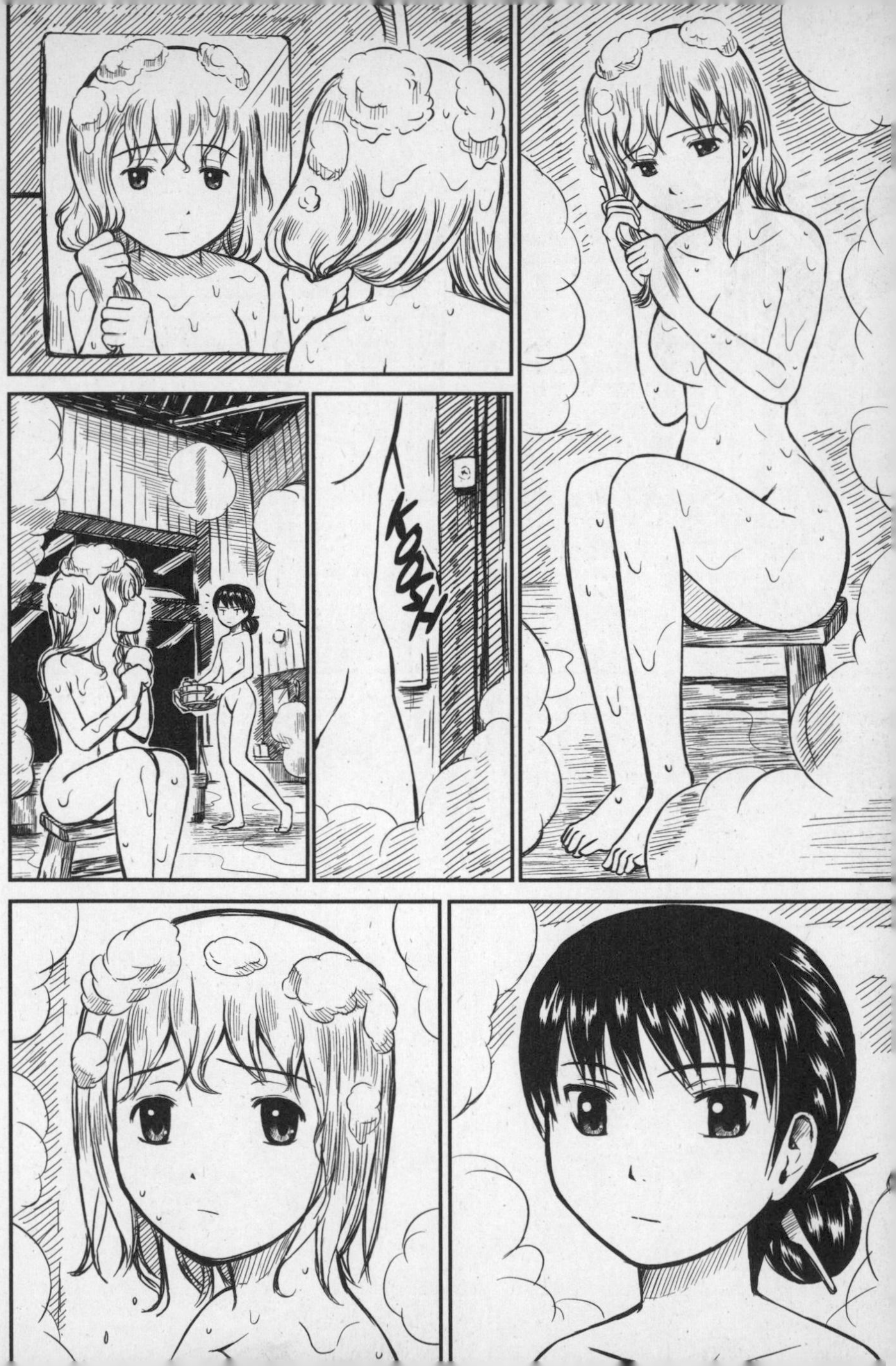
KOOSH

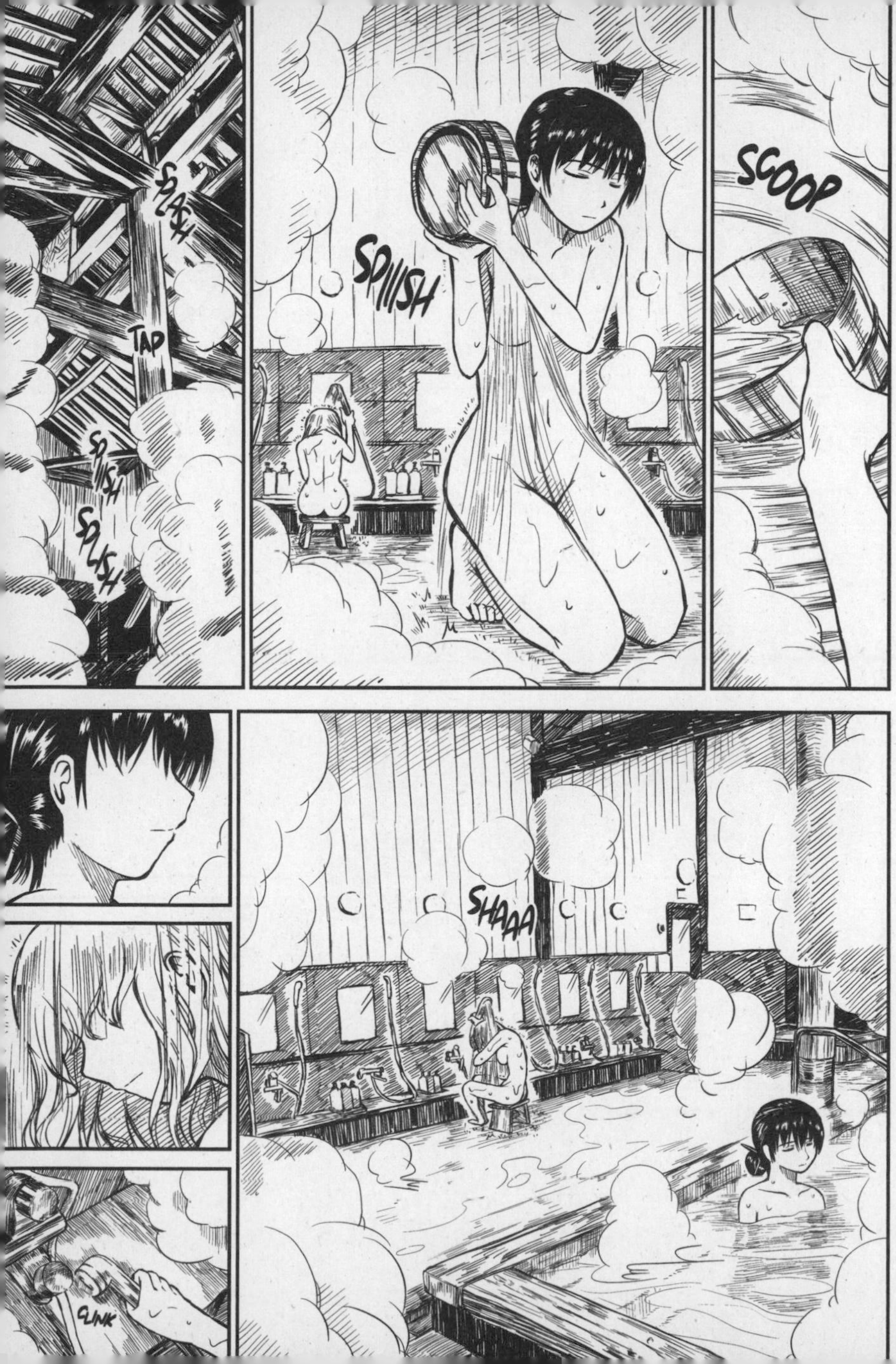
SCOOP
SPIIISH
SPLASH
TAP
SPIIISH
SPLISH
SHAAA
CLINK

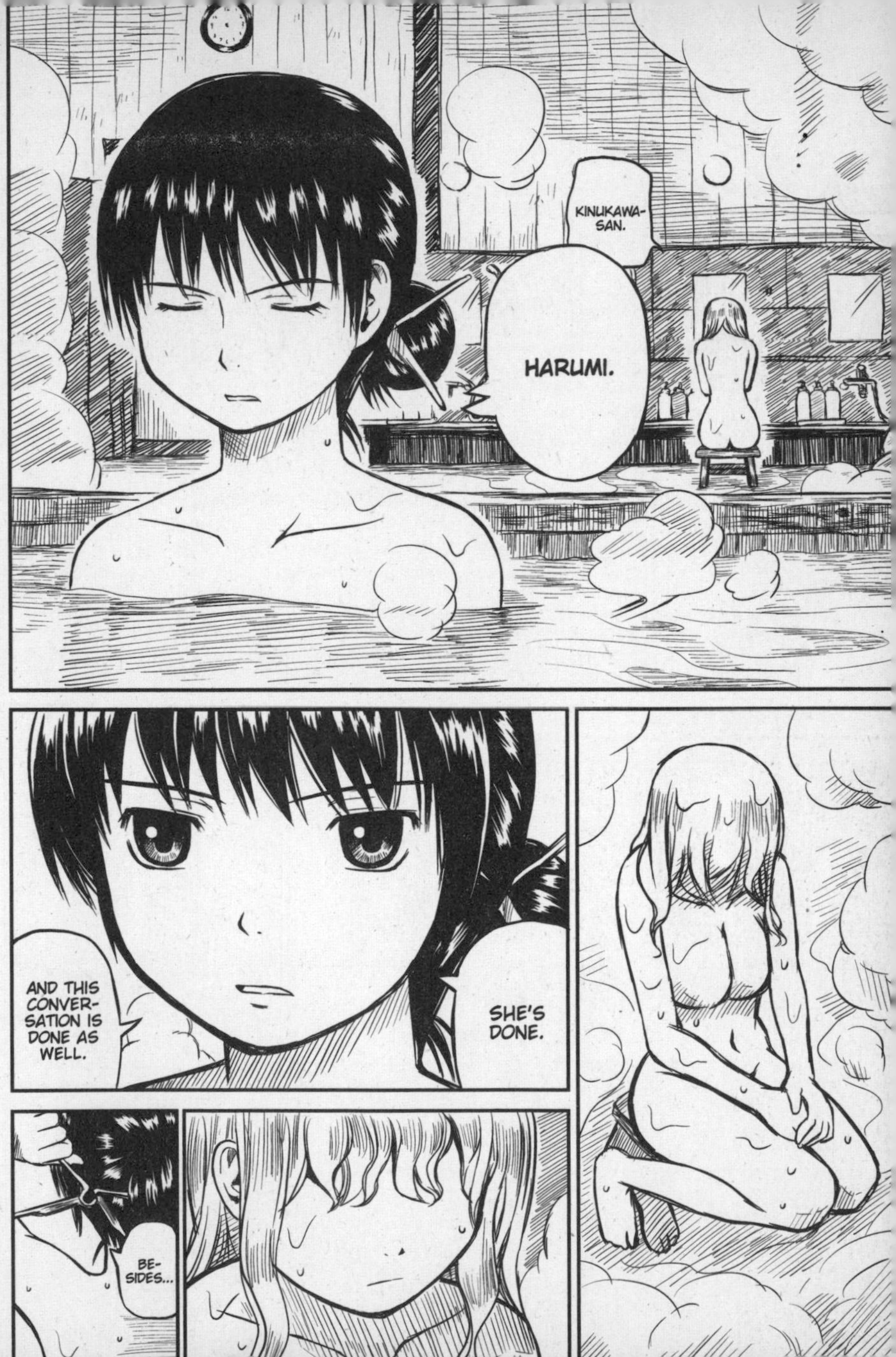
KINUKAWA-SAN.
HARUMI.
SHE'S DONE.
AND THIS CONVERSATION IS DONE AS WELL.
BE-SIDES...

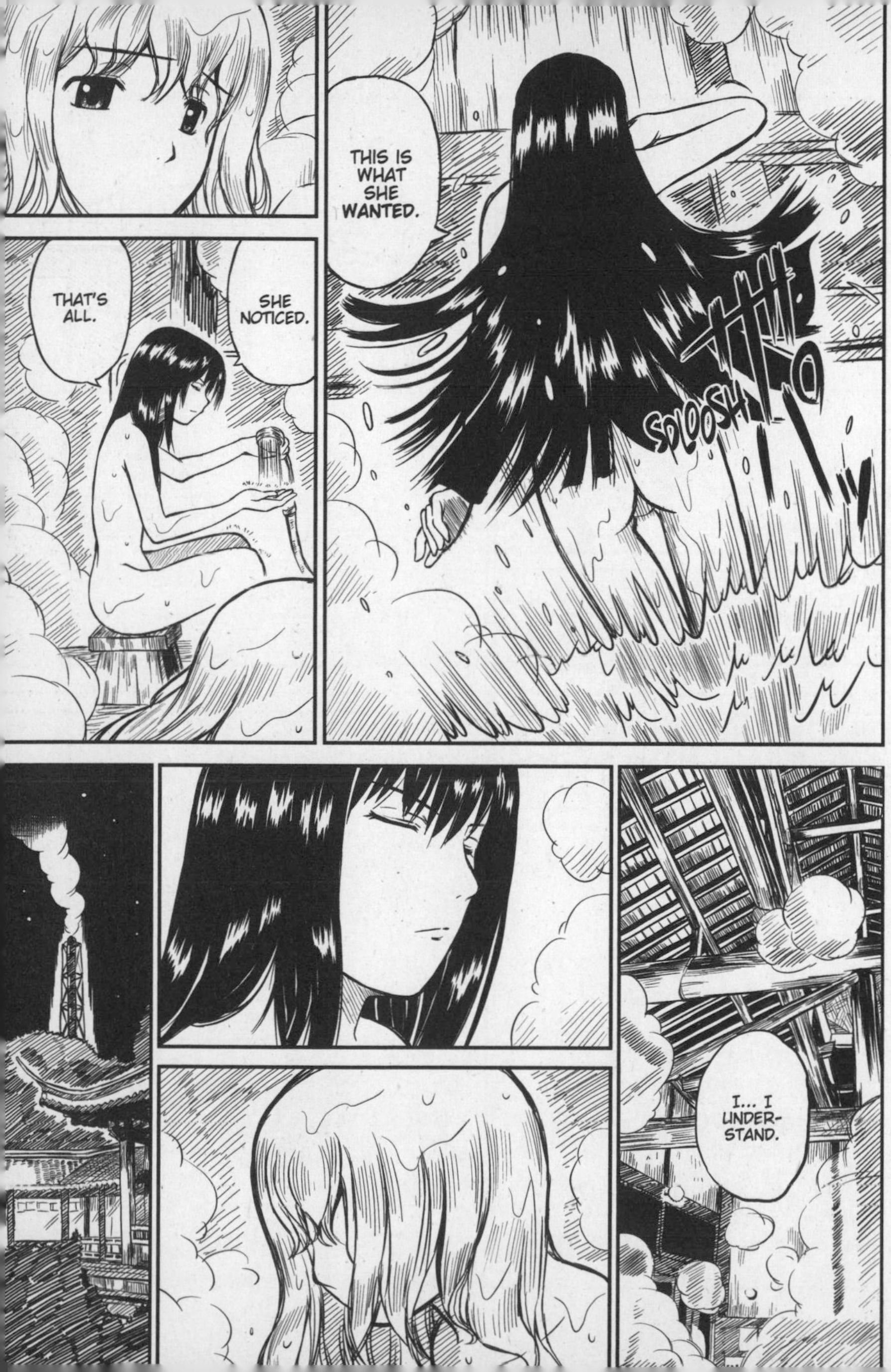
THIS IS WHAT SHE WANTED.
SDLOOSH
SHE NOTICED.
THAT'S ALL.
I... I UNDER-STAND.

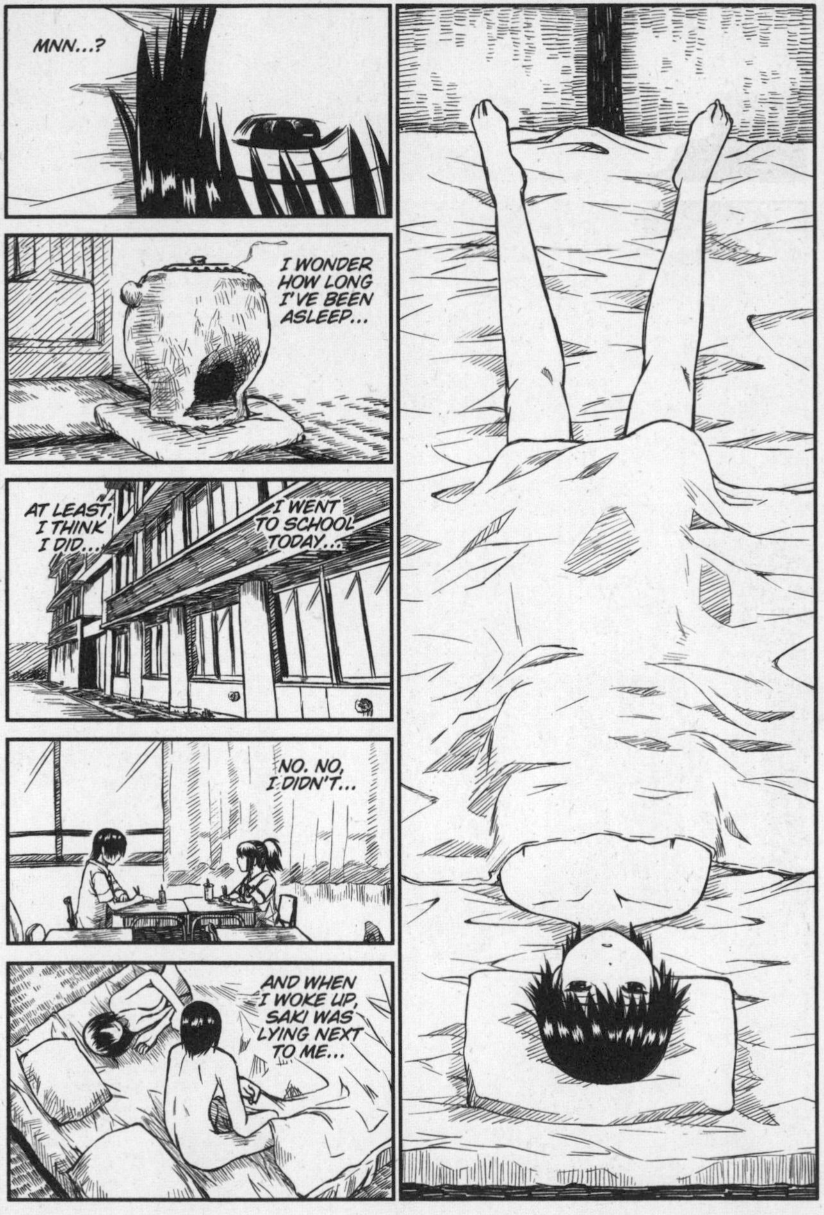
MNN...?
I WONDER HOW LONG I'VE BEEN ASLEEP...
I WENT TO SCHOOL TODAY...
AT LEAST, I THINK I DID...
NO. NO, I DIDN'T...
AND WHEN I WOKE UP, SAKI WAS LYING NEXT TO ME...

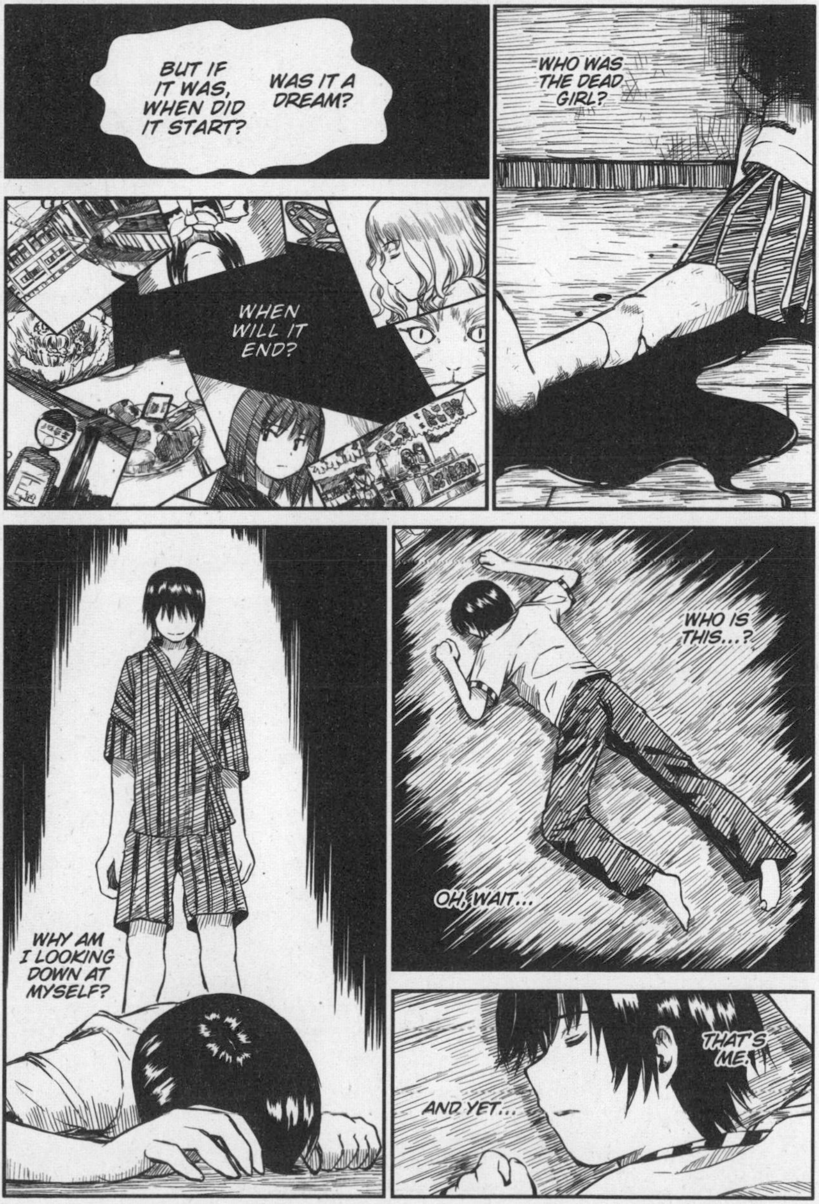
WHO WAS THE DEAD GIRL?
WAS IT A DREAM?
BUT IF IT WAS, WHEN DID IT START?
WHEN WILL IT END?
WHO IS THIS...?
OH, WAIT...
THAT'S ME.
AND YET...
WHY AM I LOOKING DOWN AT MYSELF?

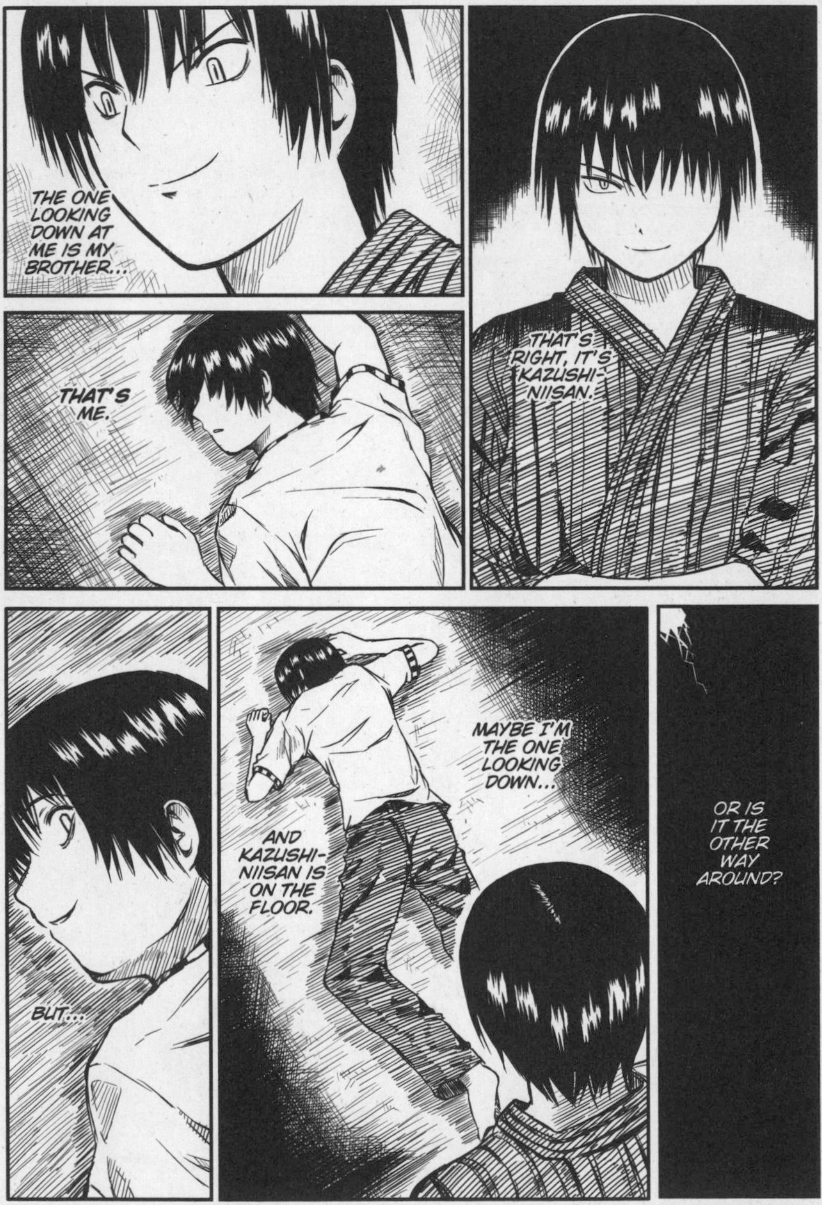
THE ONE LOOKING DOWN AT ME IS MY BROTHER...
THAT'S RIGHT, IT'S KAZUSHI-NIISAN.
THAT'S ME.
BUT...
MAYBE I'M THE ONE LOOKING DOWN...
AND KAZUSHI-NIISAN IS ON THE FLOOR.
OR IS IT THE OTHER WAY AROUND?

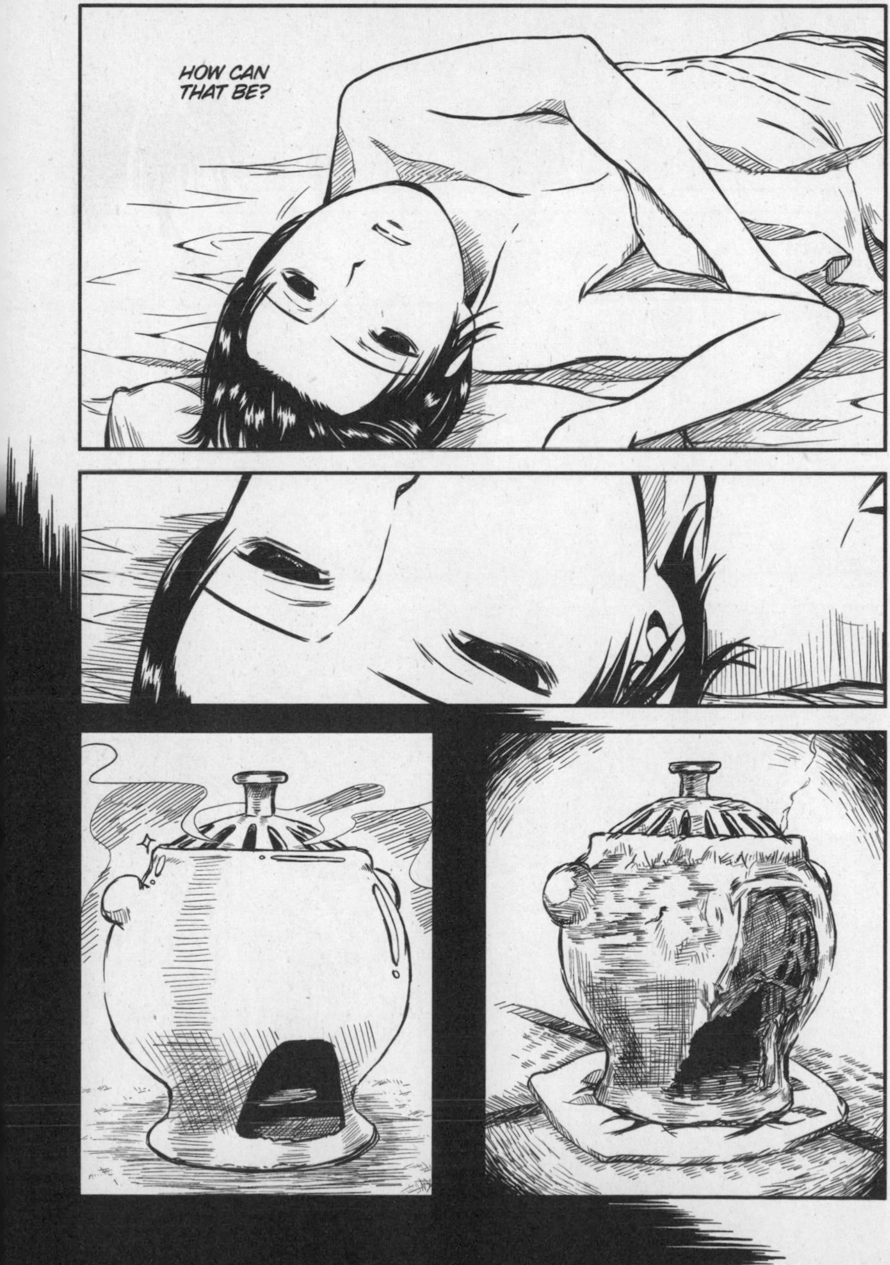
HOW CAN THAT BE?

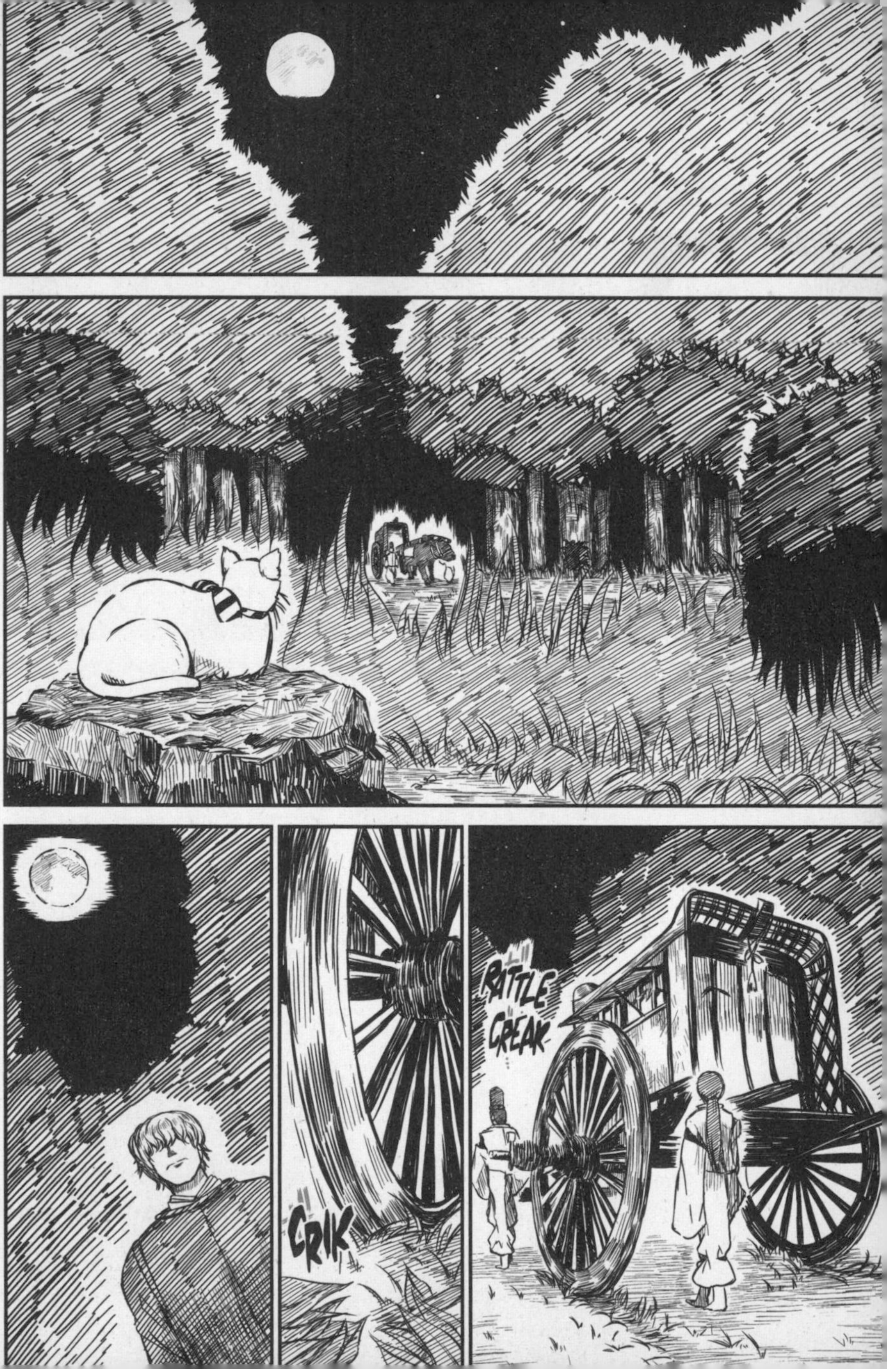
RATTLE CREAK
CRIK

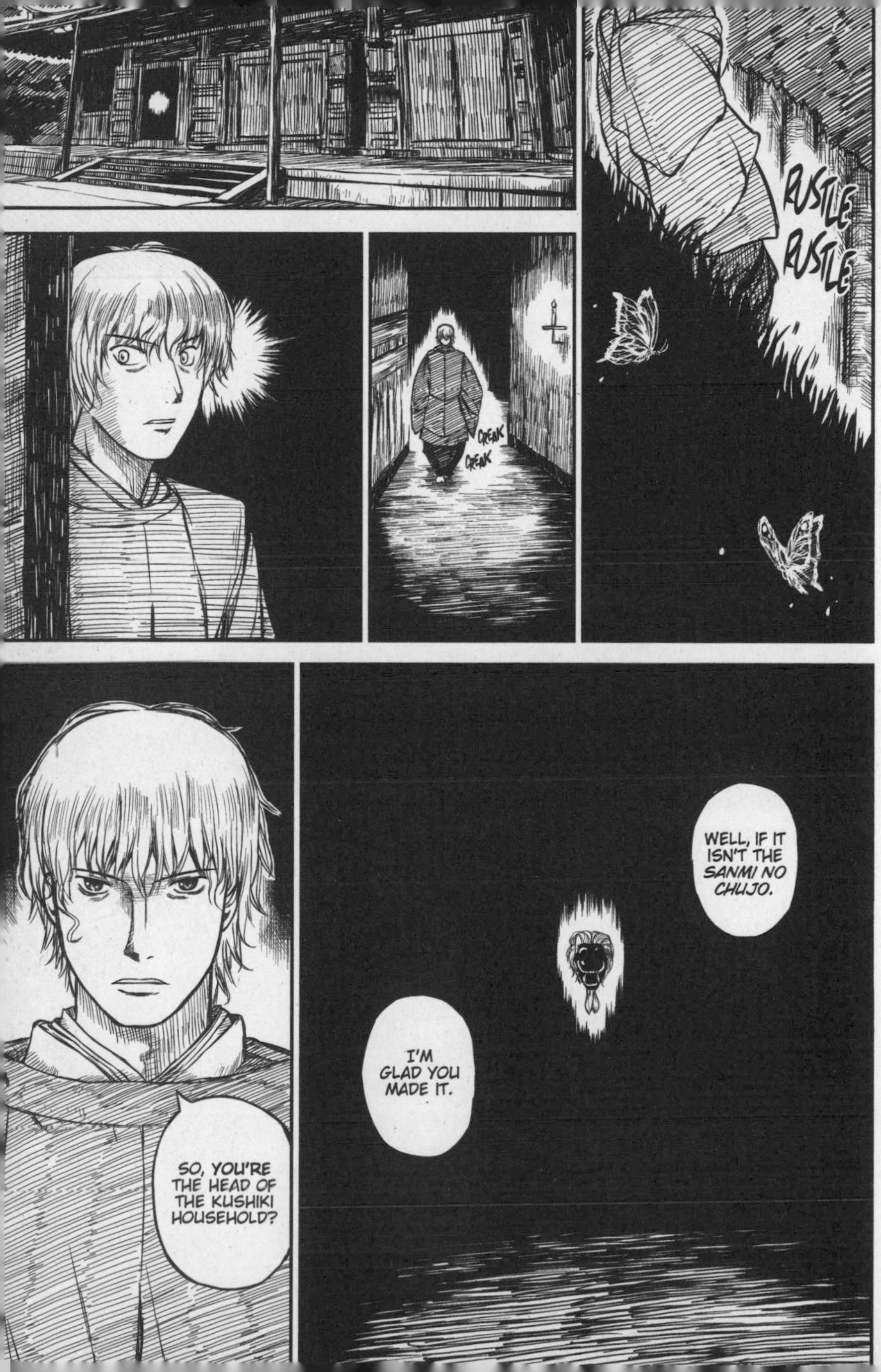
RUSTLE
RUSTLE
CREAK
CREAK
WELL, IF IT ISN'T THE *SANMI NO CHUJO*.
I'M GLAD YOU MADE IT.
SO, YOU'RE THE HEAD OF THE KUSHIKI HOUSEHOLD?

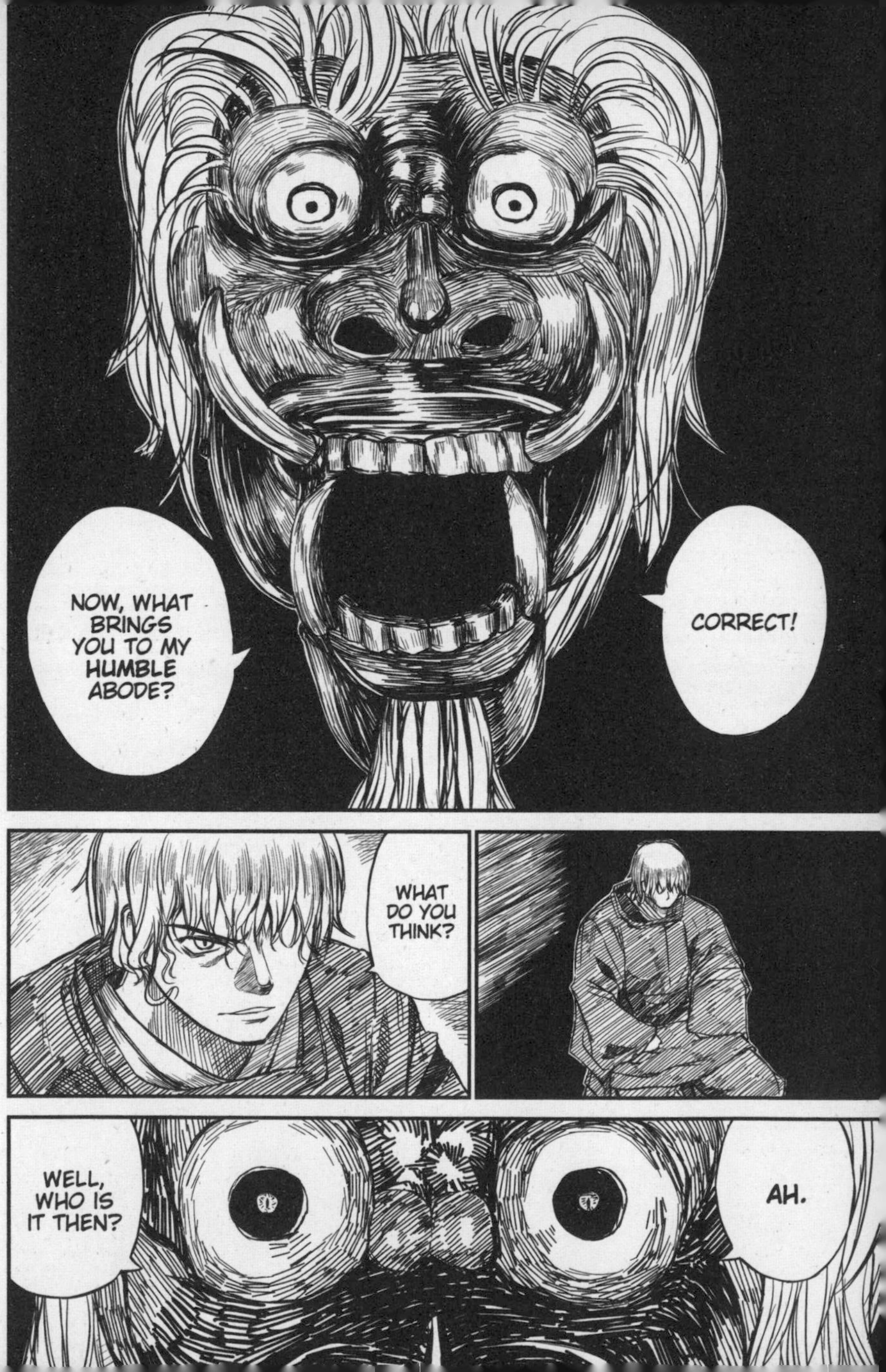
CORRECT!
NOW, WHAT BRINGS YOU TO MY HUMBLE ABODE?
WHAT DO YOU THINK?
AH.
WELL, WHO IS IT THEN?

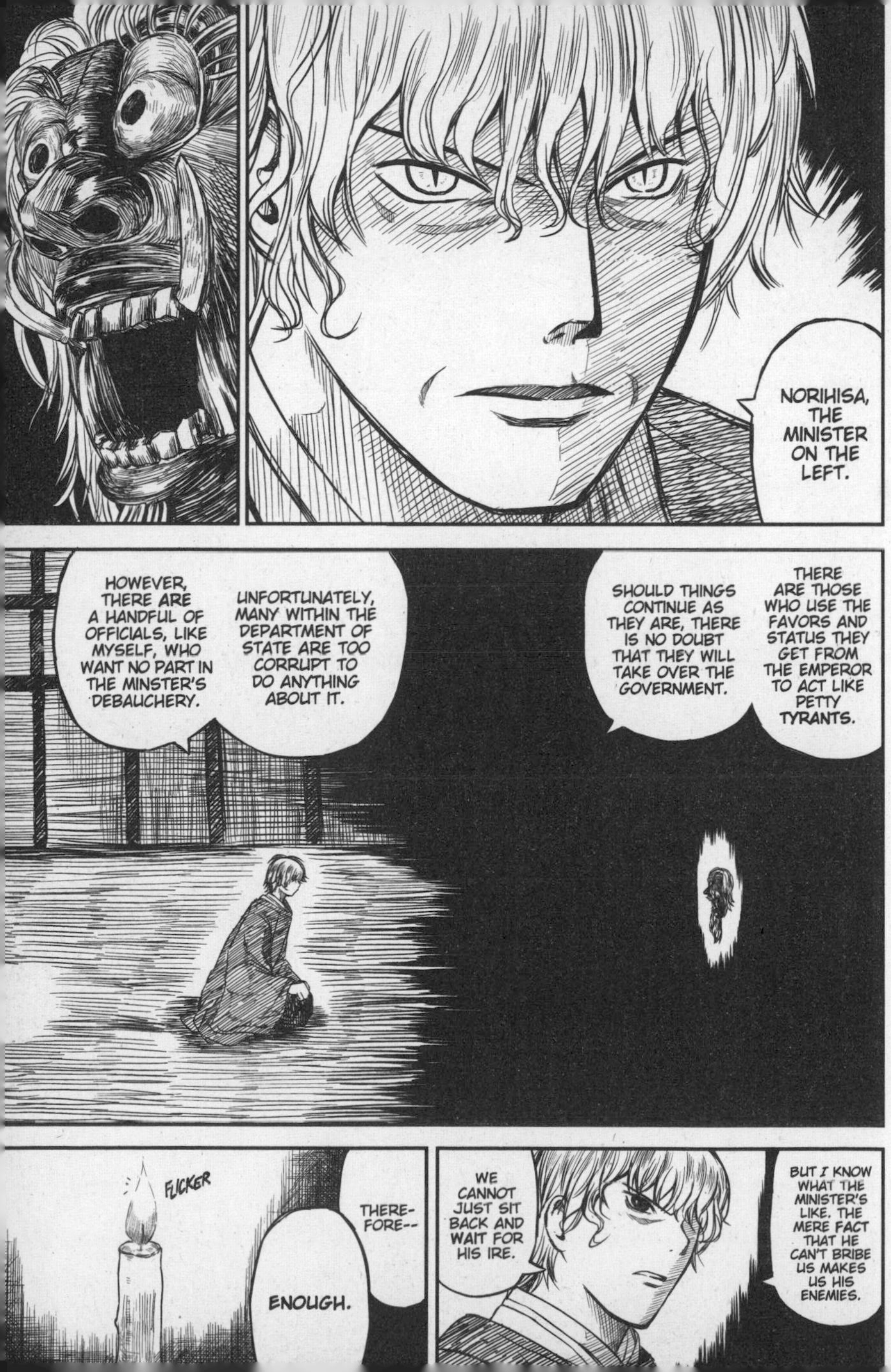
NORIHISA, THE MINISTER ON THE LEFT.
THERE ARE THOSE WHO USE THE FAVORS AND STATUS THEY GET FROM THE EMPEROR TO ACT LIKE PETTY TYRANTS.
SHOULD THINGS CONTINUE AS THEY ARE, THERE IS NO DOUBT THAT THEY WILL TAKE OVER THE GOVERNMENT.
UNFORTUNATELY, MANY WITHIN THE DEPARTMENT OF STATE ARE TOO CORRUPT TO DO ANYTHING ABOUT IT.
HOWEVER, THERE ARE A HANDFUL OF OFFICIALS, LIKE MYSELF, WHO WANT NO PART IN THE MINSTER'S DEBAUCHERY.
BUT I KNOW WHAT THE MINISTER'S LIKE. THE MERE FACT THAT HE CAN'T BRIBE US MAKES US HIS ENEMIES.
WE CANNOT JUST SIT BACK AND WAIT FOR HIS IRE.
THERE-FORE--
ENOUGH.
FLICKER

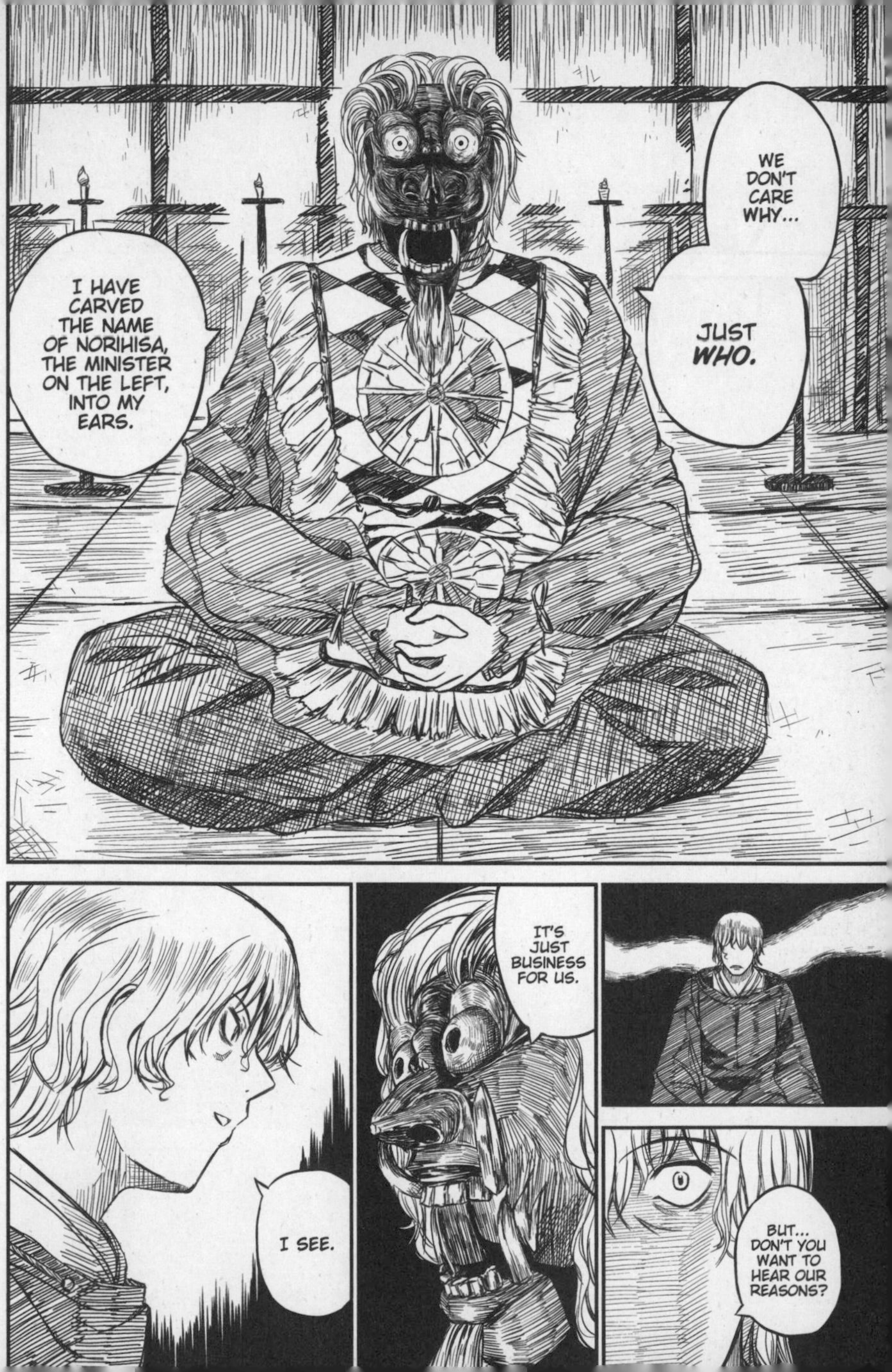
WE DON'T CARE WHY...
JUST WHO.
I HAVE CARVED THE NAME OF NORIHISA, THE MINISTER ON THE LEFT, INTO MY EARS.
BUT... DON'T YOU WANT TO HEAR OUR REASONS?
IT'S JUST BUSINESS FOR US.
I SEE.

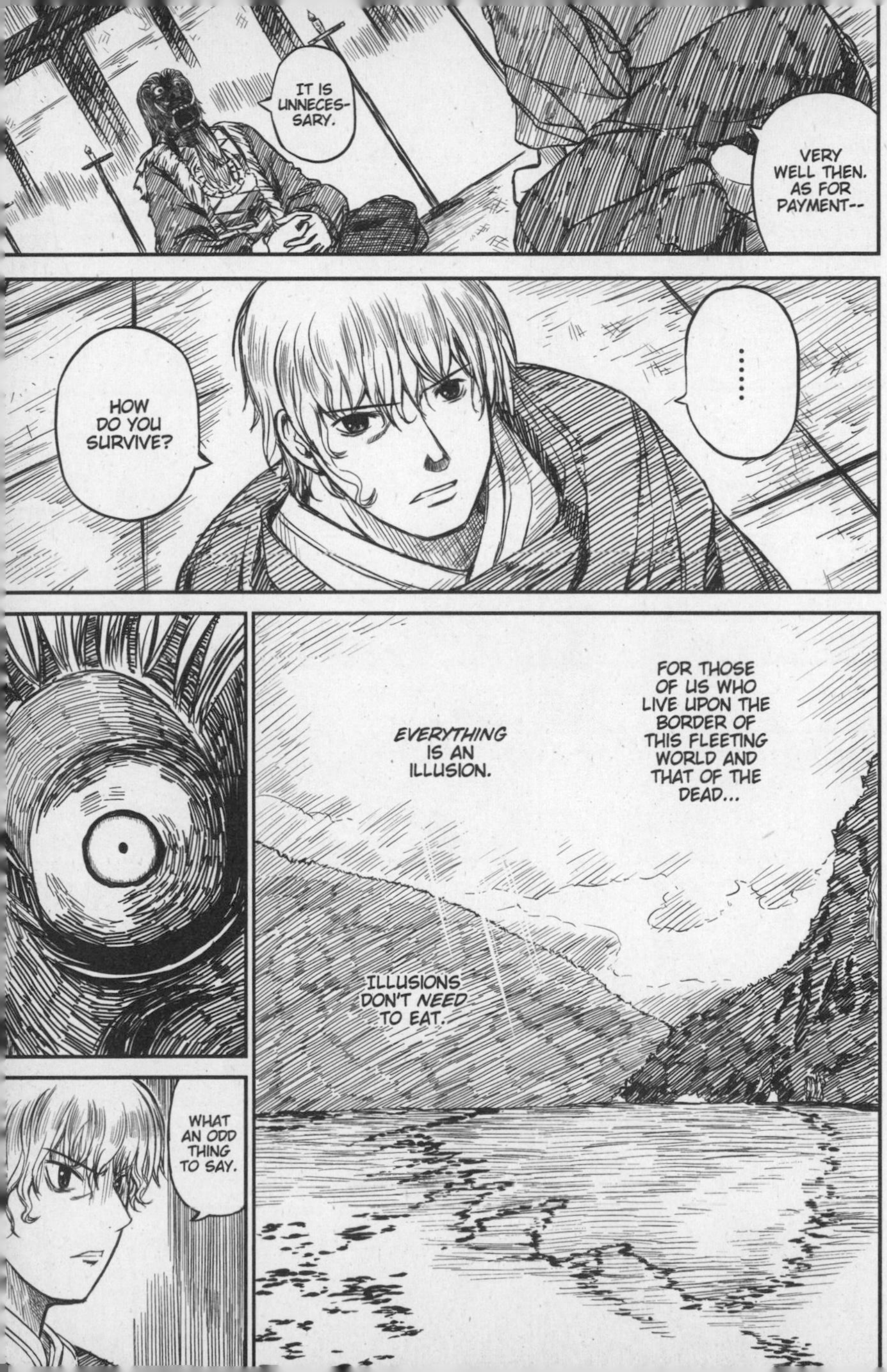
VERY WELL THEN. AS FOR PAYMENT--
IT IS UNNECES-SARY.
......
HOW DO YOU SURVIVE?
FOR THOSE OF US WHO LIVE UPON THE BORDER OF THIS FLEETING WORLD AND THAT OF THE DEAD...
EVERYTHING IS AN ILLUSION.
ILLUSIONS DON'T *NEED* TO EAT.
WHAT AN ODD THING TO SAY.

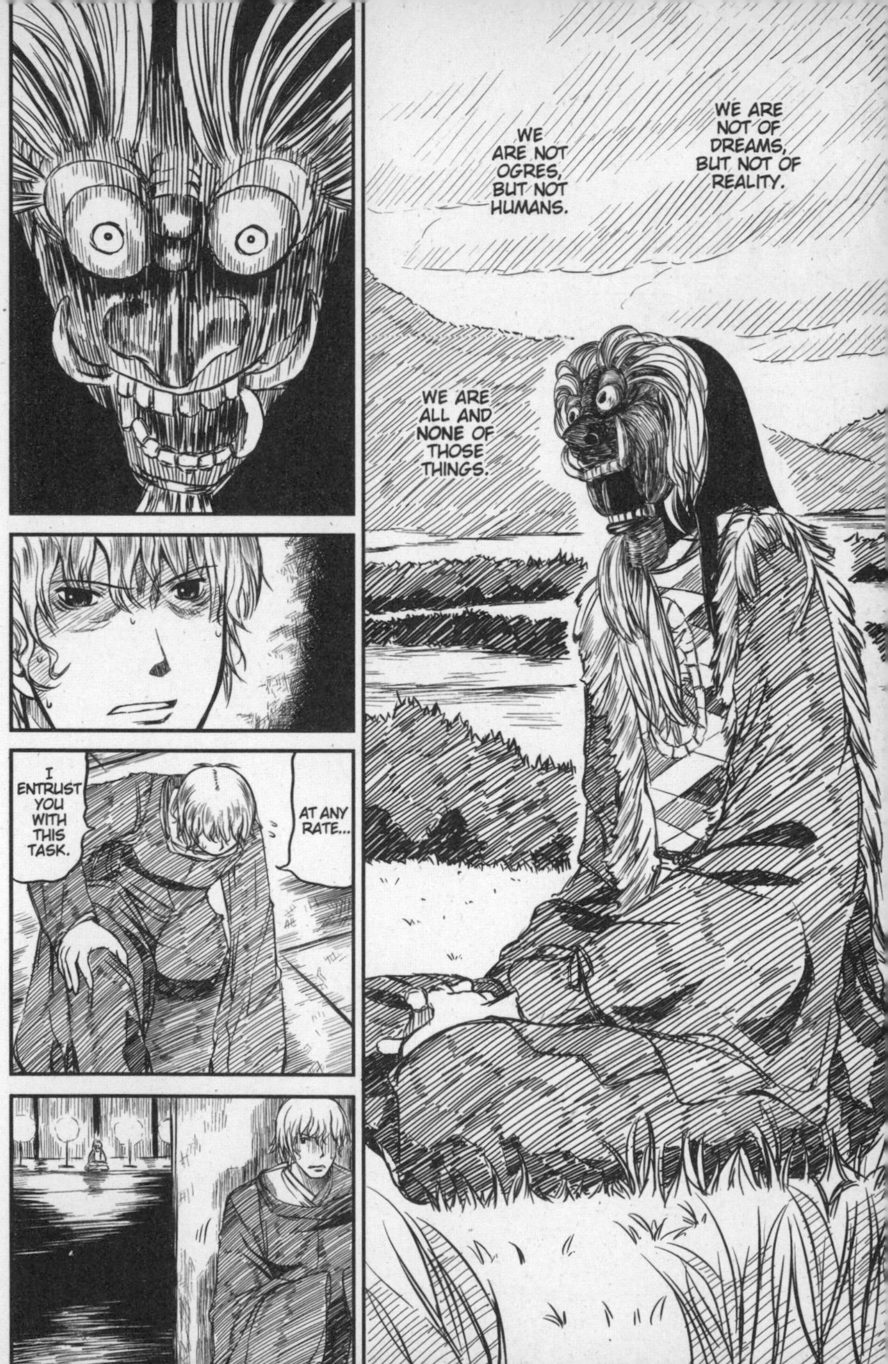
WE ARE NOT OF DREAMS, BUT NOT OF REALITY.
WE ARE NOT OGRES, BUT NOT HUMANS.
WE ARE ALL AND NONE OF THOSE THINGS.
AT ANY RATE...
I ENTRUST YOU WITH THIS TASK.

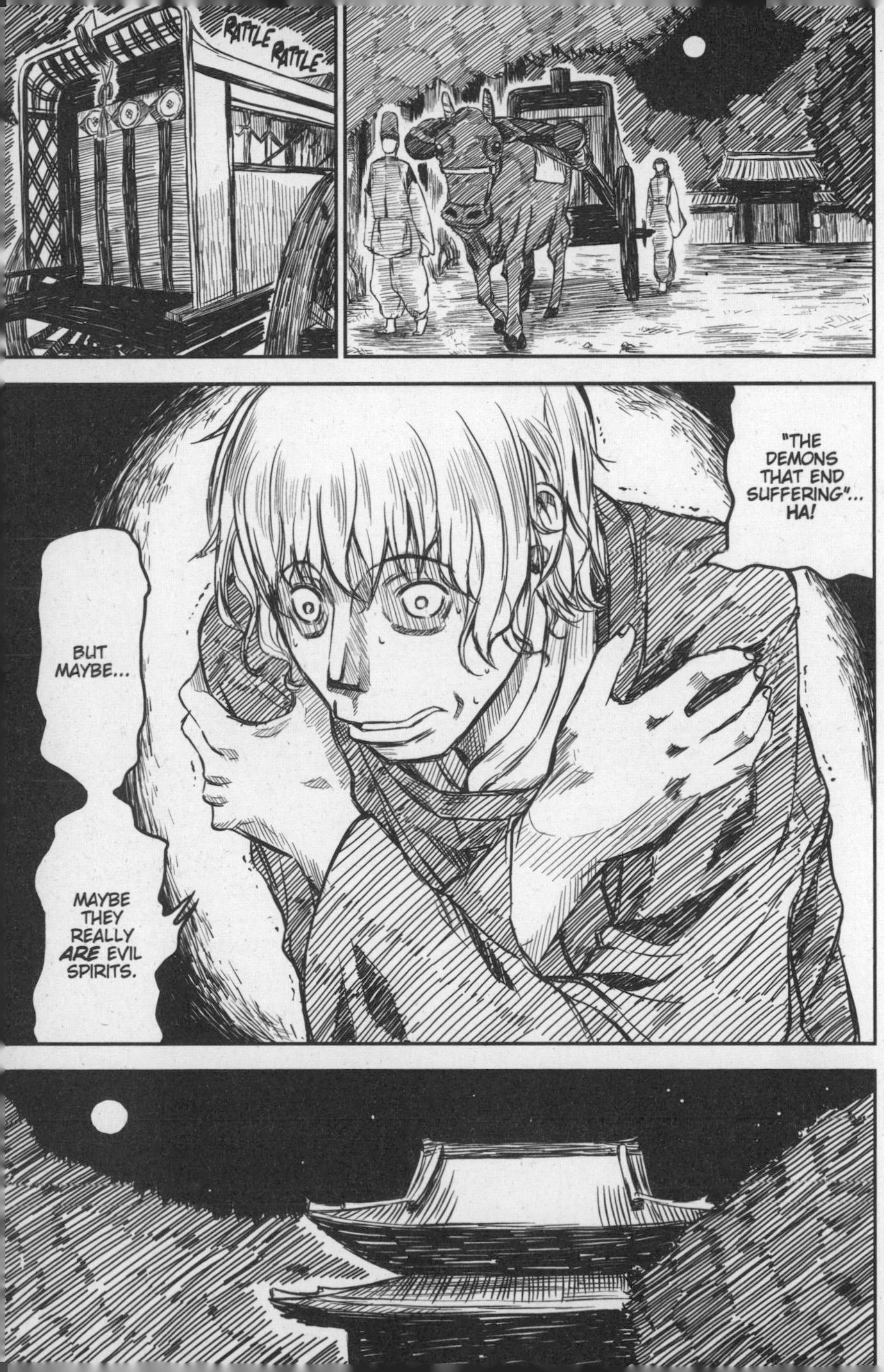
RATTLE RATTLE
"THE DEMONS THAT END SUFFERING"... HA!
BUT MAYBE...
MAYBE THEY REALLY *ARE* EVIL SPIRITS.

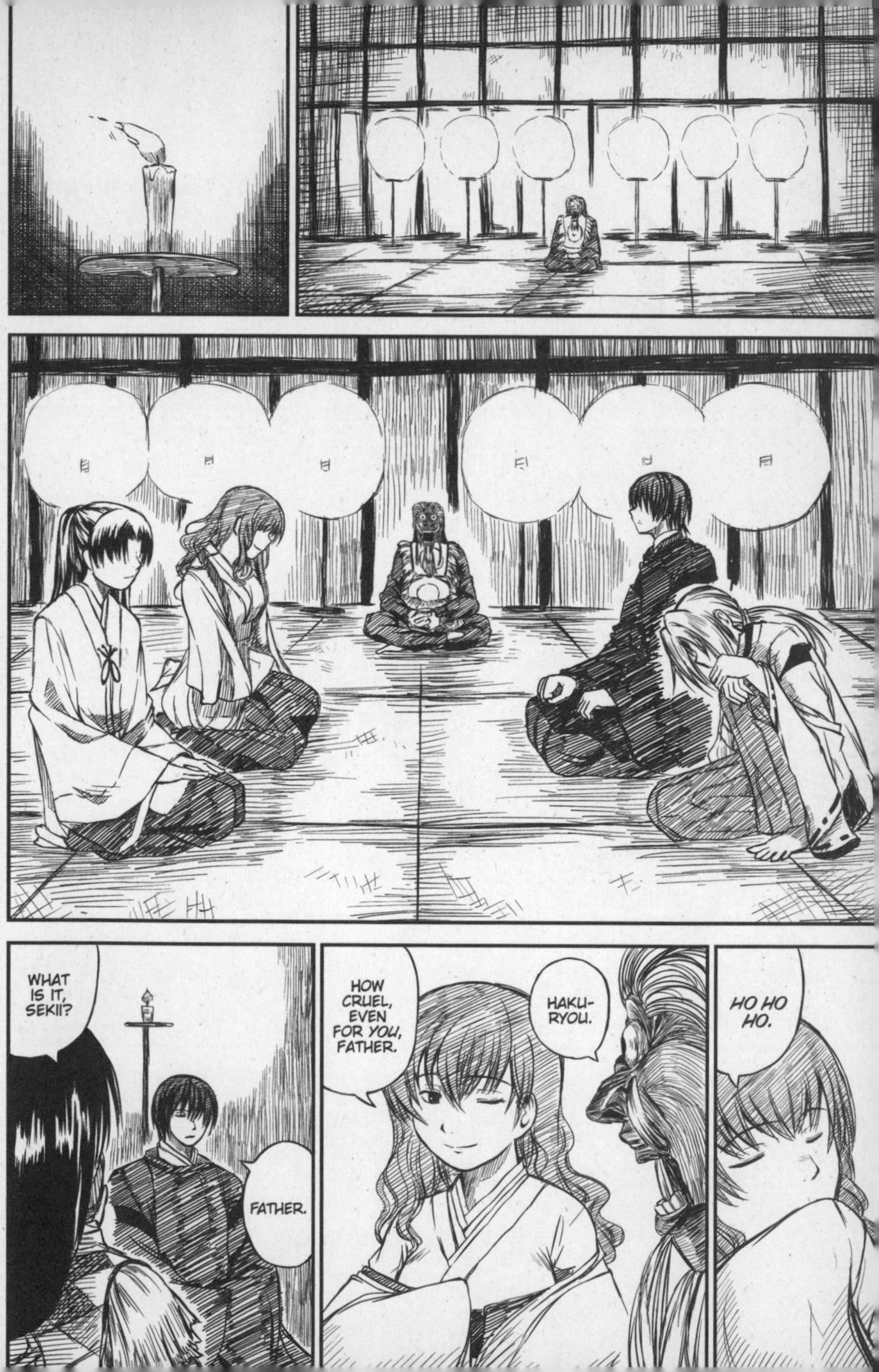
HO HO HO.
HAKU-RYOU.
HOW CRUEL, EVEN FOR YOU, FATHER.
WHAT IS IT, SEKII?
FATHER.

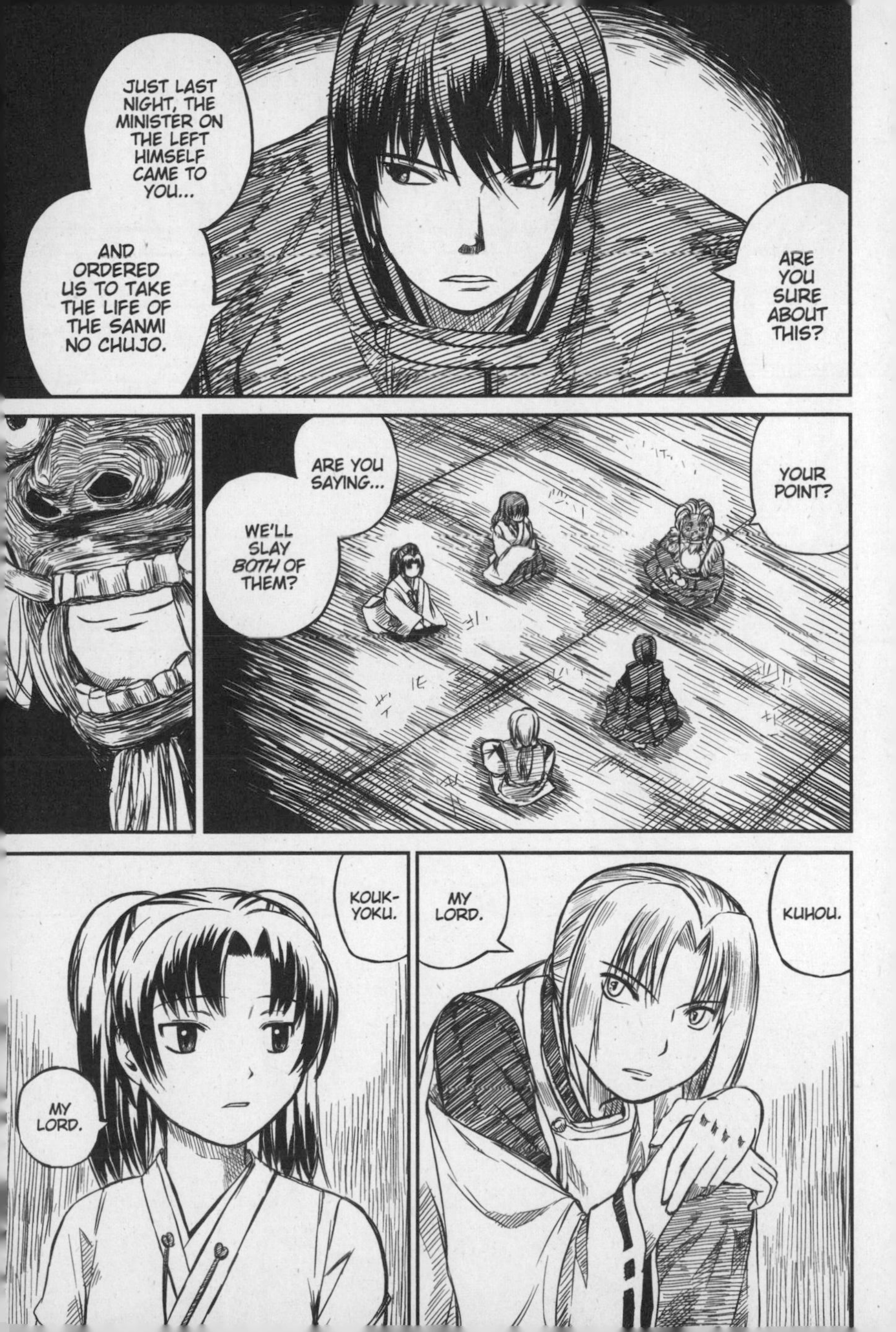
ARE YOU SURE ABOUT THIS?
JUST LAST NIGHT, THE MINISTER ON THE LEFT HIMSELF CAME TO YOU...
AND ORDERED US TO TAKE THE LIFE OF THE SANMI NO CHUJO.
YOUR POINT?
ARE YOU SAYING...
WE'LL SLAY *BOTH* OF THEM?
KUHOU.
MY LORD.
KOUK-YOKU.
MY LORD.

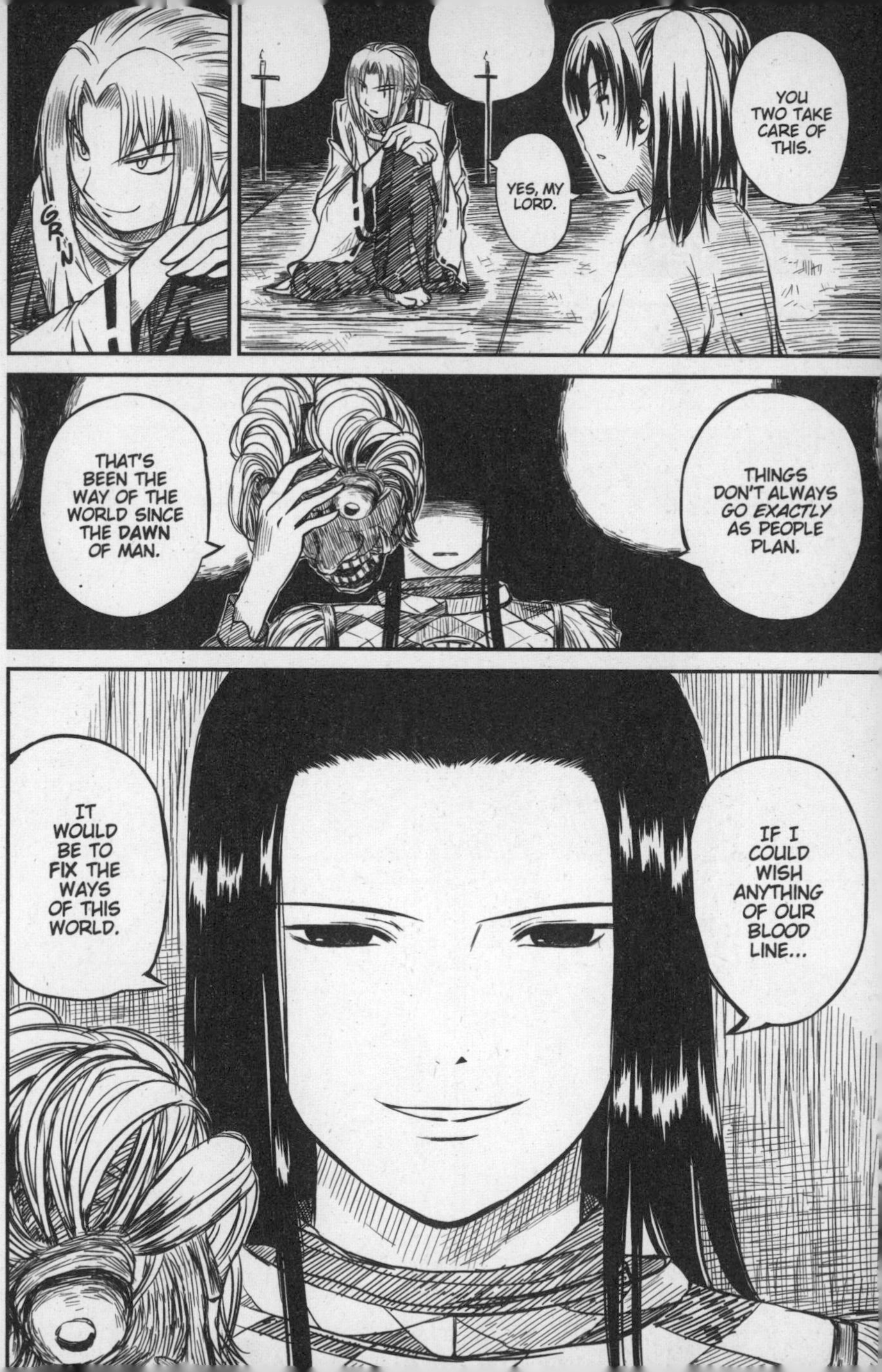
YOU TWO TAKE CARE OF THIS.
YES, MY LORD.
GRIN
THINGS DON'T ALWAYS GO EXACTLY AS PEOPLE PLAN.
THAT'S BEEN THE WAY OF THE WORLD SINCE THE DAWN OF MAN.
IF I COULD WISH ANYTHING OF OUR BLOOD LINE...
IT WOULD BE TO FIX THE WAYS OF THIS WORLD.

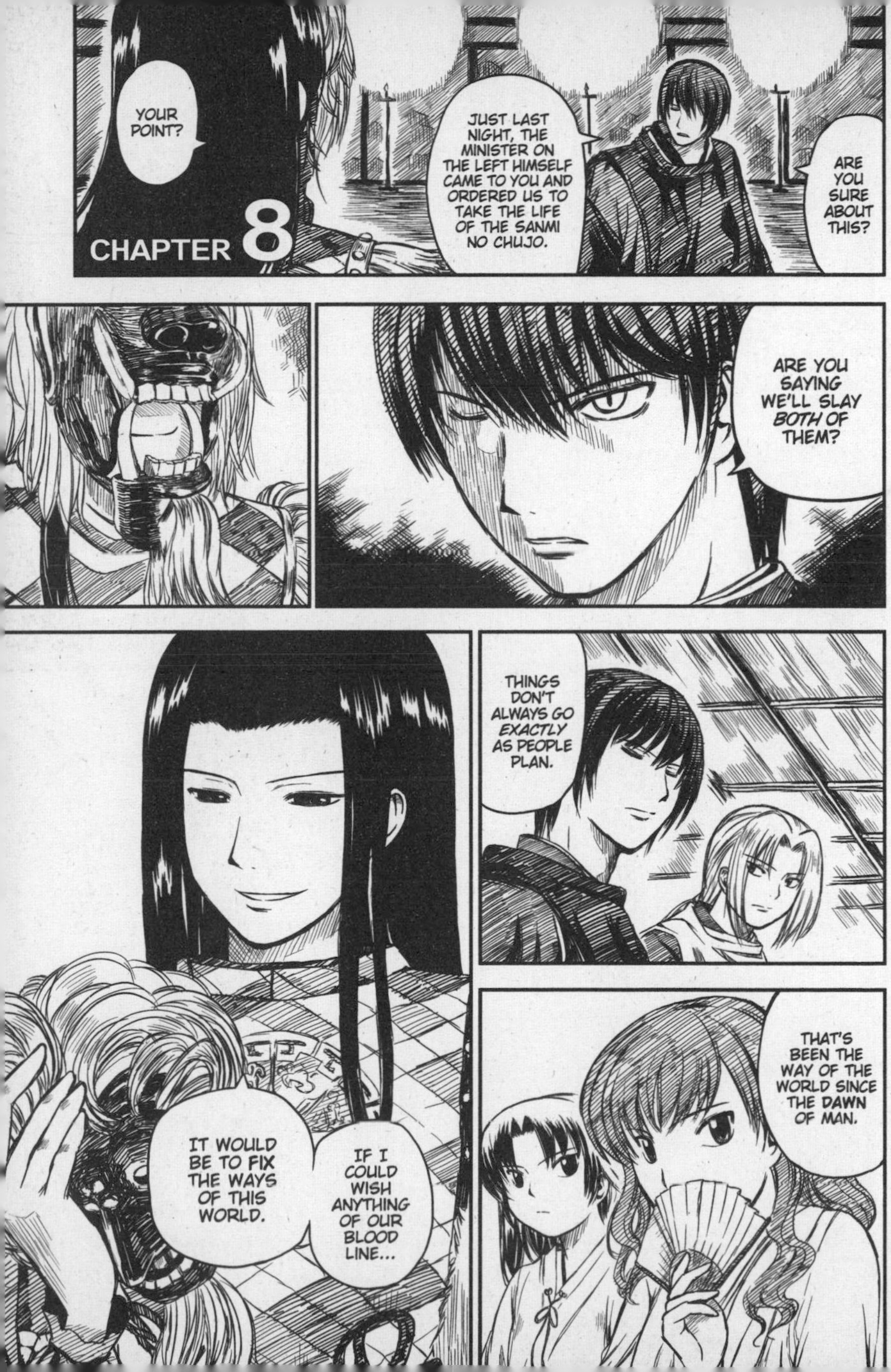
CHAPTER 8
ARE YOU SURE ABOUT THIS?
JUST LAST NIGHT, THE MINISTER ON THE LEFT HIMSELF CAME TO YOU AND ORDERED US TO TAKE THE LIFE OF THE SANMI NO CHUJO.
YOUR POINT?
ARE YOU SAYING WE'LL SLAY *BOTH* OF THEM?
THINGS DON'T ALWAYS GO *EXACTLY* AS PEOPLE PLAN.
THAT'S BEEN THE WAY OF THE WORLD SINCE THE DAWN OF MAN.
IF I COULD WISH ANYTHING OF OUR BLOOD LINE...
IT WOULD BE TO FIX THE WAYS OF THIS WORLD.

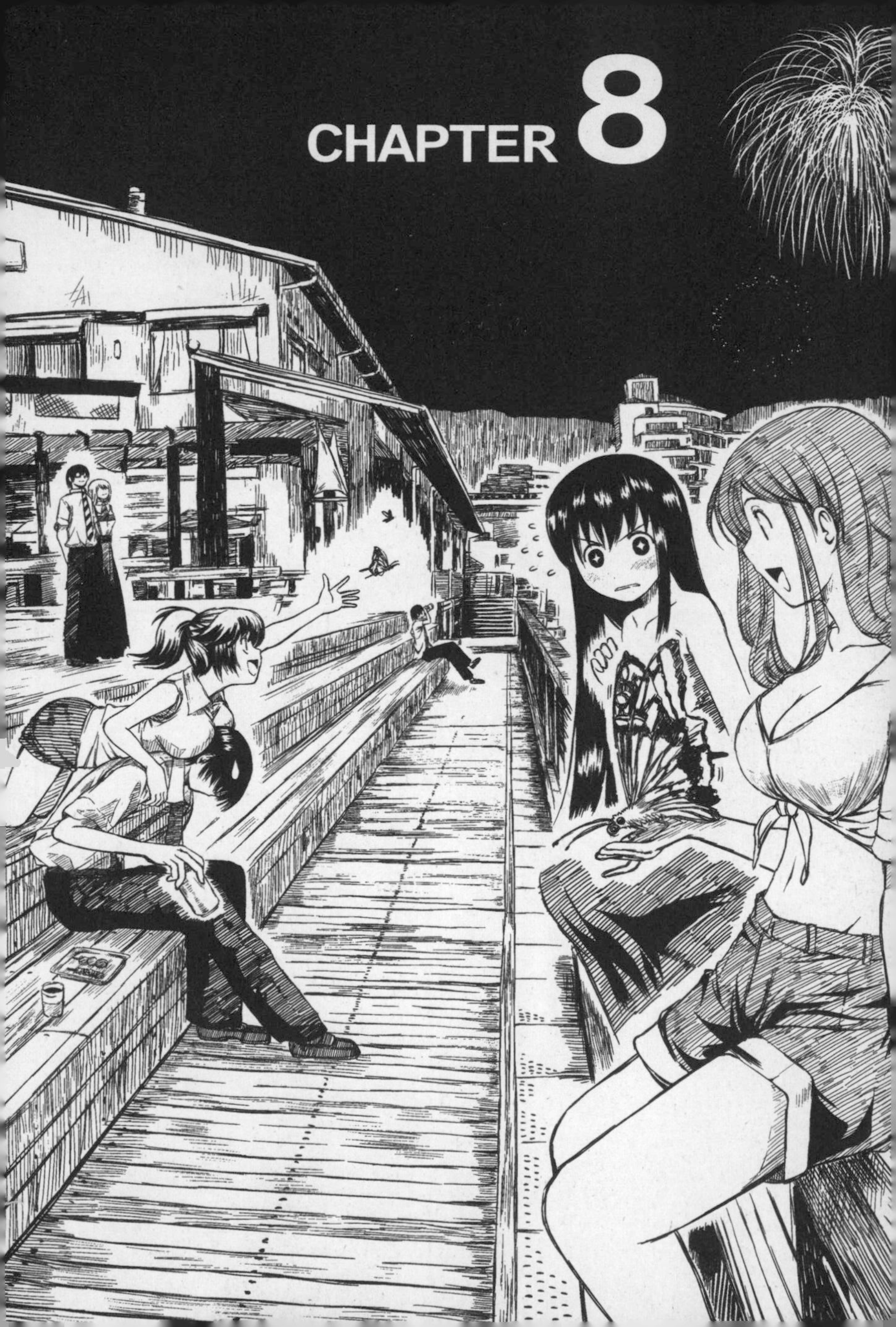
CHAPTER 8

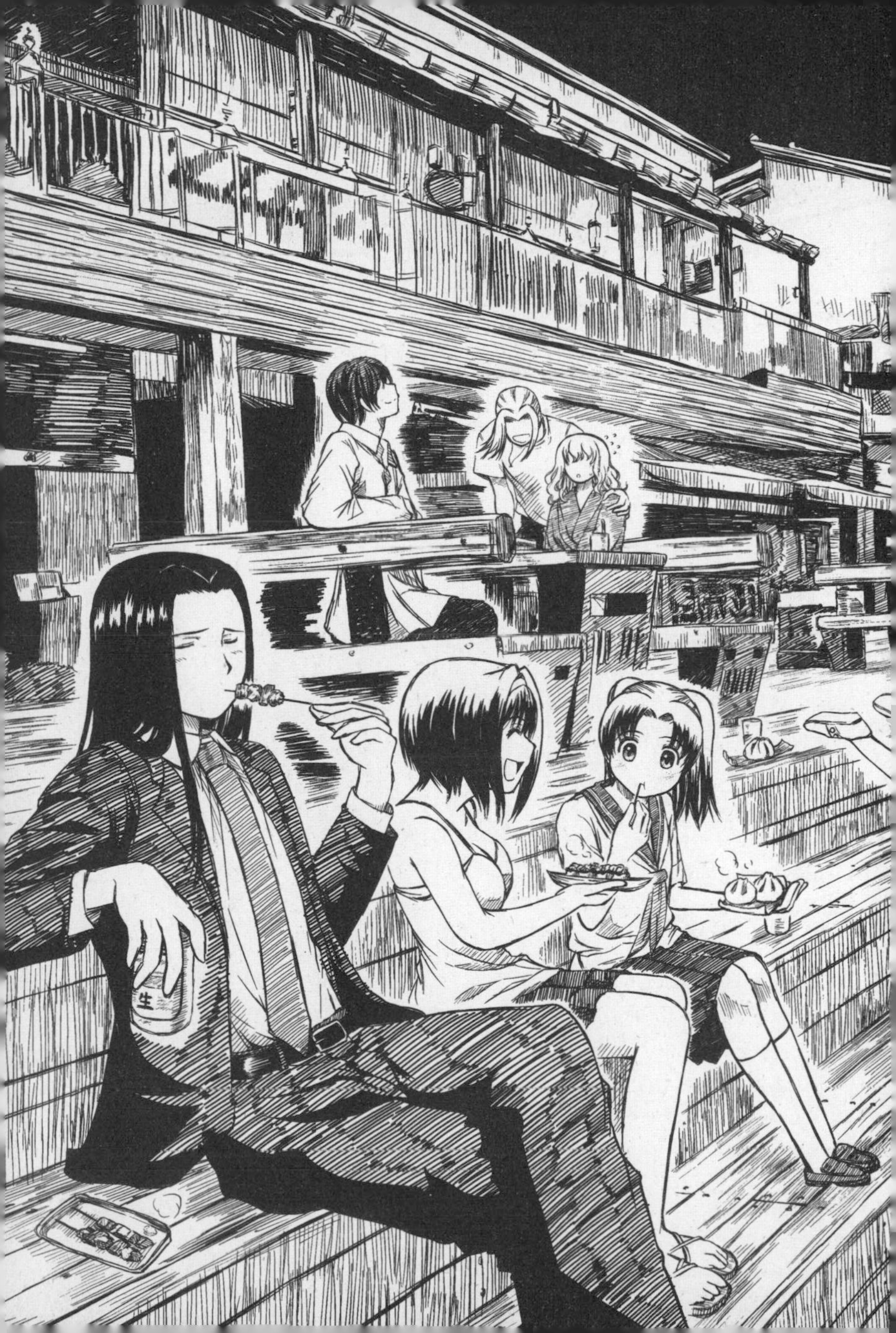
生

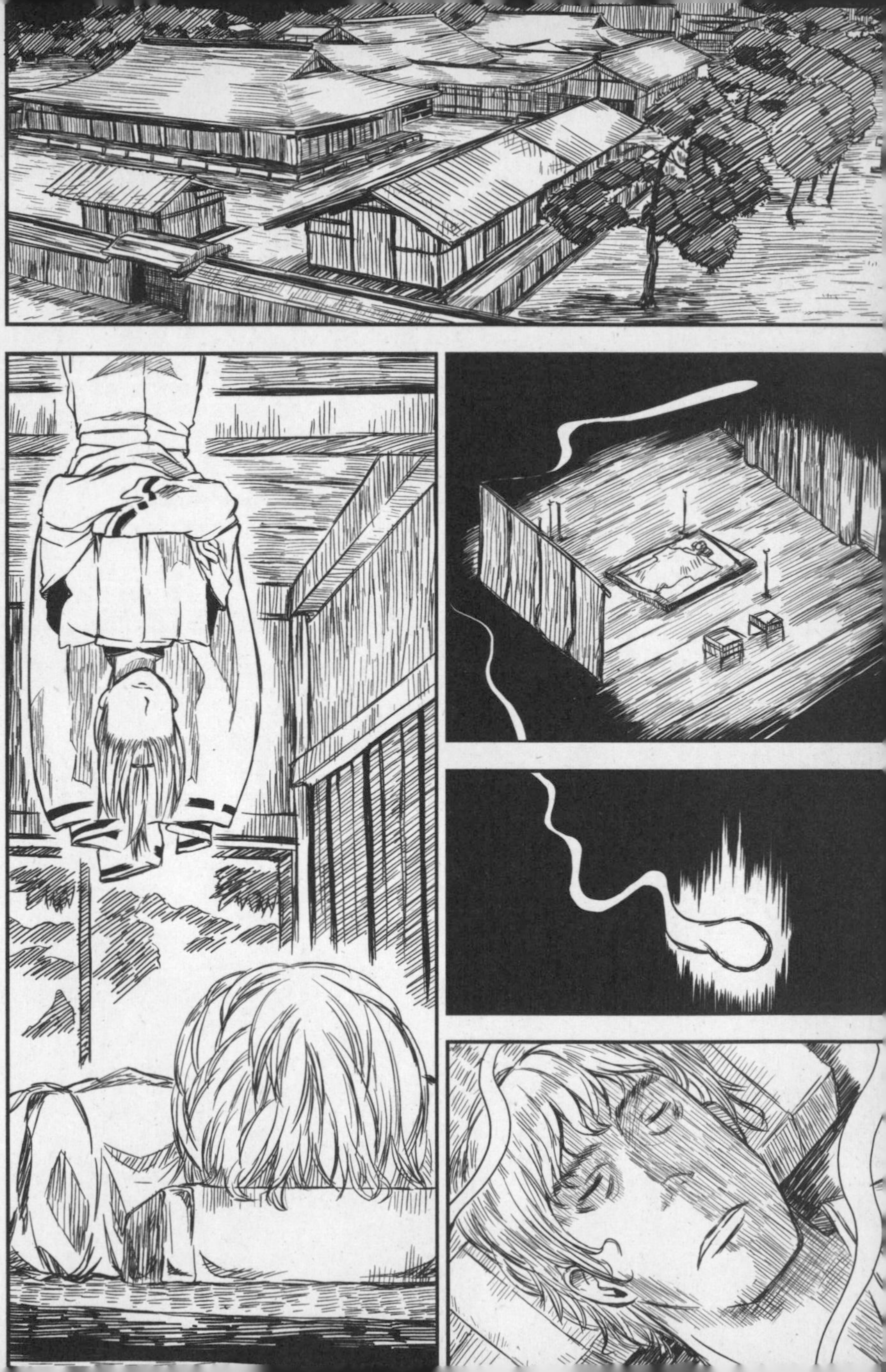

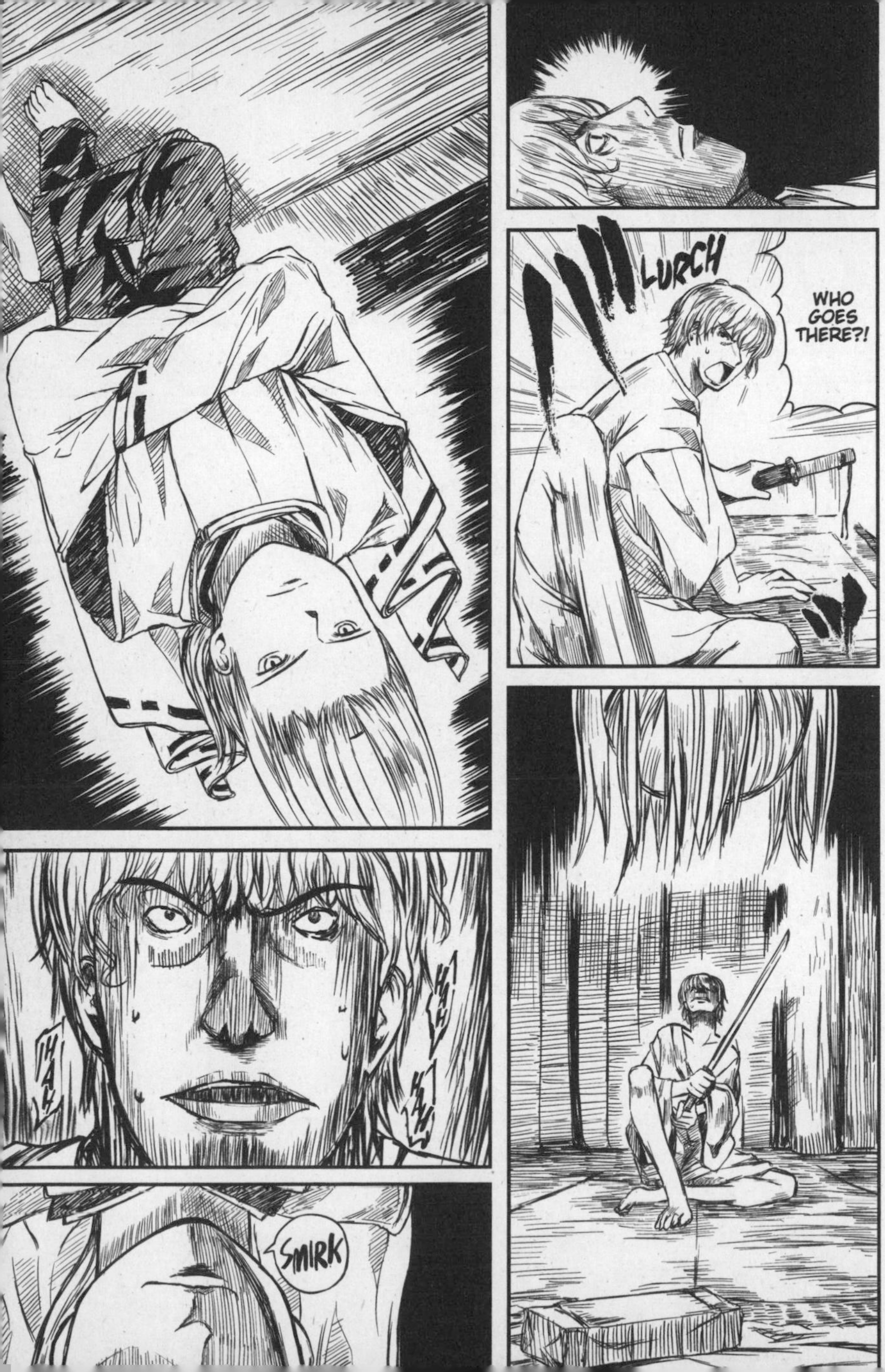
LURCH
WHO GOES THERE?!
HAH!
HAH!
HAH!
SMIRK

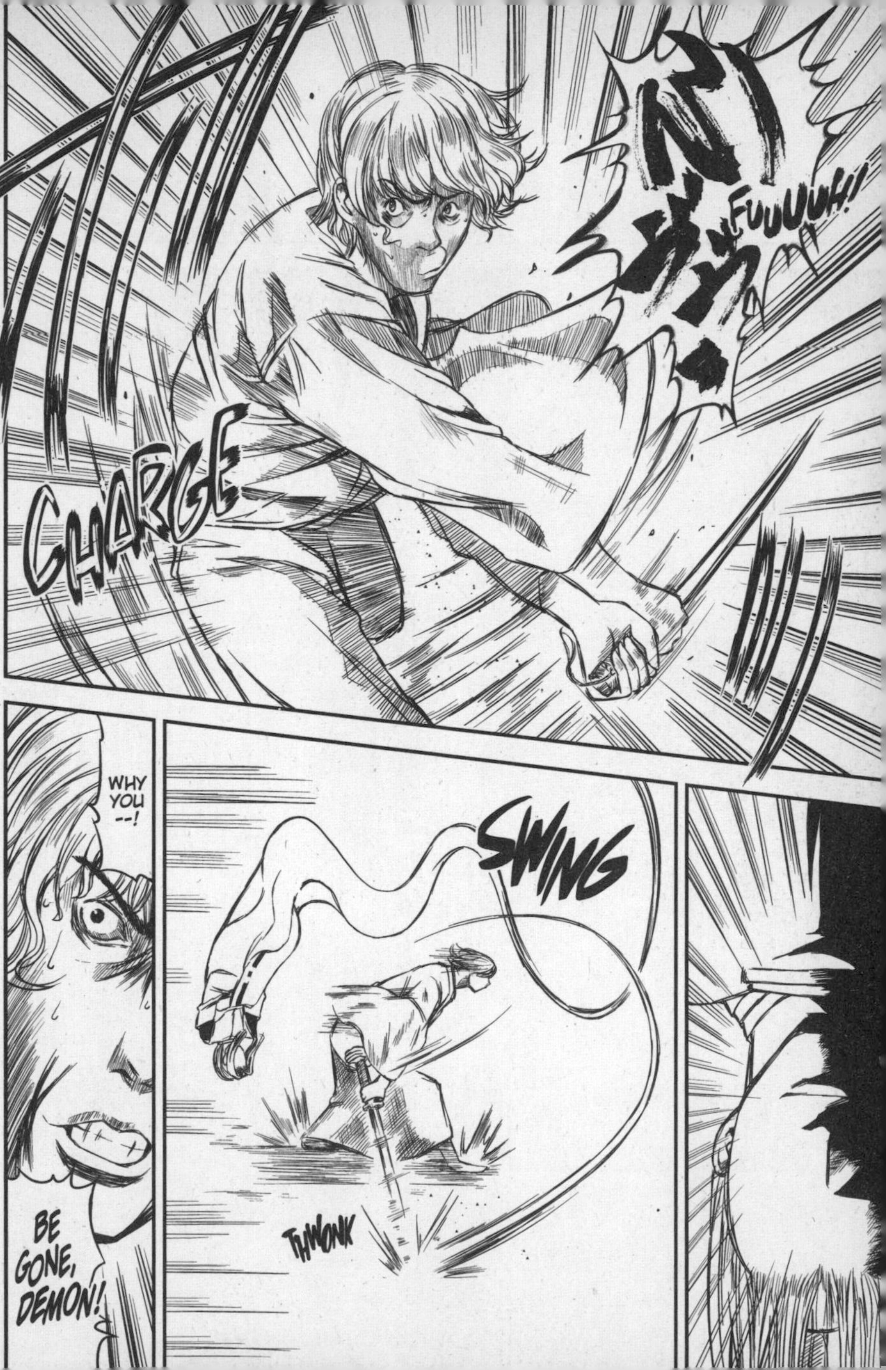
FUUUUH!!
CHARGE
SWING
THWONK
WHY YOU --!
BE GONE, DEMON!

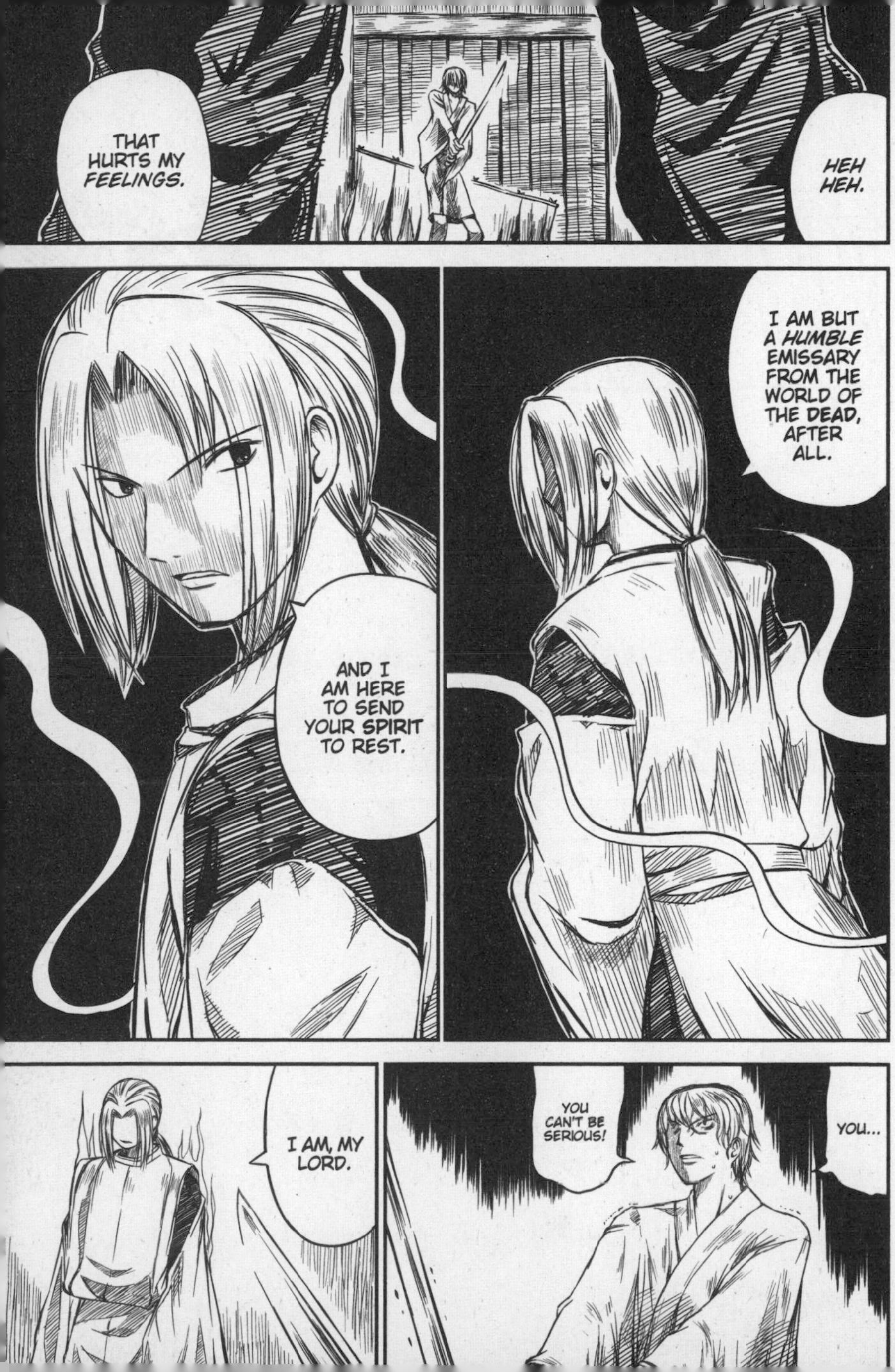
HEH HEH.
THAT HURTS MY FEELINGS.
I AM BUT A HUMBLE EMISSARY FROM THE WORLD OF THE DEAD, AFTER ALL.
AND I AM HERE TO SEND YOUR SPIRIT TO REST.
YOU...
YOU CAN'T BE SERIOUS!
I AM, MY LORD.

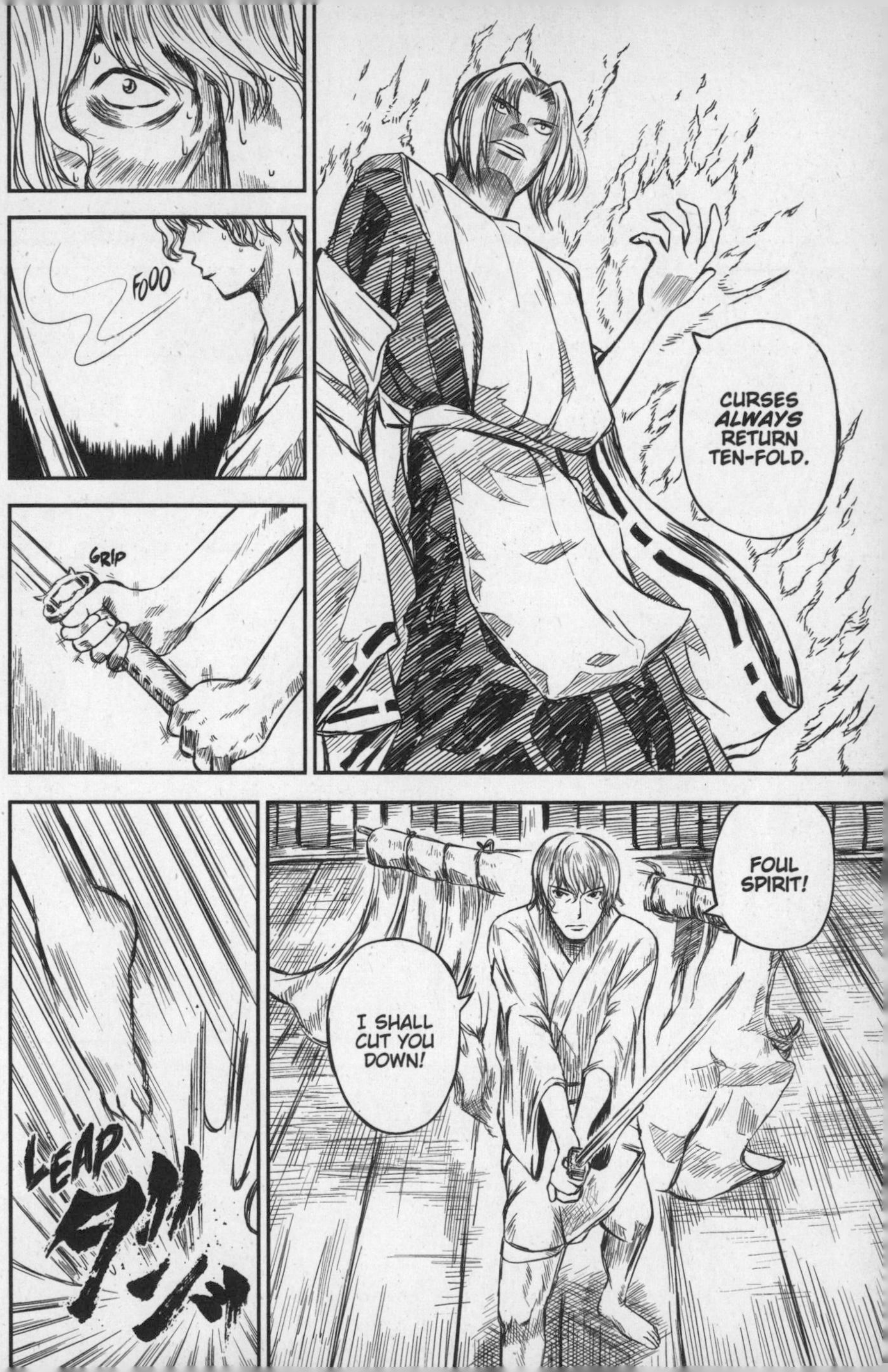
CURSES ALWAYS RETURN TEN-FOLD.
FOOO
GRIP
FOUL SPIRIT!
I SHALL CUT YOU DOWN!
LEAP

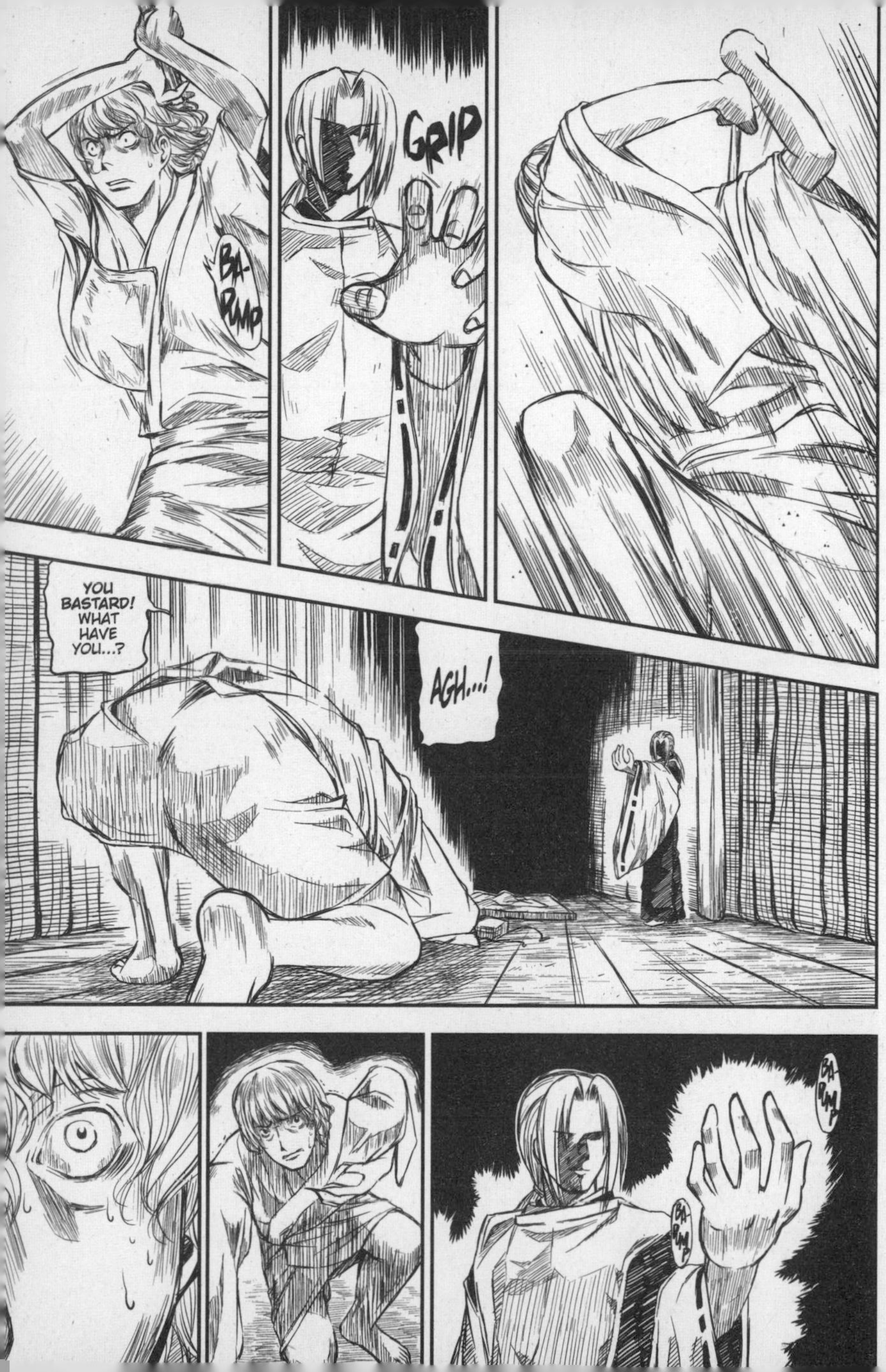
GRIP
BA-DUMP
AGH...!
YOU BASTARD! WHAT HAVE YOU...?
BA-DUMP
BA-DUMP

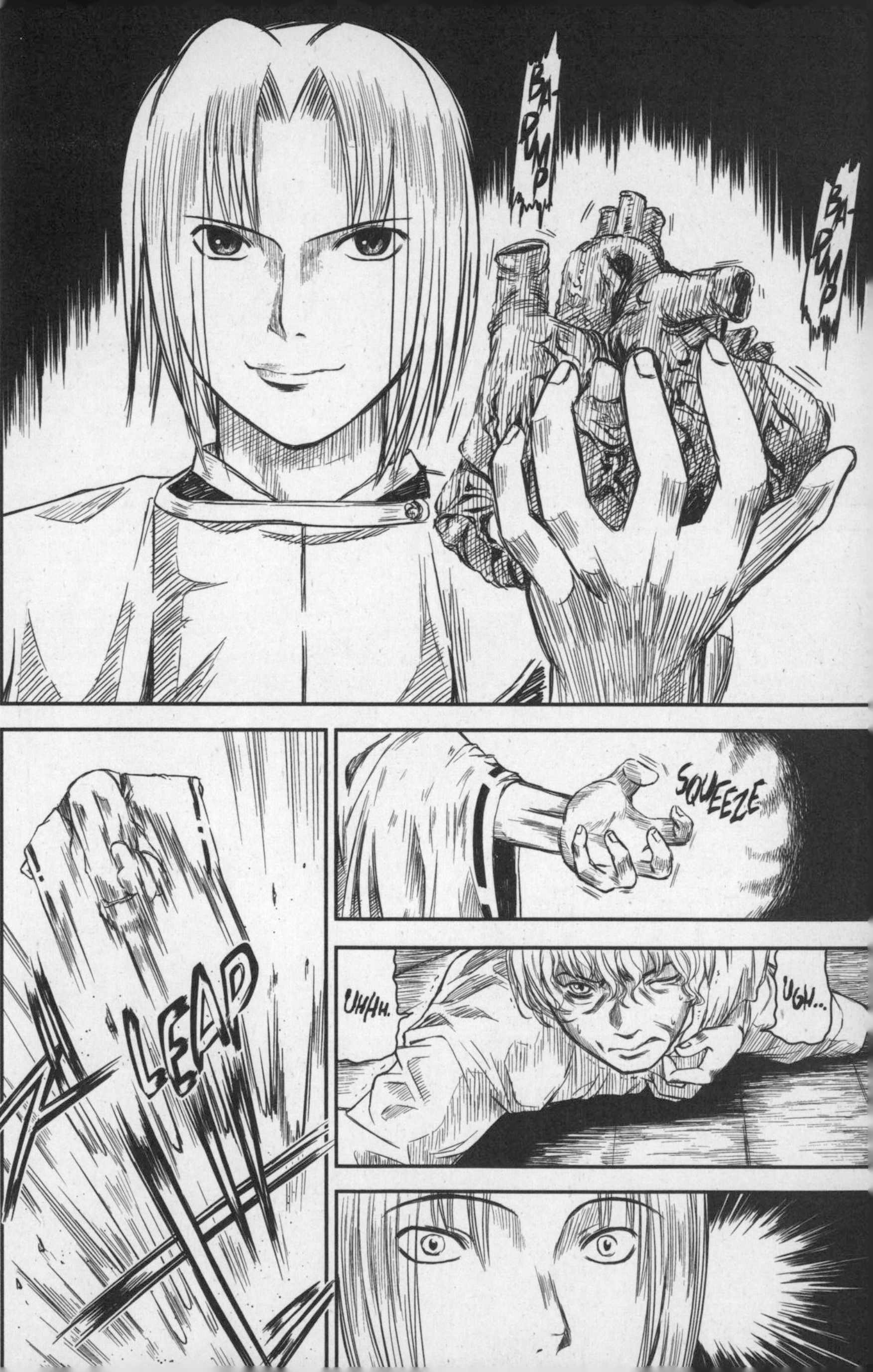
BA-DUMP
BA-DUMP
SQUEEZE
UGH...
UHHH.
LEAP

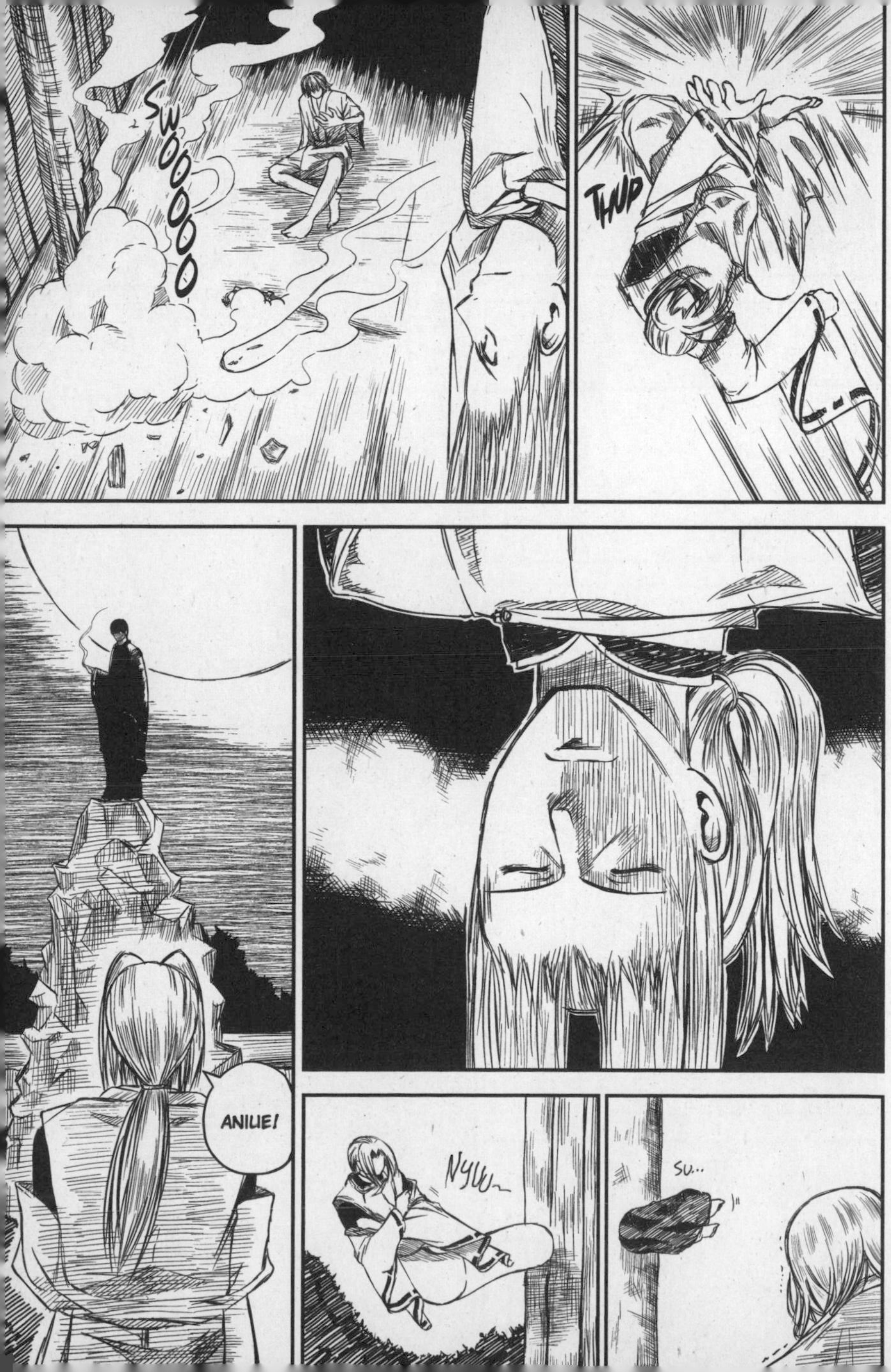
THUP
SWOOOOOO
SU...
NYUU~
ANIUE!

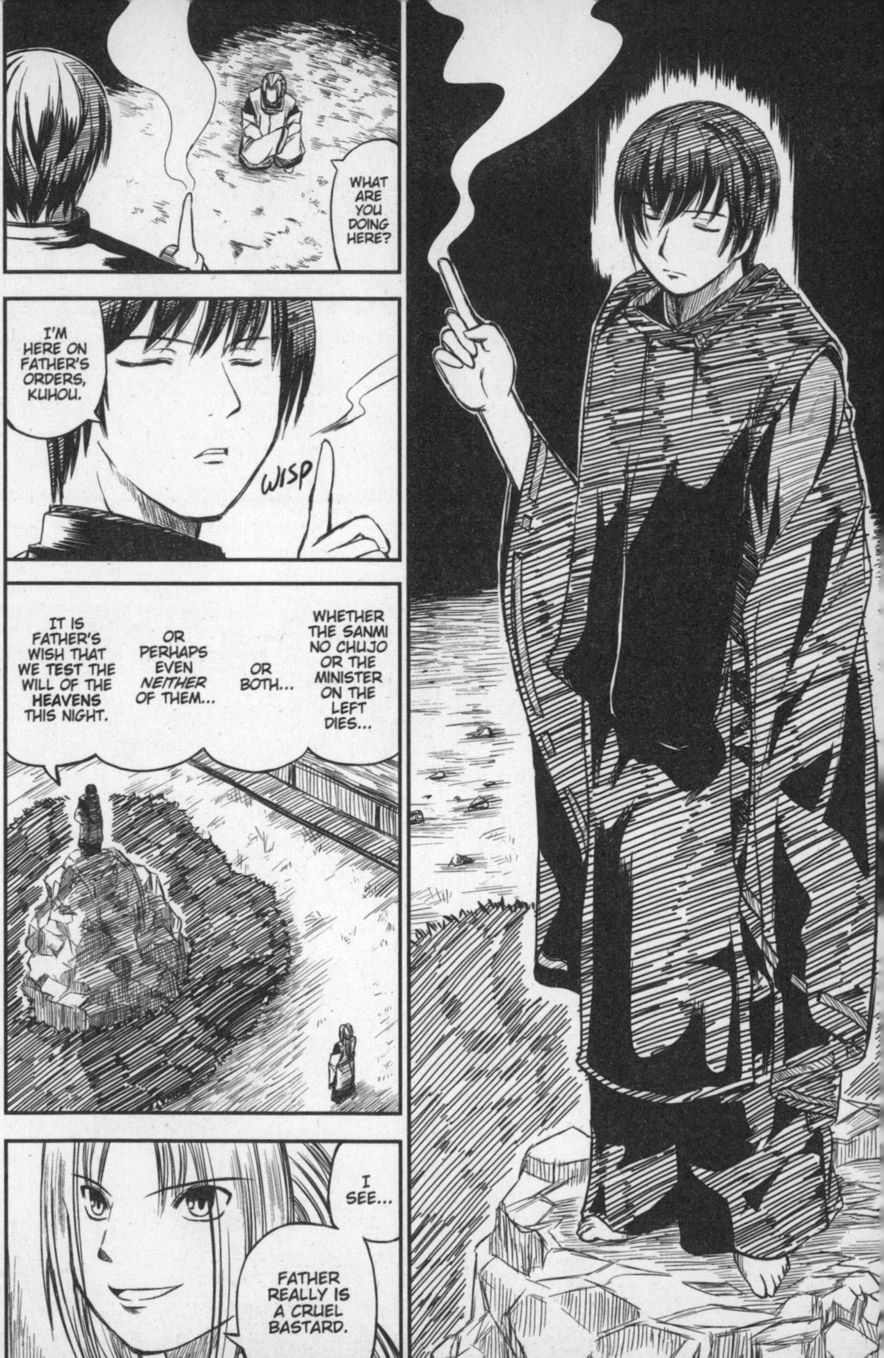
WHAT ARE YOU DOING HERE?
I'M HERE ON FATHER'S ORDERS, KUHOU.
WISP
WHETHER THE SANMI NO CHUJO OR THE MINISTER ON THE LEFT DIES...
OR BOTH...
OR PERHAPS EVEN *NEITHER* OF THEM...
IT IS FATHER'S WISH THAT WE TEST THE WILL OF THE HEAVENS THIS NIGHT.
I SEE...
FATHER REALLY IS A CRUEL BASTARD.

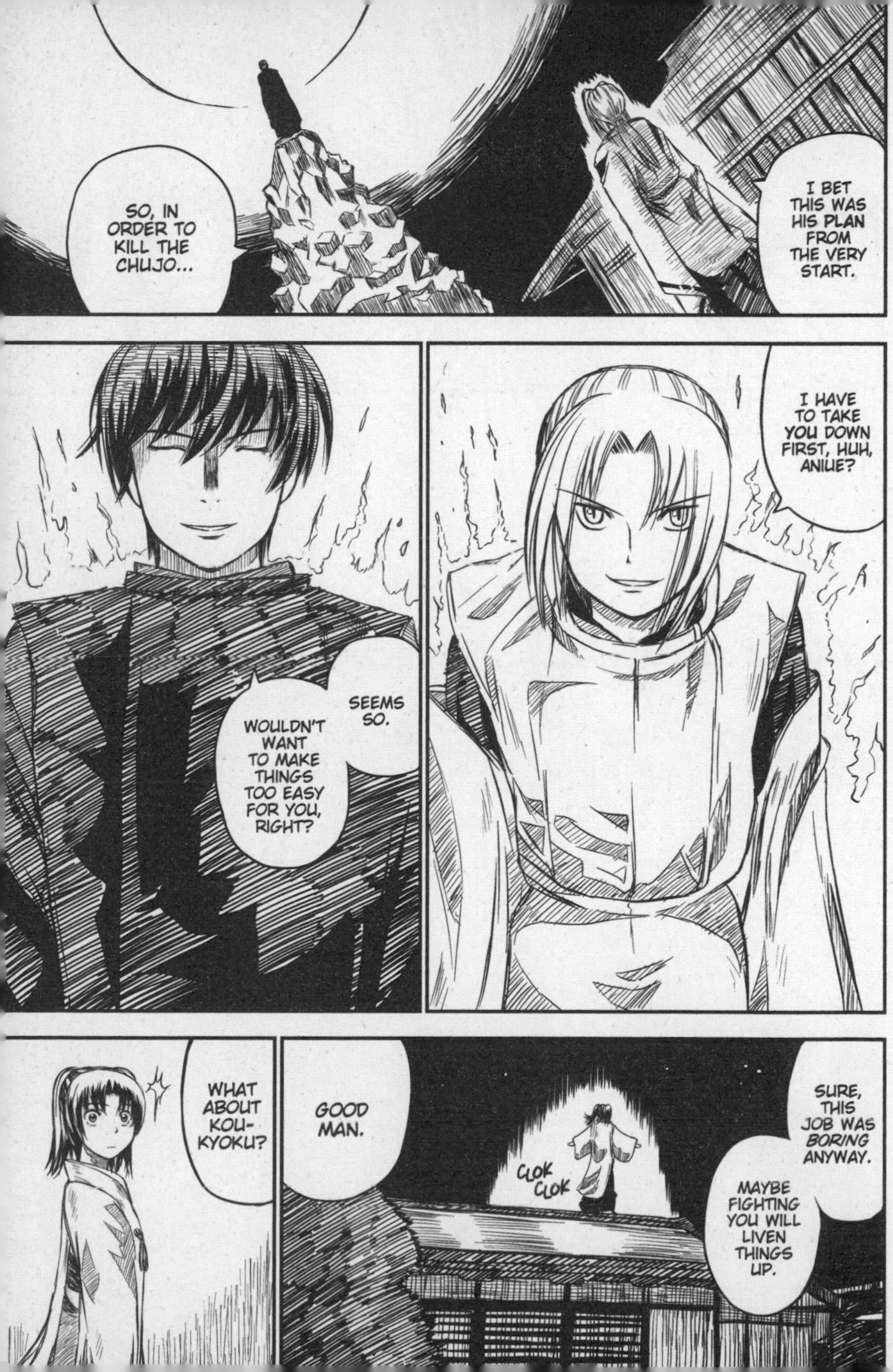
I BET THIS WAS HIS PLAN FROM THE VERY START.
SO, IN ORDER TO KILL THE CHUJO...
I HAVE TO TAKE YOU DOWN FIRST, HUH, ANIUE?
SEEMS SO.
WOULDN'T WANT TO MAKE THINGS TOO EASY FOR YOU, RIGHT?
SURE, THIS JOB WAS *BORING* ANYWAY.
MAYBE FIGHTING YOU WILL LIVEN THINGS UP.
GOOD MAN.
CLOK CLOK
WHAT ABOUT KOU-KYOKU?

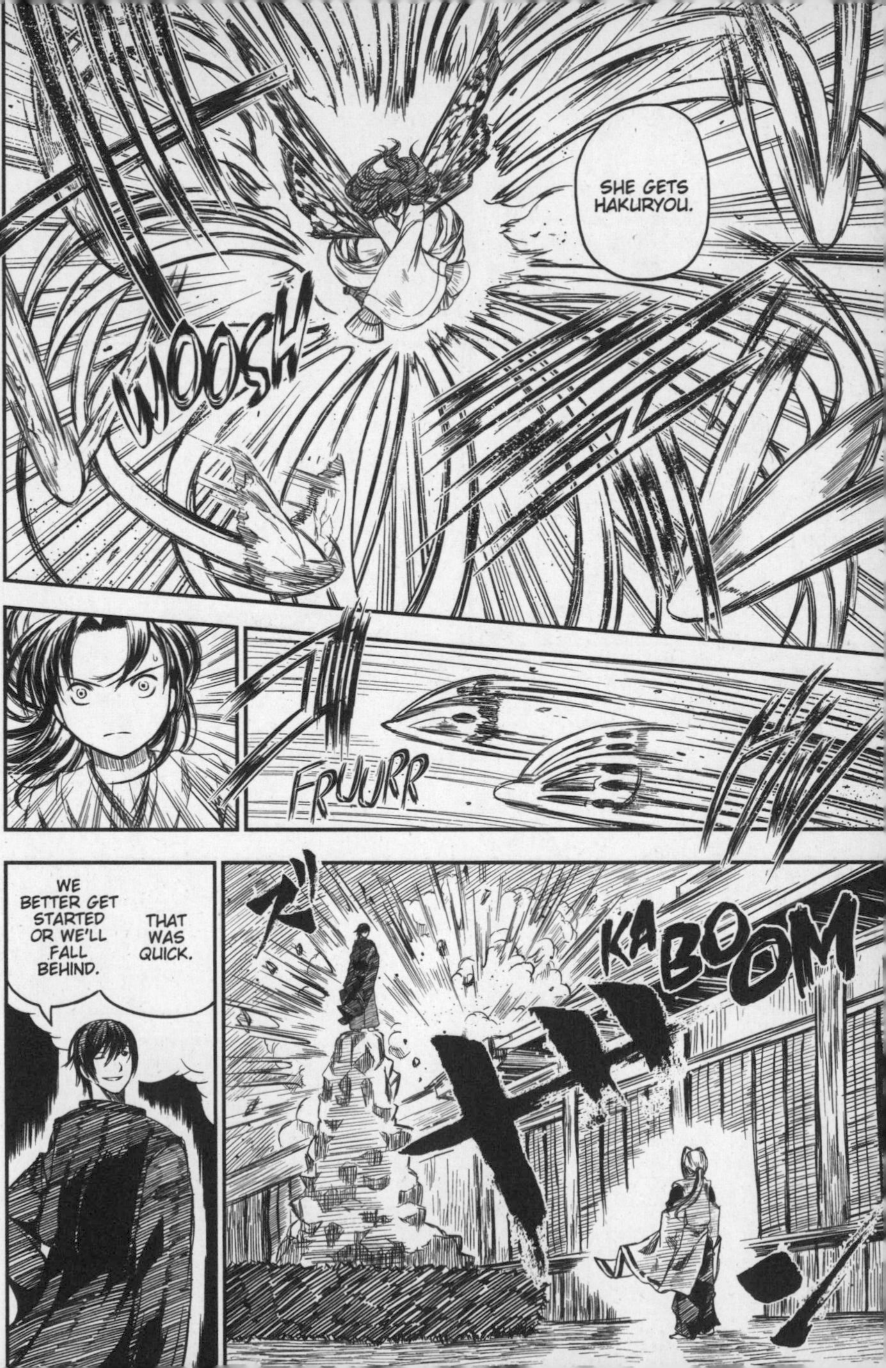
SHE GETS HAKURYOU.
WOOSH
FRUURR
KABOOM
THAT WAS QUICK.
WE BETTER GET STARTED OR WE'LL FALL BEHIND.

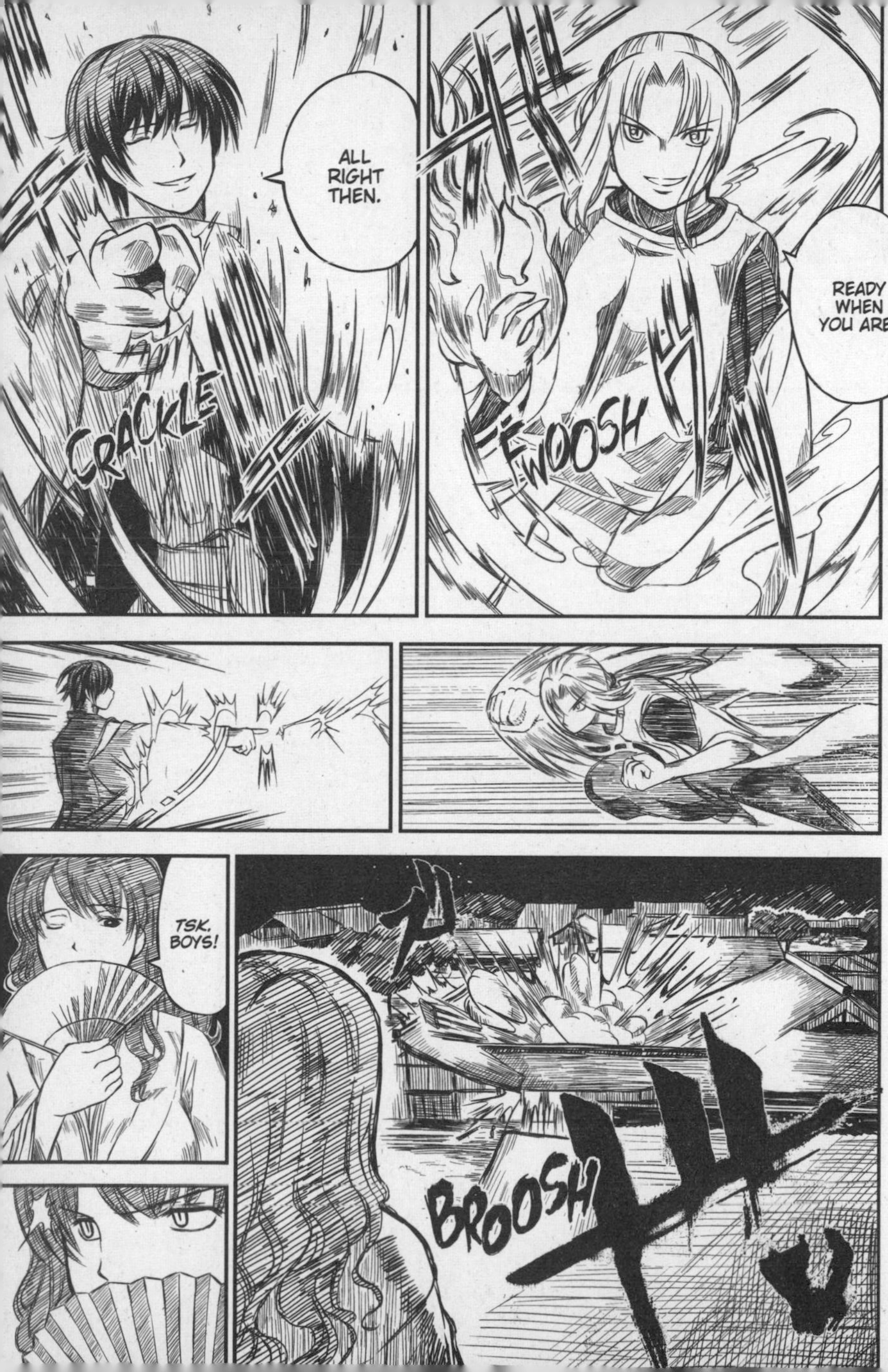
READY WHEN YOU ARE.
FWOOSH
ALL RIGHT THEN.
CRACKLE
BROOSH
TSK. BOYS!

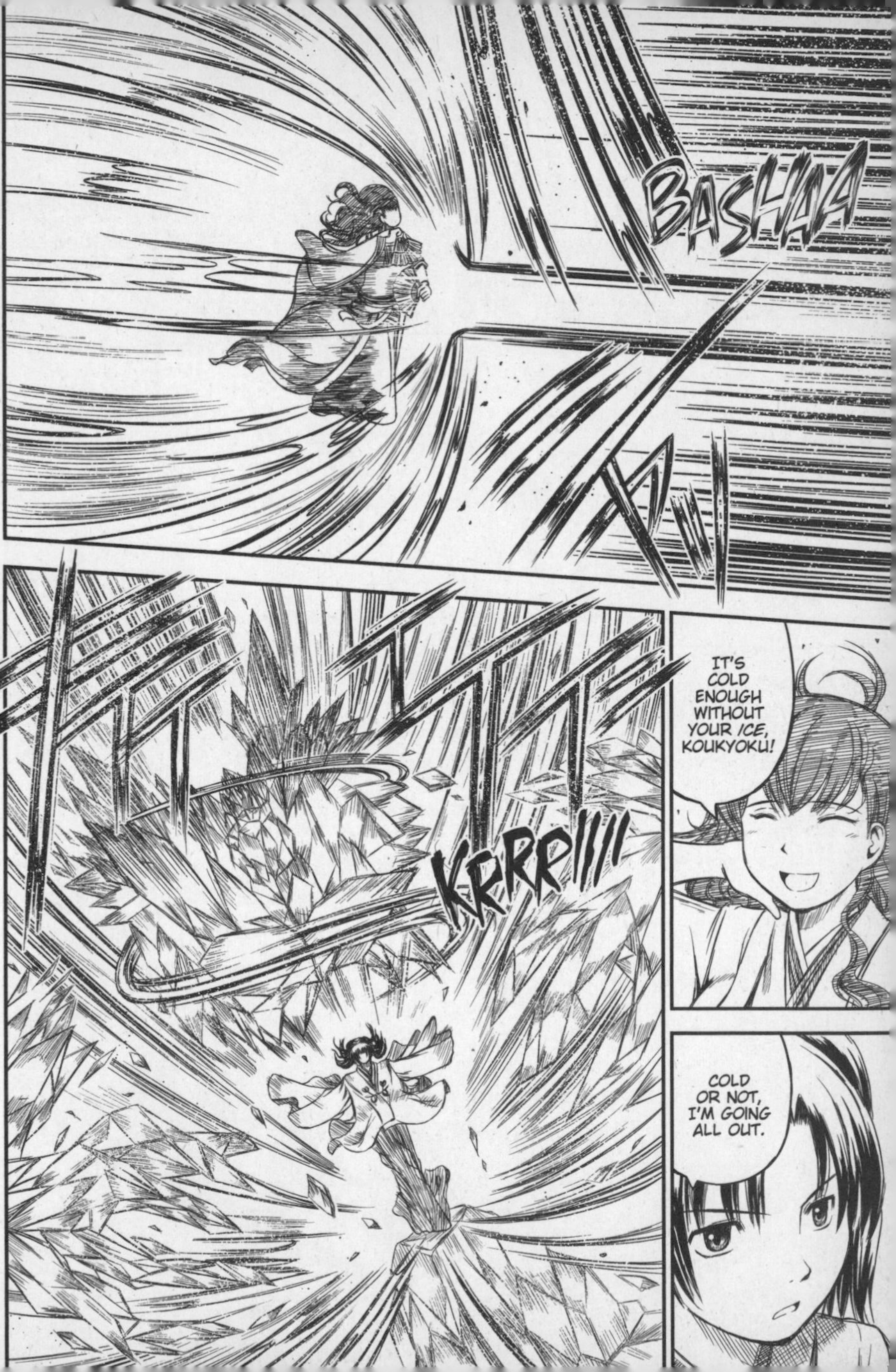
BASHAA
IT'S COLD ENOUGH WITHOUT YOUR ICE, KOUKYOKU!
COLD OR NOT, I'M GOING ALL OUT.
KRRR!!!!

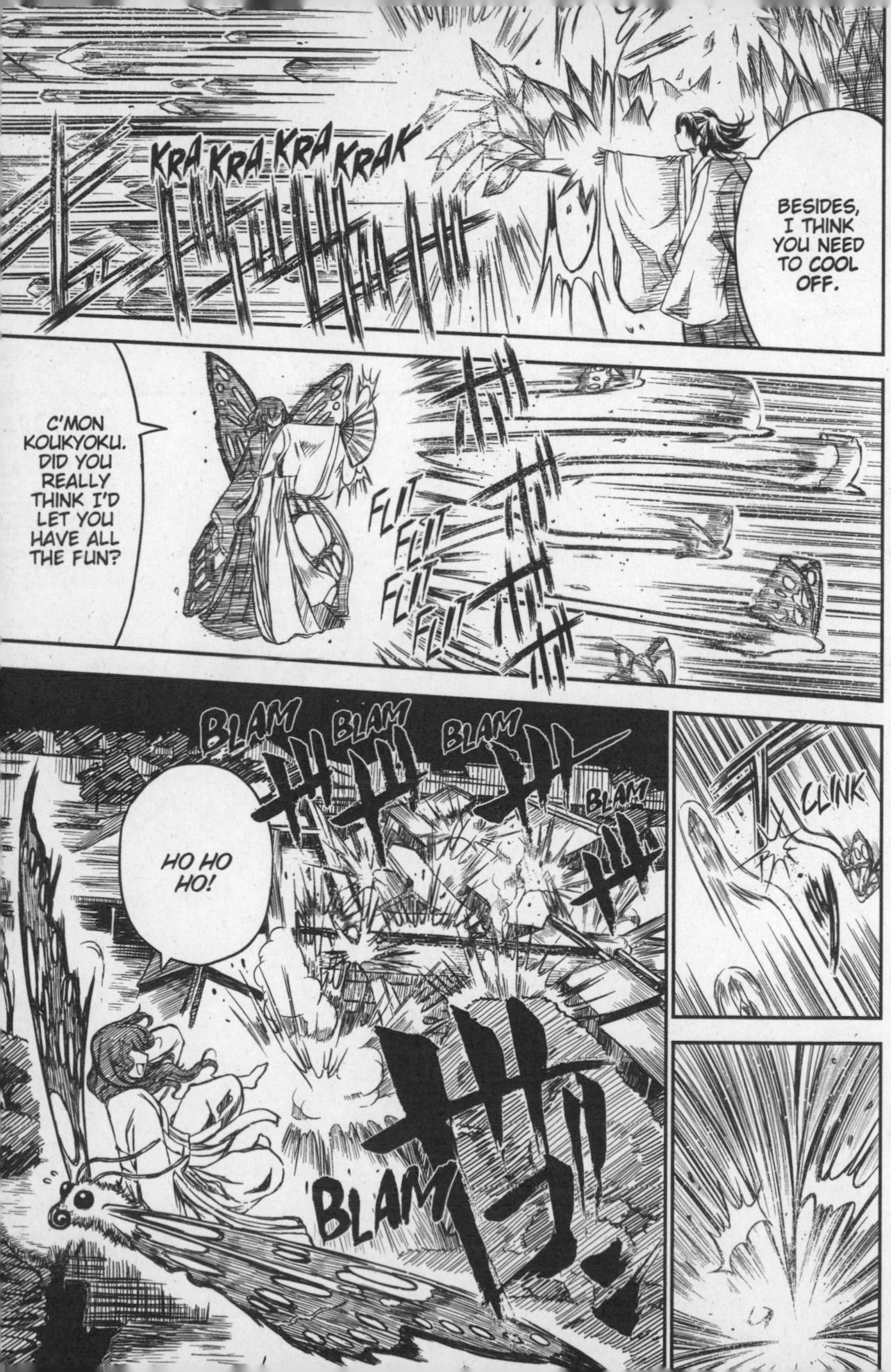
BESIDES, I THINK YOU NEED TO COOL OFF.
KRA KRA KRA KRAK
FLIT FLIT FLIT FLIT FLIT
C'MON KOUKYOKU. DID YOU REALLY THINK I'D LET YOU HAVE ALL THE FUN?
CLINK
BLAM BLAM BLAM
BLAM
HO HO HO!
BLAM

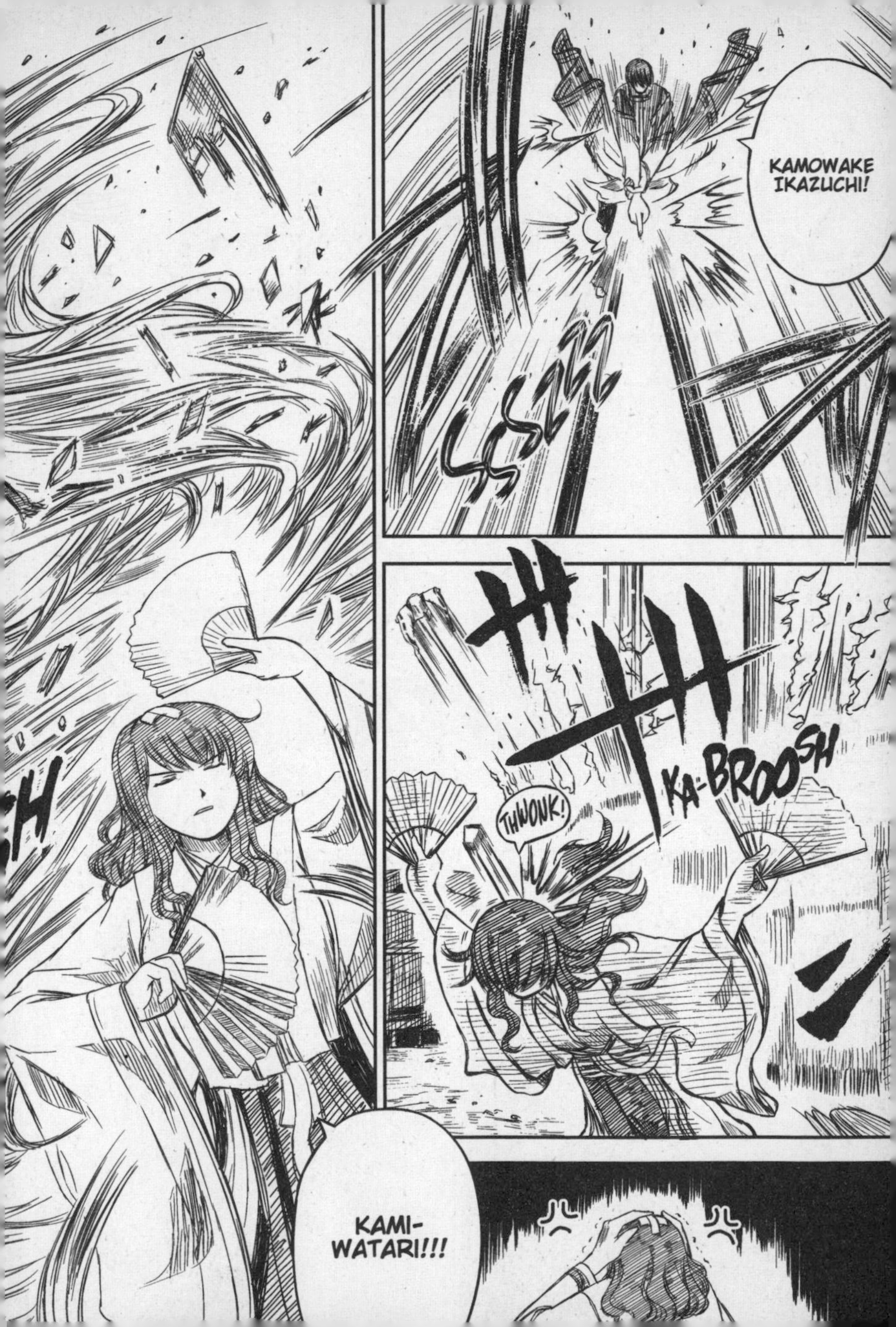
KAMOWAKE IKAZUCHI!
KA-BROOSH
THWONK!
KAMI-WATARI!!!

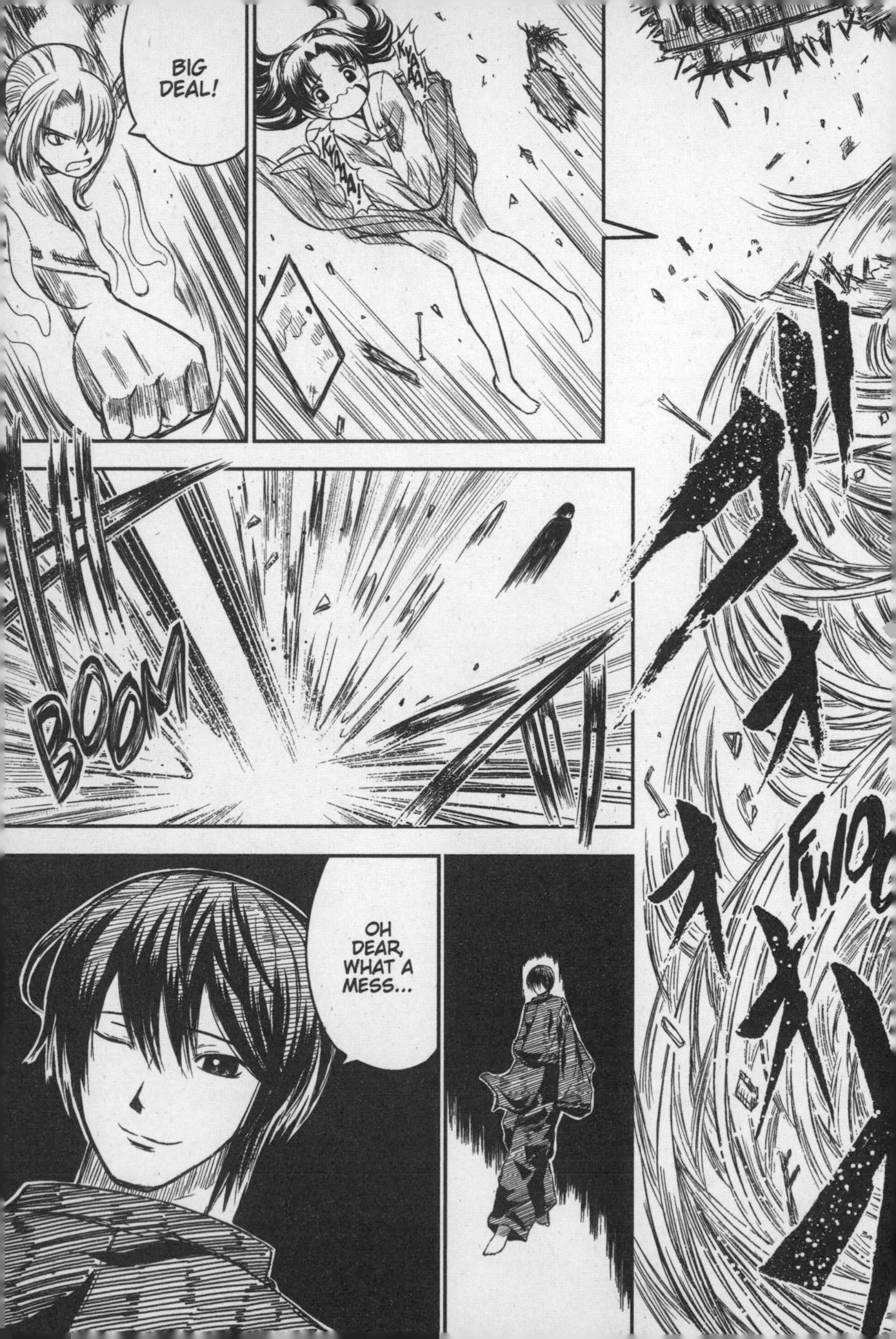

FWO
KYAAA!
KYAAAA!
BIG DEAL!
BOOM
OH DEAR, WHAT A MESS...

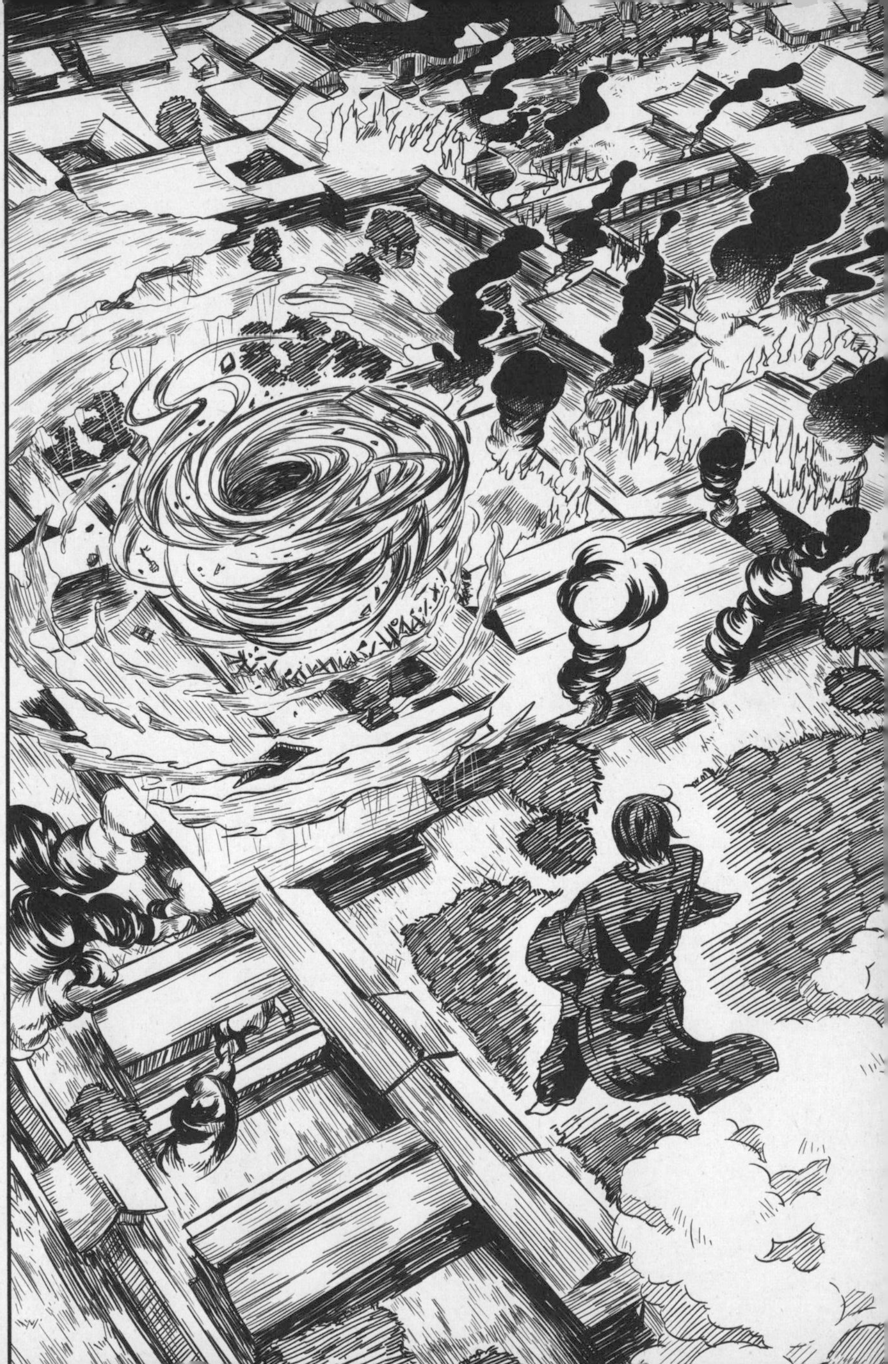

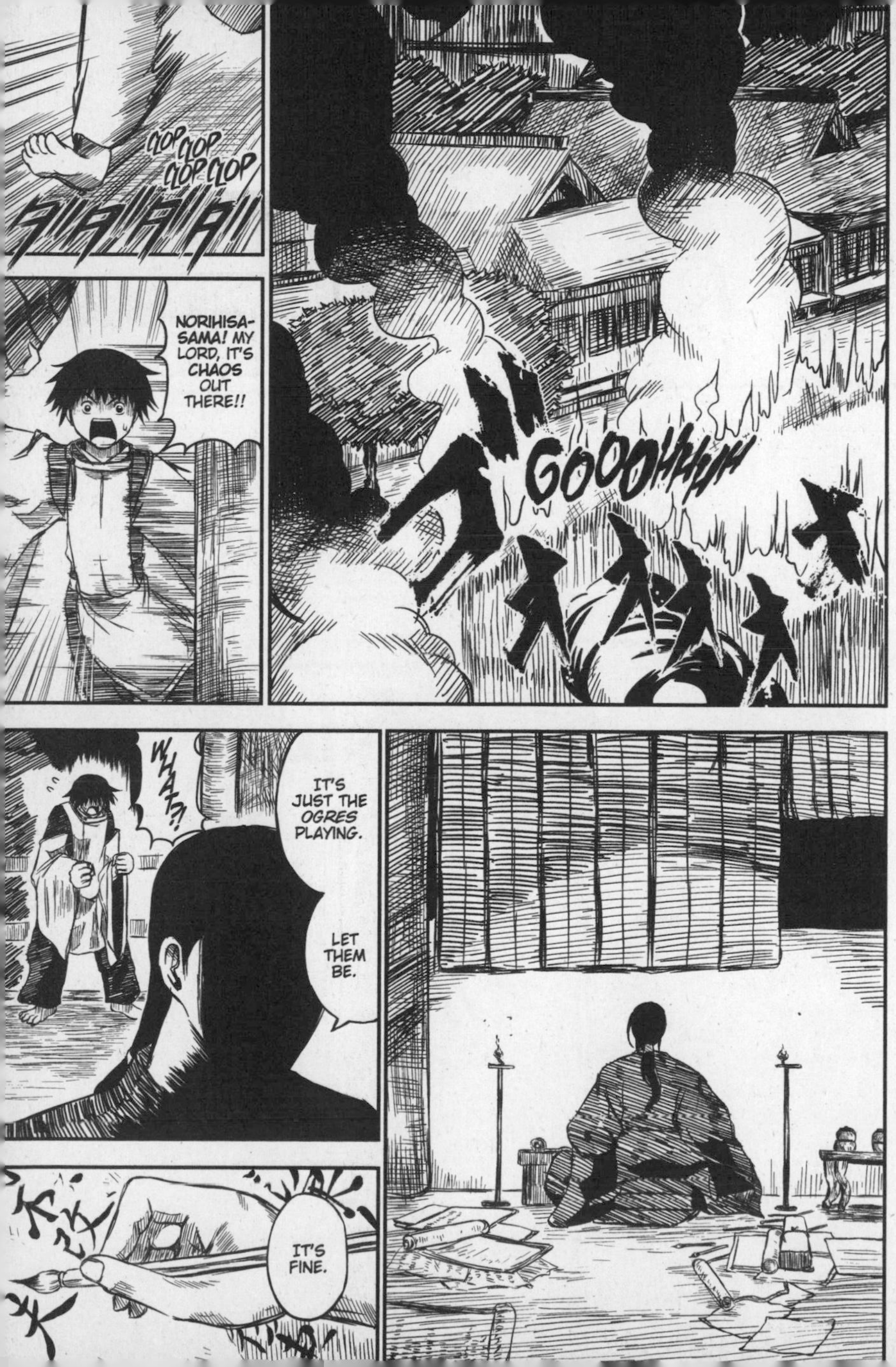
GOOOHHHH
CLOP CLOP
CLOP CLOP
NORIHISA-SAMA! MY LORD, IT'S CHAOS OUT THERE!!
IT'S JUST THE OGRES PLAYING.
LET THEM BE.
WHAT?!
IT'S FINE.

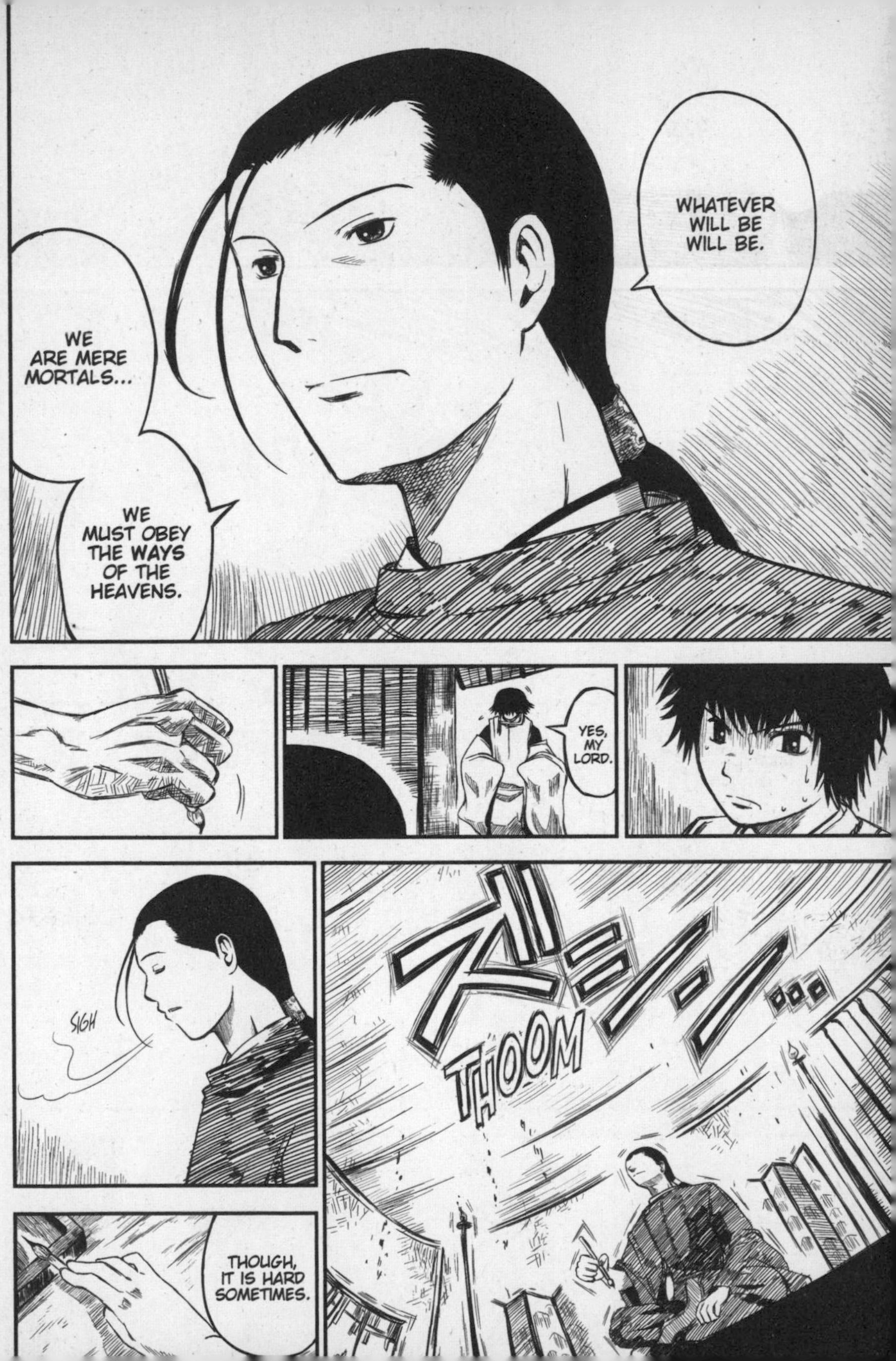
WHATEVER WILL BE WILL BE.
WE ARE MERE MORTALS...
WE MUST OBEY THE WAYS OF THE HEAVENS.
YES, MY LORD.
THOOM
SIGH
THOUGH, IT IS HARD SOMETIMES.

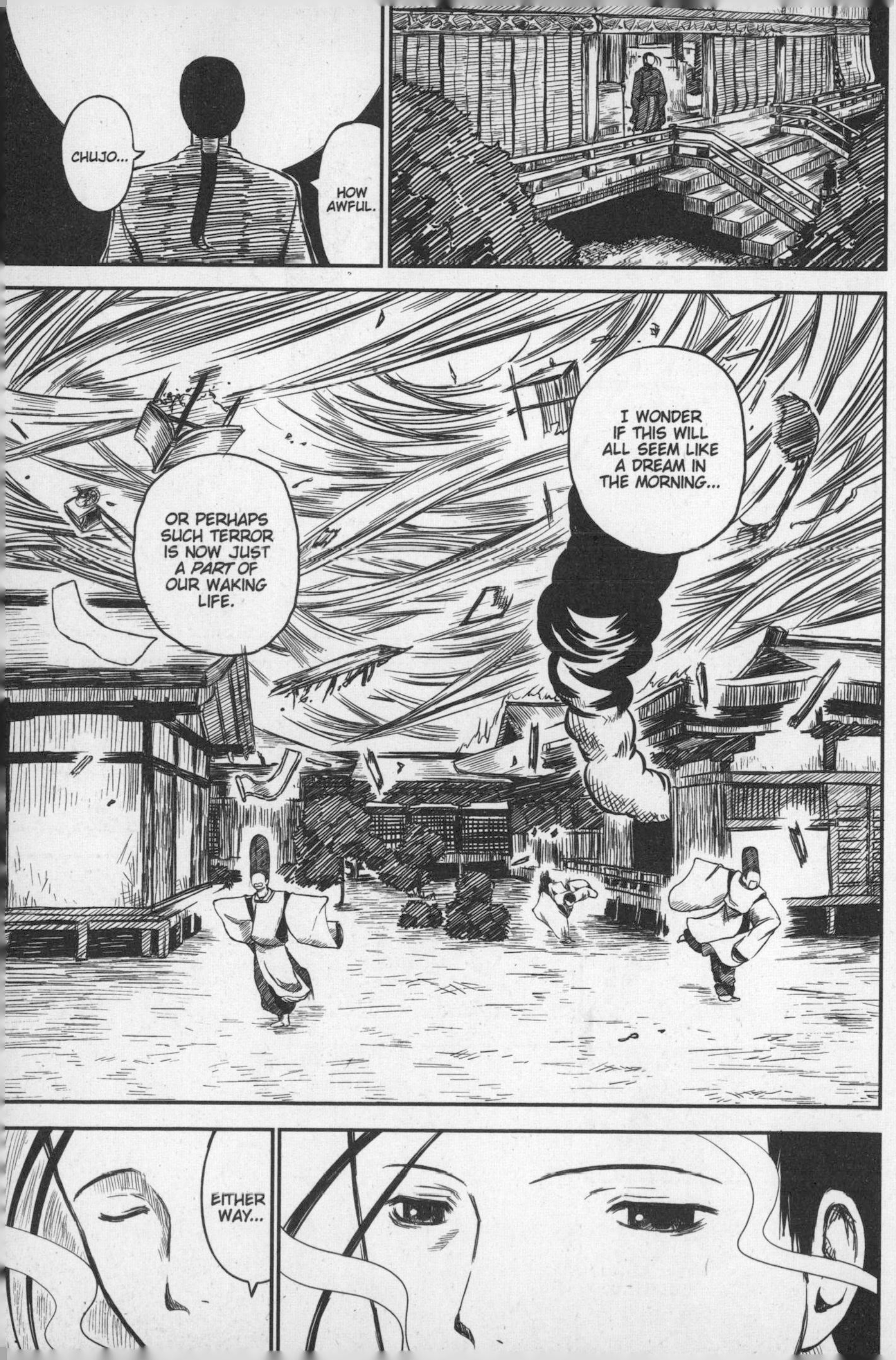
CHUJO...
HOW AWFUL.
I WONDER IF THIS WILL ALL SEEM LIKE A DREAM IN THE MORNING...
OR PERHAPS SUCH TERROR IS NOW JUST A *PART* OF OUR WAKING LIFE.
EITHER WAY...

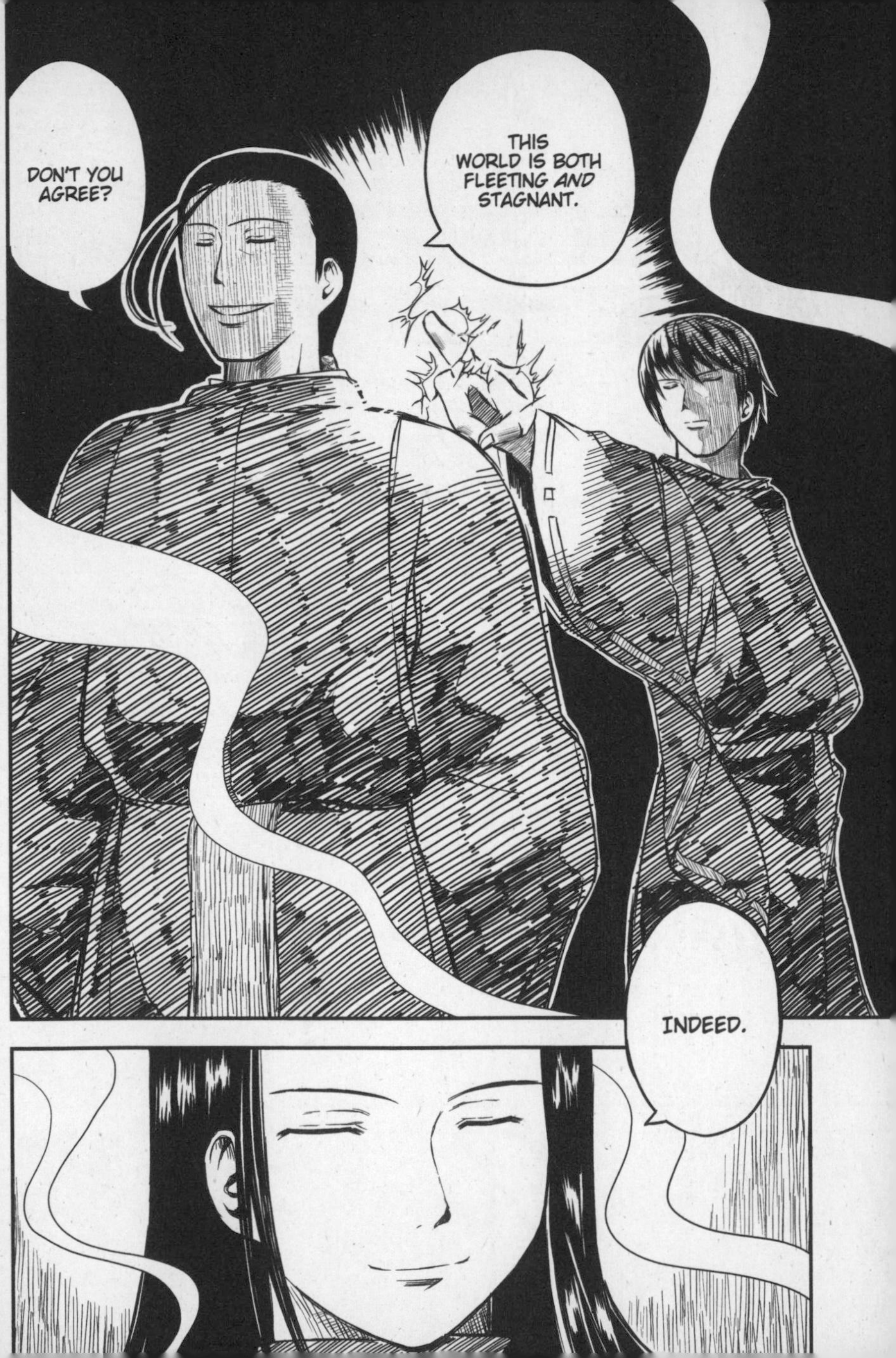
THIS WORLD IS BOTH FLEETING AND STAGNANT.
DON'T YOU AGREE?
INDEED.

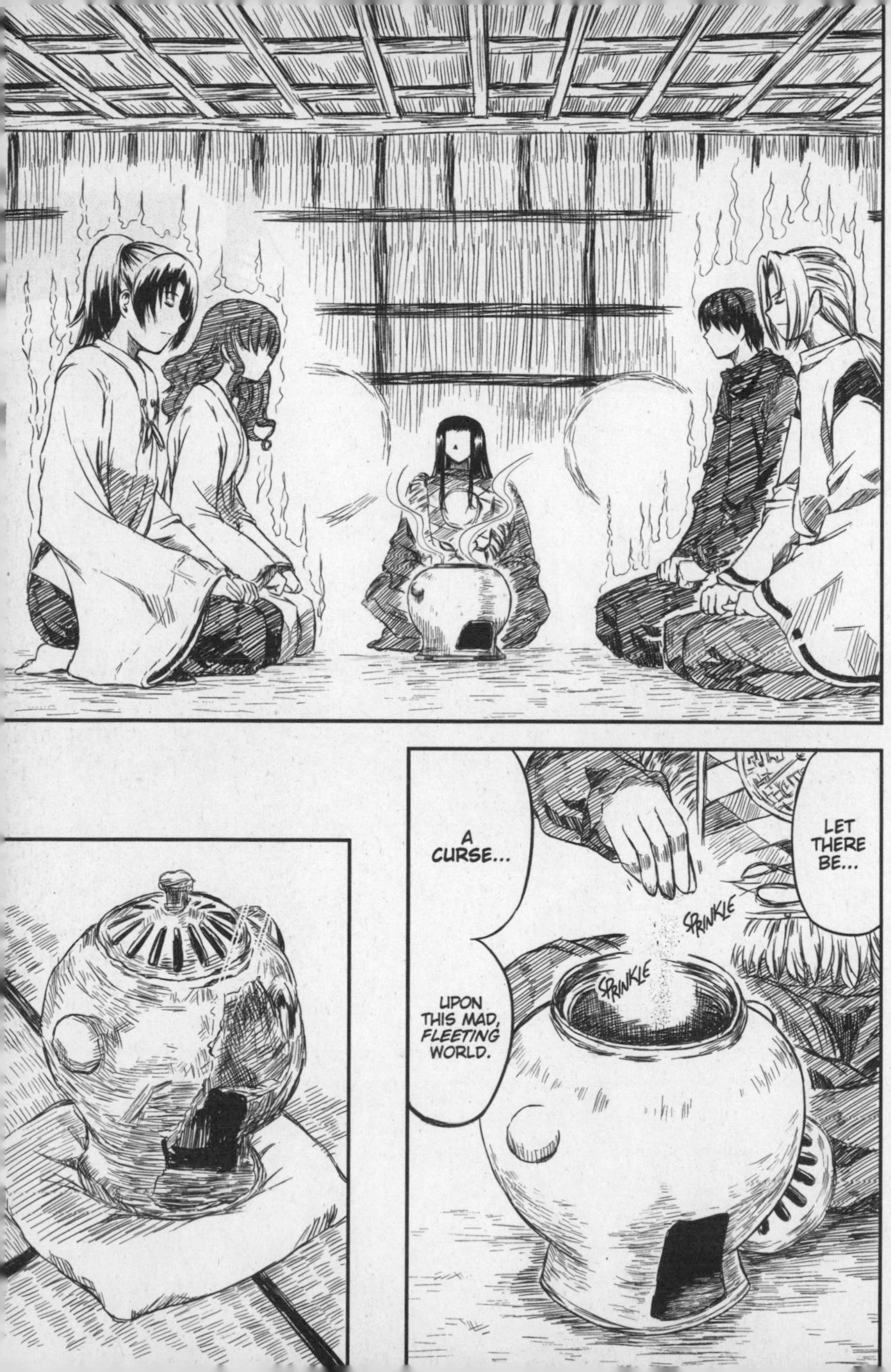
LET THERE BE...
A CURSE...
SPRINKLE
SPRINKLE
UPON THIS MAD, FLEETING WORLD.

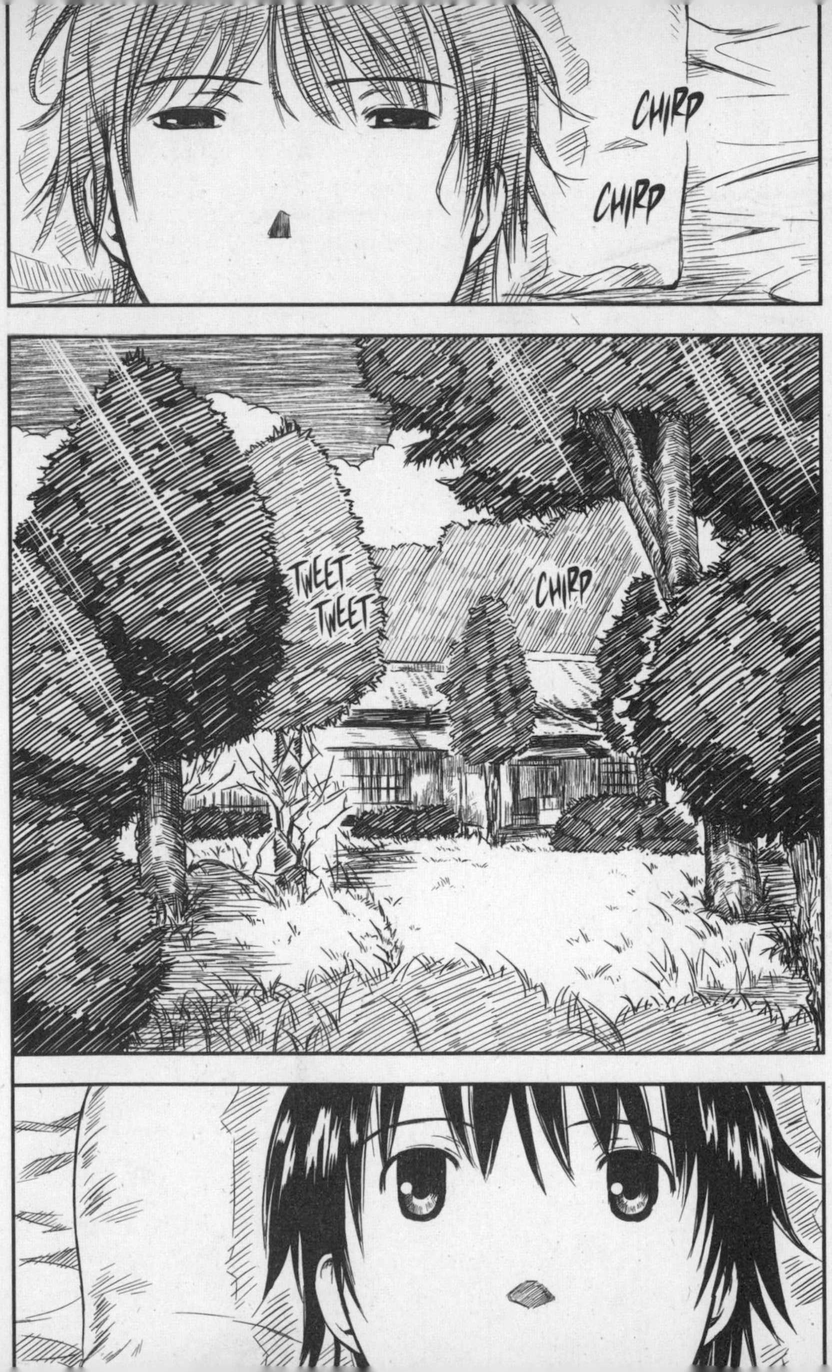
CHIRP
CHIRP
CHIRP
TWEET TWEET

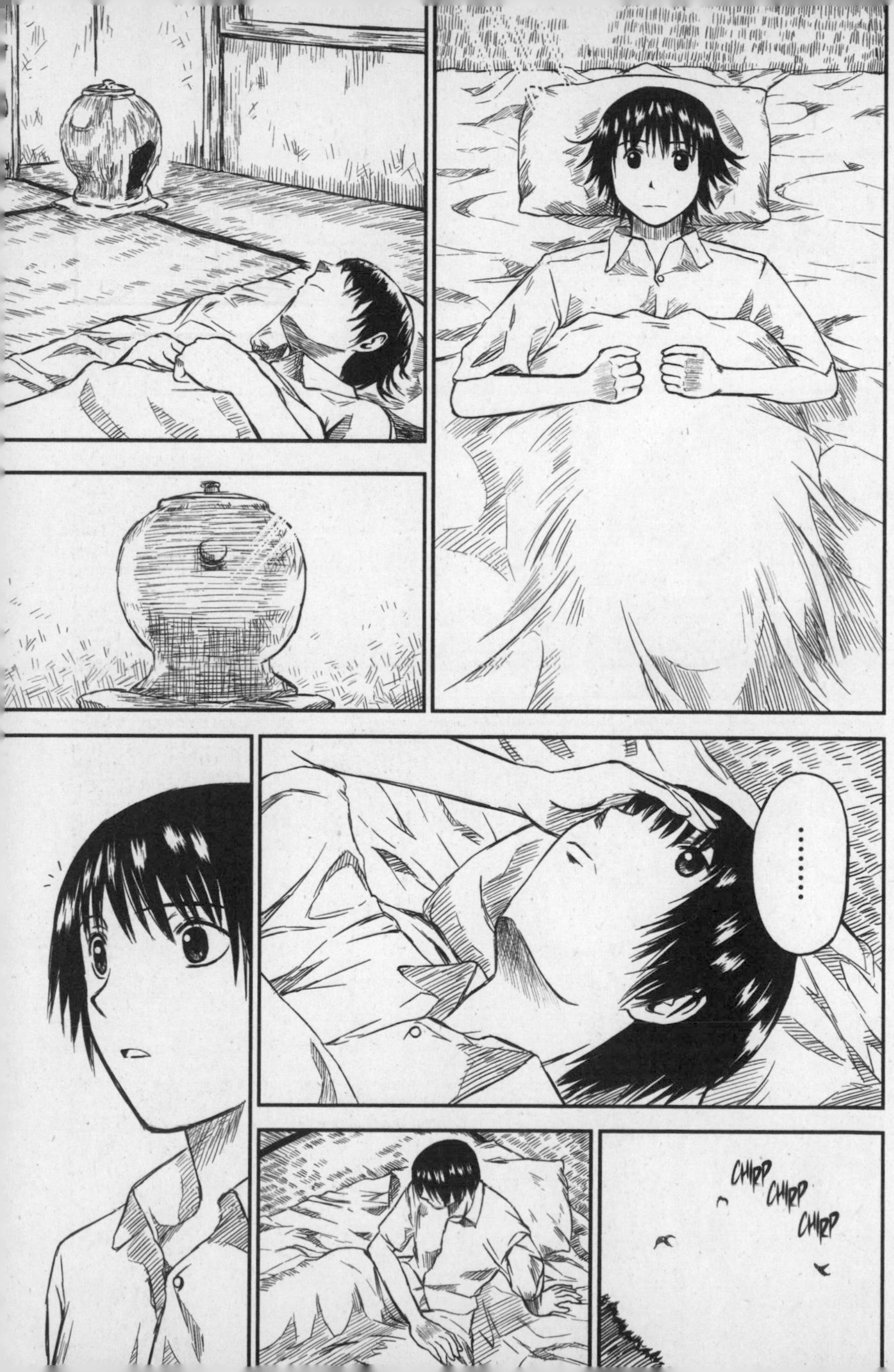
......
CHIRP
CHIRP
CHIRP

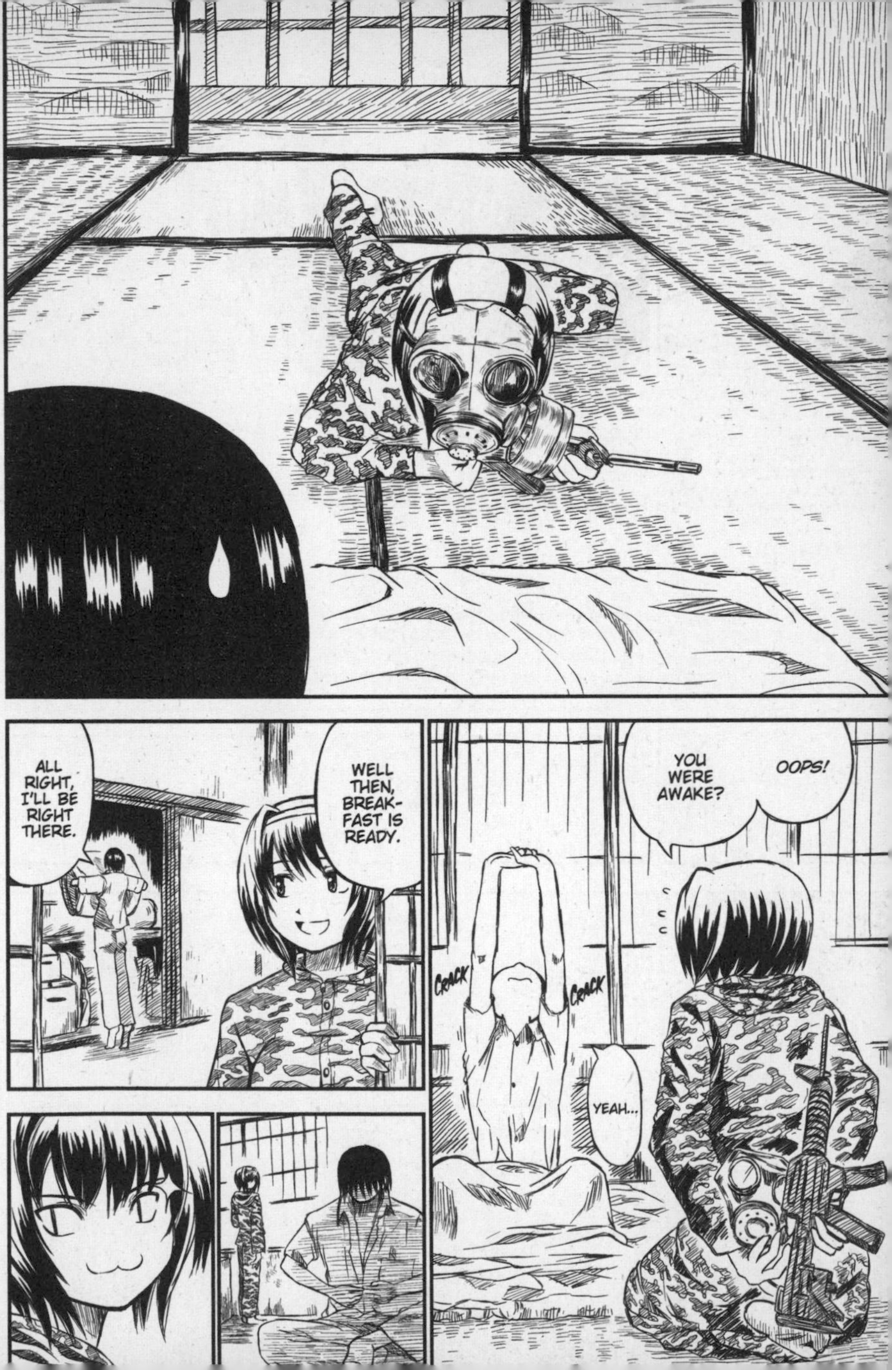
OOPS!
YOU WERE AWAKE?
CRACK
CRACK
YEAH...
WELL THEN, BREAK-FAST IS READY.
ALL RIGHT, I'LL BE RIGHT THERE.

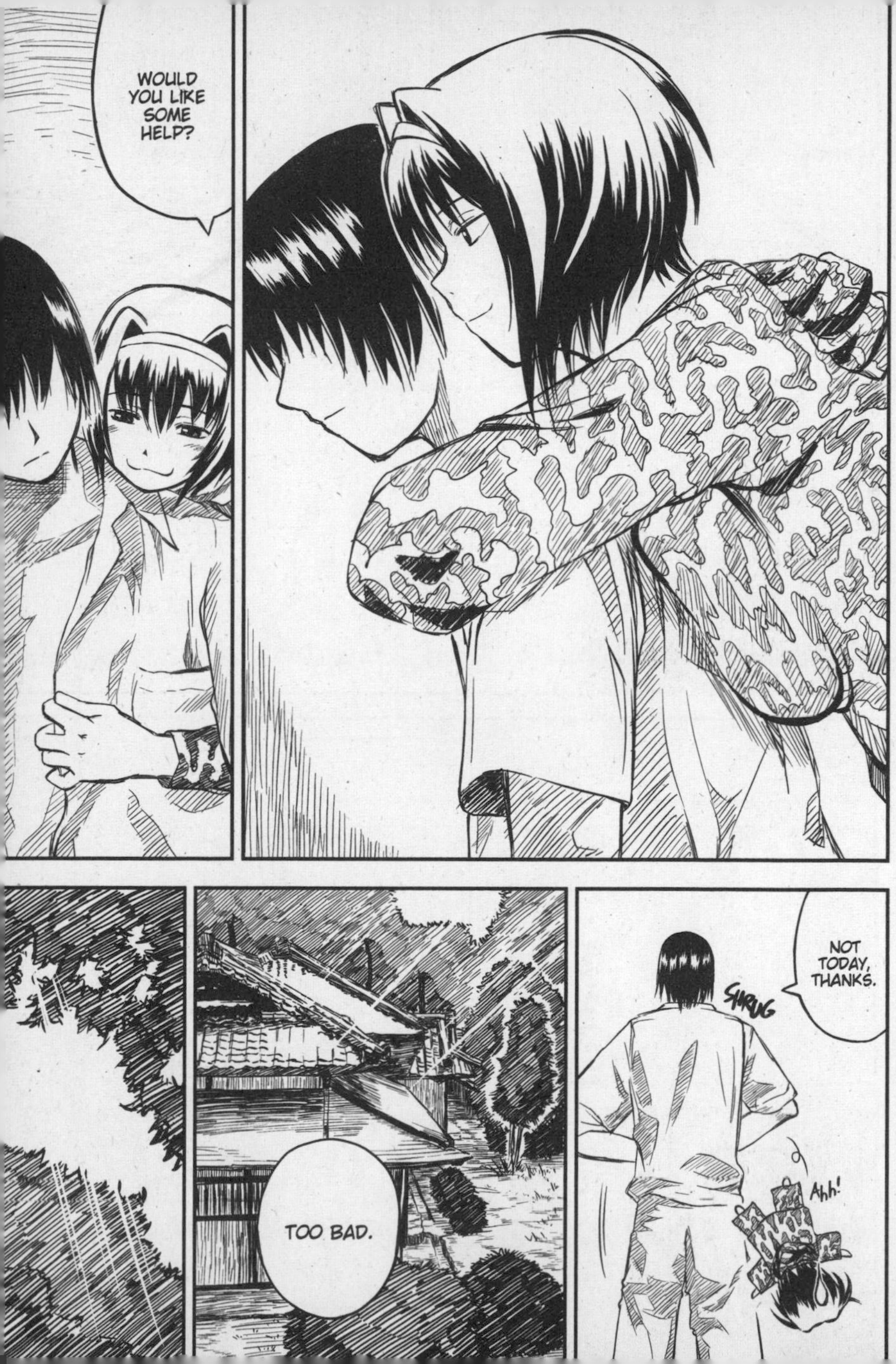
WOULD YOU LIKE SOME HELP?
NOT TODAY, THANKS.
SHRUG
Ahh!
TOO BAD.

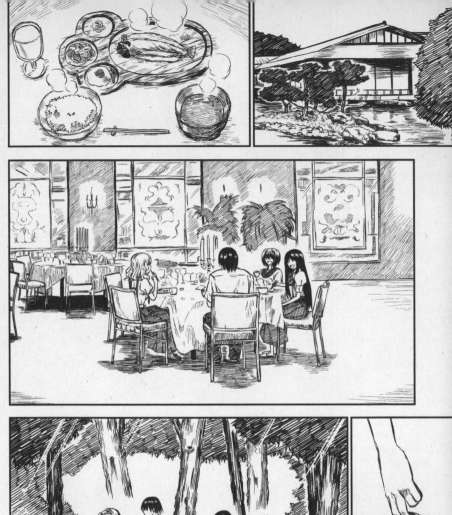

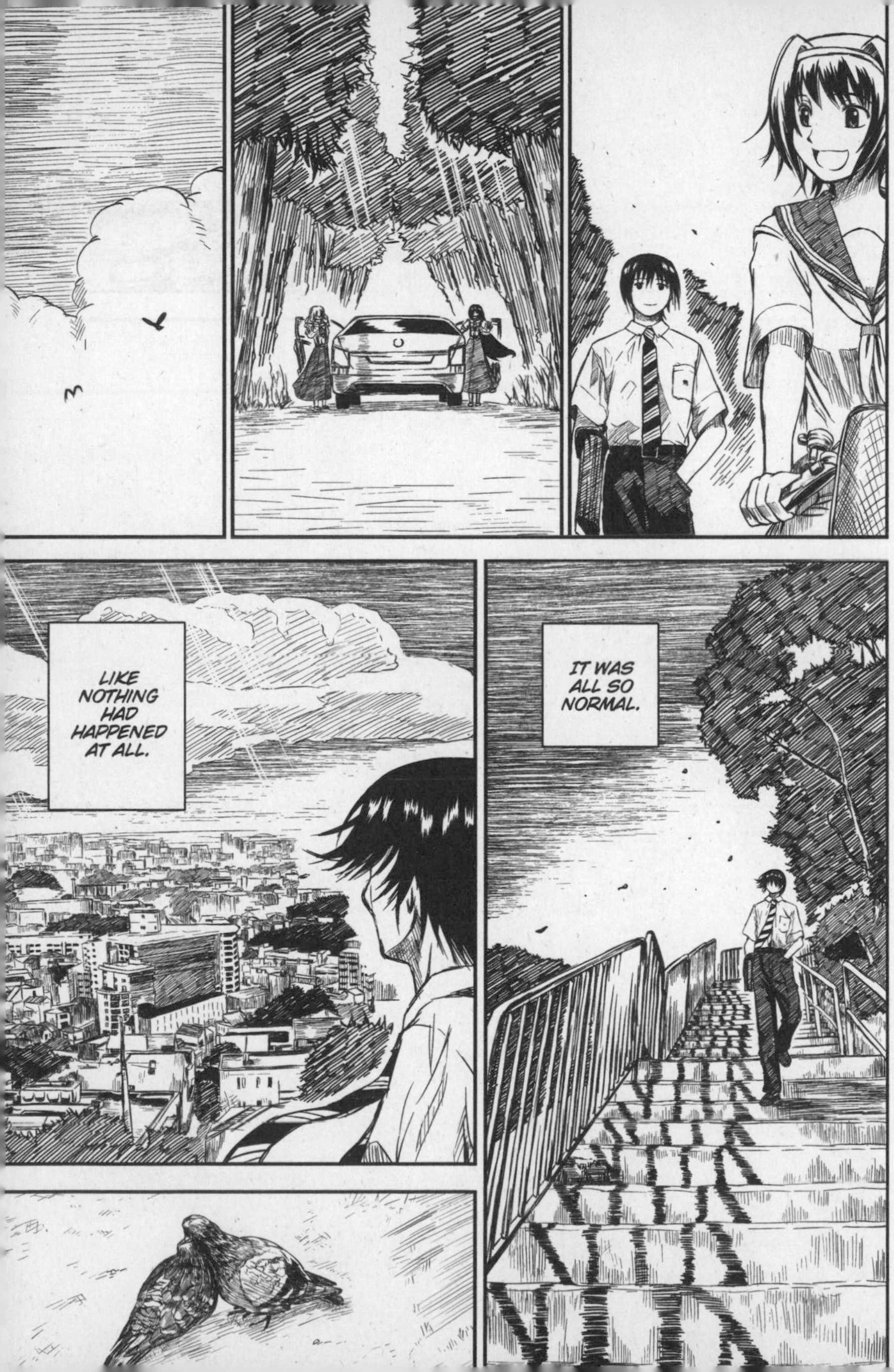
IT WAS ALL SO NORMAL.
LIKE NOTHING HAD HAPPENED AT ALL.

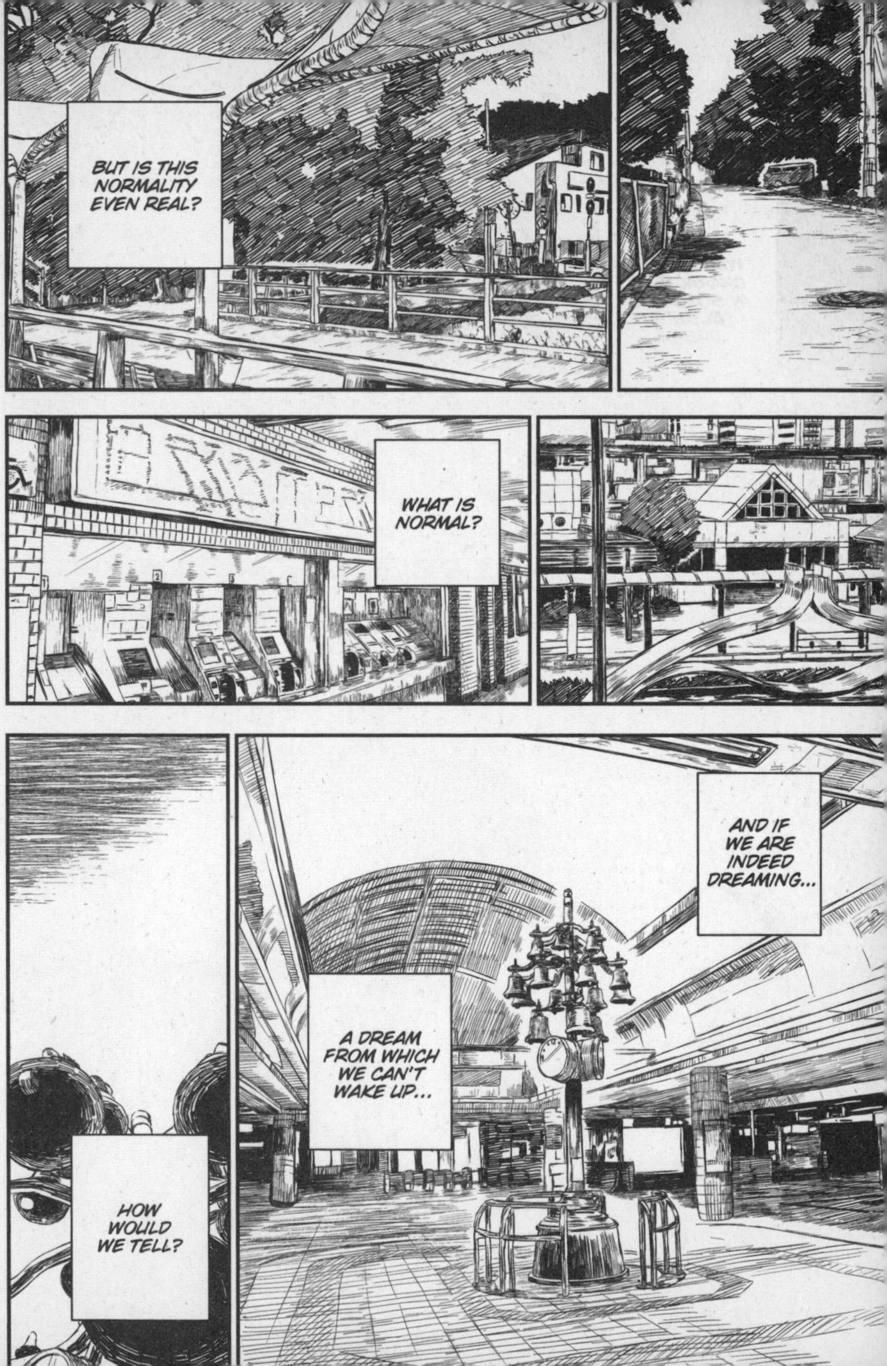
BUT IS THIS NORMALITY EVEN REAL?
WHAT IS NORMAL?
AND IF WE ARE INDEED DREAMING...
A DREAM FROM WHICH WE CAN'T WAKE UP...
HOW WOULD WE TELL?

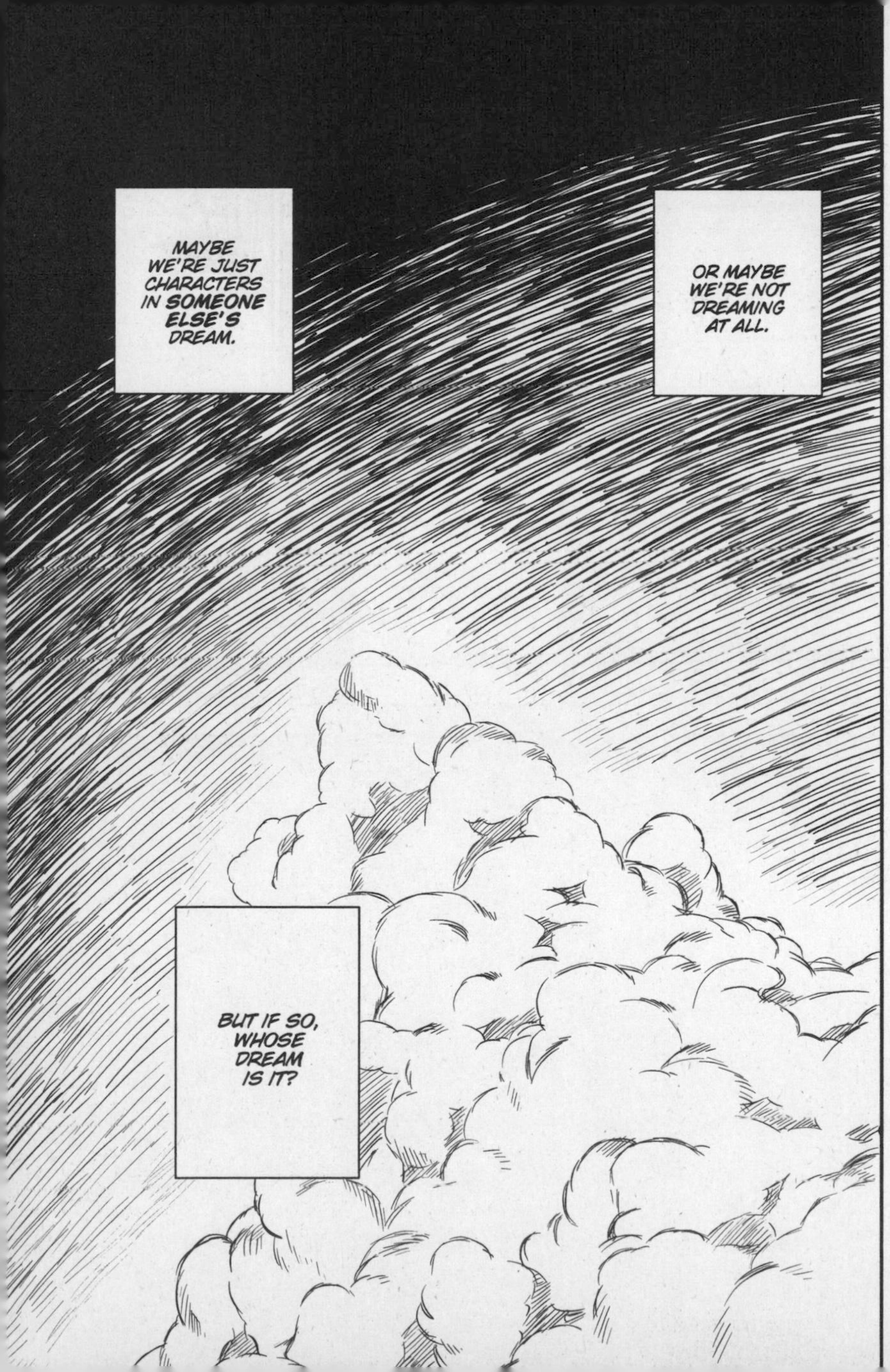
OR MAYBE WE'RE NOT DREAMING AT ALL.
MAYBE WE'RE JUST CHARACTERS IN SOMEONE ELSE'S DREAM.
BUT IF SO, WHOSE DREAM IS IT?

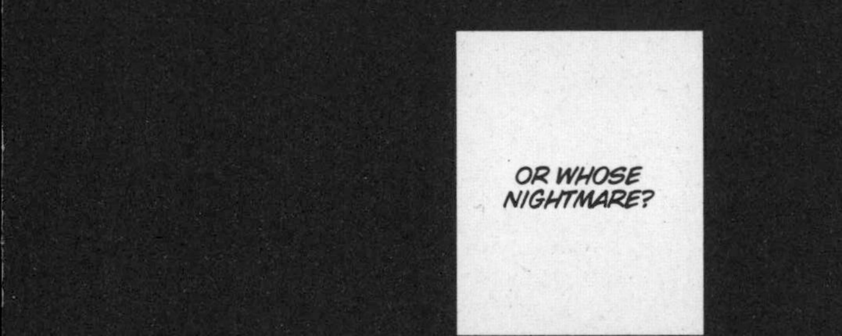
OR WHOSE NIGHTMARE?

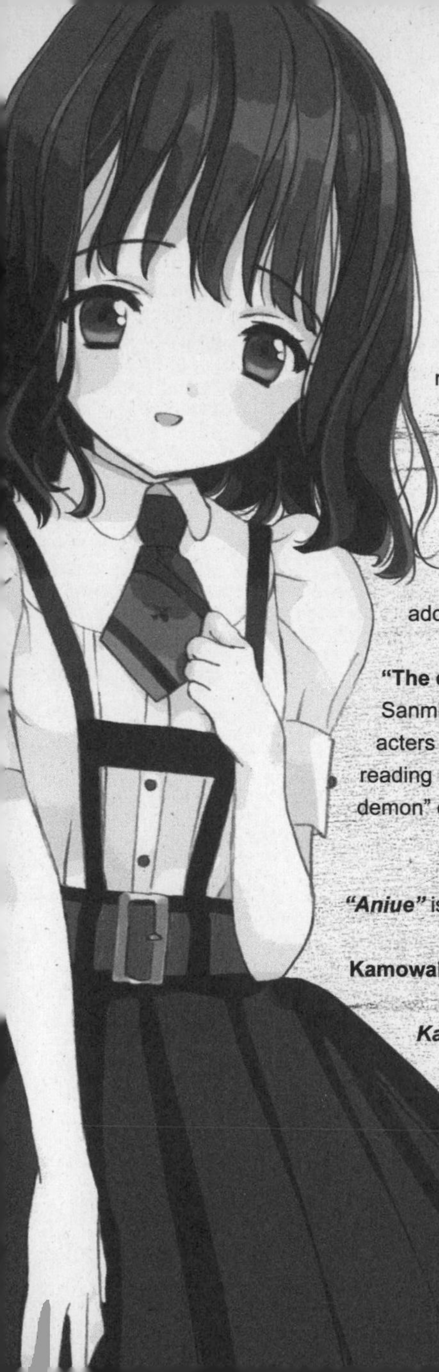

TRANSLATION NOTES

CHAPTER 5

Yakisoba Bread is a bread with fried noodles, and is apparently a popular snack at Souji and Yukako's school.

CHAPTER 7

Sanmi no Chujo – A noble who holds the third court rank during the Heian period (794 to 1185 AD). People are addressed by their titles rather than name.

"The demons that end suffering" – Here Sanmi no Chujo is commenting on the characters that make up the *Kushiki* name. A literal reading of the kanji can be "suffering ending demon" or "pain stopping ogre."

CHAPTER 8

"Aniue" is a very formal address for "brother."

Kamowake Ikazuchi is the *kami* (god) of thunder.

Kamiwatari is a phenomenon that occurs when the surface of hot springs ice over, creating pressure ridges due to the low pressure, warm water underneath.

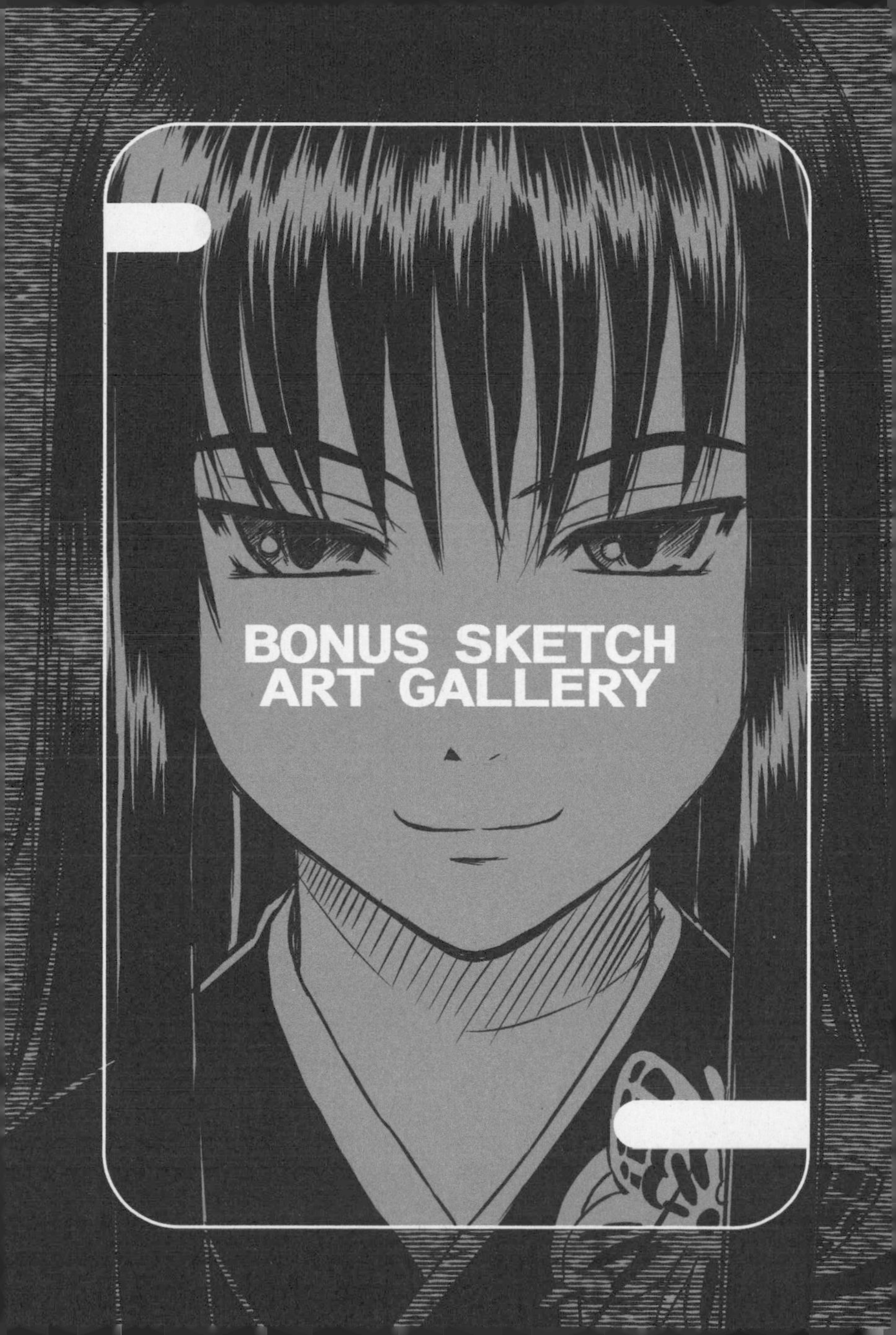
BONUS SKETCH
ART GALLERY

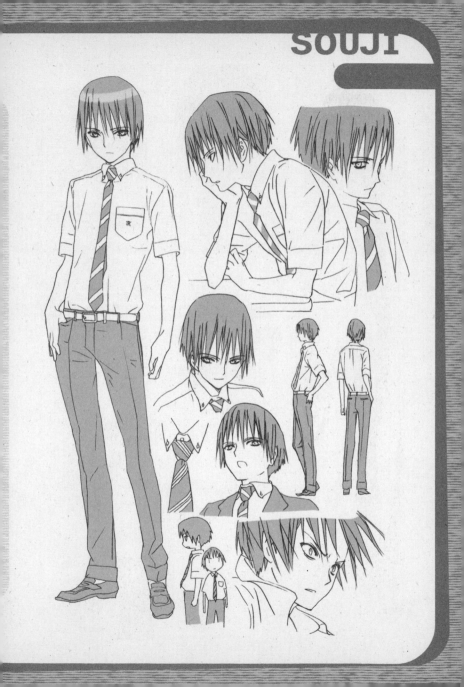

SOUJI

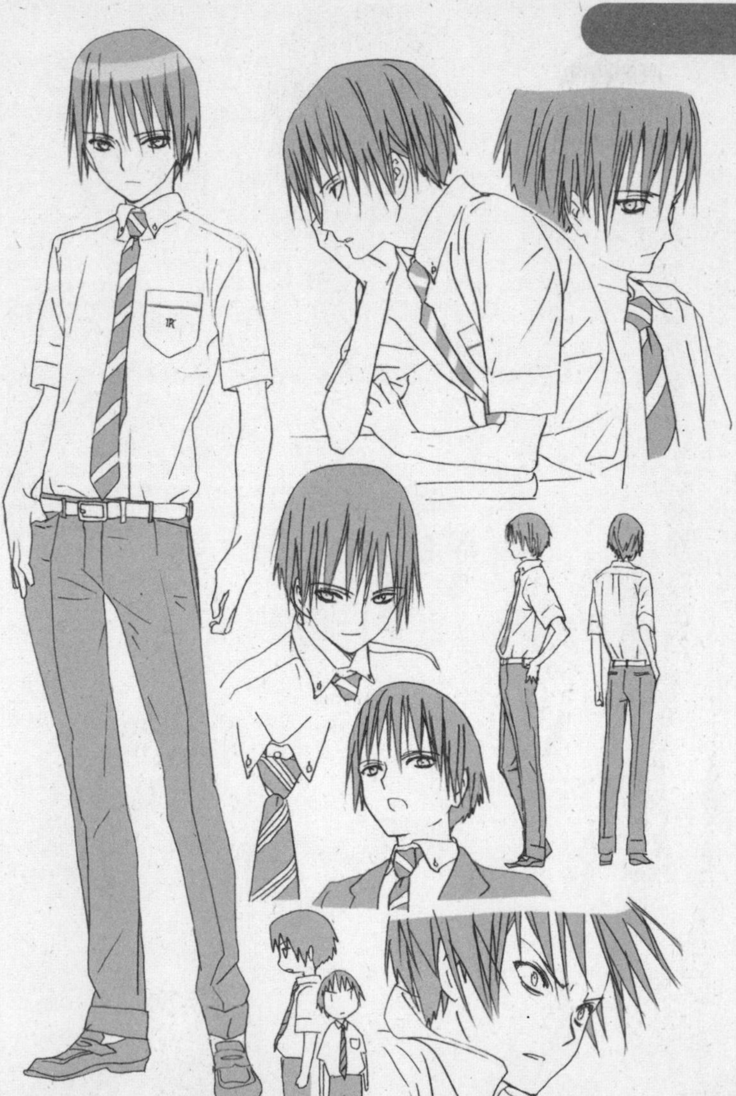

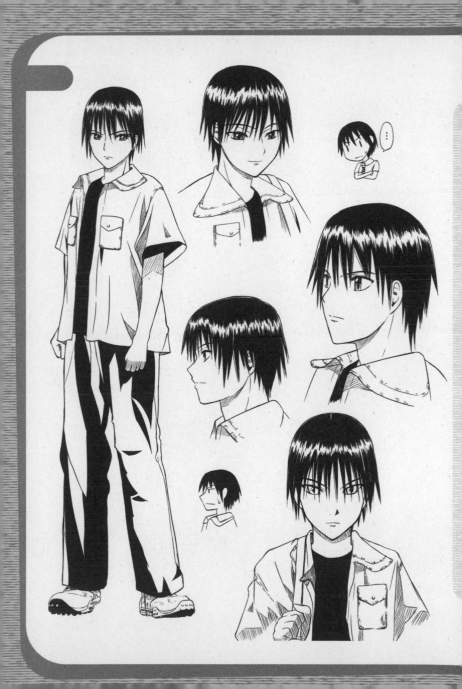

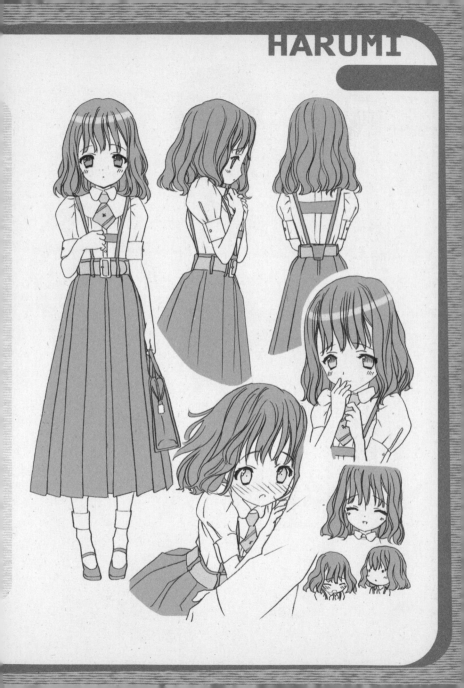

HARUMI

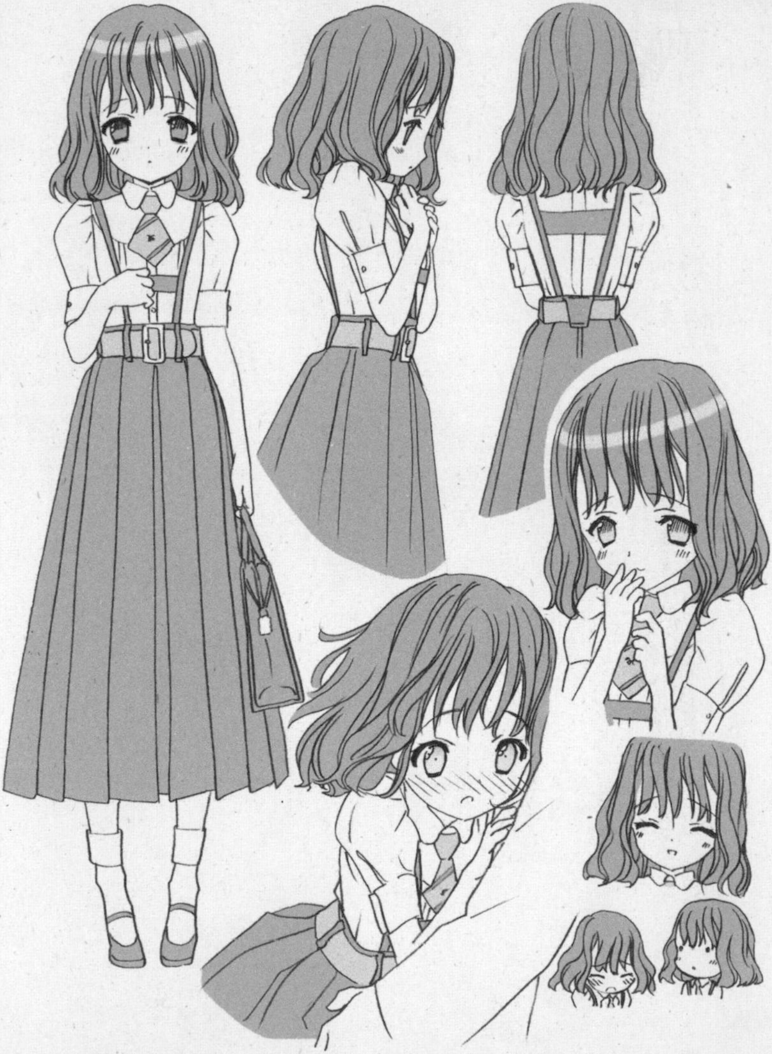

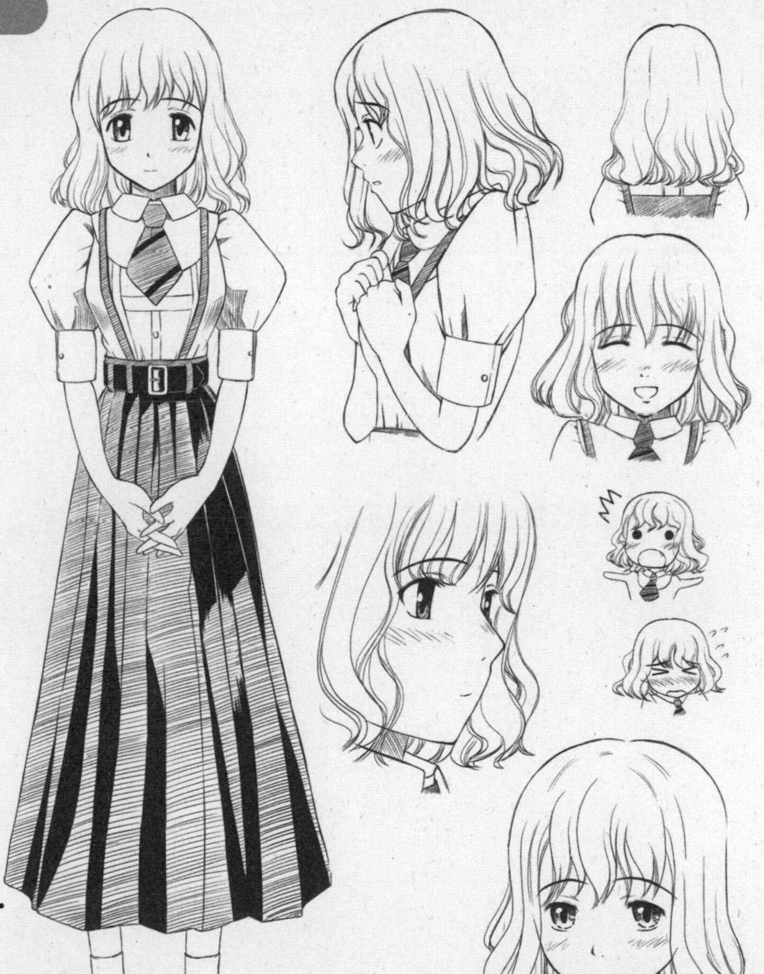

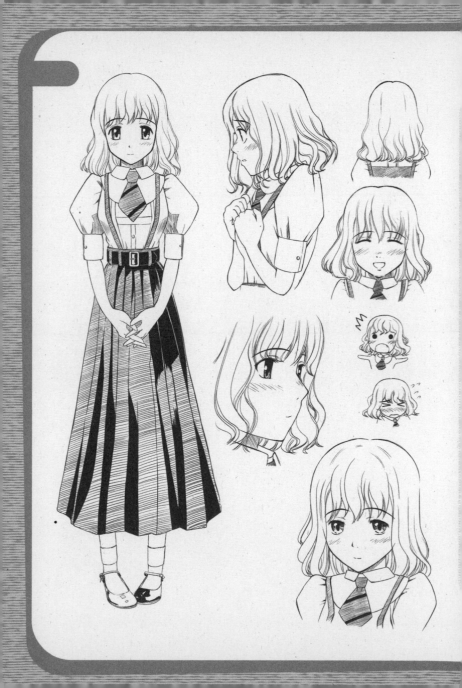

SASAI

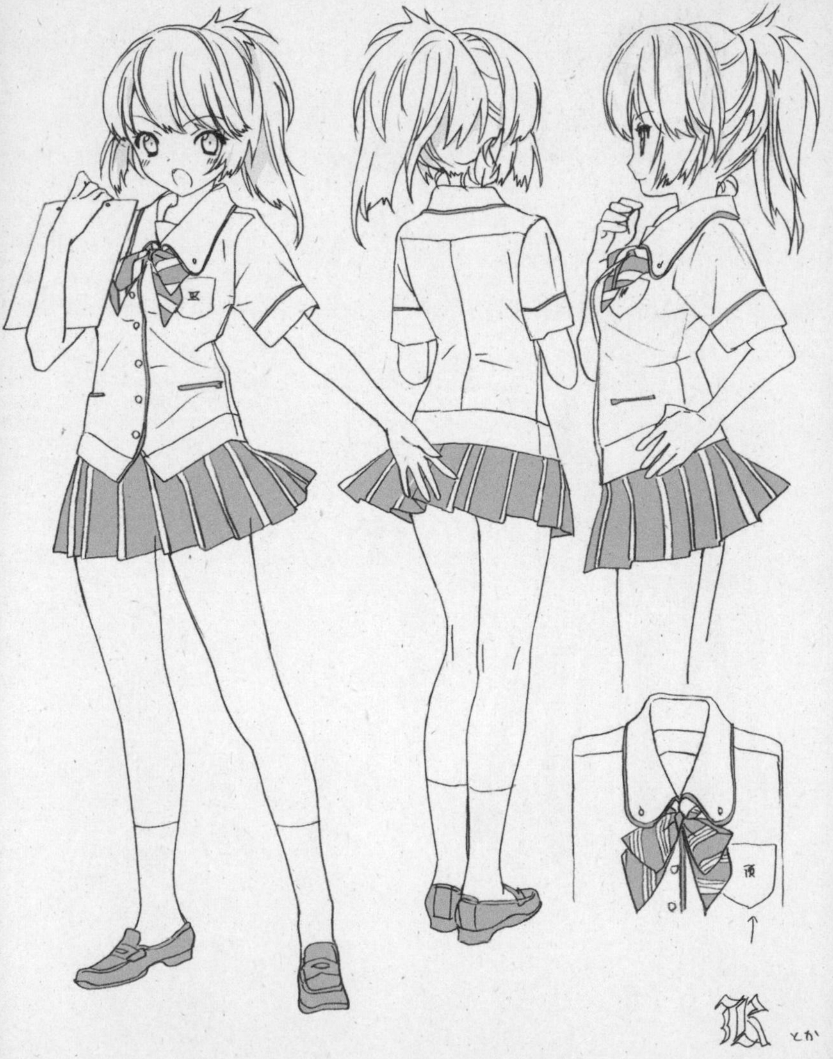
とか

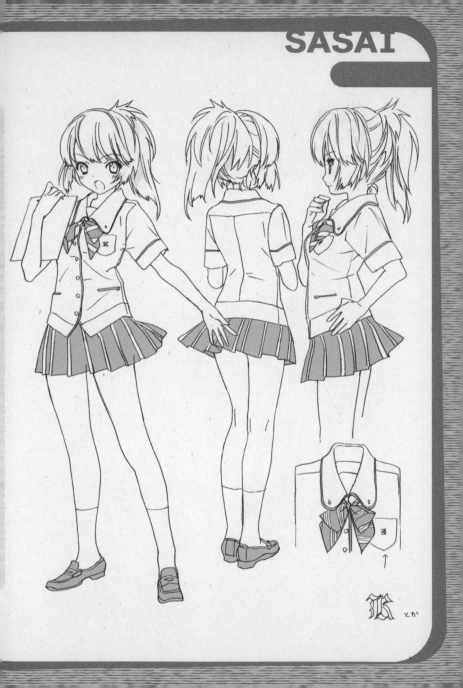

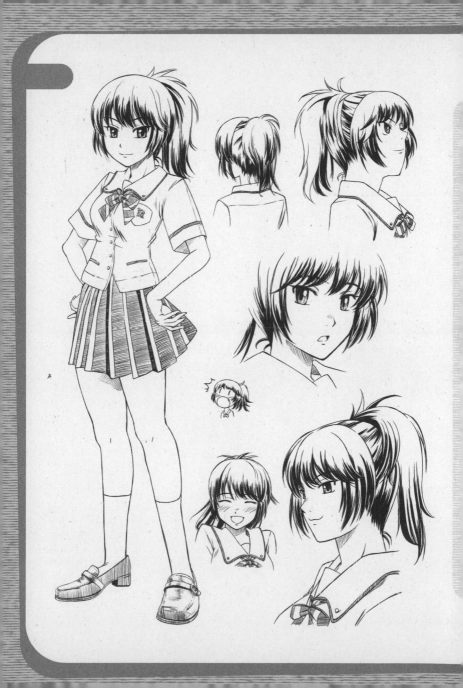

SASAI

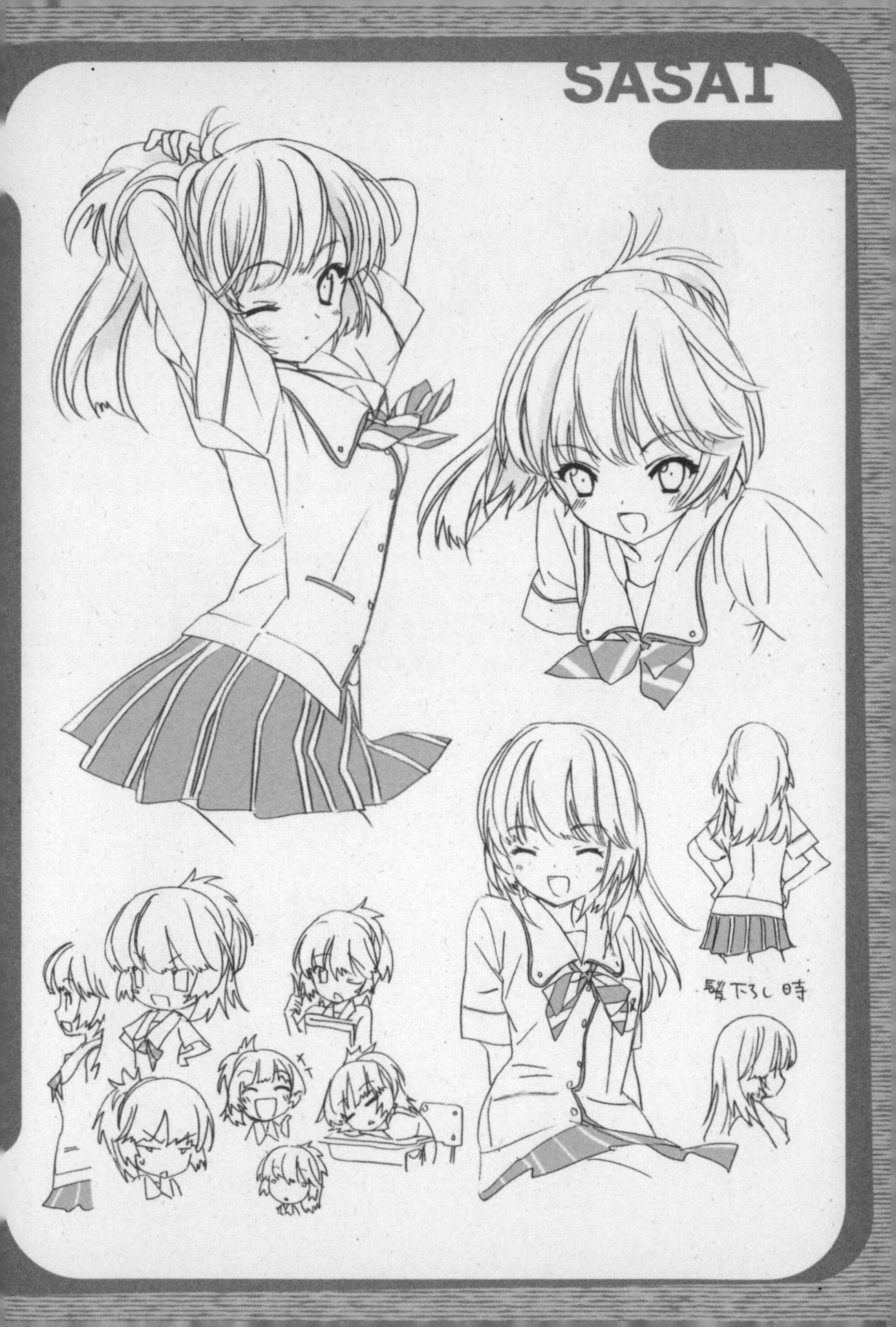
髪下ろし時

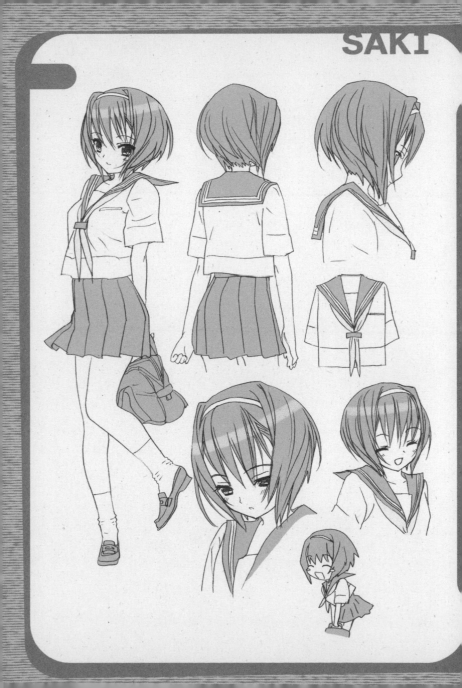

SAKI

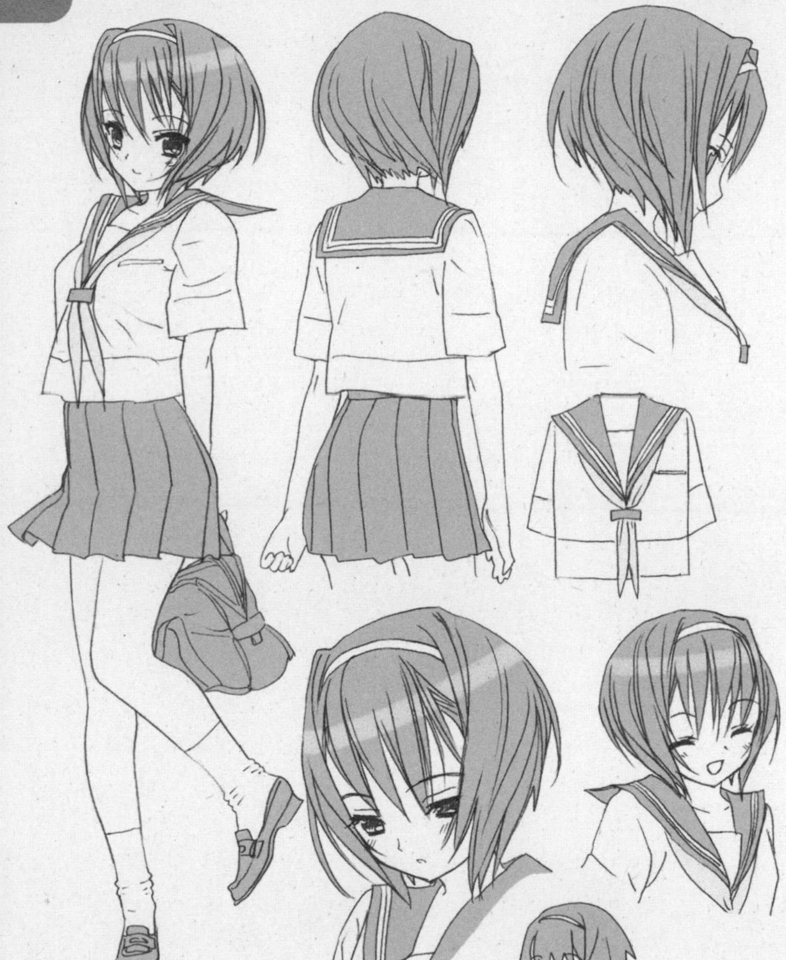

SAKI

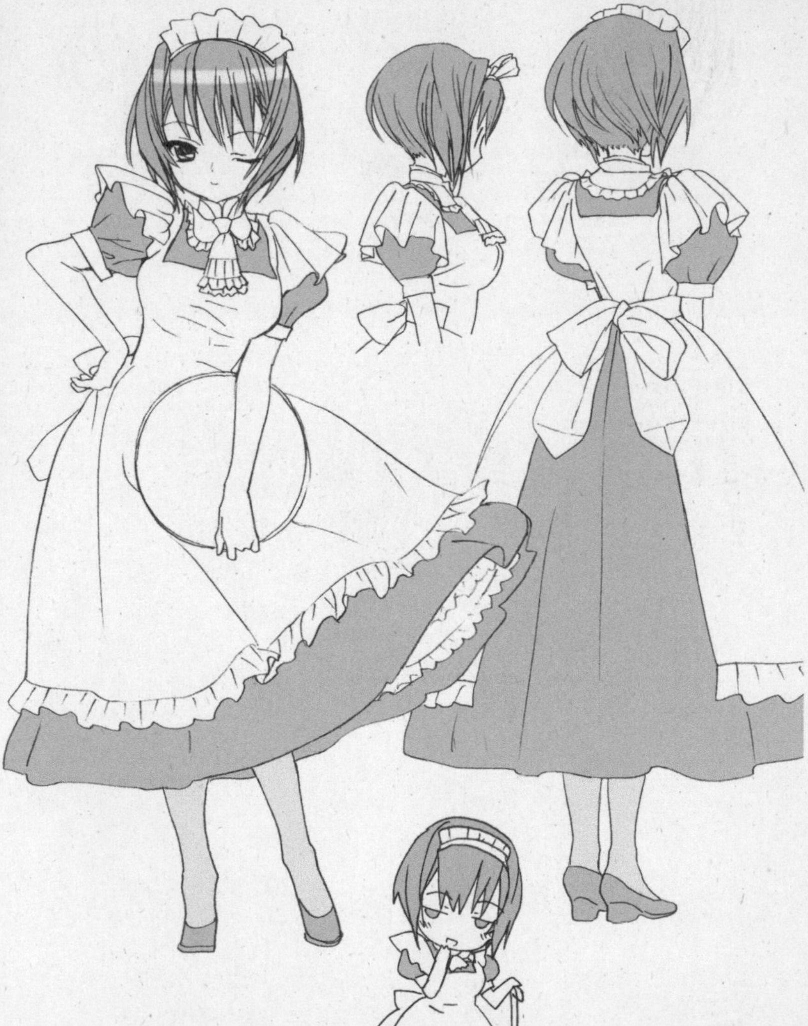

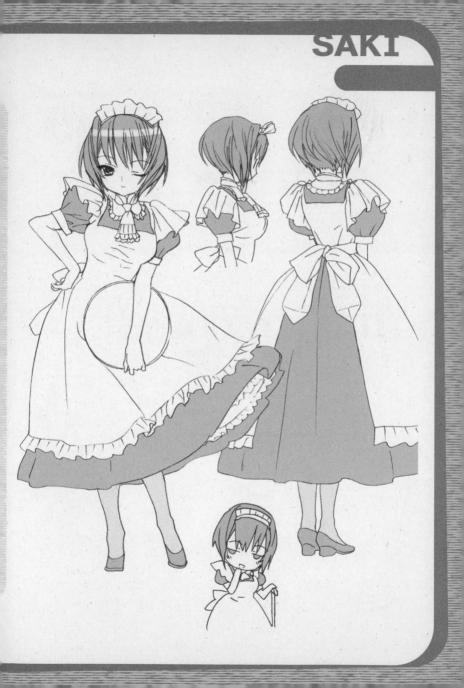

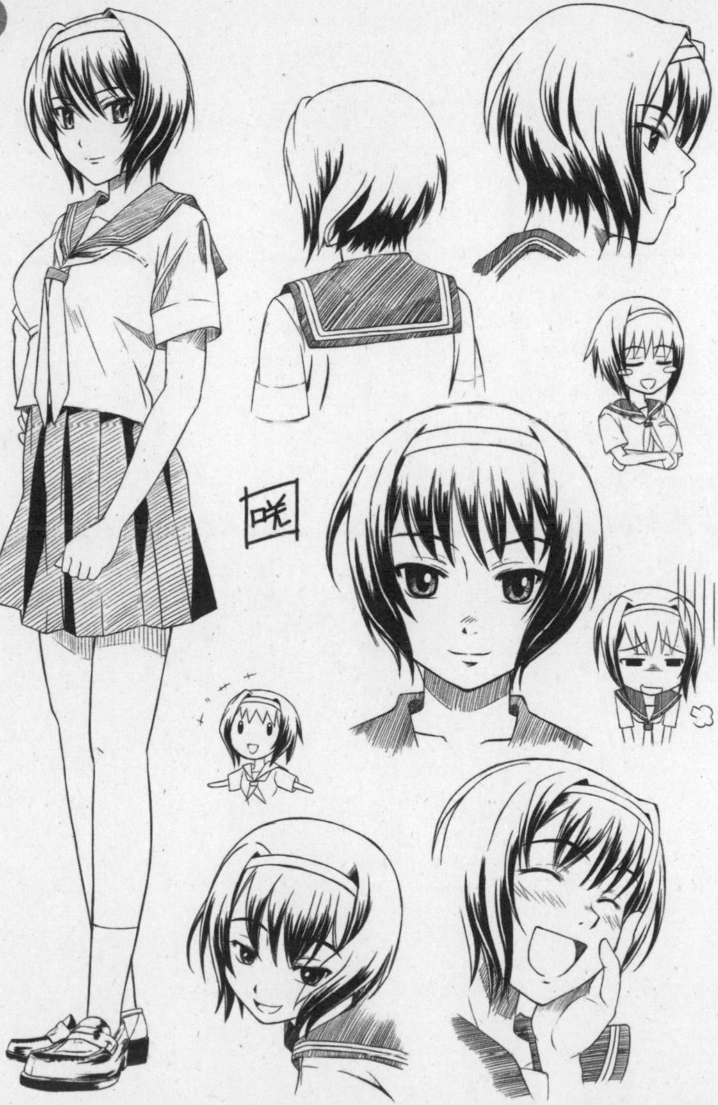
咲

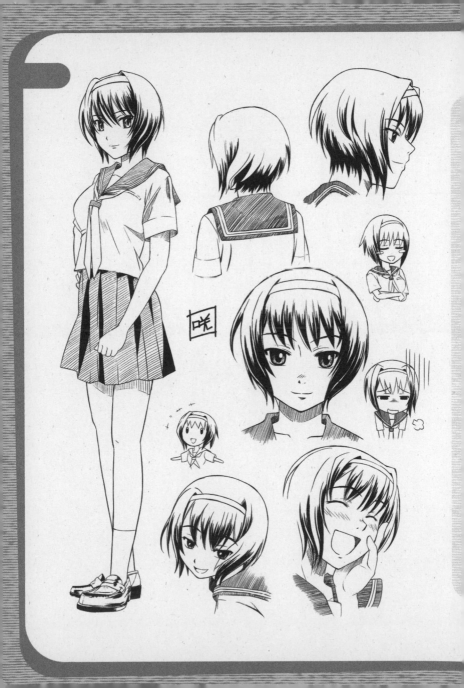

YOUKO

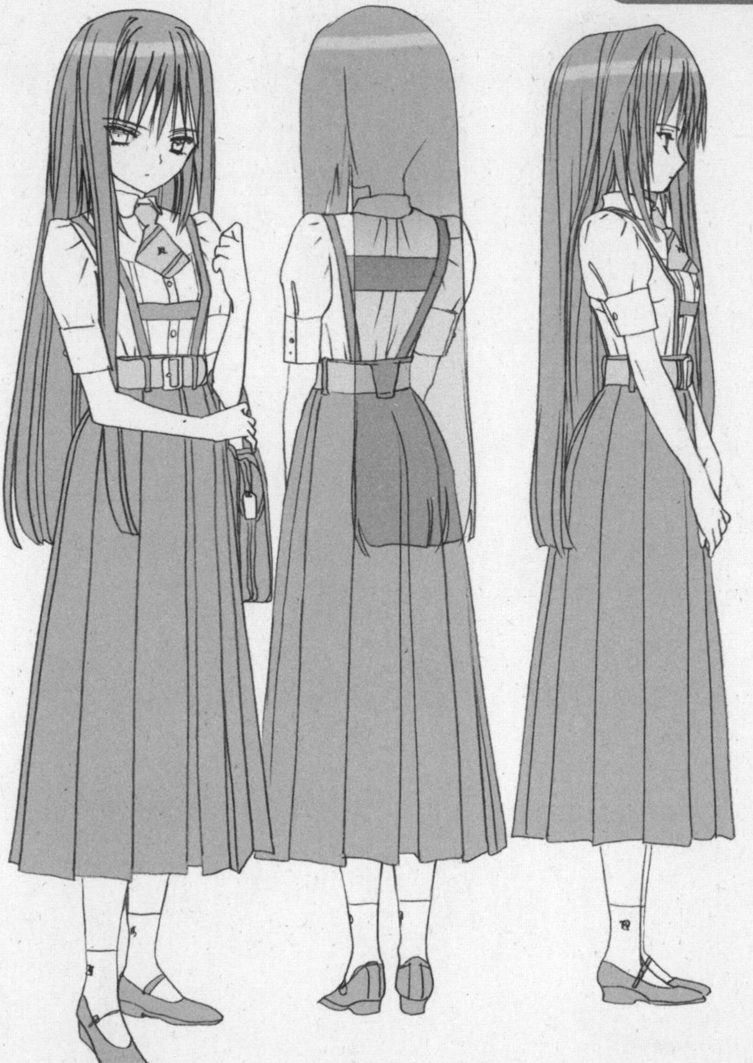

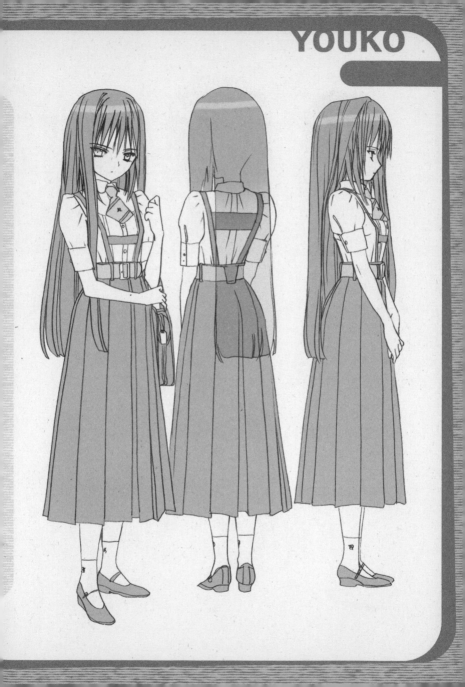

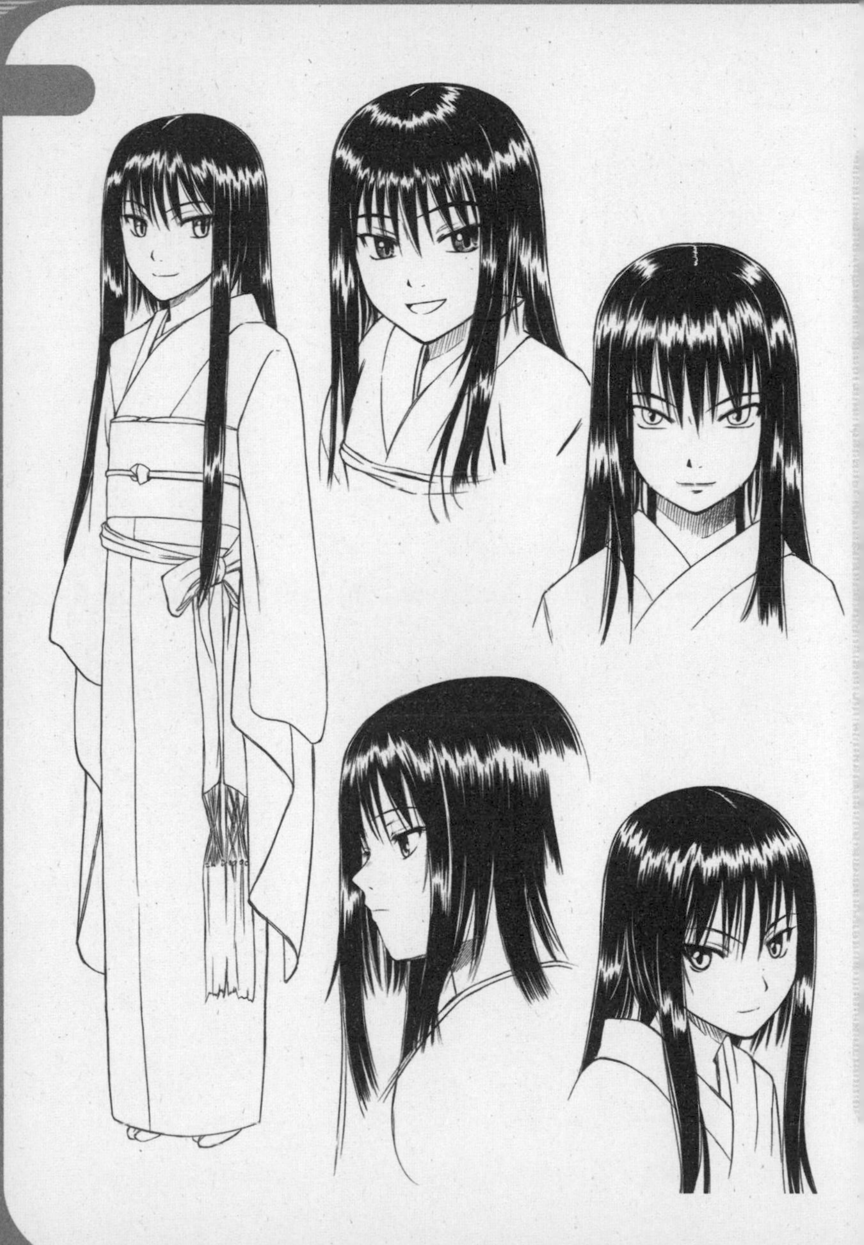

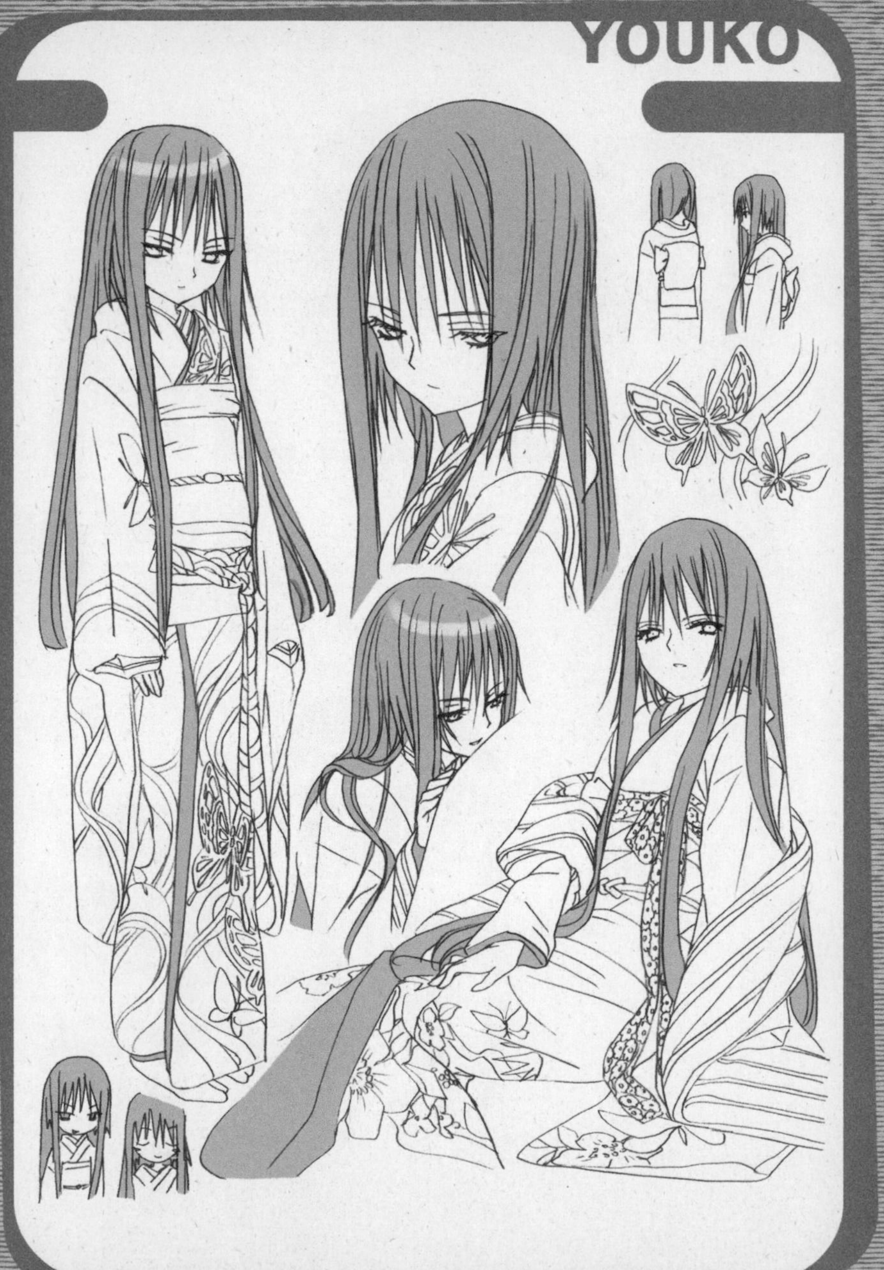
YOUKO

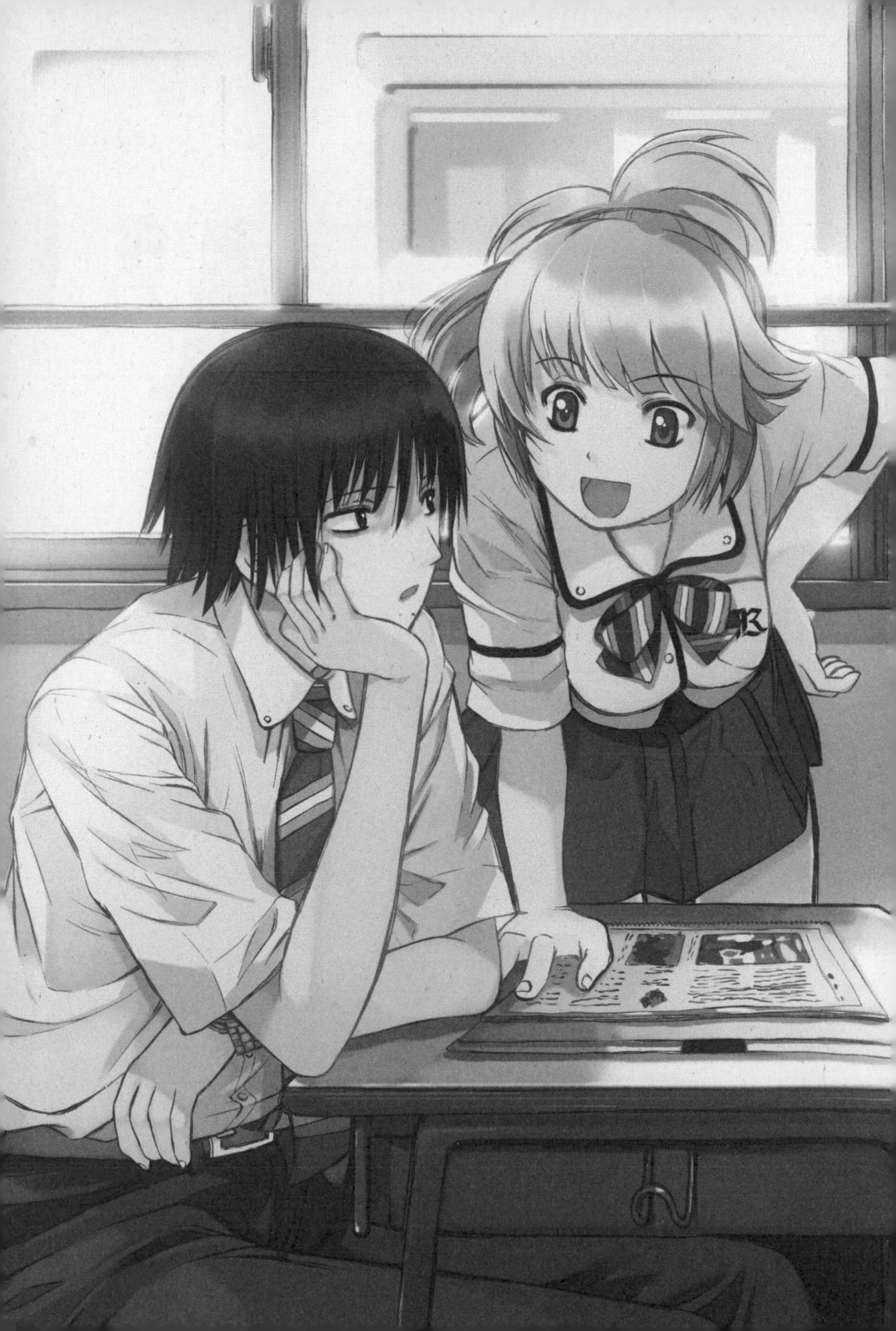

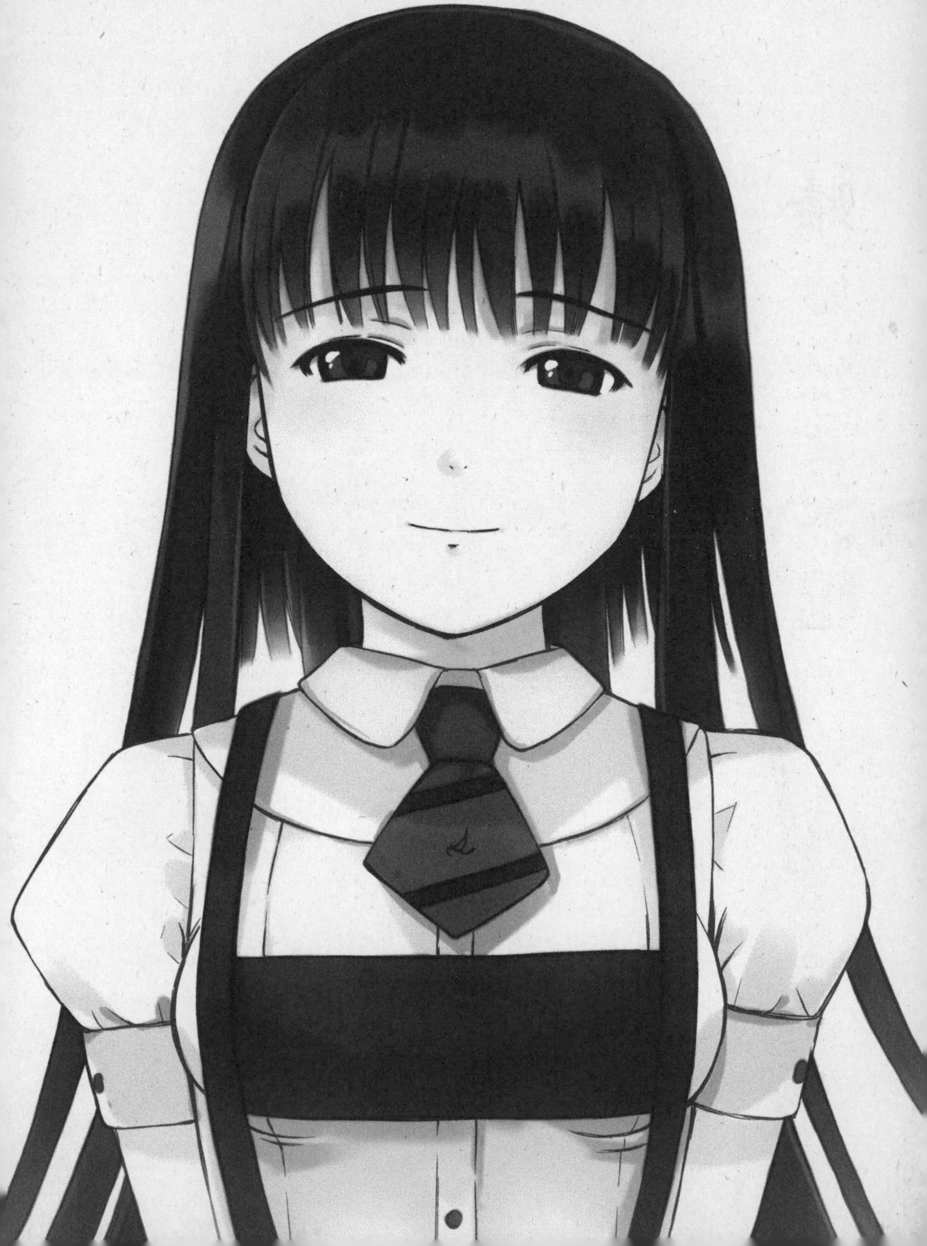

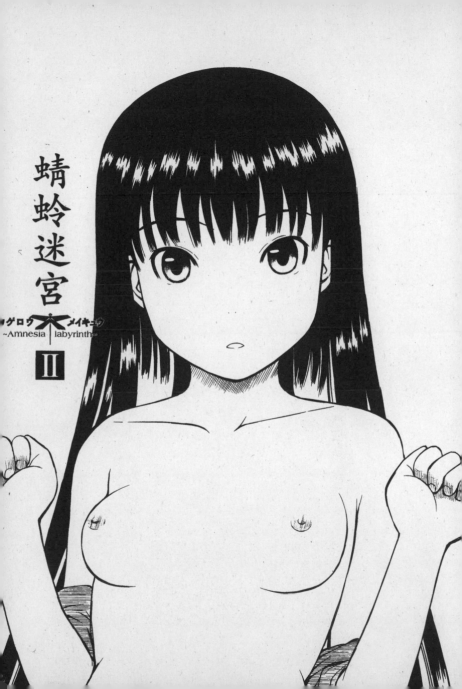

蜻蛉迷宮
～Amnesia labyrinth～
II

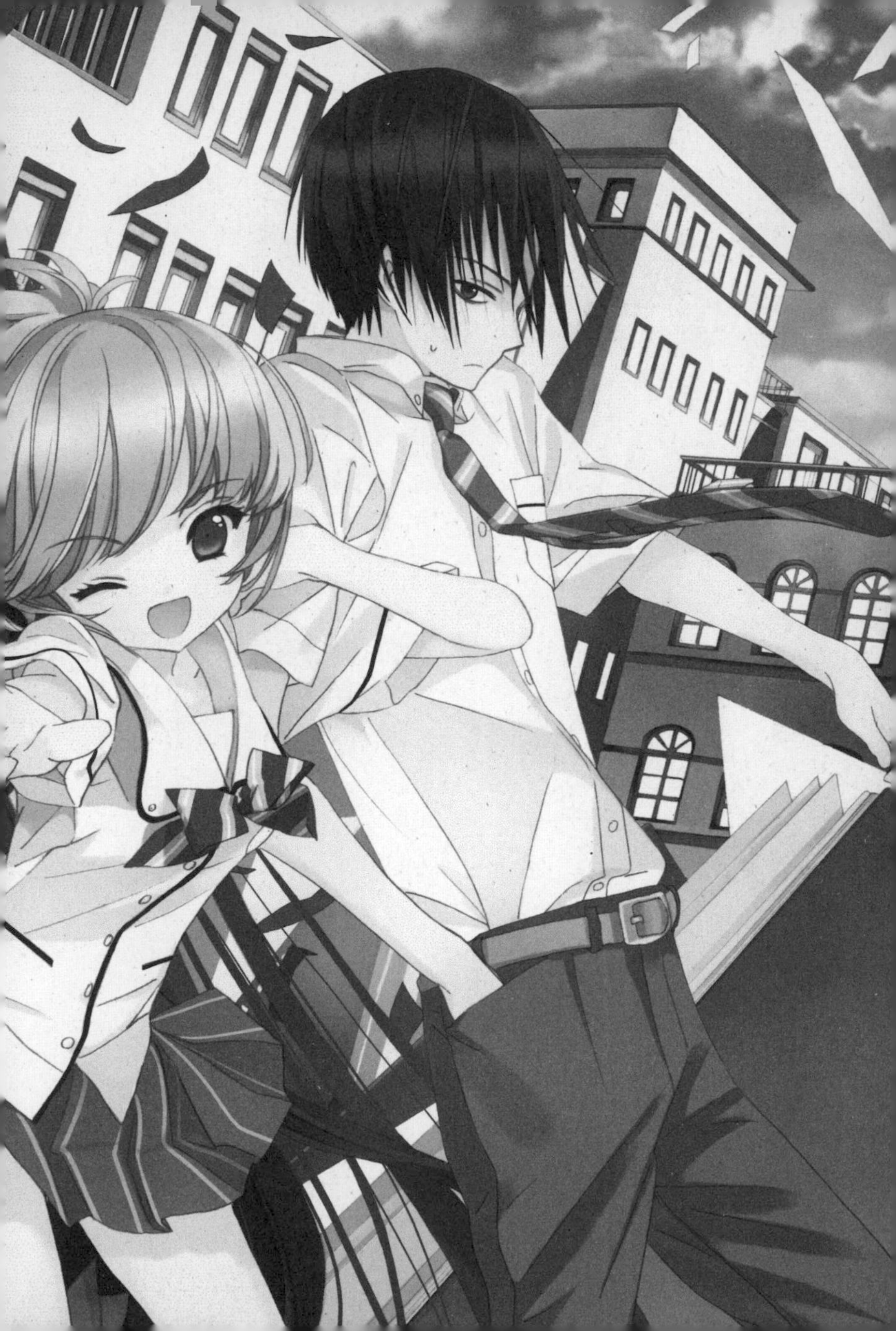

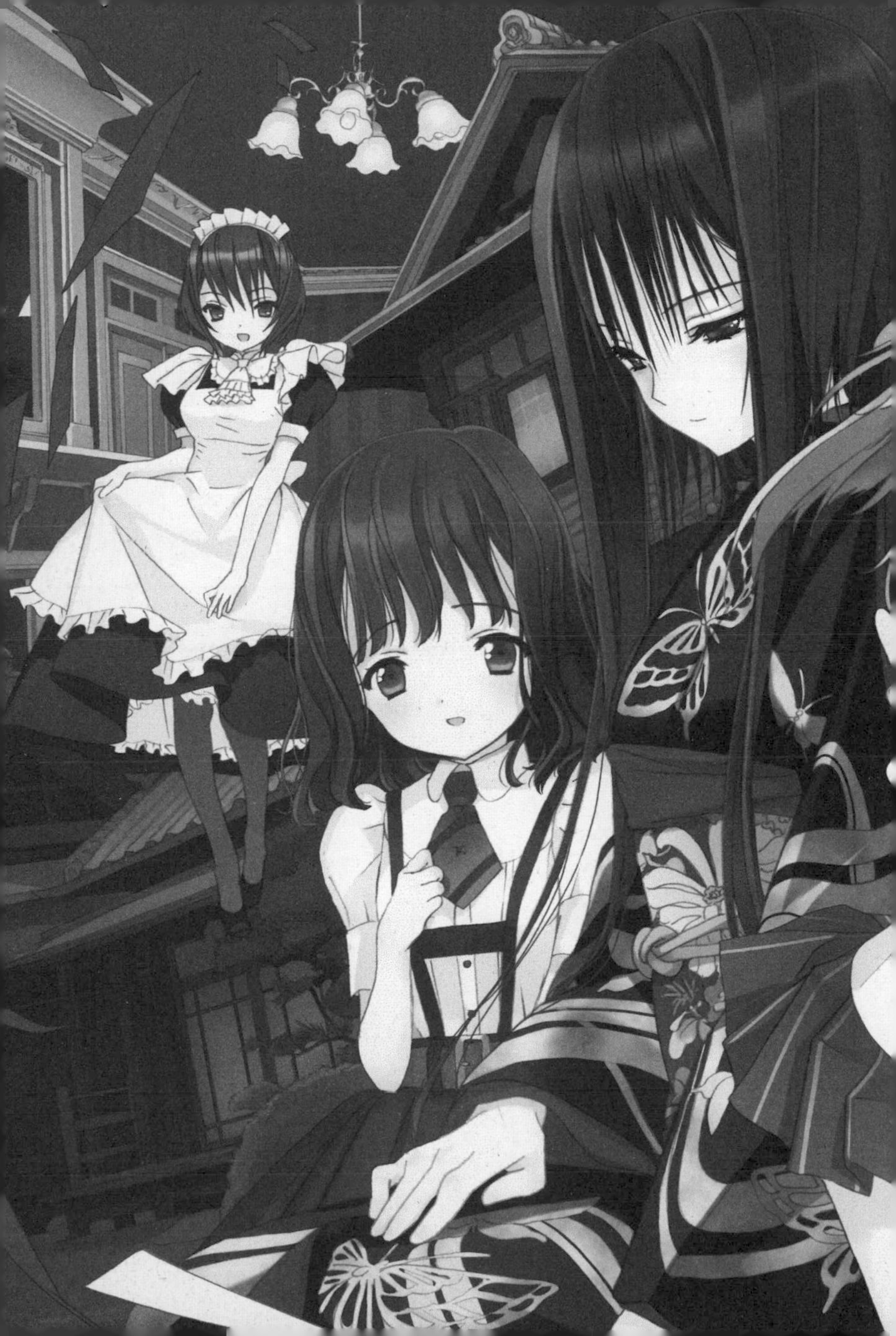

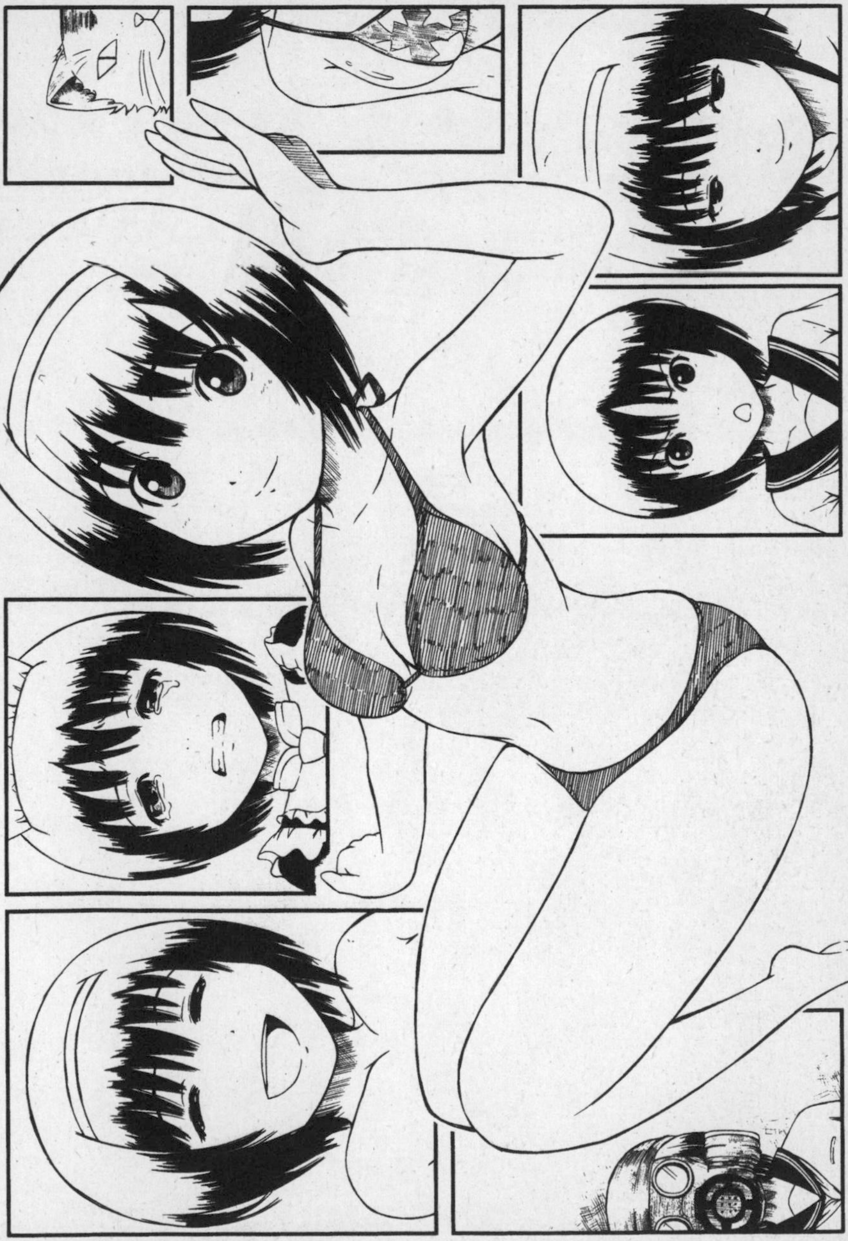

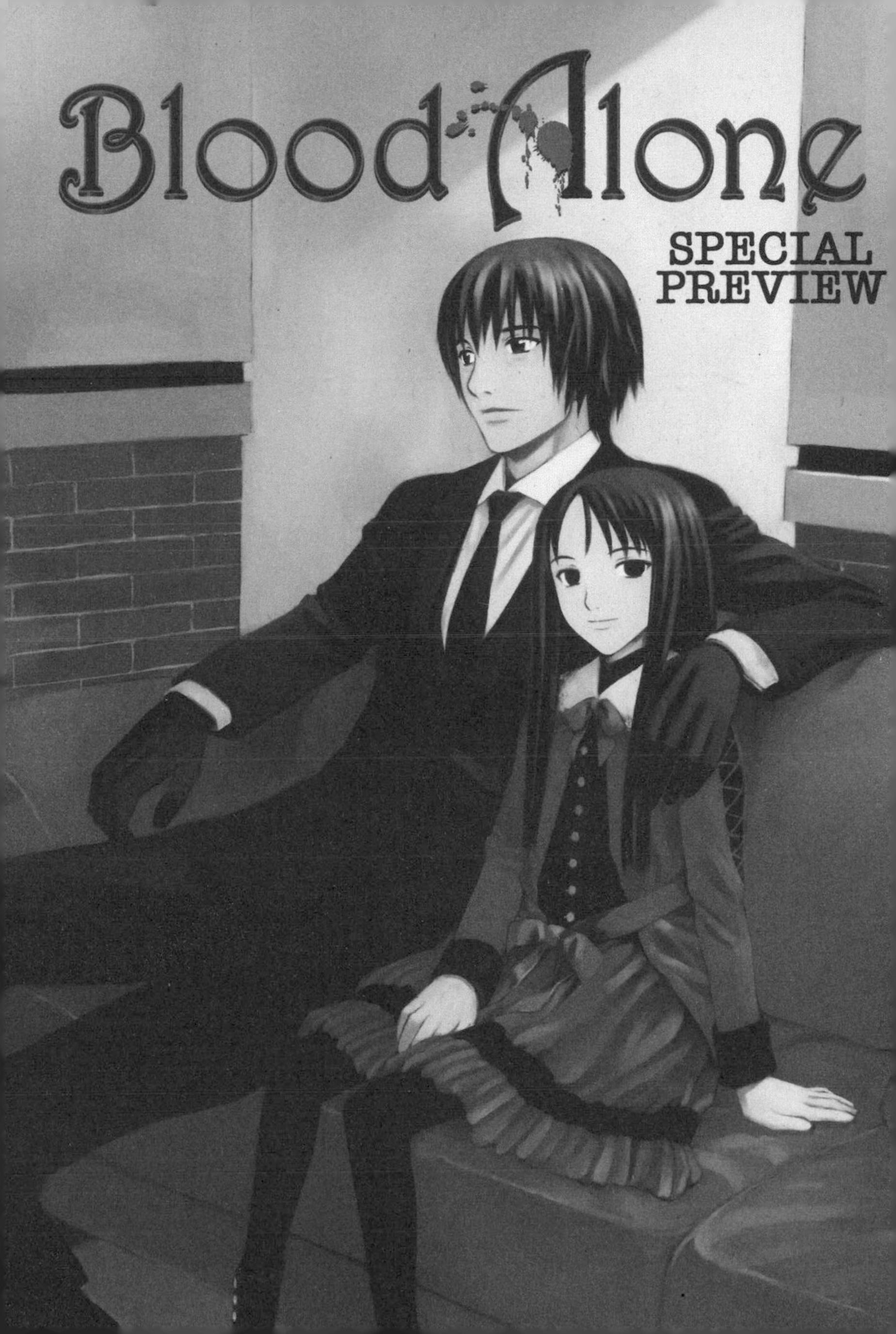
Blood Alone
SPECIAL PREVIEW

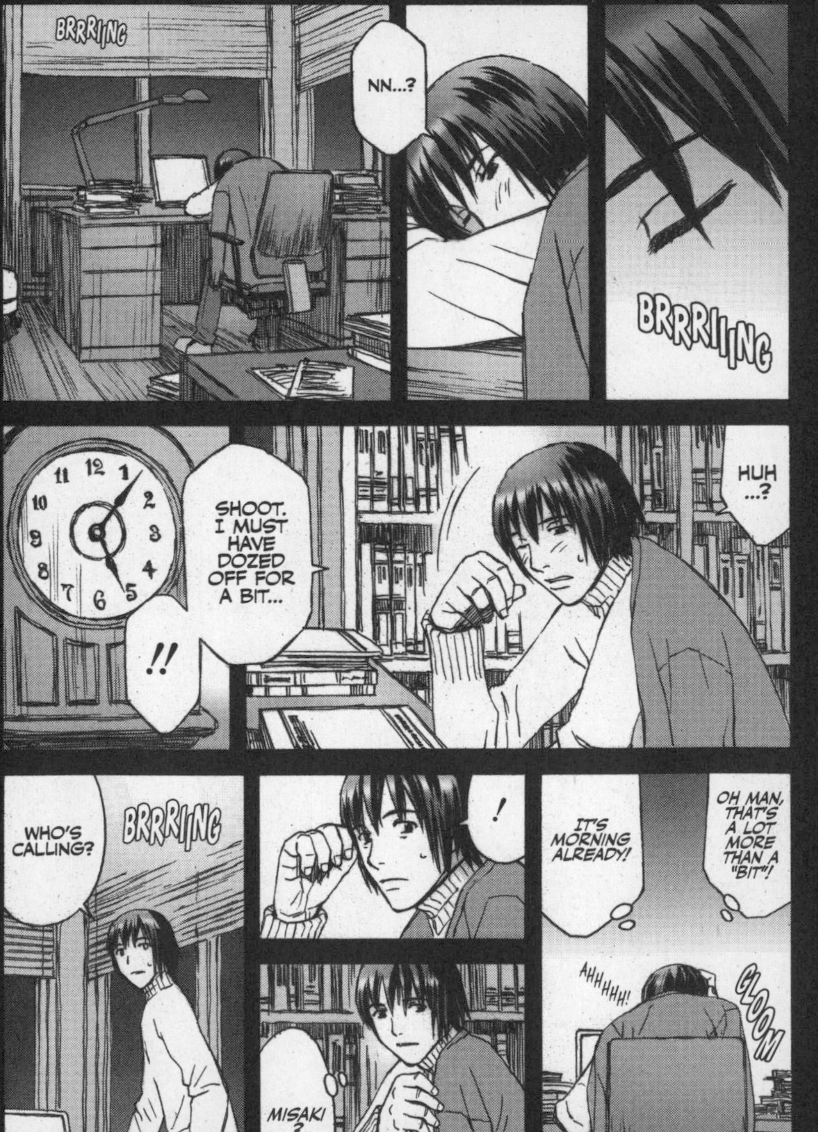
BRRRIIING
NN...?
BRRRIING
HUH ...?
SHOOT. I MUST HAVE DOZED OFF FOR A BIT...
!!
OH MAN, THAT'S A LOT MORE THAN A "BIT"!
IT'S MORNING ALREADY!
AHHHHHH!
GLOOM
!
MISAKI ?
BRRRIING
WHO'S CALLING?

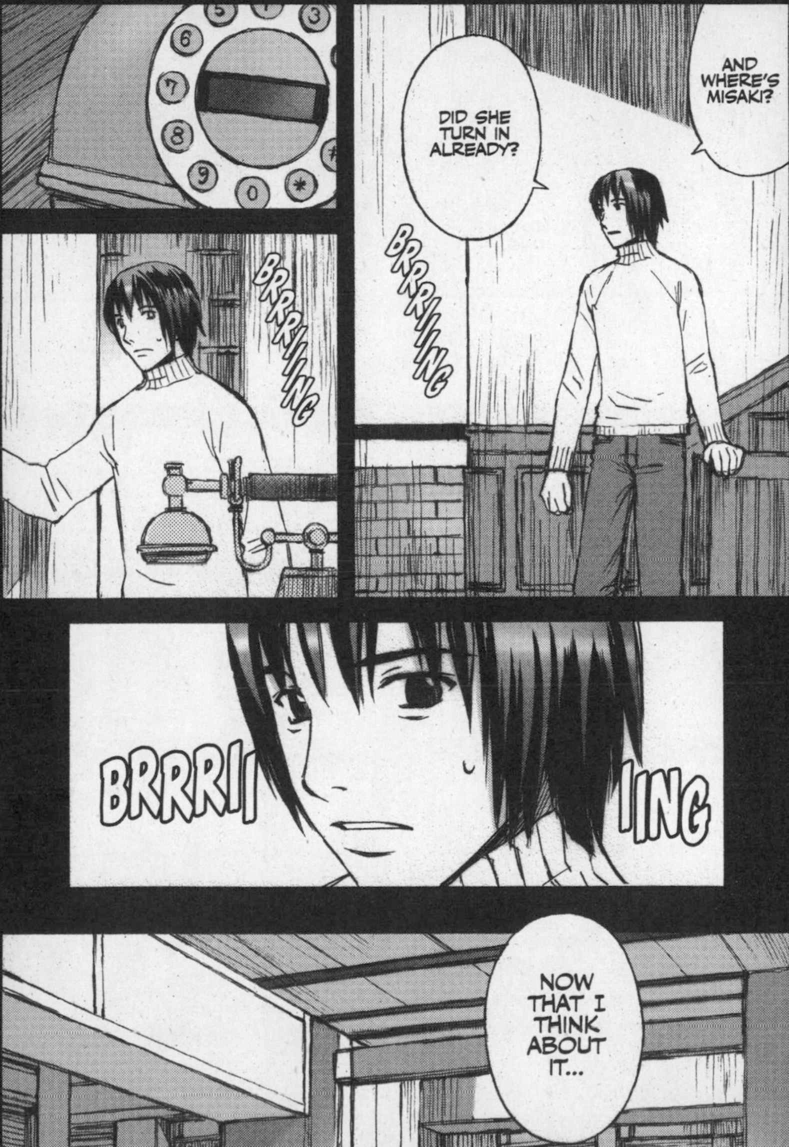
AND WHERE'S MISAKI?
DID SHE TURN IN ALREADY?
BRRRIIING
BRRRIIING
BRRRIIIING
NOW THAT I THINK ABOUT IT...

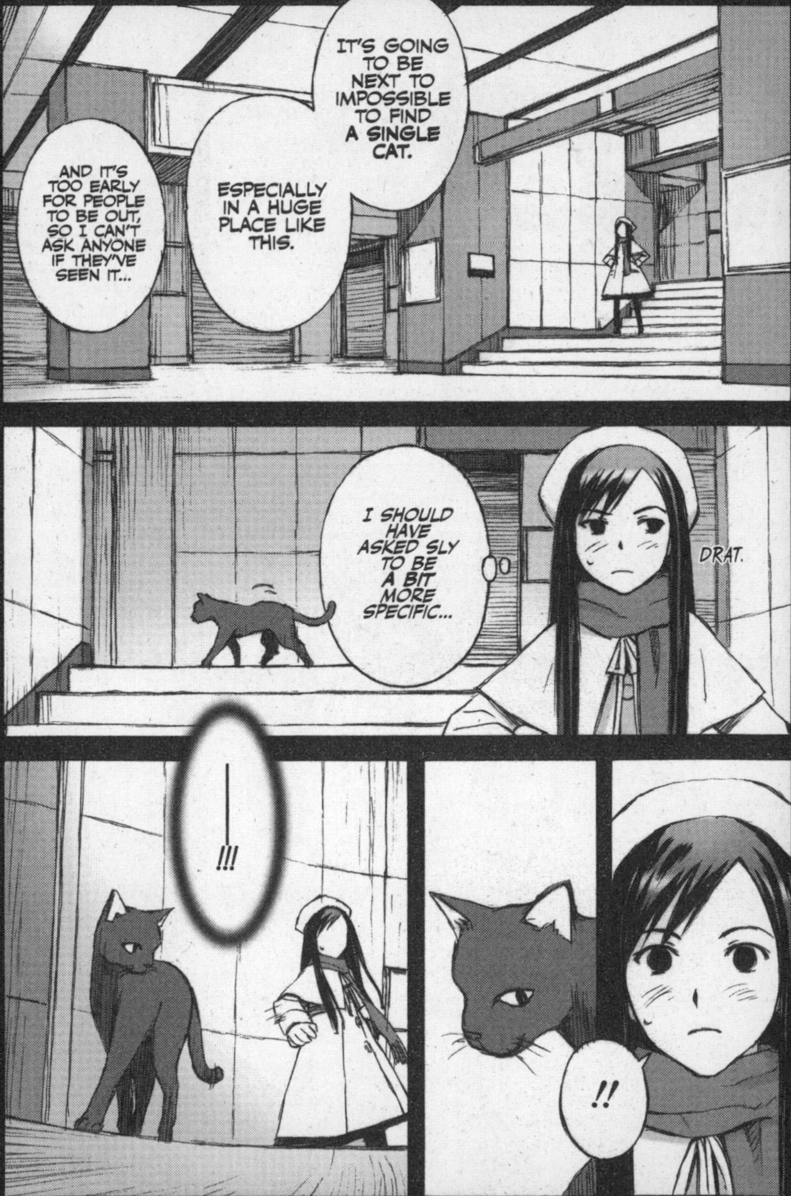
IT'S GOING TO BE NEXT TO IMPOSSIBLE TO FIND A SINGLE CAT.
ESPECIALLY IN A HUGE PLACE LIKE THIS.
AND IT'S TOO EARLY FOR PEOPLE TO BE OUT, SO I CAN'T ASK ANYONE IF THEY'VE SEEN IT...
DRAT.
I SHOULD HAVE ASKED SLY TO BE A BIT MORE SPECIFIC...
!!
—!!!

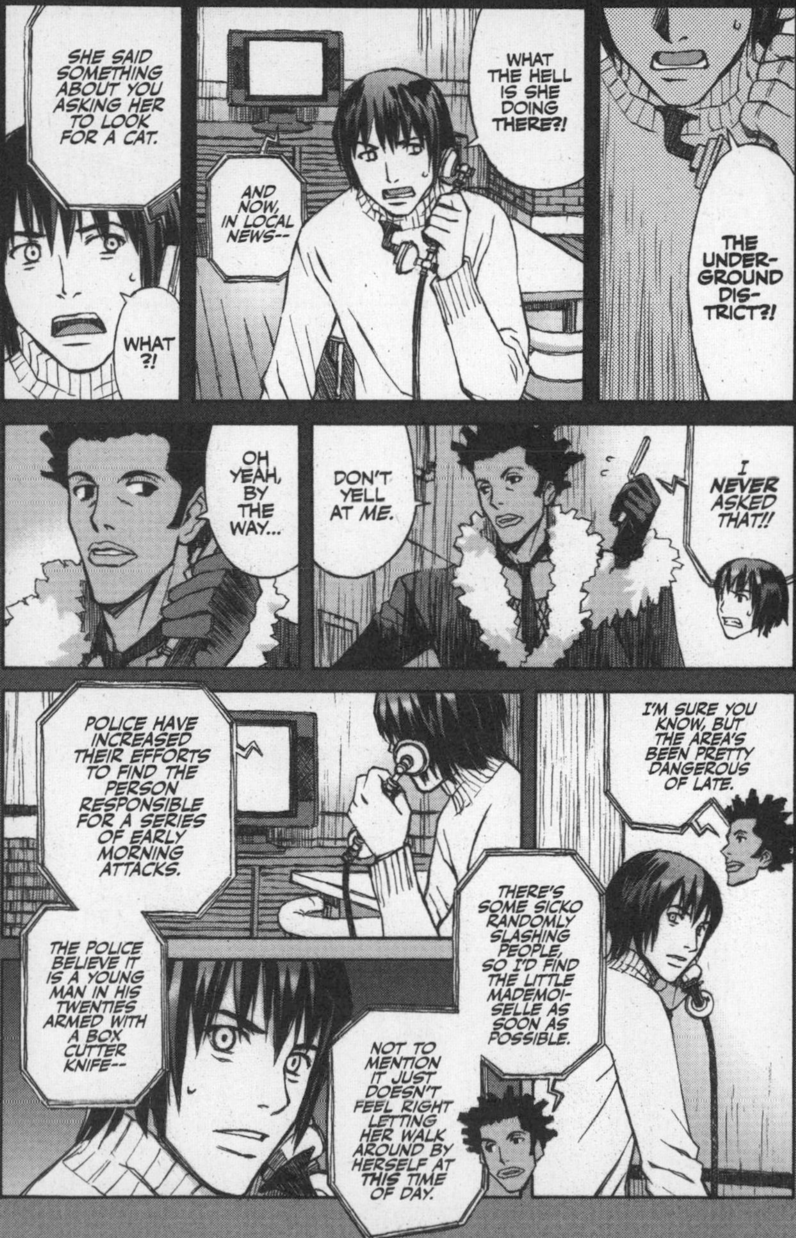
THE UNDER-GROUND DIS-TRICT?!
WHAT THE HELL IS SHE DOING THERE?!
AND NOW, IN LOCAL NEWS--
SHE SAID SOMETHING ABOUT YOU ASKING HER TO LOOK FOR A CAT.
WHAT ?!
I NEVER ASKED THAT!!
DON'T YELL AT ME.
OH YEAH, BY THE WAY...
I'M SURE YOU KNOW, BUT THE AREA'S BEEN PRETTY DANGEROUS OF LATE.
THERE'S SOME SICKO RANDOMLY SLASHING PEOPLE, SO I'D FIND THE LITTLE MADEMOI-SELLE AS SOON AS POSSIBLE.
NOT TO MENTION IT JUST DOESN'T FEEL RIGHT LETTING HER WALK AROUND BY HERSELF AT THIS TIME OF DAY.
POLICE HAVE INCREASED THEIR EFFORTS TO FIND THE PERSON RESPONSIBLE FOR A SERIES OF EARLY MORNING ATTACKS.
THE POLICE BELIEVE IT IS A YOUNG MAN IN HIS TWENTIES ARMED WITH A BOX CUTTER KNIFE--

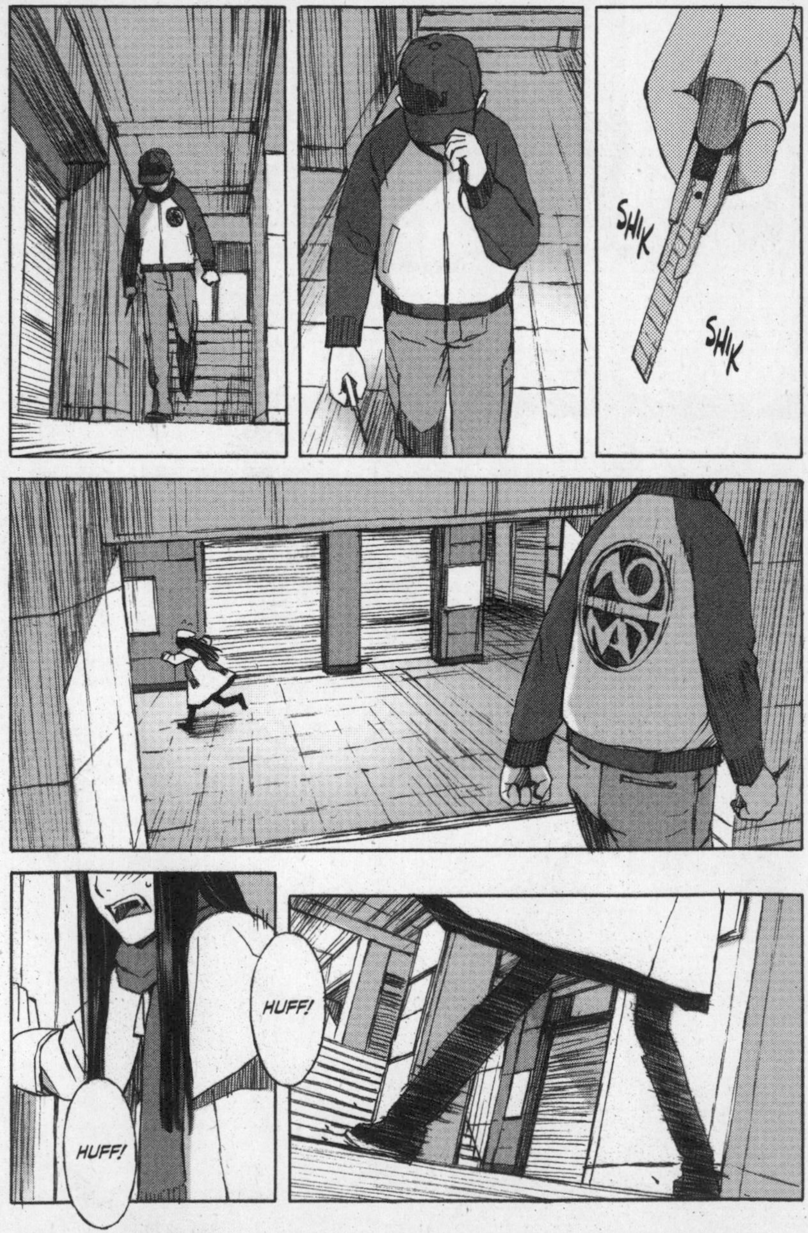
SHIK
SHIK
HUFF!
HUFF!

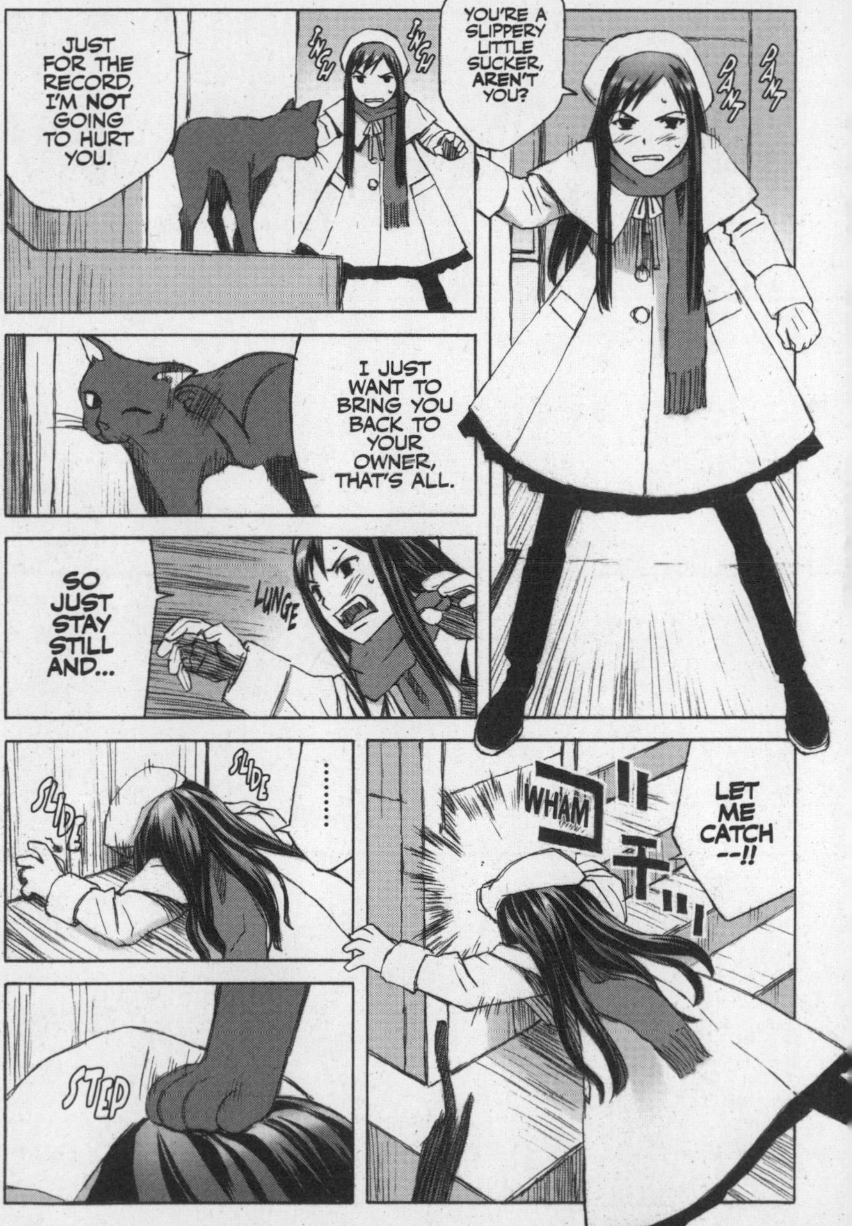
YOU'RE A SLIPPERY LITTLE SUCKER, AREN'T YOU?
PANT PANT
INCH INCH
JUST FOR THE RECORD, I'M NOT GOING TO HURT YOU.
I JUST WANT TO BRING YOU BACK TO YOUR OWNER, THAT'S ALL.
LUNGE
SO JUST STAY STILL AND...
LET ME CATCH --!!
WHAM
......
SLIDE
SLIDE
STEP

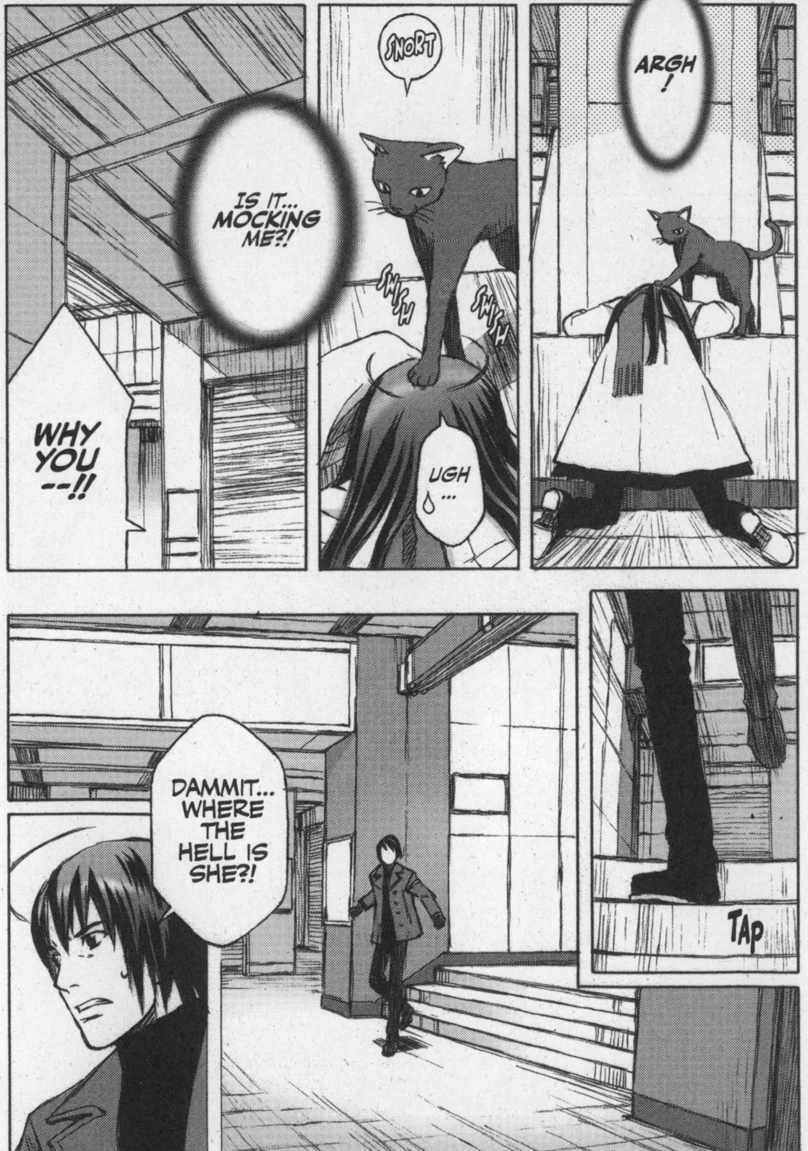
ARGH !
SNORT
IS IT... MOCKING ME?!
SWISH
SWISH
UGH ...
WHY YOU --!!
TAP
DAMMIT... WHERE THE HELL IS SHE?!

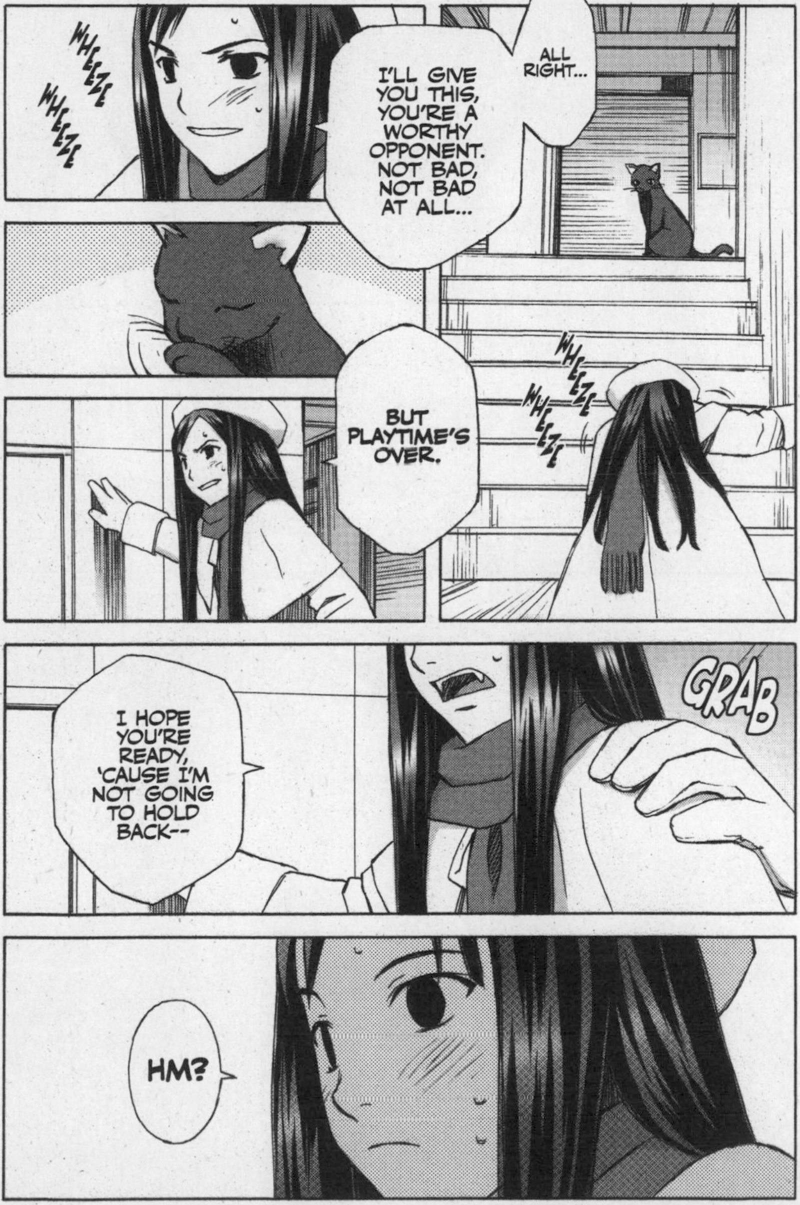
ALL RIGHT...
WHEEZE WHEEZE
WHEEZE WHEEZE
I'LL GIVE YOU THIS, YOU'RE A WORTHY OPPONENT. NOT BAD, NOT BAD AT ALL...
BUT PLAYTIME'S OVER.
GRAB
I HOPE YOU'RE READY, 'CAUSE I'M NOT GOING TO HOLD BACK--
HM?

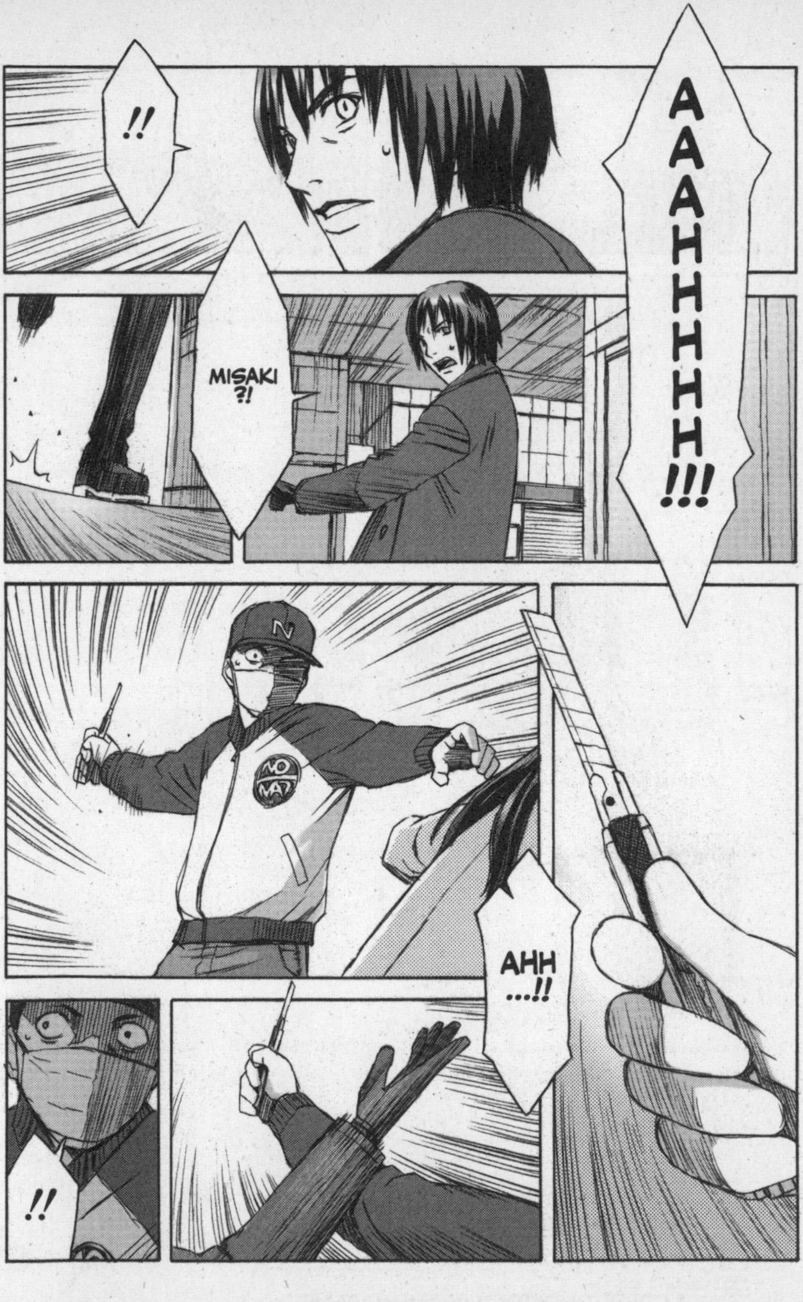
AAAHHHHHH!!!
!!
MISAKI ?!
AHH ...!!
!!

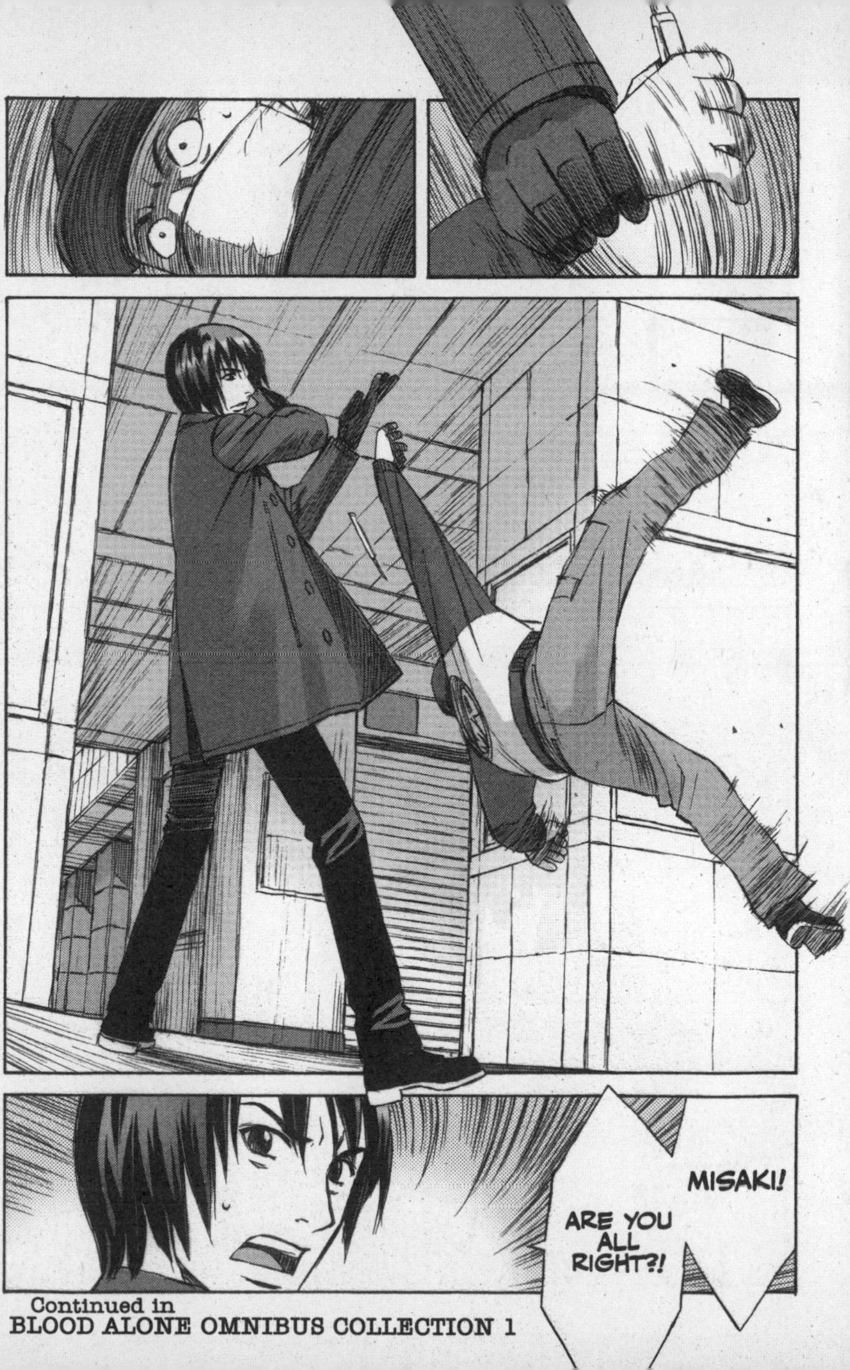
MISAKI!
ARE YOU ALL RIGHT?!

Continued in
BLOOD ALONE OMNIBUS COLLECTION 1

THE END

YOU'RE READING THE WRONG WAY

This is the last page of
Amnesia Labyrinth Volume 2

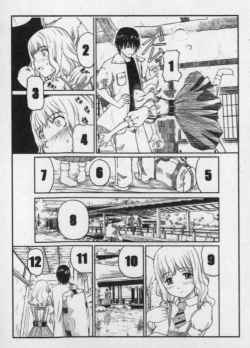

This book reads from right to left, Japanese style. To read from the beginning, flip the book over to the other side, start with the top right panel, and take it from there.

If this is your first time reading manga, just follow the diagram. It may seem backwards at first, but you'll get used to it! Have fun!